HANDBOOK ON THE KNOWLEDGE ECONOMY

Handbook on the Knowledge Economy

Edited by

David Rooney

*Senior Lecturer, UQ Business School,
University of Queensland, Australia*

Greg Hearn

*Professor, Creative Industries Faculty,
Queensland University of Technology, Australia*

Abraham Ninan

*Senior Research Associate, Creative Industries Faculty,
Queensland University of Technology, Australia*

Edward Elgar
Cheltenham, UK • Northampton, MA, USA

Published by
Edward Elgar Publishing Limited
Glensanda House
Montpellier Parade
Cheltenham
Glos GL50 1UA
UK

Edward Elgar Publishing, Inc.
136 West Street
Suite 202
Northampton
Massachusetts 01060
USA

A catalogue record for this book
is available from the British Library

Library of Congress Cataloguing in Publication Data

Rooney, David, 1959–
    Handbook on the knowledge economy / David Rooney, Greg Hearn, Abraham
      Ninan.
     p. cm.
    Includes index.
    1. Knowledge management. 2. Information technology. I. Hearn, Greg, 1957–
II. Ninan, Abraham, 1965–   III. Title. IV. Series

HD30.2.R656 2005
658.4´038—dc22

                                            2005044218

ISBN 1 84376 795 3 (cased)

Typeset by Cambrian Typesetters, Camberley, Surrey
Printed and bound in Great Britain by MPG Books Ltd, Bodmin, Cornwall

Contents

PART III   IMPLEMENTATION

Tables

Figures

Contributors

Mark Banks is a senior lecturer in the Department of Sociology and researcher at the Manchester Institute for Popular Culture, Manchester Metropolitan University, UK. His main interests are in cultural industries, creativity, work-based identities and the sociology and geography of community.

Max Boisot is Professor of Strategic Management at The Universitat Oberta de Catalunya in Barcelona, Senior Research Fellow at the Snider Center for Entrepreneurial Research, The Wharton School, University of Pennsylvania, and Associate Fellow at Templeton College, Oxford University. His most recent book, *Knowledge Assets: Securing Competitive Advantage in the Information Economy*, was awarded the Ansoff Prize for the best book on strategy in 2000. Boisot's current research explores the relationship between organizational learning and knowledge management.

Stuart Cunningham is Professor and Director of the Creative Industries Research and Applications Centre (CIRAC), Queensland University of Technology, Australia. His best-known publications include *Framing Culture*, *New Patterns in Global Television* and *Australian Television and International Mediascapes*. His recent projects include a study of popular culture among Asian overseas communities (*Floating Lives: The Media and Asian Diasporas*).

Peter Drahos is a professor in Law and the Head of Program of the Regulatory Institutions Network Program in the Research School of Social Sciences at the Australian National University. His major research interests are globalization, regulation, intellectual property and trade. He is author of the recent book, *Information Feudalism: Who Owns the Knowledge Economy?*

Brian Fitzgerald is a professor of Law and Head of the Queensland University of Technology School of Law. He is a well-known intellectual property and information technology lawyer. His latest books are *Cyberlaw: Cases and Materials on the Internet, Digital Intellectual Property and E Commerce*; *Jurisdiction and the Internet*; and *Intellectual Property in Principle*. His current projects include work on digital copyright issues across the areas of open content licensing and the creative commons, free and open source software, fan based production of computer games, licensing of digital entertainment, and anti-circumvention law.

Steve Fuller is Professor of Sociology at the University of Warwick, UK. He has been a visiting professor at UCLA, Gothenburg University, Copenhagen Business School, Tel Aviv University and Tokyo International Christian University. He is the founding editor of the quarterly journal, *Social Epistemology*, and the founding president of the Knowledge Management Consortium International. Fuller is the author of about 150 articles and ten books, including *Social Epistemology, Philosophy of Science and Its Discontents, Philosophy, Rhetoric and the End of Knowledge* and *Knowledge Management Foundations*.

Phil Graham holds a Canada Research Chair at the University of Waterloo and is Reader in Communication at the University of Queensland's Business School. He is a prolific author and is internationally recognized in the fields of language and discourse analysis, political economy of new media, and media history. He is founding co-editor of *Critical Discourse Studies* and on the international advisory boards of *New Media & Society, Cultural Politics, and Critical Perspectives on International Business*.

Greg Hearn is Professor of Media Communication and Research Development Coordinator in the Creative Industries Research and Applications Centre at Queensland University of Technology. Over the last ten years, his consulting and research have focused on the future cultural impacts and opportunities of global communication networks for organizations and communities. He has been a visiting fellow at Brunel University and Cornell University. His books include *The Communication Superhighway: Social and Economic Change in the Digital Age* and *Public Policy for the Knowledge Economy: Foundations and Frameworks*.

Paul Jeffcutt is Professor of Management Knowledge at Queen's University, Belfast and the founding director of the interdisciplinary Centre for Creative Industry. His main area of expertise concerns knowledge dynamics in the organization and management of creativity and innovation. He has also advised regional, national and international bodies on the creative industries, including the UK and Irish governments. He is the author of numerous research publications in these areas, including *The Foundations of Management Knowledge* and *Understanding Management: Culture, Critique and Change*.

Richard Joseph is an associate professor in the Murdoch Business School, Murdoch University, Perth, Western Australia. He has over 20 years' experience in the study of science and technology policy, having worked in government and as a consultant and academic. His recent research interests include telecommunications policy, information policy, and the political and social aspects of electronic business, electronic government and the Internet.

Thomas Keenan is a doctoral student at UQ Business School, University of Queensland. His research interests are in the field of knowledge management where he is particularly interested in the management of aesthetic knowledge in technology-intensive creative industries. He is an expert in ethnographic research methods and is a highly regarded singer with extensive experience in managing creative organizations.

Donald M. Lamberton is Adjunct Professor, Creative Industries Faculty, Queensland University of Technology. He is Coordinating Editor, *Information Economics and Policy* and General Editor, *Prometheus*; he serves on the editorial boards of *Economics of Innovation and New Technology*, *Human Systems Management* and *Futures Research Quarterly*. He has held positions at a number of universities, including Case Western Reserve University, Stanford University, UCLA and University of Queensland, and has undertaken work for the OECD and UNESCO. His most recent books are *The Economics of Language* and *Managing the Global: Globalization, Employment and Quality of Life*.

Stuart Macdonald is Professor of Information and Organization at the University of Sheffield. His primary research interest is in the role of information in innovation and in change more generally. Macdonald's approach makes information central to enquiry and is interdisciplinary or multidisciplinary. This inter- and multidisciplinarity is reflected in the fact that he has published in journals of many disciplines, including economics, physics, geography, history, engineering, electronics, agriculture and management.

Thomas Mandeville is Senior Lecturer in Economics at The University of Queensland. He specializes in the economics of information and knowledge, economics of innovation and information technology, and regional economics. His current research interests include: the new, collaborative, networked economy; knowledge policy and management; creative industries; intellectual property issues; complexity theory and self-organization; knowledge and innovation. He is co-founder and editorial board member of *Prometheus*.

Bernard McKenna is a Senior Lecturer in Business Communication at the University of Queensland Business School. His teaching and research interests include communication theory, corporate and scientific communication, political communication, organizational communication, critical discourse analysis and business ethics. Bernard's interest in wisdom in management arose from his deep concern with the contemporary hegemonies that regulate the discourses of corporate activity and politics, and a hope for new humanist values to provide alternative answers to the significant questions that face us.

Abraham Ninan is a senior research associate with the Creative Industries Research and Applications Centre at Queensland University of Technology, Brisbane, Australia. His key publications are in the *International Journal of Management and Decision Making*, *Management Communication Quarterly*, *Prometheus*, *Australian Journal of Communication* and the *Asia Pacific Journal of Marketing and Logistics*. Earlier, he serviced Fortune 500 clients for ten years as Director, Interactive Research, AMC Global Inc., Philadelphia; Director, Quantitative and Online Services, Sigma: Research Management Group, Cincinnati and as Research Manager, Acorn Marketing Research Group, Singapore, Indonesia and India.

Hitendra Pillay is an associate professor in the School of Learning and Professional Studies at the Queensland University of Technology in Australia. His interest in the nature and development of knowledge and systems theory has led to a diverse academic research portfolio that includes areas such as distributed/social cognition and learning, adult and community education, industry-based training and technology-based learning. He also has expertise in macro and micro aspects of social sector reform in developing countries. He has worked for the World Bank and the Asian Development Bank and on associated projects in the Balkans, the Caucasus region, the Central and South East Asian, and the South Pacific region.

Jason Reid is a research fellow with the Information Security Institute at the Queensland University of Technology. His research expertise lies in the areas of security and privacy in distributed computing systems. Particular areas of interest include: trusted systems, trusted computing and their application in mainstream commercial and government environments; authentication and access control models for distributed systems, and the theory and application of smart cards and cryptographic hardware tokens in payment systems, digital content management, e-commerce and network security. Jason is currently writing his doctoral thesis in the area of trusted systems and trusted computing hardware.

David Rooney is Co-Director of Australian Creative Resources Online, Associate Director of the Centre for Social Research in Communication and Senior Lecturer in Knowledge Management, University of Queensland's Business School. He has researched, taught and published widely in the areas of the knowledge-based economy, knowledge management, change management and the economic structure of the creative industries. He is author of *Public Policy in the Knowledge-Based Economy*.

Ron Sanchez is Visiting Professor of Management at Copenhagen Business School and the Linden Visiting Professor of Industrial Analysis at Lund University, Sweden. His research interests include theory and practice of competence-based strategic management; knowledge management and strategic organizational learning; options theory in strategic management; modularity in product, process and knowledge architectures; and strategic flexibility. Sanchez has written numerous books and journal articles on strategic management, technology management and knowledge management, including *Knowledge Management and Organizational Competence*, and most recently (with Aime Heene) *The New Strategic Management: Organization, Competition, and Competence*.

Ursula Schneider is Director of the Institute for International Management and Professor of International Management at Karl-Franzens-Universität, Graz, Austria. Her major research interests include knowledge management, intellectual capital, organizational design and international management.

Joost van Loon is Reader in Social Theory at Nottingham Trent University, where he teaches at the School of Arts, Culture and Communication. He is currently Director of the Centre for Research in Culture and Communication. He has worked at Lancaster University, the University of Wales in Cardiff and the Vrije Universiteit in Amsterdam. His books include *Risk and Technological Culture*, and *The Risk Society and Beyond*. He is an editor of the journal *Space and Culture*. His current research mainly concerns the relationship between risk, technological innovation and media cultures.

Preface

The central motivation for assembling the contributions in this *Handbook on the Knowledge Economy* derives from the observation that many in government and business seem to have taken up the challenge of putting in place whatever is needed for a knowledge-based economy or a knowledge-based organization but very few appear to be inclined to explain what knowledge is or how it works socially, organizationally or economically. While there are good reasons for this situation, not knowing what knowledge is or how it works in any detail is problematic for those who are charged with managing or facilitating it. Policymakers would not consider constructing monetary policy without the input of some detailed knowledge of economics. Managers would not implement an information system without detailed input from knowledgeable information systems experts. Similarly, good knowledge of knowledge should be seen as essential for knowledge management and knowledge-related policy.

When considering the work of knowledge managers and knowledge policymakers, any ignorance about knowledge, apart from being ironic, means that the analytical and conceptual frameworks being developed and applied by them to guide strategy, policy and tactics at macro- and micro-social and economic levels are in danger of being invalid and unreliable. If this is the case much of the effort to promote knowledge is at best incomplete and at worst counterproductive. This can hardly be considered a good situation.

In this light, it is interesting to note that very little is said in knowledge management or knowledge-related policy about some issues that would seem, even at face value, to be deeply connected to knowledge. Those issues include imagination, insight, creativity, curiosity and wisdom. These are all very powerful and necessary aspects of intellection that draw on and assist in creating knowledge. This handbook also demonstrates that an understanding of what knowledge entails raises other important (but less obvious to the casual observer) issues such as values, power, culture, communication, risk perceptions and ethics that are central to effective knowledge systems. It seems disappointing to us that so little is said in the dominant knowledge discourse about these issues. We do not want to dwell here on the absence in knowledge discourse of the topics listed above except to say this handbook demonstrates that it is important to bring them into the centre of knowledge debates and practices, and provides the conceptual and other tools for doing so.

What is encouraging is that much useful fundamental and applied research has now been done on knowledge and related topics in ways that go beyond the limited scope of classical epistemology. This new research on knowledge has been done with the specific intention of assisting managers and policy specialists to better deal with knowledge. Organizational knowledge research, social epistemology and information economics are among the key contributors here. The problem for most practitioners with this body of research is that they are not in a position to keep up with it. This is particularly so because the research is published across a wide range of academic disciplines and inter-disciplinary areas that are difficult to track without the kinds of bibliographic searching technologies that are mostly only available in university libraries. Practitioners need not feel too bad about this because it is also the case that some relevant research, such as that in consciousness studies and wisdom studies, is rarely looked at even by knowledge management and policy researchers.

This handbook has pulled together many leading researchers from a range of knowledge studies disciplines in one convenient volume. We have also asked contributors to make their chapters as accessible as possible without robbing their content of intellectual efficacy. Not all readers will find all chapters equally accessible. Readers should not be alarmed by this. Not all chapters are aimed at the same audience. Some are aimed more at policymakers, others more at business managers, while others are oriented towards professional researchers. The main reason we have done this is that the audience for knowledge research is rather wide, which is not surprising given that knowledge is integral to all aspects and levels of human endeavour. Another reason for it is that people working for knowledge need to have a broad knowledge of knowledge even if they are not specialists in more than one aspect of it. In the final analysis, knowledge economy, knowledge management and knowledge society leaders need to understand each other because all these 'sites' for the application of expertise in knowledge overlap considerably.

The recent enthusiasm for knowledge management and knowledge-based economies has led to much activity in business and government, and is commendable and exciting. Yet the speed at which the knowledge cause has been taken up, while impressive, raises some concerns. In this respect it is worth asking how much of that speed can be seen as undue haste resulting in a less considered set of methods for achieving objectives than is needed and deserved? If the knowledge cause has been taken up hastily it may be an explanation for why many of the frameworks that are now being applied to knowledge management and knowledge-related policy look more like recycled industrial and other frameworks that are simply being repurposed for knowledge-based economies. If speed is an issue it presents another explanation for why many of the people practising knowledge management and implementing knowledge-related policy do not have specific knowledge about knowledge.

As already suggested, the pace of change has been faster than it is possible for professionals to keep up with. The reality remains, though, that action needs to catch up with thinking, and this book can help with that.

The catch-up game is important because much rides on it. The enthusiasm for knowledge is going to remain for the foreseeable future and there is therefore every reason to practise knowledge policy and management better. This is particularly so because to take knowledge seriously is to see economy and society through a new lens, and this affords the ability to see new possibilities for positive action. We can for example set new objectives and reframe old ones. We can adopt new and refreshing methods of addressing previously neglected problems. Indeed, as you read the chapters in this book we hope it will be impressed upon you that we must be cognizant of the social nature of knowledge and of the need to be more humane in practising these new techniques. In the final analysis, knowledge is a profoundly human quality and is central to what makes us capable of being human and humane. We hope therefore that this volume will assist in the better understanding of what knowledge is about and how it can be used better for social and economic objectives.

David Rooney, Greg Hearn and Abraham Ninan
Brisbane, November 2004

1 Knowledge: concepts, policy, implementation

David Rooney, Greg Hearn and Abraham Ninan

This handbook is for those interested in how knowledge contributes to social and economic life and vice versa. In particular, its aim is to assist those who want to have a better knowledge of knowledge and who want to implement useful initiatives in light of the results of contemporary knowledge research. Most importantly, the structure and content of the handbook are informed by the observation that the real opportunity presented by the possibility of a knowledge-based economy or society is not simply that we can become more technologized and more commercialized but that knowledge can be put to use across the whole spectrum of human activity to yield important benefits.

While there is increasing discussion of knowledge-based economies, knowledge management and knowledge societies, little attention has been given to what knowledge really means in these contexts. Indeed, research on the assumptions underpinning contemporary knowledge-related public policy discourse (Graham and Rooney 2001) shows little evidence that it is well informed by any adequate explanation of knowledge, and that as a consequence basic conceptual shortcomings in policy formulation are common. Evidence for this is seen in policy prescriptions that focus on science, technology and engineering to the effective exclusion of non-technical knowledge. Knowledge embodied in culture, the arts and humanities, the social sciences, social skills, entertainment, spirituality and many other aspects of everyday life are not currently considered central knowledge policy concerns. These same criticisms can also be levelled against knowledge management.

The common assumption in global policy discourse is that knowledge is important for its instrumental or industrial value to the extent that knowledge and science and technology have become synonymous. Knowledge management has become largely the province of information systems. This technocratic orientation deals only with the surface features of knowledge systems and unnecessarily limit what can be seen as benefits of knowledge (Rooney et al. 2003). There are much deeper and more fundamental social, cultural and communication processes that condition knowledge creation and use, and that predispose groups to different levels and kinds of outcomes in quality of life, learning, creativity and innovation. Importantly, these deep processes lead to different profiles of consumption, production and commercialization of science and technology, and also production and consumption of cultural expression. Explanations and discussions of such fundamentals are lacking in much current policy and knowledge management discourse.

Conceptual inadequacies such as those we are concerned with result in two widespread and counterproductive outcomes. First, the social infrastructure required to develop, commercialize and diffuse new technology is ignored or mis-specified and underresourced. For example, 70 per cent of large IT projects fail because of human infrastructure problems (Hearn et al. 1998; McDonald and Thorpe 1998), and almost 50 per cent of manufacturing supply chain malfunctions are caused by human/cultural factors (Svensson 2000). We suggest that such 'human infrastructure failures' do not reflect simple human error, but rather the miscalcultaion of the educational, cultural and institutional requirements needed for creating and enacting knowledge. Second, the less immediately understood tacit aspects of knowledge systems that reside in day-to-day modes of social organization are underestimated. This is unfortunate because we know that in ecological remediation, for example, the importance of recognizing tacit local knowledge embedded in culture and everyday practice is paramount for success (Rooney 2002). We also know that wisdom, curiosity and creativity, the very foundations of all future advances for humanity, rely heavily on our tacit faculties in the form of imagination, insight and so on (Rooney et al. 2004).

Contemporary technocratic policy and management practices are a legacy of a European intellectual history extending at least as far back as Descartes. In keeping with that legacy, many contemporary practices appear to be based on assumptions that see knowledge, unrealistically, as the pursuit by individuals of certain and immutable facts about an immutable reality in order to eliminate uncertainty and impose ever greater control over reality (Welbourne 2001). However, the reality is that despite all the knowledge in the world, certainty and control are never completely won (Van Loon 2002). Furthermore, knowledge is created, distributed and used in social systems as a result of complex sets of interactions and relations rather than by isolated individuals (Granovetter 1973; Kusch 2002). It is also the case that within these interactions unpredictability inevitably emerges. This unpredictability is largely sociological, political and psychological in origin, and it is essential to healthy and vibrant societies. Importantly, innovations in knowledge frequently result from unprogrammed activity (Bryant and Wells 1998); new ideas and breakthroughs are not manufactured to order (Howkins 2001); and creativity is based in the ability to make unexpected and useful new connections between disparate ideas (Boden 2003). Knowledge-related policy and management need to reflect these realities.

While there is ample literature that focuses on functional imperatives relating to high technology in the form of industrial research and development (IR&D), and innovation and knowledge management, there is nevertheless a growing concern for the deeper fundamentals and contexts in which we create, use and diffuse knowledge, and a growing acknowledgement of the unpredictable social origins of knowledge (cf. Brown and Duguid 2000; von Krogh et al. 2000). These new foci have not been applied widely enough, though. This is an important issue for the future because in consumption-led economies, knowledge and information services such as education, government, health, entertainment, business services, financial services and the media form an important interface between consumers and knowledge and innovations of all kinds. Importantly, growth rates in these knowledge and information services sectors are often stronger than average overall growth rates for OECD countries (Rifkin 2000).

The knowledge and information services sector derives in large part from the applied social and creative disciplines, and represents 25 per cent of exemplary economies, whilst the new science sector (e.g. agricultural biotech, fibre, construction materials, energy and pharmaceuticals) accounts for only about 15 per cent of these economies (Rifkin 2000, p. 52). For example, worldwide, the creative industries sector has been among the fastest growing of the global economy, and several analysts (Creative Industries Task Force 1998; Cutler 2003; Howkins 2001; OECD 1998; Rifkin 2000) point to the crucial role they play in the new economy. In the USA, entertainment rather than defence is now the driver of new technology take-up (Rifkin 2000, p. 161). In the UK and the USA average annual growth rates for the creative industries have consistently been more than twice that of the economy at large. In addition, the economic multipliers arising from the creative industries are significant, being higher than for most other categories of economic activity (Singapore Ministry of Trade and Industry 2003). Rifkin (2000, pp. 63–4) claims that cultural production will ascend to the first tier of economic life, with information and services moving to the second tier, manufacturing to the third tier and agriculture to the fourth tier. In other words, the future is not only reserved for science and technology, and it is essential that knowledge-related policymakers are mindful of the centrality of the cultural production and services sectors in the future (Rooney and Mandeville 1998).

A key illustration of the importance of social and cultural factors contributing to the knowledge-based economy is broadband content development. Broadband content development thrives on the interactions between culture and technology, the very interactions upon which much of our future prosperity will be based. A raft of opportunities for broadband content and applications ranging from the technical at one end of the spectrum to the cultural at the other are now emerging. This also involves the intermediate use of broadband innovations in other sectors. Information and communications technologies (ICTs) will provide enabling technology for all sectors; but entertainment and the arts will shape the forms and patterns of the consumption of services in all sectors (Florida 2002) through new methods of cross-media communication.

Of course the technical end of the digital content spectrum also holds promise of strong growth outside the creative industries too. Broadband applications in for example geographic information systems, e-health and bioinformatics are growing. Moreover, digital technologies are strategically important enablers as intermediate inputs to business processes generally. In business administration, knowledge management and information systems already handle large amounts of content relevant to the conduct of business in almost all industries. It is still the case, however, that knowledge management systems are not strongly influenced by multi-media techniques such as interaction design, animation, video streaming, enhanced television and other visualization and creative techniques, but they are likely to do so in the near future.

Although current R&D strategies occasionally intimate that there should be some hybridizing of the insights of the social sciences, the arts and humanities, and science research, given the growing role of the creative and services industries we believe this hybridity should really be the *primary* principle upon which national R&D strategy is based. It is also interesting that Porter (1998) suggests the dominant structure for competitiveness in the new economy is that of clusters. These are critical masses of interlinked industry-relevant activities in one location, including suppliers, universities, government agencies, corporations and smaller companies. These affect competition in three broad ways. First, clusters facilitate close relationships, better information flows and so on; they increase the productivity and capacity of companies in the area. Second, they accelerate the direction and pace of innovation. Third, they stimulate the formation of new businesses within the clusters. What lies at the heart of Porter's innovation clusters is communication, the communication of ideas and knowledge. We argue therefore that knowledge-based economies are also describable as communication-based economies and that policymakers and managers need to be sensitive not only to facilitating knowledge but also to communication.

Governments are now attempting to advance knowledge-based economy policy models and there is a renewed sense of urgency in policy circles for such things as innovation, R&D-driven industries, science, and education and training. Clearly, if we are right, the role of government in the development of a successful knowledge-based economy needs to be much more than this. Governments need to be coordinators (mediators, organizers, transformers), and provide intellectual leadership and vision, as well as the social and cultural resources for communities so that they are knowledge and communication rich. Above all, in leading knowledge-based economies, government must be social, even gregarious, rather than technocratic, because the fundamentals of knowledge-based economies are social and cultural.

In parallel with the nuanced view of knowledge we advocate, the authors of the chapters in this volume are not simply asking readers thoughtlessly to join the knowledge-based economy dots. There is a penetrating, questioning and analytical tone that underlies these practical discussions. It has to be said that deciding how best to develop knowledge-based economy resources in the form of intelligent thinking about how knowledge works and how to work with it is essential, and this handbook contains a cross-section of resources of this type. Moreover, the discussion and advice offered is drawn from political science, economics, management studies and the humanities. We have deliberately gathered contributions from important thinkers across this broad intellectual range because readers who are serious about working wisely in relation to developing knowledge-based economies, firms and societies have to be informed in an interdisciplinary way if they are adequately to address the complexities confronting them. Knowledge, after all, is not simply synonymous with commercialization of science and technology or IT use, and so this broad perspective is essential. Knowledge must increasingly be seen to serve a greater range of interests and practices than technocratic ones.

To help understand the range of factors that affect knowledge systems, the book is divided into three parts: Concepts, Policy and Implementation. Part 1, Concepts, sets out a conceptual terrain that will help readers to better understand how knowledge fits in the context of human action and achievement. Importantly, the possession of a strong conceptual framework is a precondition for doing sound research and analysis, including knowledge-based economy research.

The first part opens with a chapter by David Rooney and Ursula Schneider, who ask the central conceptual question for any knowledge-based economy analysis: what is knowledge? They answer the question sociologically. They do so because knowledge, in the context of knowledge-based economies and societies, is relevant in terms of what people and societies do. The chapter is therefore about the processes of knowing and enacting knowledge. The chapter makes three main points. First, it explores knowledge in relation to the temporal context and material objects that are part of the situations in which people create, use and diffuse knowledge. To this end they explain that we have ideas about and because of the objects around us, and that all ideas and the possessors of ideas are influenced by their histories. Second, the chapter is important for its mapping of the often fallible enactment of knowledge. In other words, enacting knowledge is not simply about the execution of cold reason and logic. In doing this Rooney and Schneider highlight that the enactment of knowledge is also messy. Importantly, they argue that this messy fallibility is not a problem but an advantage because it drives innovation and creativity, and therefore should be valued. Finally, the chapter illustrates that the term 'knowledge' is a problematic one. Taken on its own it has little practical meaning for economic and social analysts; knowledge only makes sense in socio-economic (and politico-economic) terms when looked at as constituted by a set of social and mental processes and artefacts that include such things as memory, insight, imagination, ideas, intuition, creativity, beliefs and so on.

If there is a hierarchy of data, information, knowledge and wisdom, why stop at a knowledge-based economy or knowledge management? To this end Bernard McKenna (Chapter 3) extends Rooney and Schneider's conceptualization of knowledge by defining and discussing the highest form of knowing, wisdom. It seems impertinent to seek to improve societies, economies and firms through knowledge if we ignore the highest form of knowing. It is important that McKenna shows us that wisdom is not best seen as an esoteric, spiritual state of mind but as an everyday set of social practices and attitudes that collectively elevates ourselves and society. McKenna demonstrates that wisdom is not simply about being more knowledgeable or possessing more facts; it is in essence a balancing of rational, scientific, judgemental, evaluative and transcendent forms of knowing in a way that is steadfastly ethical and values-based. These insights have profound importance for knowledge-based economy and knowledge management practice, and can no longer be ignored. Thus, in light of McKenna's work we must ask what are the ethical dimensions of knowledge discourse, policy, work and management. Such questions are not yet routinely asked in knowledge discourse but if we are honest about the importance and value of knowledge, they should be.

Contemporary discourse on knowledge is heavily oriented towards the role that knowledge plays in reducing risks of all kinds. Risks to health, the environment and business feature prominently here. But what is the nature of the relationship between risk and knowledge at a sociological level, and can we really understand knowledge in the modern context without a clear view of what risk is? Joost van Loon (Chapter 4) broaches these very questions. In a critical reality check, Van Loon argues that knowledge might be used to solve problems and reduce risks, but the very production of knowledge also produces new risks. The chapter explores the social, cultural and political formations of the knowledge-based economy and shows that not only is there a significant social and cultural dimension to enacting knowledge, but there is a significant political economy that must be acknowledged. However, at the heart of this chapter is the observation that much of the modern passion for knowledge economies and knowledge management is underpinned by a desire to use science to make the world predictable and safe. What we find, though, is that we cannot have predictability and that the utopian dream of a society driven by science to eradicate uncertainty and instil complete control is a fool's dream, unachievable and dangerous in its own right. One conclusion that can be drawn here is that if the sole aim of knowledge policy and management is elimination of risk and uncertainty, then knowledge policy and knowledge management are unlikely to provide satisfying results.

If at the level of practice one aspect of knowledge is to address risk, it is also the case that knowledge has an interrogative dimension, that is, a core element focused on inquiry and satisfying curiosity. Thus Steve Fuller (Chapter 5) discusses normative questions surrounding knowledge and, more specifically, practices for the conduct of inquiry. Fuller is interested in showing the importance of the free flow of knowledge and how problems associated with narrow and partial views of knowledge systems must be addressed by knowledge policy practitioners. He makes important arguments about the role of universities when they are drawn into an instrumental political economy. Universities are cornerstone institutions for creating and distributing knowledge as a public good. They clearly have a necessary role to play that is important precisely because they can be outside the commodifying influence of market forces. He asks why we no longer value highly the pursuit of knowledge for its own sake. Fuller therefore provokes us to ponder the fate of the everyday interrogative value of knowledge work and curiosity. He highlights that there are real dangers in commodifying knowledge and succumbing to the narrow interests of business and neoliberal market dogmas. He is also suggesting, like Van Loon, that knowledge is political, that the political economy of knowledge is relevant to policy and management, and that in the long run, when knowledge policy professionals succumb to the narrow interests of the market, it is not necessarily good for knowledge, society or indeed for business.

In raising questions about the value of knowledge, some commentators formulate knowledge as intellectual capital or intellectual property. However, given that knowledge has intrinsic social value, we should seek to demonstrate how social values contribute to knowledge and vice versa to create positive impacts. With a special interest in developing economies, Hitendra Pillay (Chapter 6) discusses the effects of social capital and knowledge as 'assets' in development in a way that goes beyond business and commercial values. He argues that social capital in the form of social structures, norms of reciprocity, values, beliefs and so on shapes the quality and effectiveness of social interactions to the extent that they affect our ability to do things generally, and specifically for socio-cultural development. In discussing these issues, Pillay is reinforcing the central insights in Part 1: that social and cultural concerns are central to the operation of knowledge in the economy, and that essential to this are socially sound ethics and values, and a coherent cultural base. His point is that sound and vigorous socio-cultural conditions are assets (including but not exclusive to economic assets) that assist the development of a country towards knowledge-based economy and knowledge society status.

Knowledge is often thought of in economic terms as a key strategic resource. What underpins this view is a (tacit or explicit) recognition of the evaluative, interrogative and future-oriented nature of knowledge. This is an important observation and together with the public-good nature of knowledge leads us to the recognition of the need for knowledge to be factored into policy and strategy. Part 2 therefore discusses policy settings for knowledge and, in particular, demonstrates that stopping at traditional industrial innovation, and science and technology policy is insufficient.

The central observation made by Stuart Cunningham (Chapter 7) is about innovation policy. He argues that because the creative industries and cultural consumption are such major components of the economy (and are growing larger every day), it is remiss of governments to ignore cultural innovation. However, support by governments for cultural R&D activities is minimal. A risk associated with this oversight is that most countries are exposed to missing out on new waves of innovation in the burgeoning content industries. Cunningham is pointing to the fact that it is easy for policymakers to promote science and technology-led R&D agendas and that it will take a significant effort for government to get out of those intellectual tram tracks and adopt a new, broader and more effective view of innovation. He is therefore promoting the idea that cultural and creative industries' R&D activities should be seen as an integral part of the larger economy. In short, Cunningham urges that attitudes to cultural innovation have to be elevated from their current 'handmaiden' to science, engineering and technology R&D role.

Maintaining the focus on the creative economy, Paul Jeffcutt (Chapter 8), explores the organization of creativity in knowledge economies and asks how we can investigate and understand it. In doing this he raises questions about doing large-scale, indeed international-scale, knowledge and creative economy research. Jeffcutt argues for internationally comparable assessments of the construction of creativity in specific knowledge economy settings using a standard, logically consistent and yet situated analytical framework. Through an analysis of the Northern Ireland cultural economy, he redefines creative enterprises as parts of distinctive regional 'ecosystems'. He outlines how a strategic sustainable development framework can be developed by policymakers, based upon identifying the key dynamics and leverage points within each 'ecosystem'. He concludes that there are several cultural economies, not just one, each situated in specific locales with distinctive characteristics. Policymakers must insightfully work with such situated ecological information to enhance creative spaces in local knowledge economies. Jeffcutt therefore argues that there is a need for developing strategic knowledge on cultural economies across locales, globally. The challenge is to bring together local and fragmented policy actions to develop cumulative and global applied knowledge. He suggests that strong, contextualized knowledge acquisition and diffusion between distributed experts (networks of researchers, policymakers and practitioners) and other stakeholders will be most effective in managing the creation of the knowledge needed to meet the creative needs of the knowledge society and economy.

If knowledge economies are in any way indebted to culture and wisdom, then values are important to knowledge-related policy. Phil Graham (Chapter 9) argues that knowledge economy analyses must take account of values, and he provides a basis for making such analyses. He unpacks a number of incompatible forces that shape knowledge-based economy thinking through a critique of the modern-day monetary understanding of the term 'value'. He describes this state of affairs as an unfortunate product of an economic reductionism that feeds policymakers' need for objective policy production. Importantly, he shows that the 'hard science' of econometrics has rendered policy analysis of knowledge impotent because its analytical frameworks diminish the value of knowledge to price rather than a more broadly construed idea of values. Graham advocates increased use of language or discourse analysis as a primary tool in knowledge-related policy evaluation. Using these analytical techniques he illustrates how contemporary policymakers have a strong preference for language that emphasizes instrumental knowledge that will realize monetary value. He argues that the problem with this is that the assumptions implicit in such shallow practices occlude other, better ways of thinking of the value of knowledge. The paradox he exposes lies in how a thin, dry and socially barren economic rationalism contrasts with what is actually necessary for satisfying the need for a better world, and that current policy discourse actually marginalizes the deeper social and cultural values that make life truly satisfying.

Moving from a creativity perspective to innovation networks, Abraham Ninan (Chapter 10) considers innovation policy for industrial clusters. The chapter presents a review of the literature that shows the importance of location and spatiality in industrial clusters for facilitating knowledge diffusion and innovation. Ninan finds that the geography of industrial clusters matters. Geography matters because of the need for face-to-face exchange and close proximity within and between members of industrial clusters to enhance creative work and facilitate tacit knowledge spillovers. More particularly, he argues that this kind of social learning and diffusion of knowledge is dependent on a social network 'architecture' that enhances cognitive proximity and the absorptive capacity of clusters. He proposes future research inquire into and explore the different spatial levels at which innovation systems operate.

Finding the best intellectual property rights (IPRs) legislative and policy settings to enhance creativity and innovation is critical for knowledge-related policies. Peter Drahos (Chapter 11) discusses the role of IPRs and argues that they do not necessarily confer economic advantages in a straightforward way in knowledge economies. Whilst it is true that individual agents need incentives for R&D, Drahos shows that it is also true that at some point the costs to society and the economy of ever stronger IPRs outweigh the benefits. Strong IPRs can therefore inhibit innovation. In this light it is interesting to note that today significant innovation occurs in the absence of strong IPR protection, as in the case of open source software development communities. What Drahos is drawing to our attention is that there is an alarming lack of critical reflection globally in relation to IPRs and that much of what is assumed to be good about them is in fact questionable. What is also evident is that some of those unquestioned assumptions are convenient for fostering rent-seeking behaviour by monopolists. This is an unproductive and sometimes destructive aspect of knowledge economies brought about by a lack of focus on the social benefits of creativity and innovation. Drahos is clearly indicating that the often lazy or self-serving assumptions made about IPRs currently afoot in policy and business circles need to be challenged, debated and revised.

Handbooks usually place considerable emphasis on specific micro-level practices, as this handbook does. However, a strength and a weakness of knowledge is that it is important in every human activity. That means that a handbook about knowledge has to be rather selective about what activities it discusses. To help get around this problem the chapters in the Implementation part deal with some generalizable practical micro-level knowledge activities. For readers who after reading this next part still want to peruse more specific discussions in more limited areas we recommend they also consult other handbooks such as *A Handbook of Cultural Economics* (Towse 2003), the *New Economy Handbook* (Jones 2003), *The Handbook of Industrial Innovation* (Dodgson and Rothwell 1994), *The Blackwell Handbook of Organizational Learning and Knowledge Management* (Easterby-Smith and Lyles 2003), *Creative Knowledge Environments* (Hemlin et al. 2004) and so on.

We begin this part by looking at information sharing because that is a primary interaction in a knowledge economy and is essential to learning. Don Lamberton (Chapter 12), arguing from an information economics perspective, directs our attention to the fundamentals of such transactions. He argues that information sharing is a social and psychological act wherein mindsets act variously as building blocks, direction signs, filters and even obstacles. We must recognize that information is a 'structured quantity' that is a product of human minds in collaboration. Lamberton argues that we have to better understand these collective mindsets in terms of what they enable and what they prevent us from thinking and doing. Importantly, he also points out that curiosity is a valuable resource and that, generally, information exchanges are made in a climate of uncertainty. Historically, humans have relied on their curiosity to probe for answers but increasingly we seek to respond by using hierarchical command-and-control models of organization that would eliminate uncertainty. The command-and-control mindset, however, is antithetical to curiosity and, as Van Loon shows, largely denies reality. Finally, Lamberton impresses upon us that history matters in knowledge economies; that learning occurs over time, meaning that each learning process has its own social history that colours those processes and their outcomes. This observation about history leads him to argue that information sharing may be best analysed and understood as an unfolding, evolutionary social process.

Thomas Mandeville (Chapter 13), also adopting an information economics viewpoint, examines the rise of the network form of organization in knowledge-based economies. Like Ninan, he argues that networks are the most realistic way to think about interaction within knowledge economies. Mandeville's primary focus, however, is on the specific economic characteristics of information exchange to explain why cooperation and collaboration have become central to business strategy. He suggests that these networks, which are consolidated by the development of the Internet, are manifested in many different ways. Specifically, though, he concentrates on how networks within organizational structures contribute to competitive advantage by lowering transaction costs. Mandeville therefore suggests that the emergence of networks is a key issue, and creates an imperative for new policies and strategies that address the social network dynamics of collaboration. We can read this situation as one where the simplistic view that competition and cooperation are diametrically opposed is no longer useful.

If information plays a key role in the communication and creation of knowledge, so does IT. In proposing a new approach to information system design, Max Boisot (Chapter 14) interrogates the nature of knowledge in organizations. He suggests that there are three different types of knowledge, namely embodied, narrative and formal knowledge, with the first two being more tacit and the last more codified. Furthermore, he is critical of information systems that have been designed to focus on more abstract and formalized types of information because, given the social nature of knowledge and information, such designs are only partial responses to the needs of information users. Boisot argues for a contingent approach to information system design that accommodates a more dynamic, inclusive and social view of how knowledge is diffused in what he calls information space. He suggests that three key questions must guide the design of information systems: what kind of knowledge we are dealing with and where it is located in information space; what phase of the social learning cycle we are dealing with; and what institutional and cultural processes are acting to support or impede knowledge. Boisot's approach clearly demonstrates the benefits of a strong conceptual framework for the analysis, design and implementation of information systems in all organizations.

With an explicit focus on knowledge management practice, Ron Sanchez

(Chapter 15) translates aspects of knowledge management theory into a pragmatic comparison of tacit versus explicit knowledge approaches to knowledge management. Sanchez's argument is, first, that tacit knowledge resides in people, and knowledge management approaches that draw on this understanding are essentially about people management. The advantages of tacit knowledge approaches include: it is a relatively easy and inexpensive way to begin managing knowledge (for example, via intranet or database resources specifying which individuals are expert in which issues); it is motivational for staff; and the informal nature of tacit knowledge means that the leaking of critical information is less likely. Disadvantages include the difficulty of validating knowledge claims by individuals and problems associated with the fact that people are the fallible conveyers of knowledge. Management of explicit knowledge has the advantage that such knowledge is easier to capture, codify and disseminate. It also forms a baseline for the improvement of knowledge processes which is easily measured. The challenges for the explicit approach include: the resource-intensive nature of capturing such knowledge; people's fears that articulating and giving up their knowledge will jeopardize their organizational position; and that applying that store of knowledge as purposive and useful action is not necessarily an easy step. Sanchez argues that it is possible to develop a hybrid design for knowledge management practice that has the right balance of tacit and explicit approaches. He suggests that the exact formula for getting the right balance is a function of a number of factors, for example, the technology of the organization, market conditions, the role of knowledge in the business plan and strategy, attitudes of key knowledge workers in an organization, and the geographical spread of knowledge and resources. He suggests that tacit approaches are a good place to start knowledge management strategies and that they can be built into explicit knowledge management systems over time.

Thomas Keenan (Chapter 16), researching in a not-for-profit, community-based, creative organization, is another who confronts the fallible nature of knowledge work while emphasizing its relational nature. He uses the framework of social identity theory to explain how knowledge creation and diffusion is a socially conditioned process that occurs in the context of perceptions about group and individual status and people's sense of belonging. Performing arts organizations like the one in this study are in a constant process of learning and rehearsal aimed at perfecting a public performance. The study therefore provides an excellent illustration of the fact that knowledge managers need to be aware of the social stakeholders in knowledge creation processes, and that ingroup/outgroup relationships can effectively create barriers to communication, learning and knowledge acquisition that would otherwise improve an organization's (public) performance. Keenan therefore shows that group values can significantly influence the creation, diffusion and enactment of knowledge. In particular he demonstrates the importance of high-status groups effectively valuing openness and civility if an organization is to minimize unnecessary and destructive behaviours at intergroup boundaries. These destructive behaviours may not prevent the satisfactory execution of the public performance but they limit the extent to which the organization can exceed what is merely satisfactory. It is also important when considering the social nature of knowledge that these intergroup dissonances not only compromise learning but the quality of life within the organization.

Retaining a focus on cultural production, Mark Banks (Chapter 17) compares the social nature of the creative process in a range of creative industries firms. He critiques ideas of creativity that idealize individuals at the margins and instead argues that the stimulants of creativity are firmly embedded within an organization's social practices and management forms. His study of creative industries firms and their approaches to managing creativity finds a wide variety of attitudes to creativity, ranging from the view that creativity is an errant resource that must be disciplined through to very open and democratic attitudes. Banks suggests that firms wishing to stimulate creativity must consider three questions: how is creativity defined in the context of the firm; what value is placed on creativity as an internal resource; and how do intrinsic and extrinsic organizational structures enhance or undermine creativity? By answering these questions any firm is in a position to stimulate creativity.

Stuart Macdonald (Chapter 18) gives us a good example of knowledge work as a relational phenomenon in the form of an analysis of the relationships between organizations and hired management consultants. Macdonald's chapter changes the emphasis of this part of the book from mostly intra-organizational concerns to questions about how organizations deal with external sources of knowledge. To do so he advances an interesting perspective on the relationship between management consultants and the organizations and individual managers within organizations who engage them. By examining the work of consultants he is able to show that the absence of a tacit system of rules for engaging, valuing and exchanging information between consultant and client in new firms, ironically, leads to more effective use of consultants. This is in contrast to mature organizations used to employing consultants where he shows that the primary beneficiaries of the consultancy are the consultant and the individual client managers who hired them. Macdonald's study shows that the value of expert knowledge workers can be easy to over-estimate or, alternatively, easy to derive reduced benefits from when the conduct of the consultant-manager relationship becomes habituated and routinized.

While Macdonald's chapter reminds us that the contribution of management consultants, perhaps the *sine qua non* of managerial know-how, is not unproblematic, it is appropriate that Richard Joseph (Chapter 19) challenges the concept of the knowledge worker. He does this by drawing attention to two traditions, from Machlup and Drucker, of theorizing knowledge work. He suggests the dominant tradition – that of Drucker – is too Tayloristic and leads to static conceptions of the knowledge worker that reinforce unproductive control hierarchies and distinctions between knowledge work and non-knowledge work. Instead, arguing from a Machlupian perspective he advocates that knowledge work be seen as relational, and that there is a close link between learning, knowing and doing. Following Jacques, Joseph points out that it is not knowledge that is of primary importance but the ability of people to learn. Learning capacity, he points out, is a relatively constant variable whereas knowledge has a finite shelf life. Therefore if information exchange is a basic *transaction* in knowledge-based economies, then learning is a basic *ability* because the replenishment of knowledge relies on the ability to learn.

The final two chapters deal with the use of IT for knowledge work and innovation. Greg Hearn and Thomas Mandeville (Chapter 20) elucidate some general principles for enhancing productivity in knowledge-based enterprises by examining the case of ICTs. Bearing in mind debates over Solow's observations on the IT productivity paradox, they argue that the simple equation, 'ICTs = productivity' is wrong. Rather, the deployment of ICTs can either enhance or impede productivity through five mechanisms. These are: the transaction costs of the enterprise; the relationship of the enterprise to its stakeholders; the informational characteristics of the processes of the enterprise; the nature of any new products or services being provided; and the reputation of the enterprise. Individual cases of ICT deployment must be examined to see which of these factors are operative and in which direction. Like Boisot, they argue that local conditions must be examined to understand the deployment of knowledge in productive ways. More particularly, they propose a simple model which suggests that cost reduction strategies versus innovation strategies afford different outcomes. The key differentiator between these two strategies is investment in the human infrastructure required to exploit new technologies in creative ways.

The practical implications of policy debates regarding IPRs discussed by Drahos in the policy part of the book are explored by Brian Fitzgerald and Jason Reid (Chapter 21). This chapter starts by echoing Drahos's suggestion that IPRs do not necessarily confer economic advantages in a straightforward way in knowledge economies and that more open (or some rights reserved, rather than all rights reserved) access regimes are sometimes beneficial. They propose a paradigm shift in which digital rights management (DRM) is repositioned so that it includes the management of open licensing models like the creative commons spectrum of copyright licences. The chapter goes on to describe in detail how IPRs and technological innovations can be used to manage digital content for open access. The chapter provides a very practical example showing how sensitive creative (knowledge) work is to the formal, indeed, legal construction of relationships, in this case by changing aspects of intellectual property law.

Finally, an overall view of this handbook reveals some important commonalities in the way our contributors understand and treat knowledge. The most important of these is that they tend to focus on the relational characteristics of knowledge. It is also important that many contributors bring into the foreground issues such as space (situation and place) and values. These key emphases represent the state of play in contemporary knowledge research. These insights suggest that for practitioners in knowledge management or knowledge-related policy production and analysis, the coal face at which they should be working is understanding, changing and facilitating relationships, constructing places and situations that are knowledge-enabling, and responding positively to the realization that knowledge-based economies are not Cartesian, values-free machines whose only purpose is the yielding of high returns on investment. In this light, knowledge-based economies, societies and firms are communication economies, societies and firms. These places are also complex and uncertain, and depend on that complexity and uncertainty as much as they depend on their relational qualities. Essential aspects of coping with this complexity, uncertainty and relational make-up are strong, vibrant, open, tolerant, robust societies and cultures. These concerns come before science, engineering, technology and commercialization. Finally, a knowledge-based economy, therefore, is not just a place with lots of useful facts. It must also have wisdom – a purposively systematic episteme founded on ethics, creativity, insight, judgement, reflexivity, aesthetics and eloquence. If we do not have these attributes we are no better off. In working for knowledge it is the opportunity to achieve change at this level that is the real opportunity.

References

Boden, Margaret A. 2003. *The Creative Mind: Myths and Mechanisms* (2nd edn). London: Routledge.

Brown, John Seely and Paul Duguid. 2000. *The Social Life of Information*. Boston, MA: Harvard Business School Press.

Bryant, K. and A. Wells. 1998. 'A new economic paradigm? Innovation-based evolutionary systems', in *Discussions of Science and Innovation*, vol. 4. Canberra: Department of Science, Industry and Resources.

Creative Industries Task Force. 1998. 'Creative industries mapping document.' http://www.culture.gov.uk/global/publications/archive_1998/Creative_Industries_Mapping_Document_1998.htm.

Cutler, Terry. 2003. 'Research and innovation systems in the production of digital content and applications: Report for the National Office for the Information Economy'. Melbourne: Cutler & Co.

Dodgson, M. and R. Rothwell. 1994. *The Handbook of Industrial Innovation*. Cheltenham, UK and Northampton, MA, USA: Edward Elgar.

Easterby-Smith, Mark and Marjorie A. Lyles. 2003. *The Blackwell Handbook of Organizational Learning and Knowledge Management*. Oxford: Blackwell.

Florida, Richard. 2002. *The Rise of the Creative Class: And How It's Transforming Work, Leisure, Community and Everyday Life*. New York: Basic Books.

Graham, Philip and David Rooney. 2001. 'A sociolinguistic approach to applied epistemology: Examining technocratic values in global "knowledge" policy'. *Social Epistemology* **15**:155–69.

Granovetter, Mark S. 1973. 'The strength of weak ties'. *American Journal of Sociology* **78**:1360–80.

Hearn, Greg, Tom Mandeville and David Anthony. 1998. *The Communication Superhighway: Social and Economic Change in the Digital Age*. St Leonards: Allen and Unwin.

Hemlin, Sven, Martin Carl Allwood and Ben R. Martin. 2004. *Creative Knowledge Environments: The Influences on Creativity in Research and Innovation*. Cheltenham, UK and Northampton, MA, USA: Edward Elgar.

Howkins, J. 2001. *The Creative Economy: How People Make Money From Ideas*. London: Allen Lane.

Jones, D.C. 2003. *New Economy Handbook*. Amsterdam: Elsevier.

Kusch, Martin. 2002. *Knowledge by Agreement: The Program of Communitarian Epistemology*. Oxford: Oxford University Press.

McDonald, Frank and Richard Thorpe. 1998. *Organizational Strategy and Technological Adaptation to Global Change*. Basingstoke: Macmillan.

OECD. 1998. 'Content as a new growth industry'. Paris: OECD.

Porter, M. 1998. 'Clusters and the new economics of competition'. *Harvard Business Review* **76**(6):77–91.

Rifkin, Jeremy. 2000. *The Age of Access: The New Culture of Hypercapitalism Where All of Life is a Paid-for Experience*. New York: J. P. Tarcher.

Rooney, David. 2002. 'Global science', in *Encyclopaedia of Life Support Systems, 1.24. Capital Resource Issue III: Globalization and World Systems*. Oxford: Eolss Publishers.

Rooney, David, Greg Hearn, Thomas Mandeville and Richard Joseph. 2003. *Public Policy in Knowledge-Based Economies: Foundations and Frameworks*. Cheltenham UK and Northampton, MA, USA: Edward Elgar.

Rooney, David and Thomas Mandeville. 1998. 'The knowing nation: A framework for public policy in a knowledge economy'. *Prometheus* **16**:453–67.

Rooney, David, Bernard McKenna and Fred D'Agostino. 2004. 'Wisdom as an attribute of knowledge work', in *Knowledge Management in Asia Pacific (KMAP) Conference*. Taipei, Taiwan.

Singapore Ministry of Trade and Industry. 2003. 'Economic contributions of Singapore's creative industries'. http://www.mti.gov.sg/public/PDF/CMT/NWS_2003Q1_Creative.pdf?sid=40&cid=1630.

Svensson, Goran. 2000. 'A conceptual framework for the analysis of vulnerability in supply chains'. *International Journal of Physical and Logistics Management* **30**:731–49.

Towse, Ruth. 2003. *A Handbook of Cultural Economics*. Cheltenham UK and Northampton, MA, USA: Edward Elgar.

Van Loon, Joost. 2002. *Risk and Technological Culture: Towards a Sociology of Virulence*. London: Routledge.

von Krogh, Georg, Kazuo Ichijo and Ikujiro Nonaka. 2000. *Enabling Knowledge Creation: How to Unlock the Mystery of Tacit Knowledge and Release the Power of Innovation*. Oxford: Oxford University Press.

Welbourne, Michael. 2001. *Knowledge*. Chesham: Acumen.

PART I

CONCEPTS

2 The material, mental, historical and social character of knowledge

David Rooney and Ursula Schneider

It is advisable in a book about knowledge economies to say what knowledge is, and so in this chapter we set out our explanation of what knowledge or, rather, knowing entails. Our view of knowing is relevant to knowledge economies because, first, it accounts for the environment (society, economy, firm) in which knowing occurs. Taking this approach is important because when discussing knowledge economy issues, we necessarily assume that knowers function in groups that are situated in specific contexts. Second, our approach also places an emphasis on the very human, enigmatic, messy and tacit qualities of knowing, and, as we will show, these aspects of knowing are the most important but difficult ones to conceptualize, plan and manage for.

The lessons to be taken from this chapter, therefore, while abstract, are nevertheless practical. The simple point we make is that it is impractical to attempt to develop insights about the knowledge economy, and develop strategies and tactics in relation to it without sufficient understanding of the complex and differentiated nature of the subject of our concern. Our goal is to provide some intellectual scaffolding with which practitioners and researchers can plan and think sensibly about such an enigmatic subject.

Tacit knowing in theory and practice

We begin by discussing the tacit or enigmatic and foundational aspects of human awareness and knowledge of the world. Tacit knowledge is that which is not readily articulated. It consists of sentiments, feelings, emotions, hunches and so on. It is therefore different to explicit knowledge that can be readily articulated in symbolic form through texts, blueprints, numbers and the like. The difficulties attached to understanding tacit knowledge (or tacit knowing) have translated into uncertainty in knowledge management about how tacit knowing can be apprehended, represented and managed and so it should be discussed here before moving to a broader discussion.

The most promising organizational knowledge theory follows in the tradition of the social constructionist and subjectivist sociology of knowledge. Such a tradition is commonly seen as beginning with Berger and Luckmann's (1966) sociology of knowledge. In so far as this tradition is manifest in the knowledge management literature, it has a clear focus in discussions about the embeddedness (and encodedness, enculturedness, etc.) of knowledge (Blackler 1995); concern about the social processes in the conversion of knowledge from tacit to explicit (Nonaka and Takeuchi 1995; Nonaka et al. 2000); and how knowledge is established as a justifiable belief through what might best be called social epistemic testing (von Krogh et al. 2000). That is, this literature points to the ways in which knowledge can be understood as a resource waiting to be 'unlocked'. While these are legitimate views, they do not say enough about, for example, how to unlock the resources, where they should be unlocked from and how to enact knowledge.

Because the key to understanding how knowledge works is to be found in tacit knowledge, we wish to show that a more complete understanding of tacit knowing is possible. A good place to start developing this understanding is with Gebser (1985) and Mithen's (1998) research into the evolution of consciousness. Gebser and Mithen's empirical approaches, because they are evolutionary and historical, deal with consciousness in a way that allows a broader treatment of tacit knowing.

Human mental evolution
Research into the evolution of human cognition and consciousness indicates that tacit knowing is the most profound and central mental characteristic in humans. Understanding the nature of this evolution, based on its highly tacit roots, helps make it clear what the nature and importance of tacit knowledge are. The centrality of tacitness to human intellection makes it imperative that knowledge policy and management adequately allow for it.

Mithen sees the human mind as essentially tacit in nature and as forming the basis for knowing through metaphor and analogy. Indeed, Mithen (1998, pp. 171–210) describes the emergence of early *Homo sapiens* intelligence (in hunter–gatherer societies) as being dependent on abstract symbolic devices (cave art, notched 'counting' sticks, abstract maps, etc.) that precedes the highly developed explicit symbolic language such as we are acquainted with today. In large degree these forms of knowing, drawing on such abstract symbolic devices, are prelinguistic or non-verbal. Moreover, Mithen, in line with contemporary neurobiological research (cf. Edelman and Tononi 2000), persuades us that for most of the human evolutionary journey our psychology has evolved to depend and thrive on just these analogic, even unconscious, intellectual conditions to create, retain and diffuse knowledge.

To better understand the place of tacitness, it helps to understand Gebser, who expresses the fundamental tacitness of knowing in the much more abstract concept, latency (or what is concealed in our consciousness and not open to easy scrutiny). The origins of early (or immediately pre-) human consciousness, in Gebser's view, rest in the archaic stage of its evolution. At this point consciousness is entirely tacit. As difficult as this is for us to comprehend, it is a state of awareness characterized by a lack of precise, differentiated thoughts, and where consciousness is without a personal perspective, without time or space, exists as zero-dimensional mentation, and is pure potentiality. This, he argues, forms a foundation in which all awareness and thinking is ultimately rooted.

Subsequent stages in the evolution of consciousness emerge from and remain based in the archaic structure. The two evolutionary stages that intervene between the archaic and the present (mental–rational) were the magic and mythical stages. These intervening stages are still so highly tacit that they, too, may present difficulties for our understanding. Given the limitations of space, we can only broadly outline these two stages by saying that at those points in our evolution, consciousness and cognition were devoid of highly codified and explicit language but were not as undifferentiated as the archaic was. Rudimentary language (probably more accurately described as vocalizations (Mithen 1998)) emerged, differentiated ideas and beliefs emerged, and so, too, did self-awareness. Eventually, stories (myths) and other more standardized ways of communicating knowledge of the world emerged. Importantly, superimposing these new abilities on the original tacit foundations meant that reflection, imagination, intention and strategy could now occur.

With the emergence of metaphor, myth and stories, a shared social background of more or less tacit ideas, a shared phenomenological background, had arrived and enabled more complex socially oriented or purposive and strategic, abstract and innovative thinking to occur. It is important to keep in mind that despite the lack of formalism in language and knowledge in these stages of consciousness, thinking, creativity and learning readily occurred. It was not that knowledge and language were now more explicit and formal but that the tacit and explicit faces of knowing were thrust into an intellectual union to form a fertile mix. Humans were now being empowered to make better and better links between ideas, memories and so on to produce new and more complex ideas.

Humans remain highly reliant on symbolic, non-verbal thought systems, and it is significant that the power and sophistication of the modern human intellect is still based on our ability to use imagination, intuition, analogy and metaphor (Mithen 1998, pp. 244–6), all of which relate to tacit knowledge, and for linking ideas. For example, science metaphors such as 'wormholes', 'clouds' of electrons, 'selfish' genes and the like are rather common, and in fact are essential social devices for organizing, linking and effectively communicating complex ideas and for the creation of new knowledge (Mithen 1988, pp. 214–15). Knowledge in general (Berger and Luckmann 1966), including scientific knowledge (Shapin 1994), therefore, is not usually revealed impartially or objectively; it is part of a subjective, indeed, intersubjective, socially (including politically) produced conception of reality. These intersubjectivities, we argue, form the bases for relationships between the ideas that constitute a shared phenomenological background to intellection. Much of this background is prelinguistic or non-verbal (and thus tacit), and includes not only feelings, moods and emotions but also assumptions, values, ideologies, theories and propositions.

Knowledge and knowledge management

Our objective in this section is to further build upon our theorization of knowledge and to show how a fuller appreciation of knowledge can make clearer what knowledge management and policy should be most concerned with. In doing this it is useful to examine some illustrative examples of treatments of tacit and explicit knowledge in the knowledge management literature.

Articulated and unarticulated knowledge

Knowledge can be unarticulated or uncommunicated. An important observation here is that knowledge may be unarticulated now but not necessarily unarticulatable (Zack 1999). This is related to our use of the term explicit knowledge rather than codified knowledge. It is not the degree of codification that is always the most significant, but, rather, the degree to which an idea is explained or made explicit. Simply codifying will not render knowledge explicit in all cases. For example, musical notation is codified music but is only explicitly meaningful to people who can read music. Similarly, communicability is essential if knowledge is to be shared and diffused throughout a group (Rogers 1980; Winter 1987; Zander and Kogut 1995). However, because communicability is dependent on the social context in which knowledge is communicated, the degree to which we can regard knowledge as being tacit or explicit is at least partly social context dependent. This position suggests that the same knowledge in a different context or in the hands of a different person may or may not be so explicit or accessible. Context can be seen in this light as a background of potential links or interrelations between people and ideas that is not solely a property of individuals.

Extending the concept of communicability, Kogut and Zander (1993) claim that one has also to distinguish between knowledge based on its complexity and its ease of learning. The temptation here is to claim that the more complexity knowledge has, the more difficult it is to learn. For our purposes, we want to reframe this position as suggesting that two variables, complexity and social context, are interlinked to determine communicability (Granovetter 1973; Tsoukas 1996). Furthermore, we can also say that amenability to being learnt is also dependent on the degree to which knowledge is contingent on a background of shared meanings and understandings that are familiar to the teacher and learner. Thus great complexity can be inherent in knowledge but lessened by learners being joined through a rich context of shared history, learning, meanings and aspirations (Cohen and Levinthal 1990; Duck 2002; Grant 1996). If such shared cultural elements are present among interlocutors, then meaning is less problematic (less ambiguous), and the inherent levels of tacitness, explicitness, complexity and simplicity are less important. This is not to argue for a complete alignment of background characteristics between all intellectual interlocutors. That is not possible or necessarily desirable because differences are inevitable and contribute to the diversity needed for novelty. However, it is sufficient to say for now that it is important to bring people and ideas into effectively linked relationships, and, thereby access this shared phenomenological background. Knowledge, therefore, can be seen as being brought forth collectively in processes of social relations and, in particular, through processes of communication and understandings that necessarily transcend individuals.

Procedural and declarative knowledge

Moorman and Miner (1998), Sigley and Anderson (1989), and Zander and Kogut (1995) have distinguished between two types of knowledge: procedural and declarative. Procedural knowledge is treated as know-how (skill and action knowledge) or tacit knowledge, and declarative knowledge as fact knowledge or explicit knowledge. Procedural knowledge is knowledge that cannot be easily scrutinized and is used to solve a problem rather than to describe what the problem is. Declarative knowledge is found in rule-based logic and is for describing a problem rather than providing skills for solving it. Here we see another facet of knowledge. This is different to the articulability of knowledge as just discussed. From our point of view, knowledge in this form is about the relationships between the ability to know intellectually what the dimensions of a problem are and the ability or skill to perform the actions needed to solve it. Clearly, theory and action are not best seen as polar opposites but as linked or co-dependent. In the same vein, tacit and explicit knowledge are incorrectly described as two different kinds of knowledge; they are better seen as different faces of the same thing. Thus we need to deal with knowledge not just as a communicability issue but as a framework that leads from knowing about a problem to acting on it (or activity in the sense used by Blackler (1993) and Vygotsky (1986), or enacting as we describe below). In other words, there is an inescapable interrelationship between knowing and doing, and theory and practice.

Importantly, declarative and procedural knowledge are dependent on informal learning through experience (learning-by-doing, social learning) as well as on formal (institutional) learning to arrive at the desirable position where the gap between theoretical and practical knowledge is bridged in a community of practice (Lave and Wenger 1991; Wenger 1999, 2000). In addition to the relationships between knowing and doing, we argue that the bases for social learning are in networks of social relationships (both formal and informal). Therefore, if knowing is a social process, then knowing and sociality are enfolded within each other. Thus, while this position acknowledges that knowledge is brought forth in social contexts, it can also connect knowing and action to an interdependence between social structure and historically and socially shared mental processes that provide access to a larger and fertile phenomenological background (cf. Luria 1976; Vygotsky 1986). A point to be made here is that while being well integrated as a member of a community may help facilitate its members' interaction at an ideational level, those who are not members but share enough background may also be able to connect at some level to that community. In this way, a novelist who decides to live like a hermit with no social life may still meaningfully connect with a very large audience through his or her books.

Intuition
We can take our line of inquiry about the role of a tacit background further if we examine intuition. Intuition has been described as immediate (non-inferential) understanding and learning that occurs without conscious reasoning or formal scrutinizable analysis (Behling and Eckel 1991 in Brockman and Anthony 1998). It is a highly tacit process.

Intuition is knowledge that is generated and forms new schemes of meaning or insight, but its rationale is unarticulated to the knower. Intuition can also be seen as a quick and sudden, even inexplicable, new combination of elements to form a new scheme that lets things appear differently. In other words, it is about re-forming relationships between different sets of ideas. Intuition can also be seen as tacit decision-making able to be done at appropriate moments, and at speeds sufficient to deal with the minute-to-minute decision-making necessary for coping with the 'real-time' exigencies of life. Furthermore, as Whitehead (1984) would have it, intuition is also about fantasy-rich constructions that are as important to knowing as logic and coherence. To this we would add the role of memories, feelings and emotions. A relationship illustrated here is that between past, present and the future, which is infused with memories, feelings, emotions and fantasy to allow imagination, creativity and foresight (Boulding 1956). What is also important about intuition is that there is a perception by the knower of his or her correctness of judgement.

Such cognitive processes have also been the subject of research by social judgement theorists who have shown the importance, prevalence and reproducibility of judgements made by professionals (Brunswick 1956; Hitt and Tyler 1991). This reproducibility is likely to be partly a function of some kind of structured but unconscious cognitive framework (cf. Edelman and Tononi

2000) built up through years of experience and learning and can, therefore, be said to have both tacit and explicit qualities. This is not a mystical process but simply an unscrutinizable, subconscious, often non-verbal one.

It is important to realize that intuition is used to access and make sense of or link together vast sets of one's own and collective knowledge. It is therefore a nonsense to think of formal knowledge as ever being truly independent of intuition. Furthermore, assisting intuitive knowing is the degree to which complex ideas are, as it were, able to be compressed – in the sense that metaphors and analogy are a kind of meaning compression system (Chia 1998; Cohen and Levinthal 1990; Hansen 1999; Mithen 1998). This suggests that metaphor systems (which are socially produced and thus shared) are important to intuition and that intuition is critical to creatively and insightfully putting our ideas into meaningful relationships with each other. Intuition very clearly draws on a tacit background, and given the centrality of intuitive thought and judgement to human activity it clearly demonstrates the importance of tacit forms of knowing. Tacit knowing, in the form of intuitive, imaginative, creative and insightful intellection, is part of the basic platform upon which the processes of thought and knowing organize and operate.

What has emerged in our discussion so far is a picture of knowledge showing a shared phenomenological background, social context, and tacit and explicit knowledge bound in relationships of co-dependence. Vygotsky (1986, p. 218) explains that 'Every thought tends to connect something with something else, to establish a relation between things. Every thought moves, grows and develops, fulfils a function, solves a problem.' However, we need to be able to place knowing more systematically in its social, material and phenomenological contexts and in so doing we must come to understand better how societies function intellectually. An effective way to do this is to develop a sociological model that explicitly foregrounds the relational or interrelational nature of knowledge.

An interrelational model

Recent theorizing has seen organizational knowledge treated as complex, distributed systems (Chia 1998; Hansen 1999; Schneider 2001; Snowden 2000; Spender 1996; Stacey 2001; Tsoukas 1996), socially distributed activity systems (Blackler 1993, 1995; Engestrom 1991, 1993), and shared contextual spaces (Nonaka et al. 2000; Von Krogh et al. 2000). Given our focus on the interrelational aspects of knowing and the interplay between the parts as generative mechanisms, we have much in common with these approaches. However, our approach differs in that it more discretely specifies social 'structural', political, phenomenological, temporal and physical components of the system as generative mechanisms. Bohm (2000, p. 58) illustrates the importance of linking the physical, temporal and phenomenological in saying:

Indeed, all man-made features of our general environment are . . . extensions of the process of thought, for their shapes, forms, and general orders of movement originate basically in thought, and are incorporated within this environment, in the activity of human work, which is guided by such thought. Vice versa, everything in the general environment has, either naturally or through human activity, a shape, form, and mode of movement, the content of which 'flows in' through perception, giving rise to sense impressions which leave memory traces and thus contribute to the basis of further thought.

In other words, man-made objects, natural objects and other features of the environment are linked to human thought and activity in a recursive cycle. The material and mental elements are not unrelated or juxtaposed; they are parts of the same reality. Furthermore, that Bohm speaks of a recursive flow also draws our attention to time, or more precisely history. That is, knowing is situated in a social and historical place that contains objects and people with their own social histories who belong to cultures and places that also have histories. These historical experiences carry institutions, assumptions, ideologies, stories and so on that influence what and how we think (cf. David 1994).

It is now necessary to set out a model of knowledge that incorporates social and phenomenological relations, history and locations, and social behaviour. To do this we can bring together the background of shared ideas, assumptions, propositions and so on (phenomenological background) with interacting knowers, and the contextual elements of social relationships (social–relational context), interpretation (interpretative–relational context), materiality and location (situation) of intellectual labour, and the idiosyncratic messy processes of people enacting (enactment) their knowledge. In doing so, we are modelling knowledge as systemic characteristics that are emergent phenomenological properties of interrelations. It is also important to do this because if we understand each of these aspects of knowledge systems, we can evaluate any knowledge systems (society, economy, firm) relative to them and identify the generative mechanisms for knowledge, innovation and so on within them.

Social–relational context
Ideas and ideational processes are central in the interaction of human agents (Hay 2001). In other words, social practices and therefore the structures of social organization necessarily have a conceptual dimension, and should be incorporated in a model of knowing. This means that a sociology of knowledge must account not only for the conceptual side of knowledge but also (among many other things) for the organizational structures of social relations in which knowing occurs (Bhaskar 1989). Bhaskar (1998, pp. 40–41) argues that social structures are continually reproduced or transformed by active human agents who occupy 'positions', and act performing functions and tasks commensurate with those positions in the light of rules and duties, relationally.

These positions can be specified in terms of their duties and functions and also the structures (e.g. hierarchies, social networks, families, communities, etc.) they relate to. These structures, relations and positions are the social–relational context. Social–relational context, therefore, is the social 'architecture' in which knowing occurs. In looking at this architecture, we are therefore emphasizing the connections between people and that those connections can be examined for their morphology, strength, symmetry, directionality and so on (Scott 2000). The structure and qualities of particular social networks, and the effects of positions, have implications for knowledge and, therefore, for knowledge societies, economies and organizations. Granovetter (1973), for instance, famously described the advantages of weak but broadly cast social connections over strong but narrowly confined social ties for facilitating the acquisition of new knowledge.

Interpretative–relational context
While social connections can be said to be structural in some way, ideas occur in a phenomenological context that also has some order and organization. Let us begin by exploring the organizational dimension by giving recognition to the associative nature of knowledge. Knowledge and understandings are always connected to other knowledge and understandings to form a network of ideas, memories, beliefs and so on. Boden (2003) argues that the most creative people have excellent associative powers. That is, such people can make quite extensive (even unusual) associations between quite disparate ideas to come up with excellent new ones. Thus, in identifying sensemaking and understanding as requiring ideas, interpretations, memories and so on to be linked in networks, we are highlighting what we call the interpretative–relational or mental context that shapes or orders knowers' sense-making frameworks and that allows them to interpret the world around them. This context is, therefore, not the same as the social–relational (although they overlap).

Interpretative–relational context could be perceived as an abstract terrain of distributed cognitions or distributed hermeneutics available to a defined set of interlocutors. Any social interaction related to the exchange of ideas is influenced by differences in the knowledge bases and particular ideational contexts of the people involved (Lave and Wenger 1991; Luhmann 1995; Wenger 1999, 2000). Thus within the social exchange process, the interpretation of data and information is based on hermeneutics derived from the participants' contexts (including their existing knowledge, history and repertoire of metaphors) (Duck 2002; Lundberg 1974; Luria 1976; Vygotsky 1986). In such a process, the conversationalists create knowledge between them. This newly created knowledge need not be identical for all parties involved. That is, different people will often interpret an event differently.

This context acknowledges the importance of the social production and reproduction of meaning but is not simply focused at the level of interpersonal relationships; rather, it focuses at the level of cognition and awareness, and the relationships between ideas within people and between people. This context therefore can be seen as socio-cognitive or socio-phenomenological (Graham and Rooney 2001). Another way of thinking about the interpretative–relational context is that it includes those parts of the phenomenological background brought into play when a social network forms around an issue or problem.

Cultural systems are made up in part by theories, beliefs, values, arguments and propositions and so interpretative–relational contexts also have a cultural level of organization. These theories, ideas and so on exist independently of any individual person's conscious awareness of them or of logical consistencies and inconsistencies between them (Archer 1996, pp. 107–8). Theories, beliefs, values, ideologies propositions and so on, being things held more or less in common in any cultural group, are therefore independent of any individual, and are part of the shared phenomenological background and more particularly the interpretative–relational context to social activity. Indeed, culture can be defined as a shared pattern of beliefs that lead to relatively stable patterns of behaviour of groups. This stability enables intersubjectivity and intertextuality, enabling communities to work coherently and produce the ideational commonality that allows us to think, understand and act in ways that are similar to those of other people.

It has already been pointed out that society presupposes knowledge and that a society in presupposing knowledge also presupposes the existence of ideas, theories and ideologies. However, in having ideas, societies also have ideas *about themselves* and those ideas about themselves can either reproduce or transform society (Bhaskar 1998, p. 48). This is a key point for knowledge-related policy. Cultural and individual self-awareness has the potential to produce reflexivity to the extent that we can acknowledge the need (as groups or individuals) for change or to remain the same. However, the choices that are made by or for a group about changing or not are negotiated politically and are influenced by position and the distribution of power. Vision, values, ethics and wisdom are critical here because those decisions about change and strategic direction are always value judgements affected by ideology, beliefs and so on.

In short, whereas the social–relational context is about communicating or diffusing knowledge through social network structures, influenced by position, the interpretative–relational context primarily addresses how meaning and knowledge are configured or ordered, and generated intersubjectively by their relations to other meanings and knowledge (and therefore also to culture and power). Thus, to reiterate, we are connecting knowledge to the networks of assumptions, values, meaning and so on that make up the phenomenological background to social activity and which act as an organizing force for sense-making, intentionality, creativity and the like. Of course, the interpretative– and social–relational contexts are not mutually exclusive; they are two different orders of the same reality and are therefore deeply connected.

The knower

The knower, of course, is the individual. Although we have just discussed the social–relational and interpretative–relational contexts in which individuals are less than the relationship, so to speak, we cannot escape the importance of the individual as a 'doer' of things, as the base component of relationships, as a catalyst for inter-personal relationship formation, and as the possessor of the idiosyncratic mind. Therefore, 'the *generative* role of agents' skills and wants, and of agents' (and other social) beliefs and meanings must be recognised' (Bhaskar 1989, p. 98, italics in original). Individuals need to be made aware of and facilitated to effectively take their place in the overall context, and to speculate, cooperate, contest, advocate and otherwise communicate in the interest of better knowing. This also includes taking on personal responsibilities in learning, sharing knowledge, gaining general experience, being an effective communicator, being ethical and so on.

The situation

Bhaskar (1989, p. 79) says society 'is an articulated ensemble of tendencies and powers which . . . exist only as long as they (or at least some of them) are being exercised; are exercised in the last instance via the intentional activity of human beings; and are necessarily space-time invariant'. Included in our discussion of knowledge, then, is an acknowledgement that knowing occurs in defined situations. Knowledge understood in this way is said to be situated (Lave and Wenger 1991), and situations can be said to have their own situational logic (Archer 1996). For the purposes of this discussion, the knower's situation is defined by the time and space they occupy, and, more specifically, the time and space in which their impulse to act becomes action. Importantly, with the situation we seek to account directly not only for the personal, cognitive, sociological and phenomenological locations and shapers of knowledge, but now also the historical, spatial and physical elements of knowledge systems.

The physical aspects of situations include technology, and other elements of the built environment such as buildings and cultural artefacts, and the natural environment or geography (Burke 2000). We acknowledge here that at the very least society includes not only objects but beliefs about those objects (Bhaskar 1989, p. 101). We can go further than saying we hold beliefs about objects, and also say that objects can affect our moods, attitudes, memories and so on. Objects can, in other words, change how and what we think, learn and do. Thus it is also important to account for the effects of cultural and religious objects, furniture, landscape, design, colour etc. on intellection. This logic explains why the spaces in which monastic contemplation and creative brainstorming take place are very different. Additionally, because the diffusion of knowledge is frequently mediated by information (e.g. text and images) stored and transmitted on various media, we should be able to explicitly include storage, diffusion and mediating technology in our model.

Because facts, meanings, interpretations and the like are historically specific social realities, history must be acknowledged as a part of the reality of social activity (Bhaskar 1989, 1998). While many theorists acknowledge the passing of time, they do not specifically acknowledge historicity in social change. It is insufficient to provide only a temporal sequence at the expense of history. History is an unfolding of events in a complex context that must be understood. In this case history is better understood as a story of what, how and why something came to be as it is, rather than as a timeline. Those historical unfoldings and the historiographical narratives that explain them, by virtue of their influences on knowledge, affect the future (Archer 1995, p. 167) by shaping our assumptions and proposals about what could, should and will be. How the social history of individuals and groups will predispose individuals and groups to think and act is therefore salient to knowledge. If we have some idea of how history preconditions intellectual work in given situations, we can work with the force of history rather than against it by using knowledge of each other's histories as a basis for better understandings between people, and for drawing on the diversity of experiences in those histories to develop new insights and wisdom. Moreover, if we know what historical narratives are influencing knowledge, we are in a position to test or challenge the validity of the assumptions and beliefs reproduced in those narratives.

Enactment
Collective and individual behaviours are capable of developing both relatively enduring patterns and unpredictable changes (Bhaskar 1998), and this leads us to the final part of our model, enactment. It is the process of acting on our knowledge, intuitions, memories and so on that we are interested in here. In considering enacting knowledge it is noticeable that people enact what they have in their minds predictably and unpredictably, intentionally and unintentionally, rationally and irrationally. Enactment therefore highlights more than the fact that we act on our knowledge; it brings a focus to the contradictions and paradoxes associated with the social and individual application of knowledge.

People enact their intentions in a complex world, and much of this complexity is at the phenomenological level (Hearn et al. 2003). If we begin to explore these processes of production and reproduction at this level we note, first, that enactment of the sense made of our experience and position in the world occurs more or less intentionally. The effectiveness of this intentionality depends in part on knowers' conscious, intuitive, reflexive and strategic mental powers. Knowers can be seen as strategic because in being broadly intentional they generally enact their intentions purposively (strategically and politically) to realize their goals and preferences now and in the future. Hay (2001, p. 8) argues that

> to act strategically is to project the likely consequences of different courses of action and, in turn, to judge the contours of the terrain . . . to orient potential courses of action to perceptions of the relevant strategic context and to use such an exercise as a means to select the particular course of action to be pursued. On such an understanding, the ability to formulate strategy (whether explicitly recognised as such or not) is the very condition of action.

However, knowers inevitably enact their intensions in a messy way. Therefore, Hay's comments must be qualified with his further observation that any action will probably involve both intuitive and explicit strategies; and that both intuitive and explicit strategic choices are likely also to rely on incomplete or misleading information and imperfect knowledge (Hay 2001). We must also recognize that the human mind is not a perfectly rational machine, an observation that led Simon (1955, 1991) to conclude that people are boundedly rational. Bounded rational ability is only one of the limits on human intellectual capacity. Imperfect knowledge is another important limitation. This is not only about the shortcomings of information and data provision; it is also about having real cognitive limits to our capacity to know and understand, and the sheer scale of what is potentially knowable about the world (Campbell 1974). No matter how hard we try, we cannot know or learn everything. Inevitable outcomes of this are errors of judgement and fact, indecision, misinterpretation and so on. It is therefore important to recognize that the messy enactment of intentionality and strategy in a model of knowledge stands in stark contrast to the fictionally rational *Homo economicus* who is not intuitive, and has perfect information and knowledge. This fictional being, found in standard economics, indeed which underpins much of the standard economic theory of behaviour, has no place in a serious sociology of knowledge. Enactment, therefore, is the fallibly intentional and directed use of knowledge.

Further qualifying the purposive and strategic nature of enactment is the observation that people are positioned in roles that are to an extent involuntary. Different people in different parts of social systems, having different positions and roles, have different vested interests and power, and experience different rewards and frustrations. Given the extent to which those roles are involuntarily occupied and are subject to the political influences of vested interests, fluctuating levels of commitment to the functions, duties and so on attached to those roles will lead to fluctuations in the playing out of roles, resulting in either further unpredictability or inertia. Thus vested interests need to be understood in terms of interest in influencing both the *status quo* and change, what positions and roles people occupy, and what is the nature of their ethical, ideological and other commitments to those roles. These variables should therefore be considered for their effects on knowledge because position and ideological stance condition and constrain the degree and direction of interpretative freedom, the desire to be innovative, and condition judgements about what individuals and groups have to win or lose from change (Archer 1995, pp. 201–3). It is obvious that these constraints on freedoms can prevent change. What is not so obvious are the tensions they create within individuals and groups, and that these tensions can be unevenly distributed, causing more tensions. When enough tensions develop, dramatic change may result.

The above points are important because they highlight that not only is the potential for change embedded in every act of social reproduction, but also in every tension. Exploring the implications of these tensions and uneven distributions, we observe that part of the messiness of enactment is that those social–relational structures and the purposes, intentions, beliefs, assumptions, proposals and so on of agents are rarely ever consistently directed or evenly distributed. What all this contributes to our understanding of the messiness and fallibility of enacting knowledge is that such are the inconsistencies, incompatibilities and tensions in societies that

> it is only in a minority of cases that an entire social system will have all [or enough of] its components (institutions, roles and distributions) aligned in terms of one emergent core complementarity or incompatibility which . . . enmeshes all agents in the same situational logic . . . [where] all material resources are mobilized in that single direction. (Archer 1995, p. 227)

In a model of knowledge it is therefore important to account for those 'powers', tensions, inertial forces and other tendencies that reproduce or transform knowledge, assumptions, values and so on, and to recognize that the negotiation of this messiness to direct a society's ideas is done politically. This raises questions about the efficacy and ethics of the politics of knowledge and how political influences shape the kind of knowledge, assumptions, values and so on that social groups have.

Fallible enactment, therefore, also means that a knowledge system is unlikely to be highly predictable and controllable. This is a problem for managers and policy specialists who seek the very things we are denying them, predictability and control. Ormerod (1998) suggests that one way to deal with this at a policy level is to take a long-term view. He argues that collective behaviour in social systems viewed in snap-shots appears random but that over a long period patterns will emerge from the apparent randomness. It is from this long-term historical understanding that strategic interventions can be devised. Thus while one cannot necessarily predict or control for specific errors individuals and social groups might make, one can be prepared for the fact that errors do occur, and that over a long time people and more particularly societies will, collectively, tend to learn and change their commonly held beliefs, although often slowly. Indeed, Ormerod believes that the messy and chaotic nature of social systems is what sustains them and is precisely what should be preserved in them. Messy enactment suggests, therefore, that wisdom, and attention to context and process in knowledge systems are paramount.

Summary

To aid clarity about what our position means for knowledge management and policy, we list our key observations about knowledge. We maintain that:

- Learning and knowing are individual and social phenomena, where both interact with and constitute each other.
- Knowing is bound to human consciousness. Storage media contain data, texts and images but not knowledge.
- Knowing is a social and cultural process and is therefore sensitive to social and cultural conditions.
- Because knowledge is sensitive to context and is fallibly enacted, it cannot be managed. Data can be managed but context and human fallibility can only be influenced.
- Knowledge is an emergent process that is heavily reliant on tacit or unconscious processes working co-dependently with explicit knowledge, leading to fallible enactment with unpredictable and enigmatic results that cannot always be easily controlled, predicted, documented, transferred or transmitted.
- Fallibility and the enigmatic mental processes are the wellsprings of innovation and creativity.
- Tacit and explicit dimensions of knowledge are not dichotomous but interact with each other.
- There is a socially produced phenomenological organizing background that gives knowledge systems coherence, novelty, sense and their dynamics.
- The act of imposing order on messy knowledge systems is a political act and should be monitored for the inappropriate use of power and how it restricts knowledge and its enactment.

The main challenge for knowledge management and policy results largely from complex human systems that are not amenable to control-based management regimes due to the contingencies of context, situation and the fallible ways in which people think, learn, know and enact (Schneider 1999). For knowledge management and policy this presents a predicament. The system is beyond control (although it may be responsive to managed interventions), and the very intangible and emergent nature of knowledge means it is always beyond grasp. The trap is to fall for the illusion of control (of the system), and to focus only on the output rather than the underlying process and environment. It is the understanding and stewardship of interrelations within contexts, and between contexts and an environment, that needs most attention. Shaping the many and various relationships, including the contexts in which they occur, influencing the qualities of the environment and accessing the background become objectives of knowledge management and policy. The strategic questions in knowledge management and policy therefore need to be about how to access the background, and what relationships are most important and how they work. The tactical questions are about how to make positive interventions to facilitate those relationships. We need to emphasize, therefore, the *process* and *context* of knowing, and particularly those mediating and self-organizing processes that derive from relationships, communication, sociality and the tacit background.

References

Archer, Margaret S. 1995. *Realist Social Theory: The Morphogenetic Approach*. Cambridge: Cambridge University Press.
Archer, Margaret S. 1996. *Culture and Agency: The Place of Culture in Social Theory* (rev. edn). Cambridge: Cambridge University Press.
Berger, Peter and Thomas Luckmann. 1966. *The Social Construction of Reality: A Treatise in the Sociology of Knowledge*. New York: Doubleday.
Bhaskar, Roy. 1989. *Reclaiming Reality: A Critical Introduction to Contemporary Philosophy*. London: Verso.
Bhaskar, Roy. 1998. *The Possibility of Naturalism: A Philosophical Critique of the Contemporary Human Science* (3rd edn). London: Routledge.
Blackler, Frank. 1993. 'Knowledge and the theory of organizations: Organizations as activity systems and the reframing of management'. *Journal of Management Studies* 30:863–84.
Blackler, Frank. 1995. 'Knowledge, knowledge work and organizations: An overview and interpretations'. *Organization Studies* 16:1021–46.
Boden, Margaret A. 2003. *The Creative Mind: Myths and Mechanisms* (2nd edn). London: Routledge.
Bohm, David. 2000. *Wholeness and the Implicate Order*. London: Routledge.
Boulding, Kenneth E. 1956. *The Image: Knowledge in Life and Society*. Ann Arbor, MI: University of Michigan Press.
Brockman, Erich N. and William P. Anthony. 1998. 'The influences of tacit knowledge and collective mind on strategic planning'. *Academy of Management Review* 10:204–22.
Brunswick, E. 1956. *Perception and the Representative Design of Experiments*. Berkeley, CA: University of California Press.
Burke, Peter. 2000. *A Social History of Knowledge: From Gutenberg to Diderot*. Cambridge: Polity.
Campbell, Donald T. 1974. 'Evolutionary epistemology'. Pp. 413–63 in *Language, Development and Culture*, edited by D.T.E. Campbell. New York: John Wiley & Sons.
Chia, Robert. 1998. 'From complexity science to complex thinking: Organization as simple location'. *Organization* 5:341–69.

Cohen, Wesley M. and Daniel A. Levinthal. 1990. 'Absorptive capacity: A new perspective on learning and innovation'. *Administrative Science Quarterly* **35**:128–52.

David, Paul A. 1994. 'Why are institutions the "carriers of history"?' *Structural Change and Economic Dynamics* **5**:205–20.

Duck, Steve. 2002. 'Hypertext in the key of G: Three types of "history" as influences on conversational structure and flow'. *Communication Theory* **12**:41–62.

Edelman, Gerald M. and Giulio Tononi. 2000. *A Universe of Consciousness: How Matter Becomes Imagination*. New York: Basic Books.

Engestrom, Y. 1991. 'Developmental work research: Reconstructing expertise through expansive learning'. Pp. 265–103 in *Human Jobs and Computer Interfaces*, edited by M. Nurminen and G. Weir. Amsterdam: North-Holland.

Engestrom, Y. 1993. 'Work as a testbed for activity theory'. Pp. 65–103 in *Understanding Practice: Perspectives on Activity and Context*, edited by S. Chaiklin and J. Lave. Cambridge: Cambridge University Press.

Gebser, Jean. 1985. *The Ever Present Origin.* Translated by N. Barstad and T.A. Mickunas. Athens, GA: Ohio University Press.

Graham, Philip and David Rooney. 2001. 'A sociolinguistic approach to applied epistemology: Examining technocratic values in global "knowledge" policy'. *Social Epistemology* **15**:155–69.

Granovetter, Mark S. 1973. 'The strength of weak ties'. *American Journal of Sociology* **78**:1360–80.

Grant, Robert, M. 1996. 'Towards a knowledge-based theory of the firm'. *Strategic Management Journal* **17**:109–22.

Hansen, Morten T. 1999. 'The search–transfer problem: The role of weak ties in sharing knowledge across organization subunits'. *Administrative Science Quarterly* **44**:82–111.

Hay, Colin. 2001. 'What place for ideas in the structure–agency debate? Globalisation as a "Process without a subject" '. http//:www.raggedclaws.com/criticalrealism/archive/cshay-wpisad.html.24 November 2003.

Hearn, G., D. Rooney and T. Mandeville. 2003. 'Phenomenological turbulence and innovation in knowledge systems'. *Prometheus* **21**:231–46.

Hitt, M.A. and B.B. Tyler. 1991. 'Strategic decision models: Integrating different perspectives'. *Strategic Management Journal* **12**:327–51.

Kogut, Bruce and Udo Zander. 1993. 'Knowledge of the firm and the evolutionary theory of the multinational corporation.' *Journal of International Business Studies* **24**:625–45.

Lave, Jean and Etienne Wenger. 1991. *Situated Learning: Legitimate Peripheral Participation.* Cambridge: Cambridge University Press.

Luhmann, Niklas. 1995. *Social Systems.* Translated by John Bednarz, Jr, with Dirk Baeker. Stanford, CA: Stanford University Press.

Lundberg, Margaret J. 1974. *The Incomplete Adult: Social Class Constraints on Personality Development.* Westport, CT: Greenwood Press.

Luria, A.R. 1976. *Cognitive Development: Its Cultural and Social Foundations.* Translated by M. Lopez-Morillas and L. Solotaroff. Cambridge, MA: Harvard University Press.

Mithen, Steven. 1998. *The Prehistory of the Mind: A Search for the Origins of Art, Religion and Science.* London: Phoenix.

Moorman, Christine and Anne S. Miner. 1998. 'Organisational improvisation and organisational memory'. *The Academy of Management Review* **23**:698–723.

Nonaka, Ikujiro and Hirotake Takeuchi. 1995. *The Knowledge Creating Company: How Japanese Companies Create the Dynamics of Innovation.* New York: Oxford University Press.

Nonaka, Ikujiro, Ryoko Toyama and Noboru Konno. 2000. 'SECI, *ba* and leadership: A unified model of dynamic knowledge creation'. *Long Range Planning* **33**:5–34.

Ormerod, Paul. 1998. *Butterfly Economics: A General Theory of Social and Economic Behaviour.* London: Faber and Faber.

Rogers, Everett M. 1980. *Diffusion of Innovations.* New York: Free Press.

Schneider, Ursula. 1999. 'Management als Steuerung des organisatorischen Wissens', in *Managing Change, Change in Management.* Berlin: Duncker and Humbolt.

Schneider, Ursula 2001. *Die 7 Todsünden im Wissensmanagement: Kardinaltugenden für die Wissensökonomie*. Frankfurt am Main: Frankfurter Allgemeine Buch.

Scott, John. 2000. *Social Network Analysis: A Handbook*. London: Sage.

Shapin, Steven. 1994. *A Social History of Truth: Civility and Science in Seventeenth-Century England*. Chicago: University of Chicago Press.

Sigley, Mark and John Anderson. 1989. *The Transfer of Cognitive Skill*. Cambridge, MA: Harvard University Press.

Simon, Herbert A. 1955. 'A behavioural model of rational choice'. *Quarterly Journal of Economics* **69**:99–118.

Simon, Herbert A. 1991. 'Bounded rationality and organizational learning'. *Organization Science* **2**:125–34.

Snowden, Monique L. 2000. 'Modeling organizational communication and knowledge management: A systems approach to evaluation and conceptualisation', in *50th Annual International Communication Association Conference*. Acapulco, Mexico, June 2000.

Spender, J.-C. 1996. 'Organizational knowledge, learning and memory: Three concepts in search of a theory'. *Journal of Organizational Change Management* **9**:63–78.

Stacey, Ralph D. 2001. *Complex Responsive Processes in Organizations: Learning and Knowledge Creation*. London: Routledge.

Tsoukas, Haridimos. 1996. 'The firm as a distributed knowledge system: A constructionist approach'. *Strategic Management Journal* **17**:11–25.

von Krogh, Georg, Kazuo Ichijo and Ikujiro Nonaka. 2000. *Enabling Knowledge Creation: How to Unlock the Mystery of Tacit Knowledge and Release the Power of Innovation*. Oxford: Oxford University Press.

Vygotsky, Lev. 1986. *Thought and Language*. Translated by T. Alex Kozulin. Cambridge, MA: MIT Press.

Wenger, Etienne. 1999. *Communities of Practice: Learning, Meaning and Identity*. Cambridge: Cambridge University Press.

Wenger, Etienne. 2000. 'Communities of practice and social learning systems'. *Organization* **7**:225–46.

Whitehead, Alfred North. 1984. *Prozeß und Realität, Entwurf einer Kosmologie*. Frankfurt: Suhrkamp Verlag.

Winter, Sidney. 1987. 'Knowledge and competence as strategic assets', in *The Competitive Challenge: Strategies for Industrial Innovation and Renewal*, edited by D. Teece. Cambridge, MA: Ballinger.

Zack, Michael H. 1999. 'Managing codified knowledge'. *Sloan Management Review* **40**:45–58.

Zander, Udo and Bruce Kogut. 1995. 'Knowledge and the speed of the transfer and imitation of organizational capabilities: An empirical test'. *Organization Science* **6**:76–92.

3 Wisdom, ethics and the postmodern organization

Bernard McKenna

> Turning and turning in the widening gyre
> The falcon cannot hear the falconer;
> Things fall apart; the centre cannot hold;
> . . .
> The best lack all convictions, while the worst
> Are full of passionate intensity.
>
> W.B. Yeats

'Worn gears threaten derailment', stated the lead story in *The Sydney Morning Herald* (Kerr 2004). A week earlier, railway drivers had gone on strike because the rail authorities' failure to plan for driver attrition had caused a critical shortage of drivers. A concurrent inquest that found that a fatal rail accident was caused by a medically unfit driver dying at the wheel led to the disclosure that 70 per cent of country drivers were found to be medically unfit. Yet the CityRail website (http://www.cityrail.info/) tells me that it 'offers passengers one of the most cost effective, reliable, and convenient ways to travel around Sydney and beyond'; that 'All trains receive regular routine maintenance and major periodic maintenance'. They monitor their performance in three major KPIs (key performance indicators), and publish their results on the web. So, how is this relevant to wisdom and ethics? It is simply to question the wisdom and (by definition, implicitly) the ethics of a management culture within the context of a knowledge economy that supposedly delivers 'best practice' by means of auditable notions such as KPI. We need to question the very ontological and epistemological categories that underpin contemporary management practices infused with assumptions that gathering and using data improve our life.

Furthermore, I argue that we need to question the discursive inscriptions of participants in the 'new economy' organization. These two factors – a naïve management understanding of the knowledge economy and ideological inscription – I argue force management and workers into a schizophrenic set of practices based on regulation and control as oppressive at least as Taylorism (a feature of 'modern' industrial practice), while proclaiming that we are more autonomous than ever. Furthermore, I argue that valorized management practice is subject to ephemeral waves of orthodoxy. To overcome this 'widening gyre' of managerialist illusion and disillusion, I assert that the principles of wise practice – because they are timeless – should be the foundation of management theory and practice. Because excesses of postmodern theory cripple the epistemic and ethical basis of daily life, I furthermore argue that the common sense (*nous*), and inherent virtue, of wisdom will help to restore faith in the organization and regulation of our lives. Crucial to achieving wisdom is the capacity for reflexivity, which is the ability to understand the epistemic and ethical basis of our practice within its discursive domain.

The schizophrenia of contemporary life

We live in an age where individualism and choice at the level of subject and the significance of data and information at the level of object are esteemed in hegemonic discourses. Although these have been the politico-ethical features of western culture since the Enlightenment, the French, American and British revolutions, and the emergence of industrial capitalism, they have reached their apotheosis within the hegemonic discourses of neo-liberalism and neo-classical economics. Yet, paradoxically, more and more parts of our life are regulated by a technical rationality with which we must comply (e.g. the simple act of owning a pet – a timeless practice – must now be regulated by licences and local government laws).

Beck (Beck and Beck-Gernsheim 2002) argues that we are forced to be individuals in a neo-liberal hegemony, but that this individualization occurs in conditions that make it virtually impossible for the individual to achieve independence. In modern times (i.e. mid-nineteenth century onwards) individuals could make choices, but were restricted in the family and the workplace particularly, Beck argues, by bonds of authority and deference, tradition and customs, and institutions. Rose (1996) similarly describes the community and kinship of modernity as defining 'the identity of subjects from outside, embedd[ing] the person within a stable order of status, within a transcendental and implacable cosmology' (p. 301). Now, though 'liberated' from these bonds, the postmodern individual is more prone to fashions, trends and markets (see also Anderson 2001). Thus, although the postmodern subject is represented as free through choice, he or she is still limited by a consciousness drawing from the contemporary hegemonies of neo-classical economics[1] and a neo-liberal ethic. Consequently, the postmodern subject is the self-governing individual who is 'formed in relation to practices of freedom and techniques of the self' (Dean 1994, p. 195). Those values most esteemed are 'autonomy, freedom, choice, authenticity, enterprise, lifestyle' (Rose 1996, p. 320), features of active agency.

Two important effects flow from this: increasing complexity and the autonomy gap. Beck and Beck-Gernsheim (2002) claims that participation in society increasingly requires individual decision-making, even when it is not required. In some significant instances, this forces responsibility onto the individual unfairly. For example, whereas in the past a person in a superannuation scheme paid their money into a fund where 'experts' invested it wisely and prudently on their behalf, the individual is often now required to make complex financial decisions for which few people are qualified. In addition, aspects of life that were never a matter of negotiation or decision have become so. This is particularly so in the 'democratizing' of relations that were formerly governed by traditional authority (e.g. parents, teachers; husband/wife; manager/worker). Some of these have been important in the liberation of people (e.g. husband–wife relations; equal pay and conditions), but they bring with them new complexifying issues. Some 'advances' are less obvious, even retrogressive (e.g. many parents suffer unnecessary angst in regulating the conduct of their children; most teachers are not allowed to discipline to curb foul behaviour by uncontrolled adolescents). Even purchasing a phone or a hamburger is laden with complex choices. The second important effect is the 'autonomy gap', which occurs whenever an institutional or societal arrangement is premised on unreasonable expectations about individuals' level of competence (Anderson 2001). Faced with this, society can either raise the level of competence or lower the level of complexity required. Unfortunately, with reduced levels of government support as the outcome of our neo-liberal hegemony, the first of these options is rarely provided, while the second might be seen as curbing the right to free choice.

In contrast to this liberatory myth (used in the Barthesian sense), rationality, codification and measurement are the technologies that supposedly deal with complexity. As Sarup (1989) points out, the 'economic and administrative rationalization and differentiation of the social world' is a feature of modernity, not postmodernity. Yet such features continue to dominate contemporary organizational and commercial culture: organizations are founded on features of 'efficiency, predictability, calculability, and substitution of technology for human involvement' (Beyer and Niño 1998). This has led, say Schön (1995) and Jacques (1996), to a current crisis of confidence in technical rationality, because clearly it has failed to produce the certainty that it claims to deliver. Nevertheless, because we have been inducted into, and inculcated with, norms of social practice based on a technocratic rationality stripped of humanist principles (Spragens 2001, p. 56), we are left floundering in the search for epistemic and ethical certitude.

In their place, I argue that a broad commitment to wise practice would be more likely not only to produce better outcomes, but also to enhance efficiency as administrative and surveillance practices are dismantled. So how do we become wise? In the first place, being wise is not some add-on to current practice. Wise practice – like unwise practice – infuses everyday life: a caveat that should act as a warning against wisdom becoming another management fad. In a recent paper (Rooney and McKenna forthcoming), it was argued that a distillation of the wisdom tradition (from the Old Testament and Aristotle, Aquinas and Vico) produces a similar set of characteristics for being wise as that devised more recently by psychological analysis (Baltes and Kunzmann 2003; Baltes and Staudinger 2000; Sternberg 1990; Sternberg and Ben-Zeev 2001). Such a finding should provide confidence in the efficacy of these characteristics.

Definition of wisdom

From a psychological perspective, wisdom can be defined as that which:

> coordinates knowledge and judgments about the fundamental pragmatics of life around such properties as: (1) strategies and goals involving the conduct and meaning of life; (2) limits of knowledge and uncertainties of the world; (3) excellence of judgment and advice; (4) knowledge with extraordinary scope, depth, and balance; (5) search for a perfect synergy of mind and character; and (6) balancing the good or well-being of oneself and that of others. (Baltes and Staudinger 2000, p. 132)

Clearly, then, wisdom is more than a cognitive attribute: it also demands social, ethical and discursive competence. The nine characteristics of wisdom outlined by Rooney and McKenna (forthcoming) unmistakeably imply that wise action, although reasoned, requires us to act and think outside the bounds of rationality and accepted, codified knowledge; that it is grounded in worldly day-to-day activity; assumes that life is contingent; and is virtuous and humane. By distilling the Aristotelian (Aristotle 1984, 2003) and Thomistic (Aquinas 1964) accounts of wisdom as well as Vico's (Miner 1998; Vico 1982) writing, the pre-modern wisdom tradition can be said to comprise nine elements.

1. Wisdom has a spiritual or metaphysical quality that does not bind it to the rules of reason.
2. It evaluates the salience and truth-value of logical propositions when applying reason to decision-making.
3. It acknowledges the sensory and visceral as important components of decision-making.
4. The purpose of wisdom is virtuous action.
5. It is prudent and practical, displaying a sensible worldliness.
6. Because wisdom understands the contingency of life and circumstance, and the constructedness of phenomena in a spatio-temporal location, it is not reducible to method.
7. It respects and draws upon experience and tradition as a means of apprehending who and what we are.
8. It is able to clearly articulate judgements in an aesthetically pleasing way.
9. It is tolerant, born of a natural affection for humanity

The first three characteristics are now well established in empirical psychological research. Sternberg (1990) asserts that sagacity combines intelligence and creativity, and is 'more than just cognitive skills' (p. 157). The 'attitude toward knowledge as knowledge itself' is best described as a form of 'fluid intelligence', which is characterized by the capacity 'to manipulate abstract symbols' (Sternberg 1990, p. 323). The common understanding of wisdom, which psychological researchers call *folk* or *intuitive*, according to Baltes and Staudinger's (2000) surveys, is that there are intellectual, affective and motivational aspects of wisdom. The fourth characteristic roots wisdom in values and ethics, which is consistent also with psychological theory (Sternberg and Ben-Zeev 2001, pp. 231–6).

Wisdom is also essentially worldly, as stated in the fifth characteristic, even though the wise person is contemplative and reflexive. Baltes and Staudinger (2000) describe this as having rich factual (declarative) knowledge about 'the fundamental pragmatics of life'. A wise person knows how much the weekly shopping costs; what people are watching on television; and who are the heroes of sport and popular culture. For many, this may simply mean flicking through the *Woman's Day* or *Who* while waiting at the supermarket checkout, or non-judgementally leaving the radio station on the children's choice while driving them to sport. What distinguishes the wise person is the capacity to rise above these minutiae when necessary, but with an enhanced capacity to see the world as others see it.

The sixth characteristic, because of its epistemological and ontological implications, would be quite complex if fully elaborated.[2] At its simplest, it says that wise people assume that any phenomenon can be 'known' in various ways depending on the ontological categories with which we frame and apprehend it. Wise people also know that any situation has an inexhaustible number of aspects to it, but that people have a finite capacity for information. The classic example is a school teacher who punishes a child for hitting another in full public view, but may not be aware of an ongoing, subtle harassment that the aggressor may have suffered over the previous months. Rather than giving up in the face of ontological and epistemological uncertainty, wise people make decisions that are based on a reasonable judgement of relevant information. However, wise people also know that, fundamentally, they may be understanding things from an inappropriate or wrongly based ontology within a particular paradigm. Furthermore, acknowledging the contingency of life should not preclude automatized processes. In day-to-day life, wise actions can be automatized to a certain degree. For example, in some jurisdictions doctors are required to report suspected cases of child abuse. Some may reasonably argue that such a requirement reduces a doctor's capacity to make a judgement. However, such a rule might be justified to cover a possible Type 2 error (an error is not rejected even though it may be wrong in fact) rather than allowing Type 1 errors (a true state of affairs is rejected because of insufficient proof) to be made.[3] In other words, it might be better to investigate innocent situations, however troubling, rather than not investigate a situation because of doubt or fear of repercussions. Of course, although the issues of rights and privacy, among others, could be endlessly debated, on balance in some matters such as child abuse, it may be the wisest course of action to automatize a course of action provided the relevant issues have been thoroughly considered. In other words, automatized practices need not be mindless or authoritarian so long as they are well grounded, explicable, transparent and open to review in the light of practice.

Yet, although paradigm shifts may be completely appropriate from time to time, continual paradigmatic change is destabilizing. A good example of the appropriateness of paradigm change happened when the High Court of Australia overturned an 80-year-old precedent of *terra nullius* (empty land) to acknowledge that Australia was inhabited by indigenous people when the British colonized the land in the eighteenth century (Mabo 1992).[4] As a consequence of this long-overdue paradigm shift, indigenous people for the first time received legal recognition for their claims to land 'ownership' (incidentally an ontological category that didn't exist in indigenous relations). Consequently, wiser possibilities for justice, rather than mere legality, emerged.

Destabilizing paradigm shifts are most obvious in managerial faddism. Change management and 're-engineering' have become institutionalized features of contemporary organizational practice. However, encouragingly, (critical) management theorists (but also mainstream theorists and practitioners: see Axelrod 2000)[5] are strongly challenging this unnecessarily bewildering process. Among the criticisms are that contemporary management discourse mindlessly valorizes change within management practice (Zorn et al. 1999); that, despite claims to be democratic and responsive, it is in fact extremely conformist and authoritarian (Willmott 1993); that it is faddish (Valentine and Knights 1998; Zorn et al. 2000); and that its benefits are very dubious (Zorn et al. 1999). In this age where the maxim 'the only certainty is change' dominates the ethic of business practice it is crucial, indeed efficient for the organization, to know when proposals to change practice are justified. While it is certainly true, as Baltes and Staudinger (2000) argue, that a distinguishing feature of wise people is their ability to manage uncertainty (p. 126), this does not mean that wise people deliberately create uncertainty and change. It means that wise people can separate negative changes which are intended for empire building for developing and maintaining power from those that promote necessary positive change, and adapt accordingly. Often such negative changes can be as trivial as altered nomenclature (such as a university that changed its Teaching & Learning centre to a Learning and Teaching centre, or

changed its Library to a Cybrary). The no doubt well-articulated and intellectually crafted justifications for these changes are often understood only by
those who made the changes, and can be used as discursive markers to identify those 'in the know' and those who fail the discursive entry test. In this
sense, wise practice is especially relevant to our postmodern times where epistemic and axiological truths are so contested.

The seventh characteristic acknowledges the importance of tradition in
deeply knowing who and what we are. In contrast to more traditional societies,
including indigenous and Confucian, which are characterized by tradition,
stasis and elder respect, postmodern society is characterized by a culture
where youth, impermanence and change are valorized. While it is unrealistic
to attempt to appropriate another cultural characteristic to implant in our own
– most probably simply another fad – the likelihood of balance increases when
we evaluate our own cultural characteristics and reflect on others. In fairness,
it would have to be acknowledged that our western culture has delivered much
that is worthwhile in consumer goods and services, medicine, education and
travel. Certain groups of people thrive in the conditions of dynamic technological postmodernity and postmodern culture. On the other hand, we also
know that these conditions also produce anomie, rootlessness, uncertainty and
the spiritual vacuity of consumer culture. The Wisdom tradition understands
that wise people are carriers of a tradition who can draw on the deep processes,
knowledge and intuition of a reflexive humanity. It is in this sense that wise
people draw on other traditions. This does not mean that we simply ask a tribal
elder to open the proceedings of our next conference and then get on with the
real business; it doesn't mean that we feng-shui our office, though this may be
aesthetically pleasing. What it does mean is that a wise person can help to
incorporate the best of the new or the 'other' while maintaining the best of the
old.

Because wisdom is passed on, it must be articulated in a way that people
understand: the eighth characteristic. This is done in two ways: explaining
difficult decisions, and in transmitting folk wisdom. When wisdom is called
upon in action, it is invariably to resolve a complex issue. For example, judges
who decide issues of child custody and fair apportioning of income and wealth
invariably do so after all the other processes of mediation and conciliation
have failed and when grief and anger are profound. Such a judge must be able
to deliver a fair judgment, but, as importantly, to explain this to the litigants in
a way that might be understood and accepted. There are, of course, many other
complex, fraught situations, such as when people lose jobs, decide about how
to care for elderly, frail parents, or forgo a career to allow a partner to pursue
theirs. In such situations, decision-makers need to state the issue at hand, its
salient factors, the reasoning process, the human factors and the reasons for
the judgement. Such a process enhances the humane – by respecting people's

feelings – and models behaviours and processes for others to emulate. Another way to transmit wisdom is through folk wisdom. This is commonly in the form of aphorisms and sayings that are passed on from generation to generation. For example, I can still recall my Irish immigrant grandmother who raised five children as a young widow in the Depression saying 'wilful waste makes woeful want' as she stored bits of string and brown paper. As a young child, I didn't actually know what *wilful* and *woeful* meant. Nevertheless, this now fully realized aphorism comes to me almost daily as a committed environmentalist living in an excessively consumerist society as a guide to action. Baltes and Staudinger's (2000) analysis of folk wisdom reinforces the importance of this popular transmission of worthwhile behaviours. They reaffirm the claim that 'Cultural memory is the mother of wisdom' (p. 123. For more on this, see Clayton and Birren 1980; Csikszentmihalyi and Rathunde 1990; and Orwoll and Perlmutter 1990).

Finally, wise practice is humanistic in the sense that it is aesthetically pleasing and humane. The notion of aesthetics, initially, may seem odd. However, Vico's concept of *Ingenium* incorporates the capacity to 'connect disparate and diverse things', while maintaining their proportion so that decisions are 'apt, fitting, beautiful' (Vico in Miner 1998, p. 69). Management icon Chester Barnard concurs, stating that good managers have a 'sense of harmony and relevancy' (Wolf 2002). Wisdom is also concerned with virtuous,[6] or ethical, action. This was certainly as Aristotle understood wisdom in terms of both intellectual and moral virtues. As he states in the first lines of *Ethics*: 'Every art and every investigation, and similarly every action and pursuit, is considered to aim at some good. Hence the good has been rightly defined as "that at which all things aim" ' (Aristotle 2003, p. 3). Again we find concurrence between traditional wisdom and contemporary psychological theory. Sternberg (1990) identifies as characteristic of sagacity that it: has concern for others; considers advice; understands people through dealing with a variety of people; can always learn from other people; is thoughtful; is fair; is a good listener; is not afraid to admit making a mistake; will correct the mistake, learn and go on; and listens to all sides of an issue (pp. 145–6).

Wisdom and reflexivity

To sum up, then, to be wise, a person needs to display the features of reason tempered by prudence and intuition, and carries this out in reflexive praxis. Reason is fundamental to a person's capacity to deal logically and rationally with issues. To be prudent, a person must be 'able to deliberate well concerning what is good and expedient for himself' (Aristotle 1984, Bk 6, 5: 1140b, p. 105). Far from meaning greedy self-interest, prudence means that people arrange their lives to live comfortably and well, thus providing stability for themselves and others who are dependent on them. A wise person trusts and uses their intuition when appropriate. A wise person knows that the application of reason to knowledge quite often produces inadequate or inappropriate outcomes.

Wise decisions are more likely when phronesis is also applied: the practical capacity to determine the relevance of the particulars, and to identify the most relevant of these in a particular case (Dunne 1997, p. 15). *Nous* is also necessary because it operates at a supra-rational level in that the reasoner understands the truths that inform the foundational principles (Aristotle 1984, Bk 6, 1143b: 12, pp. 3–5). As there are no principles or processes to do this, one develops this capacity by being thoughtful and reflexive (Aristotle 1984, Bk 6, 1142b: 9, pp. 25–8). Combs (1995) states that 'in any area of competence it is necessary to learn the requisite skills, then to learn to relax them and regain communication with our own sensitivity and intuition' (p. 272). Phronesis must then lead to praxis, the action itself, for ultimately all wisdom must be put to worldly good. When engaged in praxis, a wise person acts publicly without ulterior purpose and without self-interest 'to realize excellences that he [*sic*] has come to appreciate in his community as constitutive of a worthwhile way of life' (Dunne 1997, p. 10).

Consequently, it is clear that a vital element of organizational wisdom is reflexivity. Essentially, reflexivity means the capacity to undertake a 'critical ontology of ourselves' so that real change can occur by transgressing the constraints of our own subjective construction (Chan and Garrick 2003). This implies that the wise manager knows that the process by which an organization is set up and maintained rests upon an ontological framework that constructs the real world in a way that makes sense to the organization (cf. McKenna 1997). This framework is also known as embedded knowledge, or 'the systematic routines' of daily practice (Blackler 1995, p. 1024). To varying degrees, employees of an organization incorporate these ontological categories in their workplace discourse. Acting reflexively in organizations requires us to go beyond instrumental critique in order to critically appraise organizational discourses. A thoroughgoing critique may be to conduct a genealogy of the issue in question by determining the context, the sets of understandings, and the rationale for something coming into existence, and then determining whether these still apply. In this way, we become autonomous, Chan and Garrick (2003) argue, by understanding, and, if necessary, disengaging from, the regulation of those internal constraints that regulate our assumptions and behaviour.

However, this supra-rational capacity is usually severely limited by the discursive constraints imposed on organizational members. That is, they simply are not allowed the discursive capacity to act in this way. For example, the concept of the balanced score card or balanced report card (BSC) (Banker et al. 2004; Kaplan and Norton 1998) has been widely and vigorously adopted.

Generally, it is used to evaluate four aspects of organizational performance: financial, customer, internal, learning and growth. While it may be admirable to attempt to expand the criteria by which the worth of an organization is assessed, in practice the internal lexis of BSC documents often constrains people to operate within a particular field of conduct, to speak in certain ways, and to exhibit particular dispositions. For example, in the Queensland Education Department document entitled *Monitoring the Implementation of QSE-2010 Using the Balanced Report Card* we are told that the report card will be a 'driver' of 'change management'; that they want to establish a 'client focus' dealing with 'customers'; that 'strategies are unique and sustainable ways by which organizations create value'; that a 'key challenge' is 'skilling Queensland – the Smart State'. To operate effectively in this discursive site, teachers and education officials need to articulate their fundamental practice – teaching – in such terms rather than in terms of the precious learning relationship between teachers and students who are not 'clients' or 'customers'. What chance would an ordinary classroom teacher have trying to enter this discursive site? In other words, someone doing the very work that the Education Department was set up to deliver – teaching students – has to adopt the discourse of economics and commerce; has to be committed to change (when tried and true methods might be more appropriate); and has to adopt political propaganda (the Queensland government uses 'Smart State' as its political branding) in order simply to be heard. The potential for wisdom to emerge from this discursive constriction appears negligible because the inherent ontological structure of such documents creates a fundamental disjunction between administrative discourse and the daily processes of the classroom and playground.

Can you be wise and postmodern?
In opening this chapter, I asserted that postmodernity provided the technological and economic conditions and postmodernism provided the ethical and subjective rationale for contemporary organizational practice. I then characterized the modernist forms of organizational regulation based on technical rationality within a postmodern ideology of individual freedom as a form of social schizophrenia. In this section I will briefly elaborate those claims.

The superordinating characteristic of postmodern theorizing (as distinct from the condition of postmodernity) is rootlessness. Simulacrous signs bear no specific referents, and cyber-reality is indistinguishable from 'reality' (Baudrillard 1994). Grand narratives that promise advance and the transcendent meta-narrative that connects historical events according to some organizational pattern are refused (Lyotard 1989). Derrida's (1998) deconstructive deferral of meaning ensures endless polysemy. The effect of this is a disabling form of epistemic and ethical relativism. Foucault referred to this as a critical ontology, which should be 'conceived as an attitude, an ethos, a philosophical life in which the critique of what we are is at one and the same time the historical analysis of the limits that are imposed on us and an experiment with the possibility of going beyond them' (Foucault 1984, p. 50). The cumulative effect of this is ongoing agnosticism, scepticism and uncertainty, which disables rather than offers freedom as is claimed.

This rootlessness provides fertile conditions for the schizophrenia of contemporary organizations where the organizational ethos is characterized by consequential pragmatism, and the organizational subject is motivated by the promise of the agency of individualism and self-interest (though this is usually far from the case). It could be argued that modern ethical (consequential) pragmatism began with Machiavelli's (1975) statement that the successful prince will maintain himself by using knowledge 'according to the necessity of the case' (p. 56). This secular consequentialism facilitated the supremacy of technical knowledge (the basis of *technē*) over the metaphysical in worldly affairs. At its simplest, this means that technology has driven much of our contemporary circumstances because of a 'we can therefore we will' force often motivated by economic imperatives. The way in which GM (genetically modified) foods and stem cell research have developed despite widespread concern typifies such an approach. The primacy of individualism and self-interest is, of course, woven into Adam Smith's justification of wealth creation for modern capitalism. However, in an age when corporate employment, not small-business ownership, is the norm, this individualism manifests itself in a different form. The 'individualistic self-ethic' (Heelas 1991), in our current enterprise culture, offers freedom and independence in the form of 'individual choices exercised in the market' (DuGay 1996, p. 77). This self-interest and consequentialism characterize the (post-)modern ethic of organizations.

Yet this apparent libertarian socio-political framework actually produces in many organizations a new kind of authoritarianism. Corporate culturism, according to Willmott (1993), produces a normative environment, which he ironically describes as one 'in which employees enjoy the security of a transcendent system of beliefs, a system that respects and indeed fosters each individual's powers of self determination' (p. 528: see also Rose 1999a, p. 119). In reality, Willmott says it produces a 'dysfunctional, individualizing, segmenting' effect (1993, p. 529).

The fundamental principle of technical rationality is the belief that 'instrumental problem solving made rigorous by the application of scientific theory and technique' (Schön 1995, p. 21) will solve organizational problems (see also Beyer and Niño 1998; Spragens 2001). Yet we know that technical rationality relies on 'pseudo-scientific' constructs (Mintzberg 2000, p. 235), and is over-reliant on formalized procedures (p. 294). A significant manifestation of this is the audit in the form of performance reviews, key indicators and the like (cf. Power 1997). The balanced score card is another such device, where it is claimed that the score card is 'like the dials in an airplane cockpit: it gives managers complex information at a glance' (Kaplan and Norton 1998, p. 123). Such processes are also applied to moral questions in organizations. Aronson (2001) labels it rule deontology that holds 'that in all circumstances individuals should follow a set of predetermined standards or rules' (p. 248).

These new orthodoxies of organizational theory and practice can produce three unhealthy tendencies that diminish the capacity for wisdom to be exercised.

Meaningless mantras   Over time, various discourses that become fashionable in management (see Abrahamson 1999; Willmott 1993) determine managers' and workers' understandings in a cohering logic of assumptions and particular ontologies that shape work practices. For the past twenty years or so, as Rose (1999b) says, management and workers are represented as 'Free individuals', 'partners' and 'stakeholders' who 'are enwrapped in webs of knowledge and circuits of communication through which their actions can be shaped and steered' (p. 147). The discourse is infused with vague but positive terms like 'quality, excellence, efficiency, and customer service' (Cheney 1999), but invariably it involves 'change' even when existing systems are working well (cf. Zorn et al. 2000). Invariably, workers and clients become inured to the mantras and the continual change, thereby developing cynicism and 'reform fatigue'.

Continual measurement   Life has become more complex under the regulation of technical rationality. Such rationality requires measurement even when to do so is inappropriate or indeterminable. Mostly, these data are used as performance indicators even when the phenomenon being measured is difficult to operationalize. Whereas in the past many organizational practices overtly drew on reservoirs of tacit knowledge and inculcation, such practices are now codified, regulated, measured, critiqued, altered and replaced. A typical example of this is a friend who has been a library aide for the past 15 years performing very competently at several well-regarded, large schools. She is now required to gain a certificate that qualifies her for the job she has been doing extremely competently, because she needs to indicate on a performance measure that all staff have met some eductional standard. Absurdly, she can avoid doing some certificate subjects if she fills in a Recognition of Prior Learning (RPL) statement. Typical of such a document is a criterion (one of about twenty) that states 'Records are created according to the standards, precedents and techniques adopted by the organization and are in accordance with industry standards' (note the lexis of control: *[industry] standards, precedents*). In answering this, the applicant had to provide extensive minute detail about a process that she has been performing autonomously, but nominally under the guidance of a librarian. When she completes all the requisite RPLs in her own time, taking literally hundreds of hours (that could be better spent with her grandchild or doing her skilled craftwork), she will then be formally recognized as having acquired the knowledge and skills that she and the supervisory librarian already knew that she had.

Breeds distrust Continuous auditing actually produces serious negative outcomes. Extensive psychological analyses show this to be the case (for a good overview see Kramer 1999). For example, Cialdini (1996) found that monitoring and surveillance systems communicate to employees that the organization does not trust them. It also destroys intrinsic motivation. These are characteristics of the misanthropic organization. Power (1997) concurs, asserting that 'audits create the distrust they presuppose and this in turn leads to various organizational pathologies, if not "fatal remedies" ' (p. 136).

These technologies of governance, no matter how much they are embellished by liberatory rhetoric about 'empowerment', 'creativity', 'autonomy' and so on, are essentially wrong-headed when they are used as extrinsic negative motivators or as a means of 'proving' excellence. This is because, as Vico pointed out three centuries ago, such approaches are based on applying a 'geometrical method', and it is simply not possible to 'draw a straight line through the curves of life' (quoted in Miner 1998, p. 71). To attempt this is to become a 'rational lunatic'. Too often, the structures of technical rationality are founded on inflexible codified knowledge, and designated organizational discourse. To some extent, regulating knowledge, especially in large organizations, is necessary as procedures are codified. This codification allows organizational members to interact internally and externally according to defined parameters of appropriate action and authority. This provides uniformity, transparency, efficiency and fairness in fulfilling the organization's purpose (see Weick and Roberts 1993, on the role of the collective mind in error-free organizations). Yet we know that knowledge is incomplete and fallible. We also know that effective organizations commonly rely on tacit knowledge to put organizational codified knowledge into proper effect (Nonaka 1994); that it is highly dispersed (Tsoukas 1996); and that people work in networks of relations (McNamee 1998) where (sub-)cultures operate and sets of knowledge and dispositions reside. This is just as true for mature industries such as food production and engineering as it is for new industries in ICT and biotehnology, according to Smith (2000). The wise manager of a large organization, then, must be skilful enough to ensure that the processes of regulated knowledge (codes, organizational practices, formal information flows) operate in a way that allows the organization to get on with its primary business. However, the wise manager also builds in processes that allow those processes to be responsive and adaptive to particular circumstance and environmental changes.

Being wiser in the future

At the root of the postmodern dilemma in postmodernity is epistemic and ethical relativism. I contend that, broadly, the impact of these disabling concerns can be minimized by adopting a form of pragmatic relativism and by firmly asserting human (or what I would call Enlightenment) values. Regarding pragmatic relativism, philosopher C.S. Peirce's (1960) advice seems useful. Accepting that 'there is nothing at all in our knowledge which we have any warrant at all for regarding as absolute in any particular', he nevertheless suggests a simple test: 'As for those things which are known by everyday experience, let him doubt them who can lay his hand on his heart and say that he does doubt them' (2.75, p. 39). Concerning ethical relativism, I have argued above that, within a neo-liberal hegemony, this relativism has become a form of rampant individualism that is susceptible to discursive claims of autonomy, freedom and wealth accumulation. Organizational theories founded in the myth of the triumphant individual (in reality, this is limited to the most powerful) need to be avoided, and should be replaced by principles of cooperation and collaboration (Bennis and Biederman 1997, p. 1) that admit tacit knowledge, practical considerations, and various perceptions and insights into wise management practice. Like Bennis (Bennis 1997), I would advocate a management philosophy that emphasizes humane values such as 'integrity, dedication, magnanimity, humility, openness, and creativity' (p. 56). Finally, it is clear that pathways must be clear so that the operation of these principles can infuse organizations: that is, there needs to be a proper context and community for wise judgement to occur and take effect. There is empirical evidence that context in the form of intrapersonal, interpersonal and extrapersonal relations significantly contributes to people's ability to demonstrate wise judgement (Baltes and Kunzmann 2003; Baltes and Staudinger 2000; Sternberg and Ben-Zeev 2001). This led empirical psychologists Baltes and Staudinger (2000) to conclude that 'One of our central theoretical postures is that wisdom is a collectively anchored product and that individuals by themselves are only "weak" carriers of wisdom' (p. 130; see also Staudinger 1996).

Technical rationality has a role to play in managing organizations. However, it is clear that orthodox contemporary practice is largely characterized by excesses of formulaic procedures, rule deontology, measurement, auditing and, contradictorily, incessant change. The wise manager for the future will be one who has the capacity to understand the secular doxology and draw from it only that which is helpful and positive; to identify the difference between ephemera and necessary change; to maintain consistent practice but to be prepared to interpret humanely and sensibly where necessary; to build trust and confidence through communicative and social practices in the workplace; to encourage themselves and their staff to use their tacit knowledge and intuition in moderation where it achieves a satisfactory outcome; to be reflexive and thoughtful not only individually but as corporate citizens; and to be joyous and positive as much as possible.

Notes

1. Neo-classical economics means here simply that the market is the primary method for determining the appropriateness of action; that government should minimize intervention in the economy; that the consumer is 'theoretically' sovereign; and that 'competition' should operate in all facets of service and goods delivery.
2. I am indebted to a colleague, philosopher Fred D'Agostino, for his advice in this area.
3. I am indebted to Professor Robert Sternberg of Yale University for his commentary on this issue.
4. One might well ask why it took 91 years for the wisest legal men to acknowledge the 'bleeding obvious'.
5. For an effective defence of change management, see Tsoukas and Chia (2002); and for its significance in organizational discourse see Faber (1998).
6. It is acknowledged that Aristotle identifies two virtues, intellectual and moral (*Ethics*, Book III).

References

Abrahamson, E. 1999. 'Management fashion: Lifecycles, triggers, and collective learning processes'. *Administrative Science Quarterly* **44**:708–40.

Anderson, J. 2001. 'Social fragmentation: Individualization, social fragmentation and the "autonomy gap" '. March. http://www.artsw.wustl.edu/~anderson/criticaltheory/.

Aquinas, S.T. 1964. *Summa Theologæ*. Translated by T.E. Gilby. London: Blackfriars.

Aristotle. 1984. *Nicomachean Ethics*. Translated by H.G. Apostle. Grinnell, IO: The Peripatetic Press.

Aristotle. 2003. *Ethics*. Translated by J.A.K. Thomson. London: The Folio Society.

Aronson, E. 2001. 'Integrating leadership styles and ethical perspectives'. *Canadian Journal of Administrative Sciences* **18**:244–56.

Axelrod, R.H. 2000. *Terms of Engagement: Changing the Way We Change Organizations*. San Francisco, CA: Berrett-Koehler.

Baltes, P.B. and U. Kunzmann. 2003. 'Wisdom'. *The Psychologist* **16**:131–3.

Baltes, P.B. and U.M. Staudinger. 2000. 'A metaheuristic (pragmatic) to orchestrate mind and virtue toward excellence'. *American Psychologist* **55**:122–36.

Banker, R.D., H. Chang and M. Pizzini. 2004. 'The balanced scorecard: Judgemental effects of performance measures linked to strategy'. *The Accounting Review* **79**:1–23.

Baudrillard, J. 1994. *Simulacra and Simulation*. Translated by S.F. Glaser. Ann Arbor, MI: University of Michigan Press.

Beck, U. and E. Beck-Gernsheim. 2002. *Individualization: Institutionalized Individualism and Its Social and Political Consequences*. London: Sage.

Bennis, W. 1997. *Managing People is Like Herding Cats*. Provo, UT: Executive Excellence Publishing.

Bennis, W. and P.W. Biederman. 1997. *Organizing Genius: The Secrets of Creative Collaboration*. Cambridge, MA: Perseus.

Beyer, J.M. and D. Niño. 1998. 'Facing the future: Backing courage with wisdom'. Pp. 65–97 in *Organizational Wisdom and Executive Courage*, edited by S. Srivastva and D.L. Cooperrider. San Francisco, CA: The New Lexington Press.

Blackler, F. 1995. 'Knowledge, knowledge work and organizations: An overview and interpretation'. *Organization Studies* **16**:1021–46.

Chan, A. and J. Garrick. 2003. 'The moral "technologies" of knowledge management'. *Information, Communication & Society* **6**:291–306.

Cheney, G. 1999. *Values at Work: Employee Participation Meets Market Pressure at Mondragon*. Ithaca, NY: Cornell University Press.

Cialdini, R. 1996. 'The triple tumor structure of organizational behavior'. Pp. 44–58 in *Codes of Conduct: Behavioral Research into Business Ethics*, edited by D.M. Messick and A.E. Tenbrunsel. New York: Russell Sage Foundation.

Clayton, V.P. and J.E. Birren. 1980. 'The development of wisdom across the life span: A reexamination of an ancient topic'. Pp. 103–35 in *Life-Span Development and Behavior*, vol. 3, edited by P.B. Baltes and J.O.G. Brim. New York: Academic Press.

Combs, A. 1995. *The Radiance of Being: Complexity, Chaos and the Evolution of Consciousness*. Edinburgh: Floris Books.

Csikszentmihalyi, M. and K. Rathunde. 1990. 'The psychology of wisdom: An evolutionary interpretation'. Pp. 25–51 in *Wisdom: Its Nature, Origins, and Development*, edited by R.J. Sternberg. New York: Cambridge University Press.

Dean, M. 1994. ' "A social structure of many souls": Moral regulation, government, and self-formation'. *Canadian Journal of Sociology* **19**:145–68.

Derrida, J. 1998. *The Derrida Reader: Writing Performances*. Lincoln, NE: University of Nebraska Press.

DuGay, P. 1996. *Consumption and Identity at Work*. London: Sage.

Dunne, J. 1997. *Back to the Rough Ground: Practical Judgement and the Lure of Technique*. Notre Dame, IN: University of Notre Dame Press.

Faber, B. 1998. 'Toward a rhetoric of change'. *Journal of Business and Technical Communication* **12**:217–37.

Foucault, M. 1984. 'What is enlightenment?' Pp. 32–50 in *The Foucault Reader*, edited by P. Rabinow. London: Penguin.

Heelas, P. 1991. 'Reforming the self: Enterprise and the characters of Thatcherism'. Pp. 72–92 in *Enterprise Culture*, edited by R. Keat and N. Abercrombie. London and New York: Routledge.

Jacques, R. 1996. *Manufacturing the Employee: Management Knowledge from the 19th to 21st Centuries*. London: Sage.

Kaplan, R.S. and D.P. Norton. 1998. 'The balanced scorecard: Measures that drive performance'. Pp. 123–45 in *Harvard Business Review on Measuring Corporate Performance*. Boston, MA: Harvard Business Review Paperback.

Kerr, J. 2004. 'Worn gears threaten derailment'. P. 1 in *The Sydney Morning Herald*. February 21–22.

Kramer, R.M. 1999. 'Trust and distrust in organizations: Emerging perspectives, enduring questions'. *Annual Review of Psychology* **50**:569–98.

Lyotard, J.F. 1989. *The Postmodern Condition: A Report on Knowledge*. Translated by G. Bennington and B. Massumi. Minneapolis, MN: University of Minnesota Press.

Mabo and Others v. Queensland. (No. 2) (1992) 175. *CLR*: 1 F.C. 92/014v.

Machiavelli, N. 1975. *The Prince*. Translated by G. Bull. Harmondsworth, UK: Penguin.

McKenna, B. 1997. 'How engineers write: An empirical study of engineering report writing'. *Applied Linguistics* **18**:189–211.

McNamee, S. 1998. 'Reinscribing organizational wisdom and courage: The relationally engaged organization'. Pp. 101–17 in *Organizational Wisdom and Executive Courage*, edited by S.S. Srivastva and D.L. Cooperrider. San Francisco, CA: The New Lexington Press.

Miner, R.C. 1998. 'Verum-factum and practical wisdom in the early writings of Giambattista Vico'. *Journal of the History of Ideas* **59**:53–73.

Mintzberg, H. 2000. *The Rise and Fall of Strategic Planning*. London: Prentice-Hall.

Nonaka, I. 1994. 'A dynamic theory of organizational knowledge creation'. *Organization Science* **5**:14–37.

Orwoll, L. and M. Perlmutter. 1990. 'The study of wise persons: Integrating a personality perspective'. Pp. 160–77 in *Wisdom: Its Nature, Origins, and Development*, edited by R.J. Sternberg. New York: Cambridge University Press.

Peirce, C.S. 1960. 'The collected papers of Charles Sanders Peirce'. Vol. 1–2, edited by C. Hartshorne and P. Weiss. Cambridge, MA: Belknap Press of Harvard University Press.

Power, M. 1997. *The Audit Society: Rituals of Verification.* Oxford: Oxford University Press.

Rooney, D. and B.J. McKenna. Forthcoming. *Knowing Well: Historical Relationships Between Wisdom, Knowledge, Ethics and Management.* MS under review.

Rose, N. 1996. 'Authority and the geneology of subjectivity'. Pp. 294–327 in *Detraditionalization: Critical Reflections on Authority and Identity*, edited by P. Heelas, S. Lash and P. Morris. Cambridge, MA: Blackwell.

Rose, N. 1999a. *Governing the Soul: The Shaping of the Private Self.* London and New York: Free Association Press.

Rose, N. 1999b. *Powers of Freedom: Reframing Political Thought.* Cambridge, MA: Cambridge University Press.

Sarup, M. 1989. *An Introductory Guide to Post-Structuralism and Postmodernism.* Athens, GA: University of Georgia Press.

Schön, D.A. 1995. *The Reflective Practitioner: How Professionals Think in Action.* Aldershot, UK: Ashgate.

Smith, K. 2000. 'What is the "knowledge economy"? Knowledge-intensive industries and distributed knowledge bases'. *AEGIS Working Papers on Innovation* 03: http://aegis.uws.edu.au/Working%20Papers.htm.

Spragens, T.A. Jnr. 2001. 'Is the enlightenment project worth saving?' *Modern Age* **43**:49–60.

Staudinger, U.M. 1996. 'Wisdom and the social-interactive foundation of the mind'. Pp. 276–315 in *Interactive Minds: Life-Span Perspectives on the Social Foundation of Cognition*, edited by P.B. Baltes and U.M. Staudinger. New York: Cambridge University Press.

Sternberg, R.J. 1990. 'Understanding wisdom'. Pp. 3–9 in *Wisdom: Its Nature, Origins and Development*, edited by R.J. Sternberg. Cambridge: Cambridge University Press.

Sternberg, R.J. and T. Ben-Zeev. 2001. *Complex Cognition: The Psychology of Human Thought.* New York and Oxford: Oxford University Press.

Tsoukas, H. 1996. 'The firm as a distributed knowledge system: A constructionist approach'. *Strategic Management Journal* **17**:11–25.

Tsoukas, H. and R. Chia. 2002. 'On organizational becoming: Rethinking organizational change'. *Organization Science: A Journal of the Institute of Management Sciences* **13**:567–82.

Valentine, R. and D. Knights. 1998. 'TQM and BPR – can you spot the difference?' *Personnel Review* **27**:78–85.

Vico, G. 1982. *Vico: Selected Writings.* Translated by L. Pompa. Cambridge: Cambridge University Press.

Weick, K.E. and K.H. Roberts. 1993. 'Collective mind in organizations: Heedful interrelating on flight decks'. *Administrative Science Quarterly* **38**:357–81.

Willmott, H. 1993. 'Strength is ignorance, slavery is freedom: Managing culture in modern organizations'. *Journal of Management Studies* **30**:515–52.

Wolf, W. 2002: 'Conversations with Chester Barnard'. http://www.the-intuitive-self.com/scripts/author.cgi?/website/author/memoir/supplements/conversation_barnard.html.

Zorn, T.E., L.T. Christensen and G. Cheney. 1999. *Constant Change and Flexibility: Do We Really Want Constant Change?* San Francisco, CA: Berrett-Koehler.

Zorn, T.E., D.J. Page and G. Cheney. 2000. 'Nuts about change: Multiple perspectives on change-oriented communication in a public sector organization'. *Management Communication Quarterly* **13**:515–66.

4 Risk and knowledge

Joost van Loon

The main question I address here is: to what extent is risk implicated in the specific social, cultural and political formations of the knowledge-based economy (KBE)? Using the example of a dramatic failure of a scientific approach to establish a low-risk and high-return strategy for capital investments, I will argue that risks provide a key function within the KBE. Risks mobilize concerns and investments in particular forms of knowledge which, in a paradoxical spiral, reinforce themselves producing an ever-increasing need for more knowledge, which is the essence of technocracy. This process, however, has a negative counterpart in that it places increasing strains on the interface between the technological/systemic and human/social dimensions of modern life. As a result, systems become increasingly self-referential, a process which can also be referred to as alienation. In order to break through this negative spiral, interventions in the visualization, signification and valorization of risk perceptions are essential. These interventions have to be geared towards increasing the public accountability of the main operators of the KBE (including the risk managers), a radical democratization of decision-making, and an ethical and moral re-embedding of risk politics in terms of the common good. Although current conditions for such interventions are not favourable, the logic of risk is such that every danger brings a saving power.[1]

In 1973 three scientists, Fischer Black, Myron Scholes and Robert Merton, produced a comprehensive formula known as the Black–Scholes model for predicting successful stock-market investments by including a means for 'hedging' risks, using derivatives.[2] Of course, financial markets operate on the basis that risk correlates with returns on investments. The higher the risk, the higher the potential profit. Finding the right balance between risk and return has always been seen as a mix of specific skills that one acquired, as well as 'talent' (Bernstein 1996; Boden 2000).

However, the Black–Scholes model heralded a new era of risk-capital regulation. Now one could have risk-free investment with high returns. The idea of risk-free investment has always been the holy grail of financial capitalism, but rather than depending on the craft skill, genius or virtuosity of stockbrokers, science would deliver it. The idea seemed too good to be true.

In the early 1990s, Black, Scholes and Merton were all involved in the setting up of an investment company, Long Term Capital Management

(LTCM), that would create investment portfolios based on the Black–Scholes model. No doubt aided by the appeal of their international fame and acclaim as Nobel Prize winners, our scientists 'sold' the use of their model of risk-free investment and persuaded major institutional (e.g. Proctor and Gamble) and individual investors to become their guinea pigs, promising them high returns for low risks (Bernstein 1996, p. 323). Whereas the decision to set up a company does not carry very high risks, the decision to invest in it does. We therefore have an interesting paradox: in order for the high-return/low-risk package to be set to work, investors have to enter it through a high-risk (and high-trust) 'portal'.

In the first three years, LTCM made record profits for their investors. However, when in 1997 the Bangkok real-estate market collapsed, and the Thai baht could no longer hold its value against the dollar, these record profits turned into record losses. Unlike most other investors, LTCM, using the Black–Scholes model, was seemingly oblivious to what was happening at the (alleged) 'fringes of the global economy'. They simply did what the model told them to do, even if experienced (but fallible) 'human' brokers – still relying on experience, artisanship, intuition, 'gut instinct' and knowledge – were pulling out, especially from East Asian markets. For two consecutive years, they made immense losses. The Federal Reserve had to rescue the company from receivership and compensate for the billions of losses. If the company had gone into receivership, it would have virtually plunged the US economy – and thus the world economy – into an instant global recession.

The problem with the Black–Scholes model was that it only works under 'normal' circumstances of relatively predictable and stable markets. It cannot deal with more extreme and excessive calamities. As soon as there is a serious disruption, the model becomes useless. This is because of its reliance on a *ceteris paribus* clause – a specific notion of instrumental reliability (reliance on an abstract model while ignoring the messiness of the real world, under the pretence that if all 'other conditions' stay the same things will go as planned) rather than trust (the embodied skills of experience) – which was deployed to incorporate and regulate contingencies.

The moral of the story, then, is that even the most scientifically advanced attempts seeking to neutralize risks are still not able to anticipate the full catastrophic potential implied in the instrumental reliability of *ceteris paribus*. In short, it shows that until further notice we must work with the assumption that risk is still fundamental to the workings of capitalism.

Technocracy and knowledge-based economies

From its very inception, the notion of capital has always already implied risk. This is why there are laws, market regulators, financial institutions and so on. This is also why economists such as Granovetter and Swedberg (1992) talk about 'trust-embedded economies' (also see Smets et al. 1999). However, if we dissect contemporary discourses on trust we quickly discover that in many discussions (and certainly in the worlds of business and finance) it refers to an instrumental notion of reliability that has become a core component of our 'high-fidelity' technocratic culture. Here, fidelity simply means a predictable and reliable mechanistic response to an input requirement (Van Loon 2002a).

I argue, therefore, that predictability is a central motivation of technocracy. Technocracy argues for a specific type of KBE, one that currently prevails in knowledge discourse throughout the developed world. From the economic theories of Schumpeter (1982), Galbraith (1977) and Kerr (1983), to the more socio-political writings of Bell (1976), Touraine (1971), Gorz (1982) and Offe (1985), as well as the contemporary sociological writings of Castells (1996), Lash and Urry (1994), Kelly (1997) and, finally, and most importantly for this chapter, Ulrich Beck (1992), despite considerable political and philosophical differences, all underscore a basic thesis, namely that *knowledge is a force of production*. This thesis is central to the very idea of a KBE.

A most pertinent effect of the growing economic centrality of knowledge can be seen in the immense expansion of increasingly specialized expertise, and our general dependence on it in the organization and regulation of both the economy and society. According to Touraine (1971), expertise forms new kinds of class relations. In particular, and central to contemporary views on the KBE, he emphasized three class types: (1) technocrats, who are central to systemic planning; (2) bureaucrats, who are mainly concerned with systemic regulations; and (3) technicians, who are involved in systemic operations. The logic of each of these functions differs, but technocracy clearly favours technocrats as planning overrules the functions of regulation and operation.

Touraine is very much in line with the classical sociological thesis that from Durkheim (1984) through Parsons (1977) and onwards to Giddens (1990) and Luhmann (1990), has comfortably held precedence in debates over modernization. The thesis maintains that growth of expertise is driven by increased complexity, which itself is driven by the (seemingly autonomous) force of differentiation. This differentiation force – which for example finds one outlet in the observable processes of individualization – is often confused with the essence of evolution itself, which is seen by many natural scientists as a movement to greater complexity and diversity of life. The underlying assumption is similar to that of biological evolution: social systems also move towards greater levels of complexity by means of increased differentiation. The question is what enables these systems to continue to 'hang together'. Whereas for Durkheim and Parsons this function of integration was to be performed by increasingly complex and abstract cultural formations (especially religion), later sociologists (especially Luhmann) have suggested that rather than increased integration, social processes have tended towards increased self-referential modes of communication. The individualization thesis, which was developed among others by Giddens (1994) and Beck (1992), is an example of the classical view as it describes the process of modernization as a shift from collectively embedded and enforced value systems and decision-making practices to more dispersed and individuated articulations of values and decisions which are increasingly seen as a private and personal affair. The integration of the latter no longer takes place through consensus-seeking value orientations, but by means of more abstract modes of regulation and governance.

The grand evolutionary speculations of classical sociology are not our only resort in explaining modernization. We can instead consider an alternative hypothesis, namely that greater complexity and differentiation is not so much a law of nature, but is the outcome of a *failure* of the cultural system to provide integration. We can explore this approach by looking at what Durkheim (1984) referred to as the *conscience collectif*. In their famous work on the structures of religion, Durkheim and Mauss (1963) suggest that as societies become more complex, the *conscience collectif* has to become more abstract to maintain a social system's integrative power. Increased abstraction can be interpreted as a narrative of *alienation* in which 'experience' becomes less and less adequate in dealing with underlying social (dis)organization. This is the essence of the late Niklas Luhmann's (1990) writings on the improbability of communication and the process of *autopoiesis* (self-creation). What is central to autopoietic systems is that as they become self-reliant and self-enclosed, they encounter increasing difficulties in communicating with other systems (they become more and more restricted by their own rules). In other words, a *translation deficit* occurs whereby the systemic demands of autopoiesis are no longer supported by other systems.[3] This, I argue, is exactly what is now happening in the KBE. Technological innovations have outpaced the ability of social systems to adapt. As a result, the interface between the spheres of technology and human sociality is becoming increasingly strained and saturated with noise.

It is with this growing awareness of the fragile nature of post-industrial financial markets, in which anticipation and expectation have become increasingly autonomous from material productivity, that we see more fundamental changes in the way in which we could conceptualize the KBE. In a world in which people trade in risk-related abstractions such as derivatives (as the price of risks), futures and real estate on financial markets where money has a price (Boden 2000, p. 184), one has to question what the nature of the dominant 'mode of production' might be. Indeed, it could be argued that alienation is not limited to 'mundane' human existence and experiences, but also operates at higher levels of abstraction, such as models and systems. Derivatives and futures markets have shifted the capitalist mode of production to such a level of abstraction that even its most cunning operators are no longer able to rely on a singular *modus operandi*.

The risk society

It is striking that, in talk about insecurity and contingency in financial markets and derivatives, very little attention has been paid to social aspects of differentiation, individualization and autopoietic systems in the KBE. Indeed, in the dominant discourse on knowledge *risks* are primarily constructed as financial and economic, and thus always capable of being converted into economic value in the form of new business opportunities. However, the logical consequences of the breakdown of the social structure not only pose problems for 'society' (e.g. public health, stress, unemployment) but also directly affect the domain of the production and management of knowledge itself. Indeed, very little thought has been given to the logical inconsistencies of the KBE itself. In the remainder of this chapter, I will show that the KBE and social breakdown are linked, and that the link can be understood through the sociology of risk. This link is generated by the translation deficit that occurs because the different systems involved in the production of information, knowledge and anticipation are increasingly incommensurable, and therefore unable to establish a stable 'social' network. One could also refer to this as a 'crisis of interfaciality': technologically driven operations become increasingly devoid of social content (the interface being a medium between two different systems, e.g. abstract versus embodied technologies). A focus on the sociology of risk will enable us to provide a more critical assessment of the translation deficit (of technological innovation into adequate modes of sociation) that is inherent in all technocratic systems and thus plagues all KBEs.

As Beck (1992), Bernstein (1996), Boden (2000) and many others have already argued, risk is a key motivator within the KBE. For example, when we consider the financial infrastructure of the KBE, we see that institutional investors such as banks, pension providers and insurance companies play a major part in almost all significant business transactions. Indeed, the very notion of investment is immersed in a logic based on risk, and this notion is directly related to knowledge and information processing. The *raison d'être* of the insurance industry is predicated upon risk constructions that are intricately intertwined with the production and literal as well as metaphorical valorization of certain forms of knowledge. For example, knowledge about probabilities related to developing debilitating diseases (e.g. under certain genetic or environmental conditions) that feeds into specific health insurance policies is based on both statistical–mathematical and clinical–medical data. The value of these forms of knowledge is at once measured in terms of scientific credit as well as financial capital. Furthermore, questions of certainty and uncertainty are deeply entangled in the specific decision logics that drive technoscientific innovation. Indeed, one could argue that the entire constitution of the KBE evolves around a continuous interchange between risks and opportunities.

According to Beck, risk is the turning point at which 'modernity' comes up against its own limits (Van Loon 2002a, p. 90). Driven by relentless economic growth on the back of an increasingly complex interplay between technological innovation and worldwide social planning and reorganization, the modern world has entered a twilight zone in which feedback loops produce ambivalent input which no longer unequivocally supports models of linear progress but has to accept ambivalence and radical contingency. That is, we have come up against the limits of growth, not only because of fundamental and irreversible ecological destabilization, but also in terms of a radical social and cultural disorganization (e.g. Lash and Urry 1994).

Risks encountered in the KBE are often non-linear (for example, genetic engineering and nanotechnology), and so their catastrophic potential cannot be mapped onto a financial scale of insurance. Non-linear risks have a tendency to become 'runaway events' (for example, futures and derivatives markets, the HIV/AIDS pandemic and nanotechnology; see Clark 1998) and undermine the very institutional ordering of rational, strategic decision-making at the level of both government and business. This can spill over into everyday life, with people being unable to maintain coherent, rational strategies (e.g. of planning one's future career, a healthy lifestyle or financial security) in the face of increasing, and often incommensurable, risks.[4]

Thus the global KBE is also part of a risk society. In this risk society, the technological framework of action has become such that in the face of its catastrophic potential (e.g. from nuclear meltdown to genetic engineering and nanotechnologies), the insurance principle has collapsed (Beck 2000, p. 220). Biochemical, nuclear and genetic risks, for example, are now incalculable in terms of probability as well as harm. Our society has created a catastrophic potential for which we have no mechanisms of control. The collapse of the insurance principle – in which money and time could be set against any possible calamity – means that modern society has outmanoeuvred itself (Beck, 2000). Insurance could be seen as the primary interface of risk management, but it is no longer capable of providing an adequate valorization of risk anticipations. In other words, systems of anticipation (of potential catastrophic events) have outpaced those of knowledge generation (of how to handle them); as a result, what used to provide a means of translation of risks into opportunities (insurance) has been relegated to a position on the margins.

The link between KBE and the risk society, however, is intrinsic at a deeper level as well. This is because by definition risks are virtual: they are always in the future (Beck 2000, p. 213; Van Loon 2000, p. 173). This means that as soon as they are actualized (are no longer in the future but an actual event, a disaster for example), risks are no longer risks. As virtual and future abstractions, risks are therefore ontologically inseparable from perceptions and knowledge. In other words, risks entail a conflation of reality and representations of reality. Risks require an information basis that in turn has to be interpreted to imagine a future state. Knowledge forms the basis of such interpretations and imaginations. On the basis of knowledge and in the face of interpretations, decisions have to be made. These decisions inaugurate risks. Without decisions, risks would not be risks but simply hazards.

Ulrich Beck's risk-society thesis suggests that transformations in science, technology, industry and culture (individualization) have engendered an increased sensitivity to risk and that whereas our awareness of risks has increased, our ability to control them has decreased. For Beck (1992) as well as Giddens (1994), risks are 'manufactured uncertainties'. The techno-scientific environment we have created for ourselves is far too complex for rational–technocratic management; attempts to manage it will further enhance risks because of the impossibility of knowing the full consequences of each decision (Van Loon, 2002a). For Beck (1992), the risk society is also an individualizing society – more and more responsibility is processed 'downwards' towards the individual, whereby risks are turned into a private affair. Thus institutional and collectively supported safety nets are being replaced by private arrangements, which depend solely on individual decisions. This is not just happening in the world of insurance, but affects nearly all domains of everyday life (e.g. from food and medication to choice of school and home security systems).

An understanding of the dynamic of the risk society adds something peculiar and paradoxical to our understanding of the KBE. The more information is produced, the more knowledge is required to enable an interpretation. The more knowledge is generated, the more complex our decisions will become. The more complex decisions become, however, the less certain their outcomes (and the greater their undecidability). The less certain their outcomes, the greater the risks; the greater the risks, the more information we need, and so on and so forth (Adam and Van Loon 2000). This is the spiral that links the KBE and the risk society as outcomes of a fatal strategy: the attempt to overcome contingency by means of anticipation.

At the same time, however, risk must be appreciated as an economic motivator, a key engine of the continuing process of modernization – despite all of its shortcomings. Fatal strategies are fatal exactly because they foreclose a turning; those ensnared by them will not succumb to apocalyptic sensibilities, because they will always translate risks into opportunities. Risks will then be simply reinforced by means of responses that are part of the same process that produced the risks in the first place.

Implications for policy and social action

The risk-society thesis has proven to be remarkably robust for describing the current global human predicament. It is vital to stress, however, that making observations about the growing importance of risk is not to claim that life has become more hazardous – but simply that the political, social, cultural and economic fields are increasingly marked by *risk perceptions*. Important for this chapter is the fact that risk perceptions depend on knowledge production systems (Adam and Van Loon 2000; Beck 1997).

If we were to present an anatomy of risk-perception construction, Luhmann's (1990) model of communication could be very useful. He distinguishes between three elements of the communication process: information, utterance and understanding. Elsewhere (Van Loon 2002b), I have developed my own triad, which is quite similar to Luhmann's. It consists of visualization, signification and valorization. These three elements, I argue, provide the basis for possible interventions to counteract the fatal strategies associated with managing risks in KBEs. In this final section, I will use this triad to present an anatomy of risk perceptions.

Starting with visualization, for risks to be perceptible, they have to revealed or visualized. Knowledge of risks is generated by expert systems. To be able to articulate risks in a technological culture, one must have access to specialist knowledge, particularly technoscientific expertise. However, given the inherently systemic nature of knowledge, the emphasis is on expert systems rather than experts. These expert systems may be embodied in technoscientific firms and organizational networks (e.g. in R&D), financial institutions; communities of specialist practitioners populated by, for example, managers or farmers; or social movements. In each of these knowledge systems a key outcome is the generation of data, and with these data experts can visualize latent pathologies.

A key issue for interventions is the extent to which visualization should be seen as the exclusive domain of experts, and the extent to which they should be subjected to public and democratic scrutiny. The articulations between risks and opportunities make the identification of particular risks a potentially lucrative business; but without any sense of collective accountability, cynical opportunism may thrive at the expense of the common good. One particular domain where this is becoming evident is genetic screening and profiling (Rose 2000). Technocratic systems are powerless against such forms of exploitation because their negative implications go largely undetected.

However, for a proper identification of risks, visualization in itself is not sufficient. Cold data are meaningless unless they are interpreted. Apart from disclosure to experts through visualization, risk perceptions also require signification for their wider dissemination. Signification is the transformation of information into a meaningful utterance. Whereas initial signification is also the domain of expert systems, the wider social articulation is primarily the work of governance and media systems. What the expert governance and media systems do is attribute 'significance'; in other words, they determine what matters (e.g. Allan 2002). Furthermore, signification is the translation of expertise into 'common sense'. For example, we can take the demonstrations performed by Pasteur to convince not only the medical but also wider political fields of his germ theories (Latour 1988). Similarly, no one is expected to read specialist publications on econometrics, but these sources are being translated by other specialist apparatuses (e.g. the *Financial Times, The Economist*) and agencies (e.g. pressure groups and social movements) into political discourse for the public sphere.

Intervention strategies have to take into account modes of dissemination as a vital element in the construction of risk perceptions. A useful way to approach this is by contrasting two undesired strategies: a 'rhetoric of endangerment' versus a 'rhetoric of containment' (Ungar 1998). In the first, risk perceptions are inflated, creating undue anxiety (e.g. around so-called 'phantom risks'; see Foster et al. 1993). In the second, risks are swept under the carpet to quell public anxieties, thereby increasing the potential for harm. One of the major weaknesses of technocratic systems is their self-referential nature. Technocratic discourse struggles to articulate anything that is not already marked by its own parameters (McKenna and Graham 2000). Essential for finding an adequate balance between the two is the active pursuit of a wider knowledge base than the one provided by the subpolitics of technoscientific expertise, and consideration of the experiences and everyday life settings of those likely to be most affected by the perceived risks.

It is not enough only to *know* what matters. For risk perceptions to obtain closure they must be valorized. Valorization is the transformation of utterance into communicative understanding (that is, it has to be shared; there has to be common ground). Understanding must not be seen primarily as a cognitive concept, but in terms of a much broader hermeneutic of sense-making which includes an attribution of value to what matters. Typically, this attributed value is of a financial, legal or military nature. In many cases, these overlap. With value attributed, risk perceptions can be ordered according to importance, severity and so on. Without the attribution of value, we would not be able to deal with the practical problem of information overload, nor would we be able to direct appropriate resources to deal with risk perceptions. Closure requires a mode of selection that is 'proper' to the prevailing (inter)systemic logic.

The technocratic nature of the KBE provides a specific closure of risk perceptions, one that valorizes risk as financial or commercial capital that manifests itself in an ever-expanding system of commodification of knowledge. Hence knowledge is commodified as 'information' and 'data' on the one hand, and 'skills and expertise' on the other. This closure ensures that the commodification process, based on a socially and culturally narrow economic value proposition that resists the possibilities for a radical overhaul of the rather self-destructive and alienating tendencies of late modernity, will not be overcome from within the system.

The policy implications for this are that if we are to be committed to an alternative, humanistic modernity that recognizes that technocracy is dehumanizing, we should be looking for a rather different type of value proposition. Not everything can or should be expressed in terms of monetary value. If we are to reject the most undesirable consequences of technocracy, we must allow for a multiplicity of valorizations and greater transparency as to how particular values have been attributed. This is a political process that should be embedded in ethical and moral concerns, rather than instrumental ones. Such an imperative cannot be expected to come from below; it does not fit in with the premises of individualization, which can only function socially by means of mutual adjustment.

The pessimism of Luhmann (e.g. 1995) – suggesting that things can only get worse – pictures a risk society in which things are always on the brink of spiralling out of control, but this is not what Beck is arguing. There is a second theoretical lineage in the risk-society thesis, influenced by Jürgen Habermas (e.g. 1989), who argues that making communicative action central to social operations will improve society. Such calls for the radical democratization of the regulation of technoscience, governance, media and commerce is echoed in the works of, for example, Irwin and Wynne (1996), Rose (2000) and Welsh (2000). Although these do not explicitly work on the basis of communicative action, they all insist on an open, deliberative, democratic scrutiny of technoscientific processes. Like Beck (and Habermas), they are deeply suspicious and critical of the subpolitical displacements[5] of decision-making to forms of expertise (also see Beck 1997).

This strong democratic drive may seem attractive and give a ray of hope to those disillusioned with modernization and who desire to bring about change. But who is going to take charge of this reinvigoration of normative rationality? Or as Touraine (1971) would say, what class/subjectivity do we expect to perform this conversion? In his later works, Touraine (1981) himself pointed to social movements. This was echoed by Habermas (1989) in his theory of the reconstitution of the public sphere. Gramsci (1971) is relevant here, for to intervene in systemic procedural rationality, one has to engage with the hegemony of expertise on exactly the same grounds as the technocrats do. Can we expect intellectuals to speak on behalf of the life world and intervene in 'the System'? What elements of 'the System' would – reasonably speaking – be willing or even able to engage with this, as it is contrary to the logic of their instrumental rationality to do so?

If, in contrast to these more idealistic social theorists, Foucault (1977) is right, then modernity is the story of an unfolding disciplinary society – based on a model of incarceration. These are the spatio-temporal enclosures of specifically engineered subjects (also incorporating their biographies), for example through the appropriation of uniforms and timetables to regulate modes of subjugation. Nothing in the disciplinary system would be amenable to communicative action. Indeed, the only normative rationality would be the rationality of normalization. Even if not totally and entirely sublated by systemic requirements, moral reasoning is still severely impaired as it becomes simply another form of discipline comprising techniques and regimented processes.

There are questions about the validity of this model in a society such as ours, especially one that is being re-engineered. Nanotechnology, for example, points to newly emergent regimes of domination. These forms of domination require neither incarceration nor strict regimes of discipline and control. Similarly, other forms of control, for example, databases and digital forms of tracking linked to GIS, do not require the compliance of docile bodies. This is the world described by Gilles Deleuze (1992) as the society of control, based not on incarceration but incorporation, not on disciplining but on inducing or coercing subjects. If this prediction is correct, then alienation itself will become obsolete; it is merely a temporary friction in a transition towards a new, post-humanist world where the logic of machines provides the new hegemony.

Both Foucault and Deleuze imply that emergent forms of power are socially driven by risk anxieties about 'pathological excesses' (e.g. crime, mental or sexual disorders, epidemics, as well as perpetual crises at more systemic levels). Such anxieties do not show many enduring signs of incorporating a scope for communicative action. To make communicative action possible, we ultimately have to embrace pedagogical strategies to transform habituses in, for example, consumption and political action. Examples of such pedagogical strategies would be consumer-led actions against GMOs, direct actions aimed at enhancing community life; the fair-trade movement, as well as various forms of 'life politics' including initiatives to protect the autonomy of families *vis-à-vis* ever-expanding state regulation (which often deploys a rhetoric of endangerment to subject parents and children to increasing levels of surveillance). Increasingly, such pedagogical strategies are focusing on 'the event', for example direct action, riots, reclaiming streets, illegal public parties and so on, which often have the opposite effect of deliberative democracy because they elicit emotive, sometimes violent, but more often hedonistic involvement rather than reflection. On the basis of this, we can conclude that radical transformation is not imminent, although it may still be immanent; that is, even if radical change is not likely to come soon, it may already be in gestation.

Notes

1. Risks are different from hazards because whereas the former only 'exist' when there is a perceived relationship between a particular cause and an effect that can be affected by particular decisions, the latter 'exist' (at least as perceptions) regardless of decision-making. Risks are also different from actual harm; they are perceived or anticipated *potential* harm.
2. 'Derivatives are financial instruments that have no value of their own. They are called derivatives because they derive their value from the value of some other asset, which is precisely why they serve so well to hedge the risk of unexpected price fluctuations' (Bernstein 1996, pp. 304–5).
3. Translation deficit simply refers to a logical hiatus between two systems operating at different speeds. As a result, changes taking place at the system operating at a higher velocity are no longer incorporated into the operational logic of other systems – there is insufficient time and shared understanding for them to recuperate and adjust to these fluxes.
4. This process could be referred to as alienation, although the origins of this term (Marxism) betray a humanistic, and indeed romanticized notion of 'organic unity' of the individual and his/her true human nature.
5. That is, shifts from the politics of representation towards decision-making practices dominated by expert knowledge and technological (rather than ethical or moral) concerns.

References

Adam, Barbara and Joost van Loon. 2000. 'Introduction'. Pp. 1–31 in *The Risk Society and Beyond: Critical Issues for Social Theory*, edited by B. Adam, U. Beck and J. van Loon. London: Sage.

Allan, Stuart. 2002. *Media, Risk and Science*. Buckingham, UK: Open University Press.

Beck, Ulrich. 1992. *Risk Society: Towards a New Modernity*. Translated by M. Ritter. London: Sage.

Beck, Ulrich. 1997. *The Reinvention of Politics: Rethinking Modernity in the Global Social Order*. Translated by M. Ritter. Cambridge: Polity.

Beck, Ulrich. 2000. 'Risk society revisited: Theory, politics, critiques and research programs'. Pp. 211–29 in *The Risk Society and Beyond: Critical Issues for Social Theory*, edited by B. Adam, U. Beck and J. van Loon. London: Sage.

Bell, D. 1976. *The Coming of the Post Industrial Society. A Venture in Social Forecasting*. New York: Basic Books.

Bernstein, Peter L. 1996. *Against The Gods: The Remarkable Story of Risk*. New York: John Wiley & Sons.

Boden, D. 2000. 'Worlds in action: Information, instantaneity and global futures trading'. Pp. 183–97 in *The Risk Society and Beyond: Critical Issues for Social Theory*, edited by B. Adam, U. Beck and J. van Loon. London: Sage.

Castells, Manuel. 1996. *The Rise of the Network Society*. Oxford: Blackwell.

Clark, Nigel. 1998. 'Nanoplanet: Molecular engineering in the time of ecological crisis'. *Time & Society* 7:353–68.

Deleuze, Gilles. 1992. 'Postscript on the societies of control'. *October* **59**:3–7.

Durkheim, Emile. 1984. *The Division of Labor in Society*. Translated by W.D. Halls. London: Macmillan.

Durkheim, Emile and Marcel Mauss. 1963. *Primitive Classification*. Translated by R. Needham. London: Cohen & West.

Foster, Kenneth R., David E. Bernstein and Peter W. Huber. 1993. *Phantom Risk: Scientific Inference and the Law*. Cambridge, MA: MIT Press.

Foucault, Michel. 1977. *Discipline and Punish: The Birth of the Prison*. Translated by A. Sheridan. New York: Pantheon.

Galbraith, John Kenneth. 1977. *The Affluent Society*. London: Deutsch.

Giddens, Anthony. 1990. *The Consequences of Modernity*. Cambridge: Polity.

Giddens, Anthony. 1994. 'Living in a post-traditional society'. Pp. 56–109 in *Reflexive Modernization: Politics, Tradition and Aesthetics in the Modern Social Order*, edited by U. Beck, A. Giddens and S. Lash. Cambridge: Polity.

Gorz, Andre. 1982. *Farewell to the Working Class: An Essay on Post-Industrial Socialism*. Translated by M. Sonenscher. London: Pluto.

Gramsci, Antonio. 1971. *Selections from the Prison Notebooks of Antonio Gramsci*. Translated by Q. Hoare and G. Nowell-Smith. New York: International Publishers.

Granovetter, Mark and Richard Swedberg. 1992. *The Sociology of Economic Life*. Boulder, CO: Westview Press.

Habermas, Jürgen. 1989. *The Structural Transformation of the Public Sphere: An Inquiry into a Category of Bourgeois Society*. Translated by T. Burger. Cambridge: Polity.

Irwin, Alan and Brian Wynne. 1996. *Misunderstanding Science?: The Public Reconstruction of Science and Technology*. Cambridge: Cambridge University Press.

Kelly, Kevin. 1997. 'New rules for the new economy'. *Wired* 5.09.

Kerr, C. 1983. *The Future of Industrial Societies: Convergence or Continuing Diversity?* Cambridge, MA: Harvard University Press.

Lash, Scott and John Urry. 1994. *Economies of Signs and Space*. London: Sage.

Latour, B. 1988. *The Pasteurization of France*. Cambridge, MA: Harvard University Press.

Luhmann, Niklas. 1990. *Essays on Self-Reference*. New York: Columbia University Press.

Luhmann, Niklas. 1995. *Die Soziologie des Risikos*. Berlin: De Gruyter.

McKenna, B.J. and P. Graham. 2000. 'Technocratic discourse: A primer'. *Technical Writing and Communication* **30**:219–47.

Offe, C. 1985. *Disorganized Capitalism: Contemporary Transformations of Work and Politics*. Cambridge: Polity.

Parsons, T. 1977. *The Evolution of Societies*. Englewood Cliffs, NJ: Prentice-Hall.

Rose, H. 2000. 'Risk, trust and scepticism in the age of new genetics'. Pp. 63–77 in *The Risk Society and Beyond: Critical Issues for Social Theory*, edited by B. Adam, U. Beck and J. van Loon. London: Sage.

Schumpeter, J.A. 1982. *Business cycles: A Theoretical, Historical, and Statistical Analysis of the Capitalist Process*. Philadelphia, PA: Porcupine Press.

Scott, Alan. 2000. 'Risk society or angst society: Two views of risk, consciousness and community'. Pp. 33–46 in *The Risk Society and Beyond: Critical Issues for Social Theory*, edited by B. Adam, U. Beck and J. van Loon. London: Sage.

Smets, P., H. Wels and J. van Loon. 1999. *Trust and Cooperation: Symbolic Exchange and Moral Economies in an Age of Cultural Differentiation*. Amsterdam: Het Spinhuis.

Touraine, A. 1971. *The Post Industrial Society*. New York: Random House.

Touraine, A. 1981. *The Voice and the Eye: An Analysis of Social Movements*. Cambridge: Cambridge University Press.

Ungar, S. 1998. 'Hot crises and media reassurance: A comparison of emerging diseases and ebola Zaire'. *British Journal of Sociology* **49**:36–56.

Van Loon, Joost. 2000. 'Virtual risks in an age of cybernetic reproduction'. Pp. 165–82 in *The Risk Society and Beyond: Critical Issues for Social Theory*, edited by B. Adam, U. Beck and J. Van Loon. London: Sage.

Van Loon, Joost. 2002a. *Risk and Technological Culture: Towards a Sociology of Virulence*. London: Routledge.

Van Loon, Joost. 2002b. 'A contagious living fluid: Objectification and assemblage in the history of virology'. *Theory Culture & Society* **19**:107–24.

Welsh, Ian. 2000. 'Desiring risk: Nuclear myths and the social selection of risk'. Pp. 1–31 in *The Risk Society and Beyond: Critical Issues for Social Theory*, edited by B. Adam, U. Beck and J. van Loon. London: Sage.

5 Social epistemology: preserving the integrity of knowledge about knowledge[1]
Steve Fuller

Social epistemology is a naturalistic approach to the normative questions surrounding the organization of knowledge processes and products. In other words, it seeks to provide guidance on how and what we should know on the basis of how and what we already know. The subject matter corresponds to what the pragmatist philosophers used to call 'the conduct of inquiry' and what may appear to today's readers as an abstract form of science policy. Social epistemology advances beyond other theories of knowledge by taking seriously that knowledge is produced by agents who are not merely individually embodied but also collectively embedded in certain specifiable relationships that extend over large chunks of space and time. Moreover, for the social epistemologist, the ends of knowledge need to be established, not taken for granted. Words like 'validity', 'reliability' and even 'truth' itself do not refer to ends inherent to the conduct of inquiry. Rather, they refer merely to constraints on inquiry that still leave wide open questions concerning the ends of knowledge: what sort of knowledge should be produced, by whom, and for whom? *Knowledge policy* captures the activity that addresses these questions, which (as discussed below) tend to be neglected by conventional science policy.

The need for social epistemology arises from an interdisciplinary gap between philosophy and sociology: philosophical theories of knowledge tend to stress normative approaches without considering their empirical realizability or political and economic consequences. Thus philosophers are much better at providing definitions of knowledge (e.g. 'justified true belief') than telling us which practices provide better and worse access to knowledge so defined. Sociological theories suffer the complementary problem of capturing the empirical and ideological character of knowledge, but typically without offering guidance on how knowledge policy should be conducted. Indeed, the sociological literature often leaves the impression that knowledge is valid only if it serves the knowledge claimant's interests. In this respect, social epistemology aims to transcend both philosophy's abstract aloofness and sociology's concrete cynicism.

Social epistemology operates with a generally sceptical attitude towards what many social theorists and science policy gurus celebrate today as our *knowledge society*. The 'knowledge society' refers mainly to the increasing role that science and technology play in societal governance and economic production. It is a tendency that has been observed by an ideologically wide range of observers since 1970, including Daniel Bell, Alvin Gouldner, Jean-François Lyotard, Francis Fukuyama and Manuel Castells. Knowledge society theorists typically valorize the progress of information technologies, the specialization of scientific knowledge and the intermediation of expertise in everyday life. These theorists, generally associated with a 'postmodernist' or at least post-Marxist political sensibility, tend to draw quite selectively on the history of capitalism to model the emerging social order. On the one hand, they highlight the conversion of knowledge work to 'intellectual capital' (or, more generally, 'human capital') that can be developed and even accumulated. On the other hand, they downplay the routinization and commodification of knowledge, as epitomized in the reduction of expertise to trainable skills that may be ultimately simulated on advanced computers, which indirectly serves to deprofessionalize the 'knowledge workers', perhaps ultimately rendering them redundant. Social epistemology draws attention to these less salutary consequences, which in many respects exacerbate the worst features of capitalism.

In a nutshell, for the social epistemologist, the knowledge society is what advanced capitalism looks like to intellectuals, once they have been assimilated into its mode of production – a classic case of what economists call the 'internalization of a negative externality'. After all, the dawn of the knowledge society has been marked by the massification of academia, from the budgets for scientific research to the number of students in search of credentials. At one level, it would seem that in our postmodern political economy, knowledge has become as central as labour in classical political economy. That may well be true – and the historical precedent should give us pause for thought. However, knowledge society discourse has given rise to a field, *knowledge management*, whose very name is a piece of Orwellian Newspeak that epitomizes the topsy-turvy political economy of the so-called knowledge society.

In earlier times, the very expression 'knowledge management' would have been heard as an oxymoron, since knowledge has generally been valued as something worth pursuing for its own sake, regardless of its tangible costs or benefits. However, now it would seem that knowledge needs to be 'managed' so as not to be left unused or allowed to grow profligate in a 'wild' state. Academics may continue to assert that knowledge is produced by hard work that is never fully rewarded, the fruits of which are nevertheless distributed as widely as possible. For economists, this is what marks knowledge as a 'public good', a distinctive product of the modern university that it manufactured by converting esoteric research into new topics for the curriculum. But for the

'KM guru', this public-good conception of knowledge merely shows that universities are not very economical in ordinary market terms. Consequently, universities are advised to disaggregate their research and teaching functions so as to acquire the 'lean and mean' spirit associated with, on the one hand, a corporate R&D division and, on the other, a vocational training centre.

The application of knowledge management to the university results in what is sometimes called a 'post-academic' conception of knowledge, which in practice levels traditional differences between knowledge and ordinary economic goods. In particular, the public-good conception of knowledge is dissolved into intellectual property rights and credentials acquisition. From the standpoint of social epistemology, this signature development of our so-called knowledge society serves to erode the autonomy of knowledge as an ideal. At a sociological level, the development corresponds to the increasing proportion of (especially younger) academics on short-term teaching and research contracts. Under the circumstances, they are more inclined to adopt what might be euphemistically called a 'flexible' and 'adaptive' attitude towards a wide range of potential employers than defend the integrity of that increasingly fickle employer, the university.

As has already been noted, the demystified – perhaps even debased – conception of knowledge in today's knowledge society has been accompanied by considerable semantic innovation, a ripe target for social epistemological inquiry. Perhaps the best display of knowledge society Newspeak is found in the glossary of *The New Production of Knowledge*, a multinational collaboration that is the single most influential academic work in European science policy circles since the end of the cold war. The notoriety of this book rests largely on the distinction between 'Mode 1' and 'Mode 2' knowledge production as a roughly two-stage process that marks the transition from 'internal' to 'external' drivers of knowledge production process. In Table 5.1, I have listed the major terms in 'Modespeak', alongside their *prima facie* innocent meanings ('not this . . .') and their more sinister practical ones ('but that . . .').

Modespeak presupposes what might be called a 'folk history of science policy' implicitly shared by many scientists and policymakers. It says that 'in the beginning' (which may be located in ancient Greece, the scientific revolution of the seventeenth century, or the rise of academic specialization in the nineteenth century), knowledge was pursued for its own sake by pure inquirers who decided if and when their knowledge was suitable for public consumption as ideology and technology. Failure to respect the prerogatives of pure inquiry led to the scientific and political enormities associated with Nazi Germany and the Soviet Union. This fixation on the epistemic value of pure inquiry is indicative of 'Mode 1' knowledge production.

However, so the folk history goes, pure inquiry generates its own kind of

Table 5.1   'Modespeak': knowledge society Newspeak

Modespeak	Not this . . .	But that . . .
'Codified/tacit knowledge' (conversion principle)	Performance/ competence (creativity)	Fixed/variable capital (knowledge management)
'Context of application'	Applied research	Client-centred research
'Globalization'	Universalization	Specialization
'Heterogeneity'	Anti-homogeneity	Anti-autonomy
'Hybrid agora/forum' (university redefined)	Knowledge unifier	Knowledge advertiser
'Informatization of society'	Knowledge mediates social relations	Knowledge alienated from individuals
'Knowledge industries'	University privileged	University deprivileged
'Massification of higher education'	Knowledge adds value	Knowledge devalued
'Pluralization of elites'	Knowledge workers respected	Knowledge workers modularized
'Reflexivity'	Critical of context	Adaptive to context
'Social capital'	Public good	Corporate property
'Social distribution of knowledge'	Integrated unit (institution)	Dispersed network (interaction)
'Socially robust knowledge'	Universally resilient knowledge (science)	Locally plastic knowledge (culture)
'Technology transfer'	Academia legitimates industry (19th c.)	Academia services industry (21st c.)
'Transdisciplinarity'	Interdisciplinarity	Antidisciplinarity

dysfunctionality when allowed to operate with impunity. Economists call it 'diminishing returns on investment'. In other words, as a research programme matures, it costs more – in terms of both time spent and materials used – to make progress comparable to that made in the past. Problems previously finessed now return to haunt the research community and typically reveal limitations in its fundamental assumptions that ultimately lead to its downfall. This captures the natural trajectory of what Thomas Kuhn called a 'scientific paradigm', an amalgam of theoretical vision, methodological principles and solved problems that set the agenda for subsequent researchers. However, as early as the 1970s, German philosophers of science under the influence of both Kuhn and Jürgen Habermas – the so-called finalizationists – began to suggest that a proactive science policy might pre-empt this tendency by channelling research effort toward standing social problems. This was beginning of 'Mode 2' knowledge production.

Over the past quarter-century, Mode 2 has migrated across the ideological spectrum from social democracy to neo-liberalism. Thus the original finalizationist proposal to harness mature science for the public good metamorphosed into an invitation for various interest groups to define more explicitly what is truly 'useful and beneficial' about the research they would wish to fund. What Jerome Ravetz originally called 'post-normal science' has now turned into 'science made to order'. In this brave new world, the Achilles' heel of Nazi and Soviet science was *merely* the prematurity with which science had been applied to policy, not that policymakers ultimately called the shots.

In more general policy terms, the Mode 1/2 distinction captures the difference between inquiry governed by strictly academic interests and by more socially relevant interests. But in practice, the scope of 'Mode 1' is much narrower than the university – closer to a discipline or research programme – and 'Mode 2' is much more diffuse than 'relevance' normally connotes – closer to a 'market attractor'. Indeed, the university is reduced from an institution with the aim of unifying knowledge to a convenient physical space that enables the 'communication' of various knowledge interests. Once again, reflecting the ideological ambivalence of Mode 2, 'communication' doubly resonates of a Habermasian 'ideal speech situation' for establishing consensus and a Hayekian 'clearing house' for setting prices. Not surprisingly, then, the overall impression the reader should receive from the tableau of Modespeak presented in Table 5.1 is that Mode 2 discourse conceals some recognizably capitalist, and even pre-capitalist, forms of domination with a pluralist rhetoric that disperses power and responsibility.

Indicative of the workings of Modespeak is the translation effected in the first row of Table 5.1: 'codified/tacit knowledge'. What academics routinely celebrate as our capacity 'to know more than we can tell' appears as a nightmare to managers trying to maintain the corporate knowledge base in the face of mobile workers in a flexible economy. When academics advise managers that our competence is not reducible to our performances, managers conclude that they must find ways of replacing that competence with a more reliable source of performances that can be made a permanent feature of corporate memory, or what Marx called 'fixed capital'. In that case, employees appear as transient sources of knowledge – or 'variable capital' – that need to be 'captured' while they are still on site. Towards this end, computerized expert systems have offered much promise to a business world that has tended to model the human mind only on a need-to-know basis. However, business is hardly alone in this regard. In fact, the succession of fashions in artificial intelligence research uncannily tracks the major models of organizational theory, starting from Herbert Simon's bureaucratically inspired 'General Problem Solver' that prevailed during the heyday of the welfare state to Friedrich Hayek's market-based parallel distributed processor model of the brain that has enjoyed a revival since the ascent of neo-liberalism in the 1980s.

For another example of the occlusions of Modespeak, compare *social capital* with a concept already raised that captured the imaginations of social scientists and policymakers in the previous generation: *public good*. The US economist Paul Samuelson invented the concept in the 1950s for goods that the state had to provide because they would never be provided efficiently in a pure market environment. These goods turned out to be the ones that would come to epitomize the welfare state over the next quarter-century: healthcare, education, utilities, and transport systems.

The defining feature of a public good is that it would cost more to restrict access to the good to just those who paid for them than to allow everyone access. Several reasons have been given for this feature of public goods. One rather traditional, but ultimately not very persuasive, reason is that some goods naturally flow to fill the available space, which means that concerted effort is needed to arrest it. In this respect, knowledge is sometimes treated as if it were a natural resource like air or water. A more persuasive account of public goods is that they require an infrastructure that is most efficiently implemented and maintained on a mass level, regardless of the capacities of particular individuals. Knowledge can be seen in this light by imagining the amount of police and judicial work that would be needed to restrict, say, access to books on nuclear physics to people who are seen as having 'paid their dues' by having acquired the right academic credentials or even the right liberal values.

Moreover, the nature of public goods is such that even free-riders may ultimately pay for their consumption by generating private and public goods of their own. For example, the flow of pirated software is both monitored and tolerated because communication among the pirates proves to be the most efficient means to discover bugs in the software. More to the point, however much it may have cost to provide the education, facilities and salaries for the medical scientists who develop a technique for treating a deadly disease, it would cost society more to restrict access to the treatment to just those who could pay market-driven prices for it than to distribute the cost across the entire society through taxation so that the treatment is free at the point of delivery. Nevertheless, public goods appear highly unattractive as investment opportunities to self-interested economic agents precisely because an investor would not be able to capture, or even regulate, the flow of profits. Of course, it would be in everyone's interest to pay *someone* to produce these public goods. That 'someone' turns out to be the state, which has the power to extract taxes from the egoists so as to provide the capital required to produce and maintain public goods.

Although the concept of social capital was not developed to replace the idea of public good, it has effectively done just that. The decline of the welfare state and the corresponding rise of neo-liberalism are once again implicated. An intuitive sense of the hidden benefits of free-riders has been replaced by a more explicit 'pay-as-you-go' sensibility. Social capital may be seen as an attempt to simulate some of the old collectivist sensibility by showing how solidarity can be in one's self-interest. The concept's popularity testifies to a profound change in our conception of who and what matters in the social order. Neo-liberalism has broken with the welfare state assumption that full employment is necessary for efficient economic growth. This, in turn, has diminished the sense of urgency with which new knowledge should be made available to everyone. Thus the state now assigns a lower priority to the main-tenance of the infrastructure for public goods, as evidenced in the decline in schools, hospitals and roads. A society (so it is now thought) may prosper, even if many of its members lag behind the market leaders.

But the impact of the state's withdrawal from the regulation of civil soci-ety does not end there: the market leaders may find it more convenient to pool their resources with people outside their own societies, causing the social fabric to disintegrate still further. This is a perennial source of deep class divi-sions in the developing world, whose elites identify more with First World elites than the masses of their own countries. The advent of computer-based information and communication technologies has only exacerbated the tendency, serving to further weaken already feeble nation-states. The concept of social capital was designed partly to halt the evacuation of money and talent associated with these transnational networks by fostering a bottom–up form of economic protectionism that does not require a full-blown welfare state, which in poorer countries never existed in the first place.

The exact appeal of social capital depends on where you live. Social capi-tal promises the poor in the developing world an oasis of economic self-deter-mination in a desert of deregulation or outright lawlessness. In the developed world, however, social capital satisfies a longing for an integrated lifestyle in these centrifugal postmodern times – the promise of higher profits from deeper socializing, or 'playmates as workmates'. Nevertheless, in the end, the concept of social capital is crafted with an eye to competitive advantage – specifically, the return to investors in a suitably dense social network *vis-à-vis* non-investors. In this respect, social capital is an example of what the economist Fred Hirsch originally called a *positional good*, that is, a good whose value is principally tied to the *exclusion* of specific consumers – the exact opposite of a public good. This point has ramifications throughout society. On the one hand, it justifies cooperative businesses that charge preferential prices to investors. On the other, it encourages stronger informal links between acade-mia and industry that result in jointly owned inventions or companies that are protected by intellectual property legislation. The perniciousness of these set-ups may not be immediately apparent but may become so in the long term, if they exacerbate existing social inequalities. (This in the import of Pierre Bourdieu's related but negatively tinged expression, *cultural capital*.) In more moralistic times, this intimate linking of social and economic interests so valorized by social capital thinking had a special, albeit now unfashionable name: *corruption*.

Ultimately, the two most insidious features of knowledge society Newspeak are: (1) the devaluation of 'knowledge', such that all organizations are now said to be in the business of producing 'knowledge' in the same sense; (2) the assimilation of democratic processes to market processes. The latter feature is symbolized in the Modespeak use of the words 'agora' and 'forum', the Greek and Latin words for the physical space in ancient cities where both business and politics were conducted. This image of a common space is then used to create a blurred image of the public character of knowledge, leading to the following confusions: free speech is confused with advertising, criticism with 'niche differentiation', the public interest with an array of 'revealed pref-erences', voting with trading, power with sales, rationality with efficiency, and progress with profits. What is perhaps most striking about all these elisions is that they happen effortlessly, largely as a by-product of the devolution of the state. This brings us to the key practical activity of social epistemology, *knowledge policy*, which is specifically designed to counteract this default sensibility.

Knowledge policy differs from conventional science policy by recognizing that policy is always being made, even when the *status quo* is maintained, or, as Karl Popper might say, induction rules. In the case of science, such *institu-tional inertia* can have significant consequences. It underlies the self-organizing, self-selecting and self-stratifying processes associated with the various levels at which 'peer review' occurs in science. Originally, peer review was limited to the publication of completed research, but in the twen-tieth century, once science was subsumed under the state, peer review spread to cover the funds required even to be eligible to do research. The result is an ever-expanding and interlocking system of elites, for which Robert Merton coined the euphemism, 'the principle of cumulative advantage'. It is tanta-mount to a 'providential' vision of history of science that would have been familiar to the early modern purveyors of what Max Weber called the 'Protestant Ethic': thus the dominant strands of scientific research would not be so well resourced and efficacious if they were not doing something right – even if we cannot as yet specify their target realities. In this context, the maxim that scientific research does not experience diminishing marginal returns on investment acts as an article of faith – that is, *any* research funded for 'enough' time will yield *some* benefit. As it happens, this maxim is invoked to continue current practices, though it could be just as easily invoked – in the spirit of Paul Feyerabend – to redistribute resources to a wider array of scientific projects. Social epistemology tends to support this redistributionist interpretation of the maxim in the name of *epistemic justice*.

Conventional science policy tends to be problem-centred without evaluating the discipline-based knowledge relevant to addressing the problems. Indeed, the science policy analyst rarely figures in *discovering* or *constructing* problems – they are simply treated as given. In contrast, knowledge policy critically examines the maintenance of institutional inertia: why don't research priorities change more often and more radically? Why do problems arise in certain contexts and not others; in particular, why is there more competition for resources within a discipline than between disciplines? These questions are addressed on the basis of three presumptions that take seriously the normative implications of the social constructivist premises of the interdisciplinary field of science and technology studies:

- *The dialectical presumption* The scientific study of science will probably serve to alter the conduct of science in the long run, in so far as science has reached its current state largely through an absence of such reflexive scrutiny.
- *The conventionality presumption* Research methodologies and disciplinary differences continue to be maintained only because no concerted effort is made to change them not because they are underwritten by the laws of reason or nature.
- *The democratic presumption* The fact that science can be studied scientifically by people who are themselves not credentialled in the science under study suggests that science can be scrutinized and evaluated by an appropriately informed lay public.

In addressing the problem of institutional inertia, the social epistemologist can begin by identifying the diverse interest groups that derive enough benefits, each in its own way, from the *status quo* that they have little incentive to change their course of action. The social epistemologist's strategy, then, would be to periodically restructure the environments in which researchers compete for resources. For example, researchers may be put in direct competition with one another where they previously were not. Moreover, they may be required to incorporate the interests of another discipline, including that discipline's practitioners, in order to receive adequate funding. This is the principle of *epistemic fungibility*. Finally, researchers may be forced to account for their findings, not only to their own discipline's practitioners, but also to the practitioners of other disciplines and the lay public. (Citizens' juries, consensus conferences and other forms of 'deliberative democracy' are relevant in the latter context.) In manipulating these variables of knowledge production, the social epistemologist can ensure that disciplinary boundaries do not solidify into 'natural kinds' and that the scientific community does not acquire rigidly defined class interests that impede communication both between disciplines and within society.

Effective knowledge policy is ultimately an exercise in 'rhetoric' in the full classical sense of using words to enable people to acquire new collective identities that become the basis of organized social action. This means that social epistemology must overcome 2000-year stereotypes of the philosopher (as Platonist) and the rhetorician (as Sophist) locked in mortal combat. According to this stereotype, philosophers invoke norms as an excuse for distancing themselves from the people, who fail to meet their lofty standards. Rhetoricians abandon norms for gimmicks that can secure short-term success for their clients. The social epistemologist's way out of this stalemate is to realize that the normative is constitutively rhetorical: that is, no prescription can have force if the people for whom it is intended refuse to obey it. This raises the question of whether knowledge policy really requires a meeting of minds or simply a confluence of behaviours. Only a philosophical conceit, backed by a dubious mental ontology, makes agreement on meanings, values and beliefs a necessary condition for coordinated action. Instead, parties to a knowledge policy decision need to realize that they must serve the interests of others *in order* to serve their own. That is, their diverse perspectives are causally entangled in a common fate, a *res publica*. Unfortunately, much public policy thinking reifies zero-sum gamesmanship, illicitly presuming that opposing interests require opposing courses of action that result in one side succeeding at the expense of the other. But the complexity of the world order makes it more likely that, in the long term, both sides to a dispute will either win or lose together.

With this last point in mind, let us return to that key battleground of knowledge management, the firm versus the university. When KM gurus want to persuade academic administrators that they should run their institutions more like businesses, they highlight the frustration that pioneering scientists (especially in the twentieth century) have felt within the disciplinary confines of their home universities. As a foil, the social epistemologist observes that it was only the subsequent establishment of academic departments and degree programmes that ultimately ensured that these initially interdisciplinary, or even transdisciplinary, fields (e.g. molecular biology, artificial intelligence) remained in the public domain as scientific knowledge, and were not converted into trade secrets and other bits of intellectual real estate.

The combined commitment to efficiency, systematicity and publicity points to the institutional uniqueness of universities. Moreover, they are virtues that even business has begun to appreciate, as firms suffer from what knowledge managers call *corporate amnesia*, the negative by-product of quickly formed, flexibly organized associations of providers and clients. While the existence of these nimble networks has enabled the business community to adapt to a changing competitive environment, the only knowledge traces they leave are those embodied in their joint products. For, once its mission is accomplished, a network's human nodes simply disperse and connect with other nodes to form new networks in pursuit of new projects.

The precedent for this diabolical situation is captured by the phrase *market failure*, which is the economist's way of talking about goods that markets fail to generate because no one finds it in their interest to produce them. This is because the cost of producing the goods can never be completely recovered in profits. In welfare economics, market failure defines the frontier where state provision of public goods begins. Similarly, we may speak of the role of universities in redressing *network failure* by reproducing and extending knowledge that might otherwise be lost through network dispersion.

Knowledge managers have yet to realize the full significance of universities in this capacity because they tend to diagnose network failure much too locally, as mere instances of 'knowledge hoarding'. The idea here is that companies become dependent on the services of certain employees – often information technology personnel – who do not make their knowledge directly available. We are then asked to envisage these human nodes as blocking the flow of information in the network by refusing to share what they know with the other nodes. Thus the knowledge hoarder appears as a moral failure who needs to be taught greater concern for her colleagues. Little is said about the emergence of knowledge hoarding as a defensive strategy for remaining employed or even employable in the knowledge economy's volatile labour market.

The targeting of the individual knowledge hoarder by knowledge managers aims to ensure that firms receive an adequate return on their 'knowledge investments', as measured by the clients, contacts or web links that employees accumulate. It is very much the point of view of managers trying to keep their firms afloat. However, from social epistemology's more global perspective, the tendency of knowledge to escape from its formative networks may be seen as a positive market mechanism for counteracting the *corporate* hoarding of knowledge, which could result in that ultimate blockage of free exchange: a monopoly.

In this context, universities are designed to permit *knowledge escape*, thereby redistributing the advantage accumulated in the staff, databases and intellectual property of corporate entities such as firms, states and even academic disciplines themselves. To appreciate this crucial point, let us return to a key point overlooked by knowledge society Newspeak: the integrity of the university as a whole is greater than the sum of its constituent departments.

The key lies in the university's status as an – perhaps even the original – 'entrepreneurial' institution, one perpetually engaged in *the creative destruction of social capital*. This Schumpeterian turn of phrase is simply another way of talking about the university's classical mission: the 'unity of teaching and research'. Research is a natural generator of social capital because those involved in its production are the primary beneficiaries. It takes further effort – often charged to others as rents, royalties and fees – to make that capital more generally available. Making that effort usually involves reducing one's own market advantage. However, that is precisely what teaching does when it makes previously esoteric research accessible to students, which then enables them to use or contribute to it. Teaching has traditionally involved synthesizing disparate cases from their original contexts of discovery and inferring larger explanatory principles, which are then subject to further study and ultimately dissemination through teaching and publication. In the increasingly practical and technical settings of today, the goal of teaching goes beyond contemplating nature's design to 'troubleshooting' and 'reverse engineering' products that may lead to their improvement and ultimately even their replacement. Precisely because their original advantage is destroyed through teaching, researchers are continually spurred on to generate new research that will once again provide them with a temporary market advantage. That endless cycle is the surest way to secure the integrity of knowledge, yet also the one most clearly under threat in today's so-called knowledge society.

Note
1. This article attempts to distil the implications of my work in social epistemology for knowledge management. The direct sources are Fuller (1993, 1996, 1997, 2000a, 2000b, 2002a, 2002b, 2003) and Fuller and Collier (2004). Related work similarly critical of knowledge management can be found in Hellström and Raman (2001). The intellectual roots of the forms of knowledge management criticized may be found in Gibbons et al. (1994) and Stehr (1994).
    Because of this approach Fuller is (with the editors' endorsement) providing a bibliography rather than a reference list and is not providing citations (ostensibly of his own work) in the text of the chapter.

Bibliography
Fuller, Steve. 1993. *Philosophy of Science and Its Discontents*. New York: Guilford.
Fuller, Steve. 1996. 'Recent Work in Social Epistemology'. *American Philosophical Quarterly* **33**:149–66.
Fuller, Steve. 1997. *Science*. Milton Keynes, UK and Minneapolis, MN: Open University Press and University of Minnesota Press.
Fuller, Steve. 2000a. *The Governance of Science: Ideology and the Future of the Open Society*. Milton Keynes, UK: Open University Press.
Fuller, Steve. 2000b. *Thomas Kuhn: A Philosophical History for Our Times*. Chicago, IL: University of Chicago Press.
Fuller, Steve. 2002a. *Social Epistemology*. Bloomington, IN: University Press.
Fuller, Steve. 2002b. *Knowledge Management Foundations*. Woburn, MA: Butterworth-Heinemann.
Fuller, Steve. 2003. 'In Search of Vehicles for Knowledge Governance: On the Need for

Institutions that Creatively Destroy Social Capital'. Pp. 41–76 in *The Governance of Knowledge*, edited by N. Stehr. New Brunswick, NJ: Transaction Books.

Fuller, Steve and James Collier. 2004. *Philosophy, Rhetoric, and the End of Knowledge: A New Beginning for Science & Technology Studies*. Hillsdale, NJ: Lawrence Erlbaum Associates.

Gibbons, Michael, Camille Limoges, Helga Nowotny, Simon Schwartzman, Peter Scott and Martin Trow. 1994. *The New Production of Knowledge*. London: Sage.

Hellström, Tomas and Sujatha Raman (eds). 2001. 'Social Epistemology and Knowledge Management'. *Social Epistemology* 15:139–262.

Stehr, Nico. 1994. *Knowledge Societies*. London: Sage.

6   Knowledge and social capital

Hitendra Pillay

Knowledge has always been at the core of economic development and social progress; however, in recent times there has been substantial interest and acknowledgement that the capacity to produce and use knowledge has much more explanatory value in understanding levels of economic (and social) welfare or rates of growth (Foray and Hargreaves 2002). However, much of the recent debate and thinking around knowledge has centred on knowledge management and has situated knowledge in the business and management disciplines with a focus on private sector enterprises. Enterprises whose practices are embedded in 'capitalist' values – maximizing monetary value of their investments which are usually achieved through exploitation of human, physical and/or social resources. The primary responsibility of management in these enterprises is to the owners of the business and shareholders rather than the 'public interest'. As a consequence the lexicon of knowledge discourse and thinking is, not surprisingly, skewed towards business and maximizing return for the financial investors.

However, a knowledge-based society should be about more than business efficiency and acquisition of wealth. It should have the capacity to regulate investment and growth for both economic and socio-cultural development, and private and public sector enterprises. Discourses such as those associated with the knowledge society and knowledge ecology imply more than the commercial enterprise – they are about a society in which commercial enterprise is but one aspect. The interrelatedness of economic performance and social and cultural conditions is well demonstrated in Knack and Keefer's (1977) study, which suggests that there is increasing evidence at a macro level that trust, civic norms and other social factors are key conditions for economic development. Further, comparative analysis by La Porta et al. (1997) confirmed that when there are two countries with similar GDP the one with higher regard for social factors tends to have more social infrastructure such as schools and hospitals, more sophisticated financial and management systems, and better fiscal policy. This interrelatedness of economic success and socio-cultural growth is increasingly being recognized and documented by development agencies such as the World Bank (2003) and the Asian Development Bank (1999).

The increasing appreciation of the link between socio-cultural and economic conditions has led to diverse but potentially confusing use of concepts such as knowledge economy, knowledge society, social capital and a plethora of conceptual hybrids. Nevertheless, despite a lack of clarity, the current debate has encouraged deeper interrogation of relevant concepts and their applications. The challenge now is to navigate through this conceptual labyrinth and maximize the potential to bring competing yet legitimate imperatives found in contemporary knowledge discourse together into a holistic framework.

Against the above backdrop, this chapter attempts first to consider (different 'forms' of) knowledge as types of asset, which are often equated to 'capital', and how these may be maximized. Second, based on the different types of capital inherent in a knowledge society, the chapter will explore ways in which one can understand and operationalize *social capital* in both business and private sector growth, and development. Based on the above, the chapter argues that there is a need to understand the complexity of the notion of 'capital' within the increasing interest in knowledge and to cast our conceptual net wider than economic and commercial imperatives. Only then can we create a new perspective or philosophy driven by intellectual and other equitable values, such as moral and cultural, that bring more sustainable benefits.

Knowledge as capital

Knowledge may be conceptualized as an asset which 'contains' some form of understanding of the nature and relationships between the various elements of things, concepts, beliefs or processes (the whole plus the elements of the whole – see William James (1909) for a detailed discussion). At its most basic level, therefore, knowledge is an individual's personal meanings derived from their understandings of those relationships. These relationships, however, are underpinned by political and cultural values and social norms. Thus, at a second level, despite relying on an individual's personal meanings, knowledge may be conceived as something that can be captured and transferred to others through training, social experiences, and cultural and technological artefacts, thereby creating a sharing of, and shared, understanding. Having knowledge (understandings) puts people, communities and organizations in a privileged position to use knowledge to leverage other assets. The aggregation of these tangible and intangible assets may be referred to as 'capital'. Bourdieu (1986), in his attempt to understand the structure and function of the social world, argued that to have a macro-level appreciation of how real economic and social growth manifests itself in real life we need to discuss capital in a way that moves beyond the economic perspective. Current knowledge commentators, building on Bourdieu's challenge, have been credited with advancing various types of capital and at different levels, such as economic, social and cultural capital at individual, organizational, national and global levels of practice (Soros 2000).

Social capital

The social structures, mechanisms, relationships and norms that shape the quality and quantity of society's social interactions are collectively referred to as social capital (Putnam et al. 1993). Putnam's thinking on social capital was influenced by Coleman (1988, p. 98), who defines social capital as a 'function of social structure producing advantage ... like other forms of capital, social capital is productive, making possible the achievement of certain ends that would not have been attainable in its absence'. Maintaining the focus on action, Putnam views social capital as the social organization of features such as trust, norms and networks that facilitate social cohesion to improve the efficiency of social institutions and relationships through collective actions. Social capital is based on human relationships and the underpinning beliefs and values held by groups of people. Putnam points out that one of the benchmarks of a successful society is when a community has shared values and morals. Social values and morals, as noted by Bergson (1956), can emanate from two sources: tribal belonging, and the universal human condition. His argument suggests that it is the latter that the advocates of social capital should strive for. Social capital transcends the local social units such as individuals and immediate social groups (friends and workmates), and focuses on macro conditions such as business and political ideologies, organizational/community health and wellbeing, and professional practices. As already noted, evidence suggests that social cohesion is critical for business and societies to achieve sustainable economic and social development (Fukuyama 1995; Osberg 2003). Social capital is not the sum of the institution and values that underpin a society; it is the glue that holds them together (Putnam et al. 1993).

Other-related capital

Social capital is significantly influenced by two other types of capital: human and cultural. Baron et al. (2000) make a distinction between human and social capital by arguing that social capital is underpinned by knowledge and intellectual understanding of the relationships concerned with issues such as distribution, equity and social cohesion. Human capital, on the other hand, is about self-development and the emotional and cognitive capabilities of individuals which, when placed in a context where certain social norms and institutional structures influence human behaviour, merge and enhance social capital. Thus investing in the development of human capital alone may not be sufficient to grow social capital.

Cultural capital is often used loosely to refer to both a historical heritage as well as contemporary practices. The underpinning knowledge needed for cultural capital is confined to certain groups drawn together by a common belief or practice, whereas social capital is more universal, transcending a number of cultural groups. Most people acknowledge that cultural capital is valuable and that it must continually evolve to survive. In the historical context, maximizing cultural capital requires interpreting and recording events/practices within the life of a culture (ethnic cultures and professional practices) rather then blindly relying on values and practices used for thousands of years. For example, the value of ancient artefacts and practices of cultural groups is not only in their direct current relevance, but also in their contribution to the understanding of historical practices which may guide contemporary vocational and cultural practices and innovations. Professional practices form professional culture, which is gradually developed by building on past knowledge and experiences. Thus cultural capital involves both professional and ethnic culture, and constitutes past and present knowledge that allows us to explain and understand our social and work-related behaviours.

Whilst these different types of capital all contribute to the knowledge society, they have different theoretical and philosophical underpinning assumptions. These assumptions presumably require these types of capital to operate under different laws of maximization. A lack of clear understanding of the underpinning assumptions and laws of maximization has traditionally led us to perceive different types of capital as competing with one another. This perception arises because we view them separately as a means to an end, rather than collectively contributing towards the growth and development of better quality of life for all. The next section discusses common tensions between social capital and economic capital that lead to the view that they are in competition.

The tension between economic and social capital

Traditionally accepted economic thinking says that increasing economic returns for investors involves the pursuit of self-interest through exploitation of resources (human, natural and other resources) to supply the demands of the market. However, with the emergence of the knowledge society and the 'knowledge worker', human resources are no longer perceived as merely a passive asset that just performs routine tasks in the cycle of production and supply. Human labour is now reconceptualized as human capital with the capacity to be innovative and thus create new demands rather than just react to the market by supplying its needs. Similarly, the market is not a passive recipient of products and services; market forces actually contribute to shape the nature of the products and services that are developed and made available. Thus, as Granovetter (1985) argues, the economically rational, self-interested behaviour assumed in many economic models unwittingly downplayed the significance of human capital and social relations in generating trust, in shaping expectations, and establishing and enforcing social norms which can be potent agents of change and growth. These social dynamics are now gaining legitimacy in the 'development' literature and are regarded as having significant influence on business success, economic reform, regional integration and security (Fukuyama 1995).

According to standard economic theory, economic growth is optimized by balancing supply and demand to achieve equilibrium. The law of maximization of economic capital entails increasing capital's value by manipulating supply and demand of goods and services – limited goods in the market means that people will pay a higher price, a price that may be more than the goods are really worth. However, to achieve and sustain equilibrium of these market factors is difficult in the face of economic agents seeking to manipulate supply and demand for their own benefit. Unlike economic capital, social capital increases its values by making itself widely available; it becomes depleted if restricted and not used. For growth in social capital, a state of equilibrium (stasis) can be seen as perpetuating redundancy and stagnation (see Burt 2000). Social capital grows from interaction within diversity and even creative conflict. For example, if everyone had the same knowledge, there would be limited need for anyone to interact with others to learn and share ideas; the social dynamic that unpins social capital becomes redundant. This social interaction is underpinned by trust, respect for individuals, social norms and so on that in turn are linked to individuals' growth and wellbeing. It includes both human and individual capital but is more about collective understanding and associated actions.

The second tension between social capital and economic capital stems from the different assumptions they seem to operate under in dealing with values. Dominant economic thinking takes into account only values associated with economic behaviour, which is directly connected to 'profiting', treats all other values as given and does not factor them into the analysis. These economic values assume that each participant is there to maximize profits to the exclusion of all other considerations. Such assumptions may not be appropriate to sustain the development of a knowledge society. Soros (2000) critiques the standard economic assumption and argues that standard economic theory may not be the best tool to deal with what must go beyond economic theory. He insists that non-economic values, instead of being taken as given, must be treated as 'reflexive'. He argues that either value can influence economic maximization or economic maximization can influence values, depending on operating conditions. Thus values have a two-way feedback mechanism that connects them to social and market reality in a holistic manner.

The third source of tension is found in the debate on the contingent nature of the various forms of capital. Putnam et al. (1993, p. 37) argue that social capital underpins good government and economic progress: 'the social capital embodied in norms and networks of civic engagement seems to be a precondition for economic development as well as for effective government'. This is contrary to current approaches to development work and government planning models, which are over-reliant on economic and financial indicators such as gross domestic product (GDP) and balance of payments. Growth in social capital often does not register on traditional indicators of GDP. For instance, better work practices in 'informal economic sectors', such as increased efficiency and cost reduction, may lead to improved wellbeing for many and yet not be counted in GDP. Equally, redistribution of resources may lead to more equity and wellbeing without any positive implications for GDP. Such redistribution could make a significant difference to the overall development of the country.

Social capital and operational issues

Having acknowledged the tensions above, we are compelled to revisit Bourdieu (1986) in relation to the convertibility of capital – how different types of capital transform from one to another and how such processes may form the basis of strategies adopted by social groups to ensure reproduction of capital. As David Suzuki argues, the world is not an infinite system: growth in one area may mean a compromise in another. Thus maximization of the different types of capital often just transforms one into another. However, short-term tradeoffs thus made may have long-term potential for a much higher net benefit to society. It is the dynamics of tradeoffs and the resultant effects that need further consideration as a tool for development and growth for a knowledge society. The above suggestion of tradeoffs is not counter to market fundamentalism; it is recognition of the changing nature of markets' responsibilities. Unless we adopt a holistic approach and combine the different types of capital that constitute the knowledge society we will continue to hinder growth and the development of a balanced global society (Nelson and Winter 1982; Soros 2000).

It appears that with the development of a global transactional economy and the pursuit of self-interest driven by capitalist ideologies, our moral and social values have been gradually transformed to support an ethic of single-minded competitiveness. Moral values related to 'social good' are being eroded by the push for a market-driven society – a world where economic maximization seems to be the only focus. This single-minded adoption of the market principle is now being perceived as market 'fundamentalism', where it is believed that the common interest is best served by an unwavering pursuit of self-interest. This has fostered a new relationship between self- and common (social) interest and is now being mandated by 'the market' to the extent that it is unclear if responsibility for the 'public good' is best met by governments and other public regulators. Whilst we may argue that the single-minded market-driven approach to national development is unrealistic, it has become doctrine in the West, and has become something to aspire to in developing countries, large corporations and public policy circles. As a result, over the last decade at least, the public sector's regulators have increasingly been shying away from responsibilities for the delivery of social sector services such as health, education, welfare and pension schemes. Arguably, there is now renewed interest in understanding if not addressing the challenges that globalization brings for governments and governance in general (see European Commission 2003).

As noted earlier, social values are intrinsic and fundamental to well-functioning communities, implying that their validity transcends prevailing conditions. Communities often fail to identify and adopt appropriate shared values due to complacency and/or a desire by individual members to increase their personal wealth through the pursuit of self-interest. In recent years, this complacency has arguably contributed to the increasing breakdown in socio-cultural values such as mutual respect, moral values and cultural tolerance. The standard model of social development underpinned by economic rationalism seems to be failing. As a consequence, in recent years many international agencies have recognized the role of indigenous knowledge in building social capital (Finger and Schuler 2004). This has become a key factor in bringing peace and relative political stability to many developing countries, which in turn has ensured a climate that attracts investors to grow these countries' economies. An example of this focus on social capital (respect, trust and wisdom of community elders) can be seen in the role of the Iraqi Governing Council, Haiti's council of community elders, Fiji's Great Council of Chiefs, Afghanistan's tribal elders. The impact of these social structures and the inherent social capital and appreciation of indigenous knowledge that they reflect are indicative of the need to engage the social networks of indigenous communities to provide the political and civic stability essential for attracting the economic investment needed for growth.

Furthermore, recognition of the significance of indigenous knowledge can be seen in the deliberations at a recent conference on drug production in Afghanistan (United Nations Office on Drugs and Crime 2004). It was noted that poppy cultivation has a long history in Afghani culture – and without a history of drug abuse. Indigenous moral and cultural values appear to have been successful in regulating the use of such substances. Even today cultural wisdom continues to play a role in the use of opium by locals – without having to resort to punitive measures and legislation. However, recent increases in the production of opium may mean more economic returns for Afghans while at the same time having a severe impact in western countries with drug abuse problems. The demand and supply of narcotic drugs is therefore emblematic of how indigenous knowledge and the dynamics of global social and economic capital can work together (see Isham et al. 2002). Practitioners need to develop a deep understanding of indigenous knowledge attributes and capabilities. Based on such understanding, a matrix comprising different social and economic institutions and their inter- and intra-relationships needs to be mapped out and juxtaposed with similar data from the West to develop an appreciation of the need for global social capital. Such grass-roots-level comparative analysis may lead to the development of sustainable interventions, unlike the current substitution model where farmers are asked to plant corn instead of poppies, with huge subsidies provided to offset the economic loss. Western industrialized nations and developing countries are concerned with different types of social capital comprising different variables, as noted by Klitgaard and Fedderke (1995). There is a need to develop more holistic models that take into consideration the full range of variables that impact on growth and sustained development of social capital for all groups of people (see Serageldin 1996).

Identifying and measuring social capital

Parallel with the theorizing is increasing interest in measuring social capital so that it may be experimented with to either maximize growth or control potential adverse effects (Portes and Landolt 1995) that may be detrimental to enhancing growth and quality of life. This is especially challenging because social capital comprises concepts such as trust, reciprocity, civic solidarity, social norms and practices, knowledge types such as indigenous, global, cultural and religious, institutional structures such as business organizations, social/community groups and governments, social networks and communication systems, all of which can be difficult to quantify. The challenge is increased when one considers that the quest is to measure not just the quantity but also the quality of social capital on a variety of scales.

Given the complex nature of the construct, even the most comprehensive definitions are multidimensional, incorporating different levels and units of analysis. Identifying core factors and developing key indicators of these factors can be very challenging as properties of many of the indicators (noted above) are inherently ambiguous. Thus social capital research cannot have (and it may not even be desirable to have) a single 'true' measure. The most useful approach will be to develop a relational understanding. As a consequence, most attempts to measure social capital have been partitioned into manageable units of this complex and multidimensional construct. However, these manageable units need to be linked to other manageable units to build a grand model, because keeping them in discrete manageable units may not further our understanding.

Attempts to measure social capital have adopted two broad perspectives which reflect Bergson's (1956) distinction between micro- and macro-levels of tribal belonging. This may be interpreted as the social capital of small units such as community groups and small business organizations. His macro-level universal human condition may be interpreted as the social capital of a number of communities, states, regions, nations and large national and multinational businesses. At the tribal level, studies such as Kreuter et al. (1998) compiled indexes from a range of approximate items for measures of trust, membership and reciprocity to measure social capital in community-based health promotion. Similarly, Parcel and Menaghan (1994) developed measures for ascertaining family social capital by measuring the extent and size of extended families and the frequency and quality of contact between members. Tribal-level research on social capital in the business sector can be seen in Chua's (2002) research on social interaction as a basis for knowledge creation in business organization. He examined structural, relational and cognitive dimensions as a basis for social interaction, which in turn is used as an indicator of social capital within organizations. Interest in studies similar to the above has been triggered by businesses embracing learning and knowledge as their key for success. It has led to business organizations experimenting with social capital indicators such as attitudes (value of self, trust/perceived safety, reciprocity, personal empowerment, diversity/openness, relationships and belongingness in the workplace (see Anderson and Miller 2003; Spence et al. 2003).

At the macro level of social capital, the universal human condition, most studies have been conducted with the support of international development agencies such as the World Bank and the Soros Foundation. One approach has been to embed attributes of social capital in the Living Standard Measurements Survey, directly seeking individuals' responses to survey items focusing on moral, cultural, social norms and relationships. Narayan-Parker and Pritchett (1997) constructed a measure of social capital in rural Tanzania, using data from the Tanzania Social Capital and Poverty Survey (SCPS). This large-scale survey asked individuals about the extent and characteristics of their associational activity, and their trust in various institutions and individuals. They matched this measure of social capital with data on household income in the same villages to link social capital to economic indicators. They found that village-level social capital raises household incomes. Another more holistic approach to measuring social capital can be seen in Grootaert's (2003) Social Capital Integrated Questionnaire (SC-IQ). It has six factors: groups and networks; trust and solidarity; collective action and corporation; information and communication; social cohesion and inclusion; and empowerment and political action that constituted social capital at the household level. They provided detailed descriptions of what may be included under each of the six factors, and also possible approaches to data analysis. For researching multi-level social capital (household, communities and organizations) there is the Social Capital Assessment Tool (SOCAT) developed by the World Bank (Grootaert and van Bastelaer 2001). This tool uses both questionnaire plus focus group interviews to collect data on community assets, governance, collective action, density of local organizations, relationships between organizations and communities. While the above research tools are useful, it is always necessary first to review the factors and items contained in these tools to assess their appropriateness to the proposed application. To make this judgement, it is important to have a full appreciation of the constructs and measuring indicators, levels of measurement and nature of context.

Alternatively, social capital proxies are identified and used as indicators of social capital. Use of proxies can be seen in Klesner's (2003) study, where he used social trust, membership in organizations, density and distribution of telephone services, and hours of television viewed daily as proxies of social capital in Mexico to ascertain the levels of political participation of people. He found strong relationships to political participation with organizational membership. His tentative explanation is that the government structure in Mexico has traditionally encouraged personal contact with officials aimed at individualized benefits rather than group-based benefits. In this, the government is supporting the pursuit of self-interest by fostering attributes of social practices that detract from pursuit of the common good.

This chapter outlined different types of capital that are often associated with knowledge management and discussed the tensions between these types of capital at conceptual as well as operational levels. It also discussed some contemporary approaches and tools to measure social capital. While the above discussions may provide insight into types of capital in a knowledge society and their management, there is a need to understand and manage tradeoffs inherent in the tensions between the different types of capital posited here. Such understanding should form the basis for developing a holistic model which may promote a balanced knowledge society.

References

Anderson, A.R. and C.J. Miller. 2003. ' "Class matters": Human and social capital in the entrepreneurial process'. *Journal of Socio-Economics* **32**:17–36.

Asian Development Bank. 1999. *Fighting Poverty in Asia and the Pacific: The Poverty Reduction Strategy*. Manila: ADB.

Baron, S., J. Field and T. Schuller. 2000. *Social Capital: Critical Perspectives*. Oxford: Oxford University Press.

Bergson, H. 1956. *The Two Sources of Morality and Religion*. Garden City, NY: Doubleday.

Bourdieu, P. 1986. *Forms of Capital: Handbook of Theory and Research for the Sociology of Education*. New York: Greenwood Press.

Burt, R.S. 2000. 'The network structure of social capital', in *Research in Organizational Behavior*, vol. 22, edited by R.I. Sutton and B.M. Staw. Greenwich, CT: JAI Press.

Chua, A. 2002. 'The influence of social interaction on knowledge creation'. *Journal of Intellectual Capital* **3**:375–93.

Coleman, J. 1988. 'Social capital and the creation of human capital'. *American Journal of Sociology* **94**(supplement):s95–s120.

European Commission. 2003. 'Second progress report on economic and social cohesion (January 2003): Unity, solidarity, diversity for Europe, its people and its territory'. Luxembourg: Office for Official Publications of the European Communities.

Finger, J.M. and P. Schuler. 2004. *Poor People's Knowledge: Promoting Intellectual Property in Developing Countries*. Washington, DC: World Bank.

Foray, D. and D. Hargreaves. 2002. 'The development of knowledge of different sectors: A model and some hypothesis', in *OECD Conference on Knowledge Management and Learning*. Oxford.

Fukuyama, F. 1995. *Trust: The Social Virtues and the Creation of Prosperity*. London: Hamish Hamilton.

Granovetter, M. 1985. 'Economic action and social structure: The problems of embeddedness'. *American Journal of Sociology* **91**:481–510.

Grootaert, C. 2003. *Measuring Social Capital: An Integrated Questionnaire*. Washington, DC: World Bank.

Grootaert, C. and T. van Bastelaer. 2001. 'Understanding and measuring social capital: A synthesis of findings from the social capital initiative'. Washington, DC: World Bank.

Isham, J.T., T. Kelly and S. Ramaswamy. 2002. *Social Capital and Economic Development: Well Being in Developing Countries*. Cheltenham, UK and Northampton, MA, USA: Edward Elgar.

James, W. 1909. *A Pluralistic Universe*. London: Longmans Green.

Klesner, J.L. 2003. 'Political attitudes, social capital, and political participation: The United States and Mexico compared'. *Mexican Studies* **19**:29–64.

Klitgaard, R. and J. Fedderke. 1995. 'Social integration and disintegration: An exploratory analysis of cross-country data'. *World Development* **23**:357–69.

Knack, S. and P. Keefer. 1977. 'Does social capital have an economic payoff? A cross country investigation'. *Quarterly Journal of Economics* **112**:1251–88.

Kreuter, M., N. Lezin and B. Baker. 1998. *Is Social Capital a Mediating Structure for Effective Community-Based Health Promotion?* Atlanta, GA: Health.

La Porta, R., F. Lopez-de-Silanes, A. Shleifer and R. Vishny 1997. 'Legal determinants of external finance'. *Journal of Finance* **52**:1131–50.

Narayan-Parker, D. and L. Pritchett. 1997. 'Cents and sociability: Household income and social capital in rural Tanzania', in *Policy Research Working Paper No. 1796*. Washington, DC: World Bank.

Nelson, R.R. and S.G. Winter. 1982. *An Evolutionary Theory of Economic Change*. Cambridge, MA: Belknap Press of Harvard University Press.

Osberg, L. 2003. *The Economic Implications of Social Cohesion*. Toronto and London: University of Toronto Press.

Parcel, T.L. and E.G. Menaghan. 1994. *Parents' Jobs and Children's Lives*. Hawthorne, NY: Aldine de Gruyter.

Portes, A. and P. Landolt. 1995. 'The downside of social capital'. *The American Prospect* **26**:18–21.

Putnam, R.D., R. Leonardi and R. Nanetti. 1993. *Making Democracy Work: Civic Traditions in Modern Italy*. Princeton, NJ: Princeton University Press.

Serageldin, I. 1996. 'Sustainability as opportunity and the problem of social capital'. *Brown Journal of World Affairs* **3**:187–203.

Soros, G. 2000. *Open Society: Reforming Global Capitalism*. New York: Public Affairs.

Spence, L.J., R. Schmidpeter and A. Habisch. 2003. 'Assessing social capital: Small and medium sized enterprises in Germany and the U.K.' *Journal of Business Ethics* **41**:17–29.

Suzuki, T.D. 2002. 'The challenge of the 21st century: Setting the real bottom line'. *Journal of Business Administration and Policy Analysis* **30**:47–66.

United Nations Office on Drugs and Crime. 2004. *International Counter Narcotics Conference on Afghanistan*. http://www.unodc.org/pdf/afg/afg_intl_counter_narcotics_conf_2004.pdf.

World Bank. 2003. *Lifelong Learning in the Global Knowledge Economy: Challenges for Developing Countries*. Washington, DC: World Bank.

PART II

POLICY

7 Knowledge and cultural capital

Stuart Cunningham

The new macro focus on the knowledge-based economy and innovation policies has been around in some form or other for some time, certainly since the information society discussions of the 1950s, with notional subdivisions of the service or tertiary industry sector into quaternary and quinary sectors based on information management (fourth sector) and knowledge generation (fifth sector). But the shorter-term influence is traceable to new growth theory in economics, which has pointed to the limitations for wealth creation of only microeconomic efficiency gains and liberalization strategies (Arthur 1997, p. 10; Romer 1994, 1995).

Governments are now attempting to advance knowledge-based economy models, which imply a renewed interventionary role for the state after decades of neo-liberal small government. There is prioritization of innovation and R&D-driven industries, intensive reskilling and education of the population, and a focus on universalizing the benefits of connectivity through mass ICT literacy upgrades.

Every OECD economy, large or small, or even emerging economies (e.g. Malaysia) can try to play this game, because a knowledge-based economy is not based on old-style comparative factor advantages, but on competitive advantage, that is, what can be constructed out of integrated labour force, education, technology and investment strategies. The cases of Japan, Singapore and Finland are exemplary in this regard.

The place of creative industries in knowledge economy strategies

It has been rare for the cultural and creative industries to be considered in knowledge economy (usually R&D and innovation) strategies, although, as we shall see, this situation is beginning to change.

Why is this? There are several reasons, principled and otherwise.

First, the great majority of the 'good news' economic data adduced to point to the economic dynamism and centrality of the creative industries to the new economy are services sector data. They relate to 'creative retail' rather than to any R&D process that may be argued to be essential to the generation of creative content.

The argument has yet to be decisively won that part of the large and growing creative industries sector which is also a part of an 'emerging industries' sector is one requiring R&D-style investment in experimental technologies or applications.

Second, both the digital applications subsector, and the larger sector from which it is growing, have been supported by public subsidy and, in those sectors where there is a fully industrialized and commercial focus, such as film, television, games or music, most countries are significant net importers of such product, with the USA and the UK as dominant exporters. So their dynamism has real social and cultural benefit for a country but problematically established net economic benefits. This can be quite sharply contrasted with the communications and ICT sector, which is perceived to drive significant productivity growth throughout the economy and to be a substantial sector in its own right, with possibly greater export potential.

But the rest of the world cannot afford to bow to a perceived iron law of comparative advantage enjoyed by the USA and the UK in creative industries' pre-eminence (note that all of Howkins's (2001, ch. 3) creative industries sectors are dominated by the USA and the UK, with very few exceptions). This fact is well accepted in the science–engineering–technology (SET) fields, where relative competitive advantage is *constructed* – in part through state interventions. In addition, the case for creative inputs across the broadening new digital economy becoming as important as ICTs must be made with a stronger evidence base and more policy traction.

Government's role is to seed risky innovation in those sectors with most potential for growth and wealth creation – just as in SET R&D. To be schematic, we move from a cultural policy to the services frame by the application of contemporary industry policies. We move from the cultural and the services to the knowledge frame by the application of R&D policies.

Another reason has to do with the thoroughly commercial nature of R&D investment in the big creative industries. Arguments for state interventions in what are, after all, massive multinational commercial enterprises and sectors may simply not be robust enough. The argument against this is essentially the same as the one above. While this may be to a significant (but by no means complete) extent true of the US economy, it is true of probably no other economy. While the private sector is the major driver of creative industries such as film, broadcasting, music, games, leisure software, architecture, design and so on, smaller economies always need public sector involvements. This is reinforced by the risk-averse nature of private sector investment in many smaller economies with branch-plant corporate structures and mentalities. R&D, properly defined, for the creative industries will always be in need of public sector involvement.

Fourth, the creative industries can be thought of as intrinsically hybrid in their nature. They are variously cultural, service (both wholesale and retail) based, R&D based, and a substantial part of the 'third', community, sector.

In this sense, one can make a general case for the creative industries being central in a knowledge-based *society*. But their specific, focused connection to the knowledge-based *economy*, and to public policy interventions specific to it, might, to some, remain diffuse.

Finally, there are inescapable pragmatics and politics. Many policy and decision makers remark – off the record – that making the whole apparatus of R&D and innovation frameworks available to content would be to open a Pandora's box of illimitable claims on the public purse, especially when these sectors are perceived to be (well?) served by cultural subsidy approaches.

The dominant view of social and cultural capital in a knowledge and innovation framework is as a handmaiden of the R&D powerhouses of science, engineering and technology. In this view, social and cultural capital provide a sort of generalized humanistic insightfulness and the management and overseeing glue that keeps the knowledge-based economy going. However true this postulation is, it is inadequate to capture the growing contribution of the content and creative industries and the social phenomena that have rapidly grown around them in contemporary societies.

Creative production and cultural consumption are an increasingly integral part of the new economy, not merely part of analysing and managing it.

Worldwide, the creative industries sector has been among the fastest-growing sectors of the global economy. Several analysts, including the OECD (1998); the UK government through its Creative Industries Task Force (1998); Jeremy Rifkin in *The Age of Access* (2000); and John Howkins in *The Creative Economy* (2001), point to the crucial role they play in the new economy, with growth rates better than twice those of advanced economies as a whole. Entertainment has displaced defence in the USA as the driver of new technology take-up, and has overtaken defence and aerospace as the biggest sector of the Southern Californian economy (Rifkin 2000, p. 161).

Rather than relegating creative production to a residual or marginal status in new economy business practice, sociologists Lash and Urry (1994) and business analyst John Howkins (2001, ch. 4) claim that it has become a model for such business practice (outsourcing; the temporary company; the 'producer' model of project management; just-in-time teams, etc.). Rifkin (2000, pp. 163–4) claims that cultural production will ascend to the first tier of economic life, with information and services moving to the second tier, manufacturing to the third tier and agriculture to the fourth tier.

Most R&D priorities reflect a science-and-technology-led agenda at the expense of new economy imperatives for R&D in the content industries, broadly defined. However, the broad content industries (or 'knowledge consumption services') sector derives from the applied social and creative disciplines (business, education, leisure and entertainment, media and communications) and represents 25 per cent of the US economy, whilst the new science sector (agricultural biotech, fibre, construction materials, energy and pharmaceuticals) for example, accounts for only 15 per cent of the economy (Rifkin 2000, p. 52).

In fact all modern economies are consumption driven (60 per cent of GDP in Australia and 62 per cent of US GDP – see Hearn et al. 1998) and the social and cultural technologies that manage and stimulate consumption all derive from the social and creative disciplines.

In Australia, these industries or enterprises are valued at between $19 and $25 billion a year (the elasticity of the figures is the tip of a large iceberg of statistical imponderability) – as much as the residential construction industry. And think how much we all place the construction industry at centre stage as an index of the nation's economic health! The creative industries are growing at a fast clip. In the high-growth areas, like digital content and applications, they are growing at twice the overall rate of the overall economy. Many Australians are involved in the creative industries, ranging from hobbyists to full-time employees and small businesspeople: 2.5 million say they work in these areas, and of those about 900 000 get paid for it.

We can no longer afford to understand the social and creative disciplines as commercially irrelevant, merely 'civilizing' activities. Instead they must be recognized as one of the vanguards of the new economy. R&D is not only required in the applied social and creative disciplines for its own commercial potential, but also because such R&D must be hybridized with science and technology research to realize the commercial potential of the latter. Commercialization depends on 'whole product value propositions' not just basic research.

The new economy requires both *R* and *D*: the contexts, meanings and effects of *cultural consumption*, in Rifkin's terms, are as important for purposes of policy development as *creative production*. The work of Richard Florida (2002) stands as eloquent testimony to this indivisibility. Major international content growth areas, such as online education, interactive television, multi-platform entertainment, computer games, web design for business-to-consumer applications, or virtual tourism and heritage, need *research* that seeks to understand how complex systems involving entertainment, information, education, technological literacy, integrated marketing, lifestyle and aspirational psychographics and cultural capital interrelate.

They also need *development* through trialling and prototyping supported by test beds and infrastructure provision in R&D-style laboratories. They need these in the context of ever-shortening innovation cycles and greater competition in rapidly expanding global markets. R&D strategies must work to catch the emerging wave of innovation needed to meet demand for content creation in entertainment, education and health information, and to build and exploit universal networked broadband architectures in strategic partnerships with industry.

Evolving innovation and R&D policies

Political economy and critical cultural studies (for example, see *International Journal of Cultural Studies*, Vol. 7(1), March 2004) might view these kinds of claims for creativity in the new economy as reductionist economism, and a 'cheerleading' boosterism fatally deflated by the dotcom bust. However, I would argue that the creative and informational economy poses a serious challenge to traditional 'scale and scarcity' economic orthodoxy as well as heritage notions of culture, and that the trends towards the 'culturization' of the economy are longer term than the hothouse events of the late 1990s and early 2000s. As Venturelli argues (2002, p. 10), 'the environmental conditions most conducive to originality and synthesis as well as the breadth of participation in forming new ideas comprise the true tests of cultural vigor and the only valid basis for public policy'. There is enough in new growth theory, and evolutionary and institutional economics, to suggest progressive new takes on traditional political economy. Creativity, once considered as marginal, has had to be brought towards the heartland of economic thought, and, with it, its values. What was once considered as the only model for innovation (science and technology) has had to make some way for creative content and process.

Despite the difficulties in shoehorning content and entertainment industries into innovation frameworks – designed as they are fundamentally for the manufacturing sector – it is beginning to occur, as innovation and R&D policies evolve. Lengrand et al. (2002) talk of 'third generation' innovation policy, while Rothwell (1994) contemplates five generations of innovation. The trend is the same, however. Earlier models are based on the idea of a linear process for the development of innovations. This process begins with basic knowledge breakthroughs courtesy of laboratory science and public funding of pure/basic research and moves through successive stages – seeding, pre-commercial, testing, prototyping – until the new knowledge is built into commercial applications that diffuse through widespread consumer and business adoption. Contemporary models take account of the complex, iterative and often non-linear nature of innovation, with many feedback loops, and seeks to bolster the process by emphasizing the importance of the systems and infrastructures that support innovation.

Innovation frameworks set the broad parameters within which R&D strategies are developed. Let's now turn to evidence that such strategies are also evolving and beginning to contemplate the role of creative content.

Canada, New Zealand, Australia and Taiwan are seeing evidence of creative industries being at least contemplated as an R&D sector and the principles for R&D intervention are interestingly to be compared with and are not mappable onto cultural and industry intervention principles. (I have addressed this issue elsewhere, see Cunningham 2002, 2004.) In Canada, there is some interesting work on stimulating Canada's broadband content industry through R&D strategies (Delvinia 2001). In New Zealand, the Foundation for Research, Science and Technology is promulgating explicit R&D policy for the creative industries, identified as a national 'Growth and Innovation Framework' priority along with biotech and ICT.

In Australia, the process to develop a set of national research priorities that were more inclusive than the original very narrow set of four 'new science' priorities (nanotechnology, photonics, genomics/phenomics and complex systems) began with 'Developing National Research Priorities: An issues paper' in May 2002. There was a sliver of a promise of integration between humanities and social sciences and science and technology in this paper, and the stated intention that there would be a second round of priority setting addressed to the humanities and social sciences. But the reason given for prioritizing science and technology was simply that 75 per cent of the country's outlays in R&D go to science and technology. Subsequently, a more inclusive set of priorities was promulgated, which requires all the major research facilities and institutions at a national level to take account of these priorities and report as to their acquittal of them. One of them is 'Frontier technologies for building and transforming Australian industries'. In this priority area there are key statements such as 'research is needed to exploit the huge potential of the digital media industry', and a number of examples of content applications such as e-commerce, multimedia, content generation and imaging are mentioned for priority research and development. In addition, under the priority goal of 'Promoting an innovation culture and economy' there is a stated intention to prioritize 'maximising Australia's creative and technological capability by understanding the factors conducive to innovation and its acceptance'.

In the context of a National Development Plan, Taiwan is linking a more 'humanistic and sustainable' approach to development to 'culturally creative industries', the goals of which are to nurture creative skills and promote the combination of culture with entrepreneurship to develop cultural industries. This necessitates setting up an organization to promote culturally creative industries, cultivating creative manpower for art and design, moulding an environment conducive to the development of creative industries and developing creative design and culture-based industries. This will articulate to the more high-tech end of the creative industry spectrum, with major new R&D investment in schools in such key areas as design and digital content, and by encouraging cooperation among industry, academia and research institutions (http://www.roctaiwan.or.kr/policy/20021021/2002102101.html).

The US R&D effort continues to be dominated by SET, and particularly defence SET, but *Beyond Productivity* is a good example of a probe from the National Academy searching for purchase for an investment strategy for the digital arts and design based on innovation (Mitchell et al. 2003).

In Europe, while innovation and R&D policy, for the most part, remains focused on big science and technology, the exception is probably digital content creation, which is beginning to slip in as part of 'technology', both at an EU and member state level (see www.cordis.lu). This is not happening at this stage through processes of explicit policy reconsideration and there are very few high-level policy documents, either in R&D or on innovation more broadly, that explicitly mention R&D for the creative industries. While there is the usual range of industry development support for creative industries (soft loans, grants, development of networks), recognition of the more particular R&D claims of creative skills and services more broadly as intermediate input into a wider range of activities, while supported in rhetoric, is not yet showing up in policy.

The European Commission's influence over R&D in member states is driven to a large extent by direct funding of its research priorities under the various Framework Programmes. If the Commission is showing an interest in funding digital content research (which it is), it doesn't mean member states will adopt that policy, but that research will get funded in those countries and will lead to pressure on national research bodies to support similar activities.

The current research programme is Framework Programme 6 and it is organized into thematic areas. Most are still science and technology focused but there are two areas – information society technologies, and citizens and governance in a knowledge-based society – that will directly support arts and humanities research. Information society technologies includes two categories of direct relevance: cross-media content for leisure and entertainment, and technology-enhanced learning and access to cultural heritage.

R&D is quite a live issue in the humanities and creative arts research community in the UK. On one hand, the Arts and Humanities Research Board is to be made into a full Research Council, with the same status as the others which deal with science and technology (and in the case of the ESRC, with social sciences). On the other hand, the same White Paper on Higher Education, which made this announcement early in 2003, makes almost no other mention of the creative industries. Nor do most of the Department for Trade and Industry policy statements on the 'knowledge economy'.

The Secretary of State for Education in early 2003 has actually needed to defend himself in the press and elsewhere from the accusation that research monies just go to big science, but there is certainly a feeling that, while support for the creative industries either as part of economic development/regeneration or as cultural policy has increased substantially, none of the sectors is yet seen as R&D based or significantly R&D influenced.

As in other jurisdictions, there is a reluctance to open up R&D programmes to creative content prototyping and production because it could 'open the floodgates'. The politics of throwing creative content's hat into the ring with SET is regarded as moot given the propensity to be marginalized by larger, more politically saleable, claims.

Final comments

There is no doubt that the dominant view of cultural capital in a knowledge and innovation framework is as a handmaiden to the R&D powerhouses of science, engineering and technology. As we have seen, in this view, cultural (and social) capital is needed to understand and manage the 'consequences of moving to a knowledge-based economy'. In this chapter, I have put the stronger view that creative production and cultural consumption are an increasingly integral part of the new economy, not merely part of analysing and managing it. This does not imply that I exclude from consideration the 'handmaiden' view, only that I think this will not produce breakthrough understandings and policies regarding cultural and creative 'capital' in the new economy. This is what this chapter has been written for.

References

Arthur, Brian. 1997. 'Increasing returns and the new world of business'. Pp. 3–18 in *Seeing Differently: Insights on Innovation*, edited by J. Seely Brown. Boston, MA: Harvard Business Review Books.

Creative Industries Task Force. 1998. 'Creative industries mapping document'. http://www.culture.gov.uk/global/publications/archive_1998/creative_industries_mapping_document_1998.

Cunningham, Stuart. 2002. 'From cultural to creative industries: Theory, industry, and policy implications'. *Media Information Australia Incorporating Culture & Policy* 102:54–65.

Cunningham, Stuart. 2004. 'The creative industries after cultural policy: A genealogy and some possible preferred futures'. *International Journal of Cultural Studies* 7:105–15.

Delvinia. 2001. 'Filling the pipe: Stimulating Canada's broadband content industry through R&D', in *Report on the National Roundtables on Advanced Broadband Content*: prepared for CANARIE inc, May.

Florida, Richard. 2002. *The Rise of the Creative Class*. New York: Basic Books.

Hearn, Greg, Tom Mandeville and David Anthony. 1998. *The Communication Superhighway: Social and Economic Change in the Digital Age*. Sydney: Allen and Unwin.

Howkins, John. 2001. *The Creative Economy: How People Make Money From Ideas*. London: Allen Lane.

Lash, Scott and John Urry. 1994. *Economies of Signs and Space*. London: Sage.

Louis Lengrand & Associés, PREST and ANRT. 2002. 'Innovation tomorrow. Innovation policy and the regulatory framework: Making innovation an integral part of the broader structural agenda', in *Innovation papers No 28*: European Commission Directorate-General for Enterprise, Innovation Directorate, EUR report no.17052.

Mitchell, William, Alan Inouye and Marjory Blumenthal. 2003. *Beyond Productivity: Information Technology, Innovation and Creativity*. Washington, DC: National Academies Press.

Organisation for Economic Co-operation and Development (OECD). 1998. *Content as a New Growth Industry*. Paris: OECD.

Rifkin, Jeremy. 2000. *The Age of Access: How the Shift from Ownership to Access is Transforming Modern Life*. London: Penguin.

Romer, Paul. 1994. 'The origins of endogenous growth'. *Journal of Economic Perspectives* 8:3–22.

Romer, Paul. 1995. 'Interview with Peter Robinson'. *Forbes* **155**:66–70.

Rothwell, Roy. 1994. 'Towards the fifth-generation innovation process'. *International Marketing Review* **11**:7–31.

Venturelli, Shalini. 2002. 'From the information economy to the creative economy: Moving culture to the center of international public policy'. Washington, DC: Center for Arts and Culture.

8 The organization of creativity in knowledge economies: exploring strategic issues

Paul Jeffcutt

Introduction

This chapter examines creativity in a broad organizational field of knowledge relationships and transactions (much in the way that innovation has recently become discussed). In considering key issues and debates across this complex field, the chapter concentrates on the key generic problems of investigating, understanding and influencing this cultural economy. A rich mix of problems and opportunities is considered and assessed, via a discussion of a pioneering in-depth study of the creative industries in a region of the UK. The chapter concludes with several key challenges for research and policy in the building of situated and strategic knowledge on cultural economies.

Creativity in the contemporary economy

Creativity has recently become a popular term with both the public policy and business communities. In one sense, this attention is obvious – which person, group, firm, city or region would aspire to be 'uncreative'? However, the recent enthusiasm for creativity needs to be put in context and, in particular, connected to a set of government and corporate strategic responses to competitive and globalized challenges (Porter 1990) in the contemporary economy. Such responses typically have two alternative cycles.

In the first, competitiveness can be maintained by downward pressure on costs that are either met by labour substitution, by the substitution of labour by technology, or by cheaper labour (usually in a different region or nation-state). In the second cycle, competitiveness can be maintained through innovation in products and services. The focus on 'price', which underpins the first cycle, has been termed 'old competition', whilst the focus on quality, innovation (and creativity) has been called 'new competition' (see Best 1990, 2001).

In the second cycle, innovation relies upon 'creativity' in the creation of novel products and services – for, in enterprises, it is the creative process that stimulates and supports the achievement of innovative outputs. Institutions may thus become configured to prize creativity and innovation (Robinson

2001) as sources of competitive advantage rather than as additional costs. Hence, the second cycle places emphasis upon loose networks of enterprises that can mix and match skills and expertise to produce short runs of new products of high quality at short notice (Amin and Thrift 1994).

Clearly creativity is at a premium in short product runs and rapidly changing product ranges. The key question that follows is how to maximize creativity in any individual, enterprise, region or economy. In order to respond effectively, one has to understand where creativity is 'located'. Obviously, individuals are a primary source of creativity, but (like innovation) it is somewhat short-sighted (although very popular) simply to seek to increase the 'creativity' quotient of each individual in the hope that this will make a significant difference.

Just as with innovation, new ideas require a context in which they may be nurtured, developed and passed on, or made into something more generally useful (Pratt 1997). Creativity does appear to flourish in some contexts and settings, but creativity is more than context – it requires both context and organization. In other words, creativity needs to be addressed as a process (requiring knowledge, networks and technologies) that enables the generation and translation of novel ideas into innovative goods and services. This key (but still poorly understood) process in the contemporary knowledge economy has been underlined by recent interest in creative industries.

The creative industries
Over the past five years in particular, influential national (DCMS 1998, 2001) and transnational (European Commission Directorate-General for Employment and Social Affairs 2001; NEF 2002) reports have recognized the value (measured by employment and turnover) and dynamism (measured by growth) of creative work to contemporary economies. In this light, a 'new' arena for policy action, the creative industries, has become constructed for the development of cities, regions and nations.

In terms of conventional indicators, the volume and value of activity in the creative industries is highly significant for western economies. For example, in the UK the creative industries have been valued at 5 per cent of GDP (£112 billion turnover per annum – approximately 170 billion euros) and assessed as employing 1.3 million people and as growing at twice the rate of the rest of the economy (DCMS 2001).

The creative industries have been defined as follows:

> those activities which have their origin in individual creativity, skill and talent and which have a potential for wealth and job creation through the generation and exploitation of intellectual property. These have been taken to include the following key sectors: advertising, architecture, the art and antiques market, crafts, design,

designer fashion, film, interactive leisure software, music, the performing arts, publishing, software and television and radio. (DCMS 1998, p. 1)

The creative industries can thus be appreciated as a desirable feature of vitality in a knowledge society – not only valuable, but also cool and sophisticated. However, what forces and dynamics are shaping this contemporary manifestation of creativity in knowledge economies? These become clearer when different processes of operational connectivity are considered.

Trans-sectoral

The creative industries are shaped by interconnection between the media/ information industries and the cultural/arts sector – this is evident at all levels of activity, from the growth of new cultural entrepreneurs to the merger between Time/Warner and AOL to produce one of the world's largest corporations.

Trans-professional

The creative industries are shaped by interconnection between diverse domains (or forms) of creative endeavour (i.e. visual art, craft, print, video, music, etc.) that are brought together through new opportunities for the use of digital media technologies. For example, over the past decade, the UK video game sector has developed from the cult activity of teenagers in suburban bedrooms to an international export industry equivalent in value to that of radio and TV (an already substantial and mature sector of the UK economy – see DCMS 2001).

Trans-governmental

The creative industries as a policy field (at whatever level) bring together a complex network of stakeholders – departments of culture and departments of industry, trade, professional and educational bodies – to try to do effective 'joined-up' policymaking and governance.

The consequences of this multi-layered operational connectivity are complex and challenging. The creative industries span a range of activities (i.e. arts, genres, crafts, specialisms and domains of endeavour), all of which have creativity at their core ('where creativity is the enterprise'). This produces a terrain with a very mixed economy of forms – from freelancers and micro-businesses to transnational organizations (encompassing the range from sole artists to global media corporations). The creative process in these organizations is distinguished by a complex cycle of knowledge flows, from the generation of original ideas to their realization (whether as products or performances). As Leadbeater and Oakley (1999) argue, the creative process is sustained by inspiration and informed by talent, vitality and commitment – this makes creative work volatile, dynamic and risk-taking, shaped by important tacit skills (or expertise) that are frequently submerged (even mystified) within domains of endeavour. Despite their contemporary influence and value, the crucial dynamics that form and transform the creative process in knowledge economies remain unruly and poorly understood.

This section of the chapter thus concludes with a rather double-edged message. Marking out the creative industries provides, on the one hand, a welcome emphasis on the significance and value of creativity for knowledge economies; but on the other hand, the currently dominant approach (i.e. derived from the DCMS definition) provides a rather arbitrary bounding of this creativity that diverts emphasis from key generic issues – such as the core dynamics of the creative process in knowledge economies.

For example, to concentrate attention on sectors where creativity is more visible in the knowledge economy does not imply that creativity is redundant in the remainder of industry. Indeed, in terms of the DCMS definition, science, technology and manufacturing are primarily 'non-creative' industries – however, this is not a depiction that fits the many highly inventive enterprises active in these fields (e.g. Intel, Dyson, etc.).

The cultural economy
The shortcomings in the definition of creative industries (from the UK government) are put into perspective by contemporary work on the 'cultural economy'. In Scott's view (see Scott 1999, 2000), the rising importance of the cultural economy signifies a phase of convergence in global capitalism in which goods and services are becoming 'aestheticized' and culture and leisure are becoming 'commodified'.

> The cultural economy comprises all those sectors in modern capitalism that cater to consumer demands for amusement, ornamentation, self-affirmation, social display and so on. These sectors comprise various craft, fashion, media, entertainment and service industries with outputs like jewellery, perfume, clothing, films, recorded music or tourist services. (Scott 1999, p. 807)

Thus, understanding the cultural economy is crucial to understanding the contemporary knowledge economy. But, as we have already seen, there is a lack of strategic knowledge about the relationships and networks that enable and sustain the creative process in knowledge economies. Recent work on these problems emphasizes the significance of particular types of knowledge relationships in particular situations.

Key knowledge relationships are articulated between the diverse contributors to the creative process (whether more engaged with the 'inspiration' or the 'perspiration') towards the achievement of successful outcomes (whether realized in terms of performances or products) in the cultural economy (Hesmondhalugh 2002). These knowledge relationships involve the bringing together of diverse expertise (both creative and non-creative) in complex value circuits of symbolic goods that connect the originators of novel ideas with the consumers of novel experiences (Caves 2000; see Scott 1999, 2000). These knowledge-intensive relationships are both situated and networked – sustained by diverse communities of activity, from project-based/hybrid/virtual organizations to cultural quarters and digital media hubs (Pratt 2002b). Clearly, these diverse relationships and networks are organized, even if they may not always be managed (in conventional terms).

In knowledge economies, these creative processes need to be understood as both transactional and contextual (see Grabher 2003; Jeffcutt and Pratt 2002). In other words, these creative processes are organized (situated in communities and spaces – local and global), networked (through dense transactions and knowledge relationships – effecting traded and untraded interdependencies) and temporal (an infinite variety of highly differentiated symbolic goods juxtapose for attention – interplaying between producer and consumer through originality, identity and market opportunity).

In this light, we must appreciate that creative processes are not uniquely found in a small number of expressive activities. Whilst there are clearly some organizational fields in which creativity is configured at a premium, in others it is either discouraged or discounted. It is thus logically consistent to undertake situated analyses and examine how 'creativity' is constructed in particular settings. In this respect, organizations operational in the cultural economy, because they explicitly produce 'creative' products, are an important and interesting particularity. However, it must be noted that cultural industries are (in principle) no more or less creative than others.

Accordingly, the chapter will proceed by examining, in turn, the key generic problems of investigating, understanding and influencing the cultural economy – this process of analysis will focus on the creative industries.

Strategic knowledge about the cultural economy

Detailed knowledge about the make-up and dynamics of particular knowledge economies is a crucial strategic resource for policy and decision-makers. A comprehensive evidence base is needed for intelligence, the analysis of key development factors and the focusing of policy action towards strategic opportunities.

However, such strategic knowledge is currently limited – in general, about knowledge economies and, in particular, about the cultural and creative industries. The major knowledge deficits can be outlined as follows.

National statistics
In the UK, as in other nations, data on the economy are regularly collected (by the Office of National Statistics), predominantly from established employers, in national surveys that are available in regional breakdowns. The data are robust and in time series, typically providing the key source for strategic decision-makers in both the public and private sectors. The main limitations are as follows:

• The statistical codes (e.g. Standard Industrial and Occupational Classification) under which data are collected and organized are agreed internationally – however, they tend to reflect an outmoded picture of the contemporary economy. Consequently, the codes do not capture the developing knowledge economy (in general) and the creative industries (in particular) at all well (e.g. despite its significance, the UK has no category of videogames yet). Furthermore, there is an approximately ten-year time lag in the substantive revision of these national statistical codes (Pratt 2002a).

• National surveys of established employers (VAT registered, in the UK) measure the established economy and tend not to capture either the self-employed or new businesses trading below the threshold of VAT registration (approximately £50 000 turnover per annum, in the UK). Consequently, national statistics do not capture many freelancers and micro-businesses that make up a significant proportion of the total of creative enterprises (e.g. such enterprises accounted for 36 per cent of total creative enterprises in Northern Ireland – see Jeffcutt 2003).

As a consequence, it has been necessary to develop methods of manipulating national statistics to provide estimates of the size of areas of activity that the coding system does not capture (such as the creative industries; see Pratt 1997 and 2002a).

Public research on economic regions
As creative industries became recognized as significant to regional economies, regional governmental bodies (in the UK, Europe and Australia) have commissioned primary data-gathering on this sector. For example, three comprehensive regional studies have been completed in the UK to date (in Yorkshire, Northern Ireland and the East Midlands). With a local focus on a rapidly developing sector of the economy, such studies have been seeking to capture both the baseline data and key dynamics that national statistics have been unable to access. The main generic limitations of such work are as follows:

- ready-made regional databases of the creative industries do not exist, they have to be compiled by the research team – this is an arduous task on a rapidly changing sector and its degree of thoroughness limits the accuracy and comparability of the results;
- a standard analytic frame for the investigation of creative industries in a region does not yet exist. Each regional study in the UK, although similar in its overall structure and approach, has made choices about sampling and analysis that reflect local priorities – this provides limits for comparability across studies;
- the detailed results of regional studies are confidential to the commissioning bodies and have only been made public in highly truncated forms – this limits the ability to make comprehensive comparisons across studies.

As a consequence, in the UK (a nation that has been recognized for its pioneering approach to this field) the public evidence base on the creative industries is patchy in its coverage and largely lacking in both comprehensiveness and depth. The major national studies that have been completed (DCMS 1998, 2001) have produced estimates of work activity and business performance derived from national statistics (on the old economy) and/or secondary sources, without making a serious attempt to examine the key dynamics that produced the results. The overall position is a surprising lack of detailed and in-depth strategic knowledge about the cultural economy in the UK.

Investigating the dynamics of the cultural economy

The work of Scott (1999, 2000) and Best (1990, 2001) has made clear that attention needs to be focused on agglomerations of diverse firms that, through dense transactions and knowledge relationships, achieve distinctive capabilities in particular areas of the cultural economy. Furthermore, these dense networks of firms of different scale and purpose (sometimes termed 'clusters') are situated in communities and spaces that are local as well as global (see Florida 2002; Landry 2000).

In this light, the comprehensive and in-depth analysis of creative industries in a distinctive economic region provides just such a locus of study. However, (thus far) only three such studies have been completed in the UK and, as was recognized in the previous section, comparative research between them is constrained. Accordingly, in order to provide a strategic context for the examination of key generic problems in investigating, understanding and influencing the cultural economy, this chapter will refer to the work of one of these studies in particular (see also Jeffcutt 2003).

Northern Ireland, the smallest UK region (with 1.7 million people spread across 100 square miles), was the setting for a comprehensive and in-depth primary study of the creative industries in the UK with some pioneering features. Commissioned by four separate departments of the regional government (i.e. Culture, Industry, Employment and Education), this study brought together a strong mix of expertise appropriate to the complexity of the creative industries (the project team included specialist researchers, creative entrepreneurs and policy-makers). The primary objectives of the study were to establish a thorough evidence base, assess critical development factors and to evaluate strategies for the further development of the creative industries of Northern Ireland.

Two major strands of fieldwork were completed (over 2001–2002). To enable the in-depth analysis of critical linkages and key development factors for the creative industries of Northern Ireland, a series of case studies of creative enterprises was undertaken. To establish comprehensive baseline evidence about the current capabilities of the creative industries of the province, a full census of all enterprises currently active in the sector (from the smallest one person enterprise to the largest) was undertaken.

Understanding the cultural economy

The study found the creative industries of Northern Ireland (NI) to be making a significant and substantial contribution to the region – these industries had grown rapidly and inhabited a complex and evolving situation:

- they contributed 5 per cent of overall NI economy (by overall annual turnover, 2001);
- they employed 4 per cent of overall NI workforce (by overall employment, 2001);
- they were building on indigenous talent and enterprise:

    - 42 per cent of creative enterprises were established in the previous five years;

- they were providing both high-skilled employment and high added value;
- they comprised predominantly micro-businesses:

    - 11 per cent of creative enterprises had over 20 employees;
    - 55 per cent of creative enterprises had under 5 employees;
    - 12 per cent of creative enterprises had over £1 million p.a. turnover;
    - 51 per cent of creative enterprises had under £100k p.a. turnover;

- they featured local enterprises that achieved excellence in global markets;

- they were largely under-recognized and under-valued in the region;
- they possessed a complex portfolio of development needs;
- they were not being supported in a coherent and integrated manner within the region.

These characterizations of the NI cultural economy are important but not unique, for they would largely apply to many of the non-metropolitan regions of the UK (see Jeffcutt 2003 for a more detailed assessment and analysis).

However, the pioneering in-depth approach of the study of NI revealed considerable distinctiveness in the local cultural economy – features which had significant impact on the regions capabilities and potential. For example:

- the impact of three distinct operational groupings (Design, Expressive, Media and Information), which both coalesced and overlapped in the multi-layered cultural economy of NI (instead of the 13 separate sub-sectors of the creative industries identified by DCMS);
- the impact of considerable local geographic concentrations of creative enterprises on a dispersed regional economy (38 per cent of the region's creative enterprises were located in three districts of Belfast);
- the impact of major skill shortages, resource and market limitations on enterprise capabilities and horizons in NI;
- the impact of access to networks of knowledge and expertise (both local and international) on the development dynamics and trajectories of creative enterprises in NI;
- the impact of fragmented infrastructure and support systems on enterprise capabilities and horizons in NI.

The NI cultural economy thus featured multiple layers, a complexity of inter-relationships and a mix of key development factors. This complex mix of interacting forces appeared to produce the fragile balance that had been achieved in the cultural economy of NI; it included both the presence and absence of key development factors and the margins and interfaces between them.

In the light of this rich picture of the creative industries of Northern Ireland, the research concluded that the region's creative enterprises should be understood as inhabiting a distinctive ecosystem. A significant contribution of the study was to analyse this ecosystem in terms of its major elements, inter relationships and key dynamics (see below). A major finding of the study was that, to be effective, the development strategy for the creative industries of NI needed to be ecological – with a coherent and integrated approach to the key elements and dynamics of the ecosystem.

The creative industries ecosystem in Northern Ireland

The core process for enterprises in the cultural economy is the building of intellectual property in a value circuit for products and services that extends from initial idea to end user. These value circuits are diverse, ranging from the relatively simple (e.g. craft) to the more complex (e.g. film) – each of which typically goes through the major phases of content origination, production, reproduction and exhibition (Pratt 1997). Enterprises occupy different niches along these value circuits, ranging from the more robust to the more insecure.

Four main generic features were found across value circuits (that were observed in the research on enterprises in the creative industries in Northern Ireland); these occurred in different mixes and strengths in different enterprises and shaped the distinctive niches that these enterprises occupied in the cultural economy. The interrelationship of these generic features of the CI ecosystem is displayed in Figure 8.1.

- *Knowledge interfaces*   The mix of social, cultural and professional relationships and networks that the enterprise possesses and can access. *Key concerns*: the range, narrowness, breadth, overlap, barriers and gaps in these knowledge interfaces.

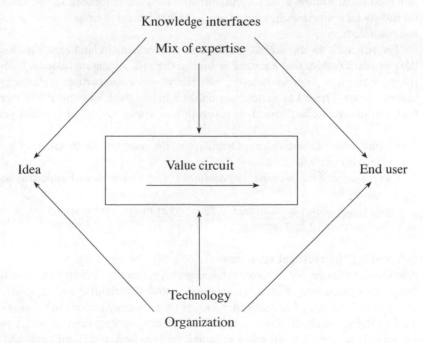

Figure 8.1   CI ecosystem: key features

- *Mix of expertise*   The matrix of expertise that the enterprise possesses and can access.
  Key concerns: the mix of specialisms (creative and business), the balance of specialisms across individuals and teams, the richness and mobility of the existing pool of expertise in the region, the availability and supply of fresh expertise.
- *Technology*   The medium of creative activity of the enterprise.
  Key concerns: the mix of craft and digital process, the uniqueness and sharedness of the technology, the rate of change.
- *Organization*   The structural and operational capabilities of the enterprise.
  Key concerns: the complexity of operations (scale and scope), the longevity and flexibility of operations (continuing/one-off), the density of transactions, the competitive position.

A cultural economy is thus made up of a rich mix of enterprises in an evolving configuration of value circuits for creative goods and services – an ecosystem of creative space. However, as both Scott and Best argue, the development factors for the cultural economy of a region extend beyond the traded and untraded relationships in any value circuit – they are embedded in the material and social context within (and from) which these value circuits develop and are sustained.

The research on the creative industries of Northern Ireland identified key development factors that enabled or limited the mix of generic features found in any enterprise (i.e. knowledge interfaces; mix of expertise; technology; organization). These key factors are outlined below (with examples) and were found to interrelate at three main levels (micro, meso, macro) of capability.

- *Individual capabilities*   Originality and potential, both creative and entrepreneurial
- *Organizational/sectoral capabilities*   The availability of expertise and resources
- *Environmental capabilities*   The market/milieu for creativity; regional infrastructure and support

Influencing the cultural economy
The dual challenge for researchers and policymakers is to better understand the crucial dynamics of cultural economies so that insightful and supportive action may be pursued in particular locales (e.g. cities and economic regions). This challenge is all the more important in a contemporary context where the outputs of the creative industries are trumpeted (as sexy and significant) and a whole plethora of policy initiatives are being undertaken (nationally and inter-

nationally, across the developed world, see Cunningham 2002), searching to expand these outcomes in the short term. A major concern is that the motivation for this activity is often the hope of joining a bandwagon (for fear of being left behind) with insufficient regard for the complexity of these creative dynamics and with little attention to the evaluation of cause and effect.

The crucial strategic logic of the research into the creative industries of NI was the finding that, to be effective, development action had to be focused on the CI ecosystem as a whole. As a consequence, any development strategy needed to be both generic and integrated rather than piecemeal – in other words, it needed to be ecological.

Importantly, the NI research reiterated that there was no 'magic bullet' for the development of a cultural economy (much to the disappointment of some local policymakers). In this light, development needs would be specific to particular cultural economies, taking account of inherited capabilities and the development dynamics of the CI ecosystem. The necessary starting point for any development strategy was thus a detailed appraisal of these circumstances and a realistic evaluation of both capabilities and opportunities.

The worst-case scenario would be a policy of late 'me too' – an economic region that, from a situation of unexplored disadvantage, desires to imitate the economy of elsewhere in the vain hope that their success will also arrive once a copy (of what is believed to be the secrets of their success) is established locally. This naïve imitative process is perhaps best described as a policy-maker's 'cargo cult' in which the totems of aspirational development are regularly constructed (with the help of 'witch doctors') but the spirits of success are rarely bestowed. As Scott (2004) has argued, despite the many attempted imitations across the world, there is still only one Hollywood.

In contrast, the real development work for policymakers in economic regions is the complex and longer-term strategy of building capability across a portfolio of areas of development need (see also Landry 2000; Best 2001). Considering the dynamics of the ecosystem of the creative industries in NI, a development framework for the sustainability of the cultural economy was proposed in which development action would be focused on key dynamics and leverage points. A strategic framework for sustainable development was recommended, with a series of action lines in five main thematic areas (see Figure 8.2):

1. Creative learning – improving the supply of new entrants to the sector
2. Creative opportunity – developing the existing workforce in the sector
3. Creative business – developing enterprises in the sector (new and existing)
4. Creative sector – developing sectoral infrastructure (hard and soft)
5. Creative governance – developing 'joined-up' policy for the sector.

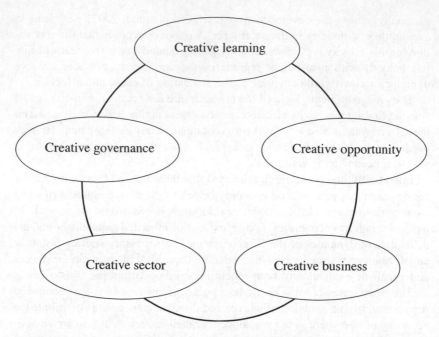

Figure 8.2   CI ecosystem: development framework

The rationale for this approach was that although Northern Ireland had recently developed a significant creative industries sector, this rapid growth had largely been driven by creative entrepreneurs, without effective support and resource systems that could sustain the medium and longer-term development of the sector in NI. Hence the strategic framework sought to address the breadth and diversity of the needs that had been exposed (in the research) by building sustainable pathways for development (across the value chains of the CI ecosystem) that brought together key stakeholders in effective partnerships and programmes of coherent and coordinated action. In essence, the development strategy was ecological, being built around enabling initiatives (e.g. interfaces, brokerage and intermediaries) that could bridge gaps and enhance relationships between creative enterprises and the existing support and resource systems of NI. As a whole, the portfolio of actions was focused on sustaining the regional knowledge economy of NI in a crucial area of opportunity – the creative industries.

Conclusions

The chapter has considered key issues and debates across a complex field concerned with creativity in knowledge economies, examining the key generic problems of investigating, understanding and influencing the cultural economy. This process has necessarily considered a rich mix of problems and opportunities, situating these in a discussion of a pioneering in-depth study of the creative industries in an economic region of the UK.

The first main conclusion is that there is not one cultural economy but many. Each cultural economy will be situated in a particular locale with distinctive layers, features, dimensions, knowledge relationships and capabilities. Hence any analysis of and action on the cultural economy needs to be both situated and strategic. Such work necessarily involves a number of challenges, which can be outlined as follows:

- The key research challenge is to insightfully analyse the ecosystem of creative space in particular knowledge economies. This involves examining multi-layered knowledge networks and transactions that are glocal, temporal and mobile but organized. This organization is realized as an evolving order, articulated by an emerging dynamics of interconnection (i.e. clusters, interfaces, margins and hybrids).
- The key policy challenge is to insightfully work with this situated knowledge (and its stakeholders) to enhance the creative space of particular knowledge economies. This involves an ecological approach that is generic, integrated and which focuses on key dynamics (i.e. enabling connections at interfaces through brokerage and intermediaries).

The second main conclusion is that there is a need to build strategic knowledge on cultural economies (across locales) that is thematic, flexible and responsive. Such work necessarily involves a number of challenges, which can be outlined as follows:

- The key research challenge is to overcome existing problems in the availability and sharing of detailed research knowledge on particular cultural economies and establish a generic framework for knowledge building. This knowledge is necessarily interdisciplinary and inter-operational (see Jeffcutt et al. 2000; Jeffcutt and Pratt 2002).
- The key policy challenge concerns the numerous and diverse policy actions that are being undertaken (across the developed world) in particular cultural economies. These are largely local and fragmented and are rarely being coherently evaluated in ways that will enable the strategic development of cumulative applied knowledge (within and across locales).

As has already been seen, the key socio-economic problems of the twenty-first century don't come conveniently sectioned up in terms of pre-existing structures – hence to address them effectively we are required to work in ways that are more interactive, distributed and dynamic. Because of its dynamics of connectivity, the field concerned with creativity in knowledge economies should be capable of rising to the above challenges and pursuing more boundary-crossing approaches to the development of strategic knowledge. It is clearly a field of distributed expertise (between researchers, policy-makers and practitioners) built around multiple networks that do not value convention. It is also a field of multiple stakeholders, where key questions need to be framed and reframed across contexts in an interactive process of analysis, response and action.

Arenas that practise such strongly contextualized co-development between distributed expertise and stakeholders have been characterized as fields of 'mode 2' knowledge (Gibbons et al. 1994; Nowotny et al. 2001) and are thought to be more effective at dealing with the challenges of complexity in knowledge societies. Within the field concerned with creativity in knowledge economies, there is a growing recognition of the importance of 'mode 2' methods of knowledge development. In essence, this work is concerned with the building of an effective 'in-between' – characterized by sustainable pathways and effective partnerships between research, policy and practice. Such work is not only crucial for the development of creativity in knowledge economies, but also for the development of 'mode 2' knowledge.

References

Amin, Ash and Nigel Thrift. 1994. *Globalization, Institutions and Regional Development in Europe*. Oxford: Oxford University Press.
Best, Michael. 1990. *The New Competition: Institutions of Industrial Restructuring*. Cambridge, MA: Harvard University Press.
Best, Michael. 2001. *The New Competitive Advantage*. Oxford: Oxford University Press.
Caves, Richard. 2000. *The Creative Industries*. Cambridge, MA: Harvard University Press.
Cunningham, S. 2002. 'From cultural to creative industries'. *Media International Australia* **102**:54–65.
Department of Culture, Media and Sport (DCMS). 1998. *The Creative Industries Mapping Report*. London: HMSO.
Department of Culture, Media and Sport (DCMS). 2001. *The Creative Industries Mapping Report*. London: HMSO.
European Commission Directorate-General for Employment and Social Affairs. 2001. *Exploitation and Development of the Job Potential in the Cultural Sector in the Age of Digitisation*. Munich: MKW Wirtschaftsforschungsgesellschaft GmbH.
Florida, Richard. 2002. *The Rise of the Creative Class*. New York: Basic Books.
Gibbons, M. et al. 1994. *The New Production of Knowledge*. London: Sage.
Grabher, G. 2003. 'Learning in projects, remembering in networks'. *European Urban and Regional Studies* **11**:99–119.
Hesmondhalugh, David. 2002. *The Cultural Industries*. London: Sage.
Jeffcutt, Paul. 2003. *Creative Enterprise: Developing and Sustaining the Creative Industries in Northern Ireland*. Belfast: Centre for Creative Industry, Queen's University.
Jeffcutt, Paul and Andy C. Pratt. 2002. 'Managing creativity and the creative industries'. *Creativity and Innovation Management* **11**:225–33.
Jeffcutt, Paul, John Pick and Robert Protherough. 2000. 'Culture and industry: Exploring the debate'. *Studies in Cultures, Organizations and Societies* **6**:6.
Landry, Charles. 2000. *The Creative City*. Leicester, UK: Earthscan.

Leadbeater, Charles and Kate Oakley. 1999. *The Independents*. London: Demos.

NEF. 2002. *Creative Europe Project*. Funded by the Network of European Foundations for Innovative Co-operation (NEF).

Nowotny, Helga, Peter Scott and Michael Gibbons. 2001. *Rethinking Science, Knowledge and the Public in an Age of Uncertainty*. Cambridge: Polity.

Porter, Michael. 1990. *The Competitive Advantage of Nations*. New York: Free Press.

Pratt, Andy, C. 1997. 'Employment in the cultural industries sector: A case study of Britain, 1984–91'. *Environment and Planning* A: **29**:1953–76.

Pratt, Andy, C. 2002a. 'Understanding the cultural industries: Is more less?' *Culturelink* Special issue:51–68.

Pratt, Andy, C. 2002b. 'Hot jobs in cool places: The material cultures of new media product spaces – the case of San Francisco'. *Information, Communication and Society* **5**:27–50.

Robinson, K. 2001. *Out of Our Minds*. London: Capstone.

Scott, Allen. 1999. 'The cultural economy: Geography and the creative field'. *Media, Culture and Society* **21**:807–17.

Scott, Allen. 2000. *The Cultural Economy of Cities*. London: Sage.

Scott, Allen. 2004. 'The new map of Hollywood'. Paper presented at the Centre for Creative Industry, Queen's University, Belfast.

9 Analysing policy values in a knowledge economy

Phil Graham

It has been noted more than once that capitalist social relations have led to a purely monetary understanding of the term 'value'. Classical political economy, regardless of its many flawed assumptions, sought to achieve an understanding of human interaction that embraced the entirety of human experience. In its original form, political economy emerged from the more general field of moral philosophy. However, since the mid-nineteenth century, political economy has withered in its scope while enjoying an ever-broader sphere of influence. Because it is a collection of quantitative terms, the price system has thrived under post-Enlightenment science. It has become the single most important public expression of value. In mainstream economics, price has become the primary measure of value for policymakers (Graham 2002). The gradual withering of political economy to 'economics', a science of pure price, has had far-reaching implications for the production and analysis of policy. The monetary reductionism of economics has been further exacerbated by the allegedly 'neoliberal' policy agenda that has been in play throughout developed countries since the late 1970s.

Ignoring the various meanings of what might be understood by the 'liberal' part of neoliberalism, the basic tenets of neoliberal economic theory are as follows. First, competition for resources, market share, more skilled or cheaper labour and so on is assumed to be beneficial regardless of its consequences. Second, such competition is assumed to be global, natural and inherently efficient, producing the best outcomes for individuals and societies. Third, any interference to competition is tantamount to a crime against society, as evidenced in the many legal challenges launched by one government against another in extrajudicial contexts such as the World Trade Organization. Fourth, government is expected to promote and enforce competition, even between its own departments. Finally, it is assumed that the benefits and effects of competition can be understood solely in terms of price. Put as simply as possible, neo-liberal economic theory is based on perverse interpretations of Adam Smith's 'invisible hand' and Charles Darwin's theory of natural selection.[1] Its analytical framework, at least where policy is concerned, is the field of econometrics, a highly abstract, though mathematically rigorous, set of tools that has an often tenuous relationship with reality. In the econometric framework, the whole of reality is reduced to models of the price system – past, present and future.

Any contemporary study of the knowledge economy must take the influence of neoliberal discourse into account. It must also consider the social function of policy as well as *how* it is made. Policy, and political science more generally, is more expressly concerned with how we ought to live. In other words, the 'political' part of political economy has been charged with legitimate authority over social outcomes. Yet the framework within which political science operates, whether at the level of bureaucratic process or political discourse, is influenced and shaped by the tenets of modernist science, as is the 'economic' part of political economy. In other words, policy must be based on 'good science', or at least be seen as such.

The scientific impetus of modernity raises problems for contemporary policymakers. 'Good science' is objective, replicable, universal and, most important of all, 'value free'. Therefore policymakers, who are charged under the tenets of their discipline with legitimate moral authority, must, according to the tenets of 'good science', divest themselves of their values in order to make 'good' policy. This presents a great deal of difficulty for policymakers. To produce objective, value-free policy requires the reduction of the social world to a set of universal, objective, value-free, quantitatively derived 'laws'. Econometrics and quantitative sociology supply laws such as these.

The paradox of contemporary policy goes to the heart of arguments about the differences between 'hard' and 'soft' science. Good 'hard' science is based on experimental methods that produce predictable and replicable results across multiple and often unrelated contexts: Newton's laws of gravity, for example, are assumed to be the same on earth as they are on Mars, or as they are in yet-undiscovered galaxies and solar systems. Further, such laws are assumed to be valid throughout eternity. Yet any social science that produces replicable results across all contexts, cultures and times can probably be described as either fallacious, tautological or uninformative. That is because societies and cultures of all kinds change over time, at least to some large extent. Social science that can only show that which does not change, or that which is not different across different social contexts, is therefore of limited use. But the various forms of social science that focus on change, difference and especially on non-quantitative aspects of human experience are generally held to be 'soft science' and therefore unsuitable for making policy.

For these reasons the contemporary policymaker is subject to a number of conflicting forces, the most apparent of which are: the unruly characteristics of social life and the unpredictability of social change; imperatives to do replicable, quantitative experimental science that is most amenable to the system of monetary values which dominates international political economy; and the tenets of neoliberalism. Policymakers are required to formulate policies that are evidence-based, scientifically valid and economically sound. Policy must also be presented in appropriate forms of language. The language of science is the language of *fact*. It is the language of objective, expert descriptions based on verifiable, quantifiable, predictable and replicable aspects of experience. Policy documents therefore appear as a collection of scientifically derived *propositions* (or statements and descriptions). However, to be effective, policies must also function as a collection of *proposals* (specifically, commands or exhortations) that result in people acting and interacting in specific ways.

The language of fact and description is very different from the language of command and exhortation, even though the two can spill over into each other in functional terms. This functional spillage can be demonstrated with a simple example. Almost every parent has been confronted with a child who says: 'I'm hungry', a clear truth claim. Now the nature of propositions, and what defines them as such in distinction to proposals, is that they are open to argument, whereas proposals are not (Halliday and Martin 1993). The child who says 'I'm hungry' is putting forward a proposition that a parent can argue with. Usual arguments would include 'but you just had lunch . . .'; 'you can't possibly be hungry'; and so on. However, as most parents understand, when a child says 'I'm hungry' what he or she means is 'Feed me!' What happens here is that the child draws upon social and cultural relationships to turn a proposition (I am hungry) into a proposal (Feed me!): it is, in most cultures, the obligation of a parent to provide food for his or her children, a social fact understood by both the child and the parent, however implicitly. The obligation that a parent feels is an expression of a long-standing value system that is often referred to as 'family values'. It is from this pool of family values that the utterance 'I'm hungry' derives its social force as a command. It is in the realm of cultural values that the functional transformation between statements of fact and demands for action is operationalized.

The same functional transformation is constantly operationalized within the realm of policy. That is a matter of necessity. Because contemporary policymakers must present their products as the result of a scientific process, contemporary policy relies upon operationalizing what can only be described as an ongoing naturalistic fallacy: a continual movement from 'is' to 'ought', from fact to exhortation. As in the example of the parent–child interaction I have described above, policymakers rely on a multitude of social and cultural patterns to produce a functional transformation from statements of fact to mass exhortations (Graham 2002).

My emphasis on language in the analysis of policy is of threefold significance in the context of a knowledge economy. First, it is axiomatic that what we call knowledge is inherently bound up in language: how we know is shaped to a large extent by what we say to each other, and by how we say it. Therefore language assumes the utmost significance in any knowledge economy. Second, the 'commodities' of the knowledge economy are necessarily products of more or less valued types of language. Finally, language (whether mathematical, spoken or written) is at the same time a key means of production and distribution for knowledge commodities. To further complicate the matter, policy is almost entirely an achievement of language and exists to propagate new cultural patterns of evaluation – it is simultaneously an expression and legitimation of particular value systems designed to produce specific actions and outcomes by drawing on cultural patterns of evaluation. Further, in a knowledge economy, policy is a most valuable commodity. Billions are spent each year on its production, purchase and dissemination, and much of it has global implications.

Two further problems face evaluative analyses of contemporary knowledge economy policy. The first is the characteristic tendency of policy authors to rely on extremely abstract nouns to convey meaning (Halliday 1994, p. 21; Lemke 1995, pp. 59–65; McKenna and Graham 2000). The second is in the essentially future-oriented nature of policy: it is essentially hortatory; its primary function is 'to get people to do things' (Muntigl 2000, p. 147). In the case of the current knowledge economy, this consists of getting people to know particular things in particular ways. However, in operationalizing the hortatory function of policy, contemporary authors are driven by technocratic imperatives to 'rationalize' exhortations with 'facts', and then to turn facts into exhortations. The hortatory content of knowledge economy policy is therefore usually implicit, disguised as ostensibly 'value-free', 'objective', statements of fact (Lemke 1995, pp. 60–61; McKenna and Graham 2000).

These aspects of policy introduce the need to make some very basic distinctions. Because the objective of policy is always future-oriented, time and tense, especially in the interplay between proposal and proposition, become problematic – there is little point in trying 'to get people to do things' in the past; the explicit and implicit proposals in technology policy are only ever a future-oriented, *irrealis* (roughly, potential or imagined) function of language (cf. Lemke, 1998, p. 36). For the same reasons, the propositions of policy are similarly oriented, often concerning themselves with describing future circumstances (Graham 2002).

There is a distinct division between aspects of language that can describe the world in terms of *substance* and those that can describe the world in terms of *space-time*; or, between language used 'to specify a set of properties' for, or predicates of, a particular thing (substance language), and the language used to locate a particular thing at a particular time and place (space-time language) (Harvey 1973/1988, pp. 38–40). The confounding aspect is that 'space itself can enter into either language but in different ways' (ibid., p. 39). So can time. Spatial and temporal positioning are necessarily properties of particular substances (cf. Aristotle 1999, p. 439; Harvey 1973/1988, p. 41). One of the main distinctions I wish to emphasize here is between two broad 'types' of evaluations made in policy language: those 'belonging' to substances and those 'belonging' to processes.

Substances (which can include particular people or groups of people) are realized, explicitly or intertextually, as having attributes that define them in relationship to *other* substances within particular conceptual or ideational spaces (geographical, social, aesthetic, scientific and so on). In latinate grammar, substances would generally be identified by their status as nouns, indicating that they are tangible 'things' of one type or another that occupy space and have a static, or at least irreversible, aspect to them (Harvey 1973/1988, ch. 1). In process relationships, the time element – movement and action – is foregrounded. Substances (and substantial spaces), as well as other processes, are set in various relationships to one another over more and less specific periods of time, with causal and functional effects implied or expressed. These two aspects of language are marked by grammatically and conceptually different types of evaluative possibilities in language, but are nevertheless ultimately interdependent aspects of language. Consequently, to pull them apart and analyse them in complete independence from one another would be synthetic and impractical.

The approach to analysis that I am advocating here recognizes that both substance and process aspects of language are invariably present in any evaluative representation, even though they are in many respects irreconcilable. The main differences between them are that specific substances are delineated in terms of their attributes in relation to other substances. Process language, on the other hand, defines time-bound relationships of causation between substances and other processes. In more concrete, or 'everyday', language, we would expect to see substances described and delineated by the deployment of 'relational processes' that are deployed to assign attributes to things ('He *has* beautiful eyes'), and to situate them in hierarchical or taxonomic relation to others ('That *is* a much better house than the other one') (Halliday 1994, pp. 124–9). Process language is typically realized in everyday language by the deployment of material, transitive processes (John *kicked* the ball). But because of the heavy reliance on nominalization in technocratic discourse, and because the purpose of policy is to translate words into future action, analysis cannot easily delimit realizations along these lines (cf. Graham 2002; Halliday and Martin 1993).

Following is an examplary policy text that can help us understand how values can be seen in the broader terms I have described so far. The following two paragraphs are from a World Bank publication, *Public Policy For A Knowledge Economy* (Stiglitz 1999) and will serve to illustrate the usefulness of the analytical approach I am proposing:

Development is about the transformation of societies which ultimately involves people changing how they think. External agencies cannot force people to change how they think or what they believe. People can be forced to adopt certain behaviors and to utter certain words, but they cannot be forced to change their hearts or minds. That, they can only do themselves.

In industry, the shift towards a knowledge-based economy involves a shift in organization away from top-down hierarchical structures to flatter structures such as networks of semi-autonomous teams. Tayloristic vertical structures were designed to enforce and coordinate certain physical behaviors while knowledge-based work organization involves greater recognition of the autonomy and self-direction of the mind. Knowledge is best acquired not by passive rote memorization but by the active involvement of the learner. Learning is by doing, not by watching or memorizing. (Stiglitz 1999, p. 6)

Although the entire passage quoted above comprises propositions in the form of statements of fact, it is remarkably open in its emphasis on the need for people to relate, act, organize and think in new and different ways in order to achieve some future outcome. There is an overt Idealist philosophy underpinning the policy here: people must first change *how they think* and *what they believe* for *development* to happen. According to this logic, underdevelopment is merely a function of people thinking incorrectly and believing in the wrong things.

The orientation of the World Bank towards development foregrounds the future orientation of policy. Development is presented as a substance rather than a process, because it compresses an enormous amount of social and technological processes into a noun. In this context, development is defined by particular attributes: it is about the transformation of societies and involves people changing how they think. Further, it is an *irrealis* substance, a potentiality that can only emerge at some time in the future, and only then if people adopt certain behaviours, change their hearts and minds, think in new ways, and believe in new things. In a knowledge economy, autonomy and the self-direction of the mind are key factors in successful industry. These are presented as being somehow different from physical behaviours that Tayloristic organizational structures were designed to enforce and coordinate. In other words, Stiglitz is suggesting that success in the knowledge economy is about building the best organizational structures for managing people's minds: knowledge-based work.

According to Stiglitz (1999), successful knowledge industries are organized in semi-autonomous teams: structures designed to extract products from semi-autonomous minds. Autonomy of the mind can only be, at best, semi-autonomy – the self-direction of the mind essential to the production of new knowledge is regimented according to new management principles, at least to some significant degree. That is a function of defining and regulating what counts as 'useful' knowledge as that which can be turned into economic gain.

This limits the kinds of knowledge that attract investment in a knowledge economy. Unless a particular form of intellectual labour is oriented towards specific outcomes even before it has started, it is unlikely to attract investment, whether as wages or venture capital. The most likely outcome of this orientation is the constant 'reverse engineering' of what already exists in industrial commodity forms (new ways to produce food, transport, advertising, entertainment, weapons, soap, etc., none of which is necessarily more efficient than its predecessors). Put more strongly, there is no space whatsoever in such an approach for development; there is only the possibility of new technology – new means to old ends. It is inherently conservative and permits of little or no qualitative difference in terms of development.

Many contradictions of an officially mandated knowledge economy are realized in the World Bank text above. For example, while the author claims that development is a function of how people think, and that systems of management designed to regulate physical activities are of little value in a knowledge economy, the long-standing tensions between Idealism and Materialism become manifest when the topic of knowledge labour is broached. Knowledge, like development, is presented as a 'thing' that people acquire by doing material activities, not by watching or memorizing. In other words, the most important knowledge is practical knowledge: knowledge created by material rather than intellectual labour; it is knowledge created by material means that can be applied in ways that realize a price. And it is specific classes of activity that shape people's ability to know in appropriate ways to produce commodifiable knowledge. By extension, it is the modes and means of ownership over these activities and their products that defines social relations in a knowledge economy – implicit in this conception of development in a knowledge economy is a social separation between knowledge, its owners, its 'renters', its managers and its producers.

Semi-autonomous knowledge labour dedicated to the production of commodities is by definition alienated labour – it is not the labour of knowledge for its own sake, or for the labourer's own sake. To be of use in a knowledge economy, activity must be oriented towards net economic gain within an industrial–commercial framework – it must be saleable, reducible to price. The autonomy of the mind must be harnessed by technical and institutional means and reduced to semi-autonomy; creative processes of cognition thus become primary objects of commercial enclosure, commodification and expropriation. Consequently, in a knowledge economy, intellectual property law assumes the utmost importance, and the ability to delineate and isolate ideas that can be turned into money becomes the very definition of valuable property.

All these aspects of our emergent knowledge economy can be understood when it is seen as emerging from the industrial, commodity-based framework most often called capitalism. Capitalism has for many years taken on the appearance of a system designed for making money, and making money has become synonymous with 'making a living', whether as employee, manager, share owner, or business owner. The 'underdeveloped' society in contemporary policy parlance is a society that does not have the means to make money by participating in capitalist endeavours. Any ills such societies and cultures suffer are generally construed in policy as the result of a lack of capitalist entrepreneurialism, never as a result of capitalist practices destroying different, supposedly 'backward' ways of living. Yet at the same time, many of the most lucrative knowledge economy initiatives are oriented towards capturing 'traditional' knowledge from such cultures, especially in areas such as medicine and pharmaceuticals for use in biotechnologies (Sunderland 2000). Put plainly, stocks of social knowledge in non-capitalist societies are at least as valuable to capitalist knowledge enterprises as the products of the technologically complex laboratories and research institutions of developed societies.

The bias of 'developed' societies is evident later in the text from which the above quote is taken:

> First, in the long run, success in the knowledge economy requires creativity, higher order cognitive skills *in addition to* basic skills. Those countries that find ways of fostering this kind of creativity will, in the long run, have more success in the competition of the knowledge economy.

> Second, also key to success in the knowledge economy is training in science and technology. There are good grounds for government subsidies to science education: Because those engaged in research so seldom capture the full benefits of their work, there are, as we noted earlier, real externalities. These externalities may be most marked for graduate education. (Stiglitz 1999, p. 21)

It is paradoxical that Stiglitz, one of the most realistic economists who has inhabited the higher echelons of world knowledge policy production in recent years, and who is well acquainted with the complexities of allegedly underdeveloped economies, should emphasize an entirely 'western' view of knowledge underpinned by the tenets of neoliberalism and its technological biases. Learned skills, both basic and higher cognitive, are construed as creativity, and training in science and technology is seen as essential to development. This of course means 'western' science and technology. While earlier asserting that knowledge is best created in free and relatively open social contexts, the emphasis on demonstrably closed and destructive 'western' ways of knowing, and of applying knowledge, are promoted to the extent that no other 'road' to development is even considered. Success in the knowledge economy is realized by winning an economic competition. Neo-liberalism is realized here in the pretence that human achievement is a function of competition rather than cooperation, one of the most flawed assumptions of contemporary policy.

Much more could be said about the narrow value system that pervades contemporary knowledge economy policy and, indeed, policy more generally. Even more could be said about the very human values that are *not* represented in contemporary policy: beauty, happiness, and the value of knowledge for its own sake; respect for nature, culture, and alternative forms of wisdom; in short, practically every system of values that stands outside the price system has been removed from policy contexts. The slow elision of these values from policy has taken centuries to achieve. Its effect has been the production of a complex of hard, dry and brittle policies that has led to the antagonistic fragmentation of human social systems, whether religious, cultural, familial, or political. The pseudo-Darwinian assumptions of competition that underpin the econometric price system entail the competition of everyone against everyone, and between humanity and the rest of nature.

These aspects of policy are achievements of discourse – specifically, the development, institutionalization and mass deployment of technical languages over many years – and are realized in the language of policy. Policy production is an iterative process of institutional editing according to specific value systems, and the struggle over words and their meaning in this process is intense and self-conscious (Muntigl 2000). Policy analysis therefore necessitates an engagement with the language of policy. But analysis must also realize that policy itself is, or at least has become, a commodity in the political economy of knowledge: it is produced by experts to promote and operationalize very specific values. This is achieved by changing the way people act, including how we think, what we believe, how we express ourselves, and most of all, how we evaluate each other and each other's social contexts.

Note
1. The argument about whether my interpretation of Smith or Darwin is incorrect or perverse is a sidebar to this chapter. Darwin's theory of evolution through natural selection is a macro theory of how species have come into being over many centuries, not a theory of the quotidian. Adam Smith's mention of the 'invisible hand', read in context, has clearly been blown out of proportion in respect of the rest of his theories. Also, most neoliberal readings of Smith entirely ignore his equally important *Theory of Moral Sentiments*. It seems clear to me, whether for better or worse, that human beings are, as Aristotle pointed out, social animals. Our survival as a species has relied upon cooperation, not competition.

References
Aristotle, A. 1999. *The Metaphysiscs*. Translated by H.C. Lawson-Tancred. London: Penguin Classics.
Graham, p. 2002. 'Predication and propagation: A method for analysing evaluative meanings in technology policy'. *TEXT* **22**:227–68.
Halliday, M.A.K. 1994. *An Introduction to Functional Grammar*. London: Arnold.
Halliday, M.A.K. and J.R. Martin. 1993. *Writing Science: Literacy and Discursive Power*. London: Falmer Press.
Harvey, D. 1973/1988. *Social Justice and the City*. London: Blackwell.
Lemke, J.L. 1995. *Textual Politics: Discourse and Social Dynamics*. London: Taylor & Francis.

Lemke, J.L. 1998. 'Resources for attitudinal meaning: Evaluative orientations in text semantics'. *Functions of Language* **5**:33–56.

McKenna, B. and P. Graham. 2000. 'Technocratic discourse: A primer'. *Journal of Technical Writing and Communication* **30**:219–47.

Muntigl, P. 2000. 'Dilemmas of individualism and social necessity'. Pp. 145–84 in *European Union Discourses on Unemployment: An Interdisciplinary Approach to Employment Policy-Making and Organizational Change*, edited by P. Muntigl, G. Weiss and R. Wodak. London: Benjamins.

Stiglitz, J.E. 1999. *Public Policy For A Knowledge Economy*. Washington, DC: World Bank.

Sunderland, N. 2000. *Beer, Bread, Cheese, and Heat Resistant Pigs: Reflections on Politics and Discourse in the Modern Biotech Debate*. Queensland University of Technology: Working Paper Series, Centre for the Study of Ethics.

10 Knowledge issues and policy in the operation of industrial clusters

Abraham Ninan

In his definitive work on international competitiveness, Michael Porter (1998) argued that a nation's leading export firms are not isolated success stories but successful groups of rivals within related industries. Implicit in Porter's theory of industry strategy is a concept of how knowledge regions work in both traditional and 'new' industries.

Although there are important caveats to the observations, clusters operate geographically, often regionally. This is despite globalization and technological mediation. I argue that this is because of a number of knowledge mechanisms that must operate in clusters, namely:

- horizontal and vertical links in clusters;
- five factors in Porter's competitive model (1998) – local context; firm strategy, structure and rivalry; factor input conditions; demand conditions and related and supporting industries;
- close geographic proximity;
- face-to-face communication and exchange for creative work;
- social network memberships within clusters;
- cognitive proximity;
- absorptive capacity;
- spatial levels of analyses: regional, national and international.

Reviewing Porter's cluster model: definitional elasticity
In policy terms, the cluster approach, while not without critics (e.g. Garlick 1996; Meyer-Stamer 2002) is still in the ascendancy. Using a knowledge management perspective, I suggest policy imperatives for the operation of clusters – the fundamental engines of industrial organization and innovation.

Porter (1998) used the term 'clusters' to describe the cluster concept; this refers to sets of firms connected by horizontal and vertical links of various kinds (including, but not confined to, input–output trading associations). Further, according to Porter (1998), the significance of these industrial clusters resides in the interactions between five sets of factors that constitute a 'competitive diamond':

1. Local context
2. Firm strategy, structure and rivalry
3. Factor input conditions
4. Demand conditions
5. Related and supporting industries.

The more developed and intense the interactions between these five sets of factors, the greater will be the productivity of the firms concerned. Also, the intensity of interaction within the competitive diamond is enhanced if the firms in the cluster are geographically localized. According to Porter (1998), the geographical concentration of firms in the same industry is common around the world; the most globally competitive industries of a nation are also likely to be 'geographically clustered' within that country. Cluster theory was originally devised as a way of decomposing a national economy, where clusters represented groups of interlinked industries and associated activities. That theoretical underpinning has since evolved to become a spatial metaphor, with clusters now representing geographically localized groups of interlinked businesses.

However, Porter (1998) posits that the competitive diamond is the driving force for cluster development, and simultaneously that the cluster is the spatial manifestation of the competitive diamond. The systemic nature of the diamond produces local concentrations of leading rival firms, which in turn magnifies and intensifies the interactions between the factors. He suggests that the process of clustering, and the intense interchange among industries in the cluster, work best where the involved industries are geographically concentrated.

Porter also uses the term 'cluster' to characterize new public–private avenues for constructive action. Porter suggests that 'the way clusters operate involves a new agenda of collective action in the private sector' (1998, pp. 88–9). He argues that the new role for governments in the new economies is a departure from the old industry policy of picking winners and developing trade restrictions. In contrast, the aim of a cluster policy approach is to reinforce the development of all clusters by providing inputs such as educated citizens and physical infrastructure. According to Porter (1998) it may also involve establishing the rules of competition by, for example, protecting intellectual property or enforcing anti-trust laws. Various authors in both the UK (Leadbeater 1999; Mulgan 1997) and Australia (Byrant and Wells 1998) advocate this very emphasis of providing key inputs to clusters. In view of the rise of emergent forms like 'industry networks' it is imperative that the viability of extending this provision of key inputs to a network of such industry clusters be considered.

Martin and Sunley (2001) propose that a key reason for the popular acceptance of Porter's model is the very nature of the cluster concept. They explain that Porter's cluster metaphor is highly generic in character, being sufficiently indeterminate to admit a very wide spectrum of industrial groupings and specializations from footwear clusters to wine clusters to biotechnology clusters, demand–supply linkages, factor conditions, institutional set-ups, among others, while at the same time claiming to be based on what are argued to be fundamental processes of business strategy, industrial organization and economic interaction.

Geography matters in economic knowledge management

Blandy (2002) aptly summarizes Porter's competitive advantage position when stating that Porter makes the case for a new approach for both understanding and creating economic success in a global economy. Using cases from around the world, Porter relates the competitiveness of nations and regions directly to the competitiveness of their home industries. Moreover, he argues that in advanced economies today, regional clusters of related industries (rather than individual companies or single industries) are the source of jobs, income and export growth. Specifically he states that 'these industry clusters are geographical concentrations of competitive firms in related industries that do business with each other and that share needs for common talent, technology and infrastructure' (Blandy 2002, p. 15).

Moreover, Blandy (2002, p. 19) suggests that 'the emergence of clusters in non-location sensitive activities, not normally thought of as subject to clustering, can also be identified in Omaha in telemarketing, South Dakota in credit card processing, Ireland in back office processing for financial services, Sydney in information processing, Bangalore in software services, and Manila in data entry'. He states that 'these are only a few examples of mobile activities that one generally thinks of being decentralised *from* places rather than being decentralised *to* places . . . the fact that such "placeless" activities have even shown tendencies to cluster indicates the strength of the phenomenon' (ibid.).

As Audretsch and Feldman (2003, p. 31), indicate,

perhaps the greatest development in the literature on the economics of innovation and technological change in the last decade has been the insight that geography matters. A long tradition of analysing the innovative process within the boundaries of the firm and devoid of spatial context has given way to the incorporation of spatial context in models of innovation and technological change. Incorporating spatial relationships into the model of knowledge production function has redeemed the view that knowledge inputs are linked to innovative output. While the boundaries of the firm still matter, so do the boundaries of spatial agglomerations. Geography has been found to provide a platform upon which new economic knowledge can be produced, harnessed and commercialized into innovations. Thus, the model of knowledge production has been found to hold better for spatial units of observation than it does for enterprises studied without reference to their spatial context.

The geographical anchoring of clusters may be explained by some knowledge-related issues.

Mechanisms facilitating transference of knowledge in clusters

Location and transference of creative knowledge
Addressing issues relating to the importance of location in the transfer of knowledge in clusters, Henton and Walesh (1998, p. 14) claim that

> creative work occurs primarily in face-to-face exchange largely within teams, where people live and work in close proximity. Although electronic communication is important, it is not a substitute for the trust, sharing, and intense interpersonal interaction essential for the creative process. Although the same types of work can be done remotely via personal computer, the creative heart and soul of the new economy will continue to be tied in place.

Location and transference of tacit knowledge in epistemic communities
Adding to the above perspective on mechanisms influencing the transference of knowledge in clusters, Håkanson (2003) suggests that the location of epistemic communities, which are dependent upon social network memberships, determines knowledge spillovers more than does the nature or coding of knowledge type in such a population. He states that the

> access to knowledge and specialized expertise is clearly of vital importance. But such knowledge and expertise, regardless of how it is articulated and codified, can only be accessed and exploited by individuals who are members of relevant epistemic communities. The location of such individuals and the communities to which they belong are the decisive determinants for knowledge spillovers – not the nature of the knowledge (tacit or otherwise) in question. (2003, p. 20)

In the above context, Giuliani (2003) and Cowan and Foray (1997) confirm the importance of the role of geographic proximity in epistemic communities when stating that knowledge that is transferred is likely to be partially unarticulated, rather than tacit, and as such based on codes and technical terms that have been developed to applied practice and confrontation. In a way, geographical proximity may influence the production of a common and local technical code that may be developed by knowledge-skilled workers to fix location specific technical problems.

Bergman et al. (1996) also underline the importance of the geographical location of clusters in the transference of tacit knowledge. They state that tacit knowledge makes geographical location more important because propinquity greatly affects the ability of people and firms to share this sort of knowledge.

Research outcomes link location and knowledge transfer in clusters
There is strong evidential support from several studies that reiterate the importance of geographical clustering for knowledge transfer and related innovation activity. For example, Dahl (2001) and Breschi and Lissoni (2001) note that within the last decade or so many studies have been published which take advantage of the sizeable sources of information on innovative activity from patent counts, patent citations, innovation counts and qualitative surveys. These new sources have enabled researchers within this field to make larger studies of the geographical dimension of innovative activity. More or less all of these sources have had the intention of highlighting and demonstrating the existence of geographically bounded knowledge spillovers, which lead to the geographical clustering of innovative activity.

Networks in geographical clusters further facilitate knowledge transfer
Blandy (2002) adds new light to the mechanics of knowledge transfer for innovation purposes in geographical clusters when arguing that a defining characteristic of the new economy is the networking of firms. He states that 'small, medium, and large firms collaborate on projects and later compete on other projects in a process of continuous networking. These firms share the common pool of talent and intellectual capital within a geographic area' (2002, p. 23). Blandy also states that 'firms of all sizes develop webs of relationships to help them achieve the speed, quality, flexibility, and knowledge essential for competitive advantage' (ibid.); he refers to work by Henton and Walesh when adding 'the shift to a new economy and the changing nature of work place a premium on regions as important places. They do so because the networks which lie at the heart of the flexible specialisation model function most effectively when clustered geographically in a region' (ibid.).

However, some researchers have questioned the assumption that local networks based on trust-based, embedded relationships are likely to generate much innovation (Boschma et al. 2002). This may be explained in terms of 'weakness of strong ties'. Essentially, it refers to poor capacity to interpret new information or to adjust, due to loyalty and long-term commitment, at the expense of hampering the innovative and learning capacities of the individuals who network to facilitate knowledge transference in geographically proximate clusters, as such a mix of 'embedded' and 'market relationships' is more likely to generate innovative behaviour. In this light, Uzzi (1997) has claimed that there exists an optimum in terms of adaptive capacity when the network consists of a mixture of arm's-length ties (which keeps the firms alert, open-minded and flexible) and embedded relationships (lowering transactions costs and facilitating inter-organizational learning). Cecil and Green (2000) describe a similar idea.

Thus the literature on clusters has mostly concentrated on the analysis of local learning mechanisms, emphasizing the strength of clusters as engines of endogenous knowledge creation. At the same time, the mere reliance on localized knowledge can produce the 'entrophic death' of the cluster that remains locked in an obsolete technological paradigm. Giuliani (2003, p. 4) states that 'in laggard regions or clusters such as those in developing countries, the dependence on external knowledge is strong and the degree of openness is crucial to avoid lock-in'. For this reason, different contributions have now emphasized the importance of cluster's cognitive interconnection with external sources of knowledge (Albino et al. 2000; Bell and Albu 1999; Camagni 1991; Freeman 1991).

Cognitive proximity: redefines location and knowledge transfer in clusters
The whole idea of geographical proximity and its implications for cluster literature takes a radical turn when 'distance' is discussed in a new light – that of cognitive proximity, which is dependent upon firms' knowledge bases in the cluster. Giuliani (2003) explains that

> firms with higher absorptive capacity are more likely to show a higher degree of local interconnection, so that they transfer knowledge to other local firms. At the same time, the cognitive interconnectedness between the technological gatekeeper(s) and other local firms are bound to be tied to cognitive proximity of firms' knowledge bases. (Giuliani 2003, p. 7)

The above suggests that

> the exchange of knowledge in clusters is not even across firms, but it is driven by the existence of overlapping knowledge bases and of cognitive proximity among firms. It is therefore possible to develop a scenario in which firms occupy different cognitive positions in the cluster according to their knowledge bases. [Consequently,] firms with very low absorptive capacities could be too distant, from a cognitive point of view, to interconnect with the technological gatekeeper or with other local firms. They would, therefore, tend to isolation and be cast apart from the local knowledge system. (Ibid.)

Absorptive capacity: redefines location and knowledge transfer in clusters
Giuliani (2003) suggests that it is

> firms with higher absorptive capacities that should be more likely to interconnect cognitively with external sources of knowledge. This is theoretically explained considering cognitive distances between firms so that firms with higher absorptive capacities are thought as being more cognitively proximate from frontier/extra-cluster knowledge than those firms with lower absorptive capacities ... firms with higher absorptive capacity are more likely to expose themselves to extra-cluster knowledge flows and be cognitively interconnected with external sources of knowledge. (Giuliani 2003, p. 6)

Some measures to improve absorptive capacities of clusters may include the adoption of an incubator model, where a geographical cluster imports experts in a 'knowledge area' to a specific location, and through informal and formal training of other co-workers (e.g. an observe-and-follow or a more structured, hands-on approach), increases the absorptive capacity of the cluster. This in addition to the presence of a 'network star' (expert) will increase the potential for the cluster both to attract resources as well as to develop its own brand equity in the local, national and international marketplace.

For now, based on the discussed alternative meanings of distance-affecting knowledge transfer for innovation, as in cognitive proximity and absorptive capacity, the chapter analyses, at a more macro level, the operation of such mechanisms. Specifically, it seeks to identify the relevance of spatial levels at which innovation systems operate and how these relate to knowledge transfer and the efficacy of supportive mechanisms.

Spatial levels affect knowledge transfer for innovation

The chapter has so far established links between location, distance, alternative meanings of distance, networks and how these affect knowledge transference for innovation in clusters. Audretsch and Feldman (2003, p. 8) best broach the topic of spatial levels of such knowledge transfer when stating 'innovation clusters spatially where knowledge externalities reduce the costs of scientific discovery and commercialization'. Pre-empting, as it were, the importance of spatial levels as units of analysis for measuring knowledge transfer, they indicate that 'firms producing innovations tend to be located in areas where there are necessary resources: resources that have accumulated due to a region's past success with innovation. In this way, firms and resources are endogenous' (ibid). Jacobs (1969) adds that cities are the sources of significant innovation because knowledge sources are most diverse in urban spaces.

Audretsch and Feldman (2003) indicate that emerging empirical evidence points towards location and proximity as being central in knowledge spillovers. They state that

> the geographic estimation of the knowledge production function, however, is limited because there is no understanding of the way in which spillovers occur and are realized at the geographic level. The pre-existing pattern of technology related activities makes it difficult to separate spillovers from the correlation of variables at the geographic level. Economic activity may be co-located, but the pattern of causality is difficult to decipher (p. 13).

Future research agenda: metrification of units of analyses
There is much ongoing debate that aims to resolve the best spatial levels at which innovation systems must operate. Many authors claim that regions are the appropriate unit of analysis (e.g. Braczyk et al. 1998; Acs 2000), while

others believe that technological systems function internationally (e.g. through cooperative networks between multinational firms). By contrast, Lundvall (1988) and Nelson (1993) have stressed that the interplay between geographical, cultural and cognitive proximity is most effective at the national level. Carlsson and Stankiewicz (1991) support this when stating that geographical and cultural closeness facilitates effective interaction and suggest that national borders tend to enclose networks of technological interaction (p. 102). While research has not yet established precise metrics or units of measurement for gauging degrees of interplay between geographical, cultural or cognitively proximate factors affecting knowledge transfer for innovation, it has established secondary evidence for links between these factors. Also, it is more important that such interplay could happen at several spatial levels of analyses, for example regional, national or international. Future research must consider the fine-tuning of such spatial levels as units of analyses to help establish and measure relationships between various knowledge transfer facilitative mechanisms in clusters to help promote innovation. The custom metrification of such knowledge transfer and innovation facilitative measures for the regional, national and international levels of analyses will ease the task of policy-makers in particular. It will give them a better grasp on methods to measure, monitor, facilitate and govern regional, national and international economies with a view to effectively promoting economic growth with optimum benefits for clusters and their citizens; all this, while harnessing location- and cluster-specific competitive advantages.

Policy issues
Despite caveats to the precise mechanisms of and levels at which clusters operate, public support for innovation has certainly moved from help for firms and individual projects to start-up aid for 'collective topics'. These topics relate to helping firms seek for cooperation among themselves and for encouragement of projects that house the potential to develop networks and spread demand for innovation.

> Successful innovation requires the correct combination (or package) of innovation inputs – knowledge, technical expertise, design, finance, managerial expertise, marketing expertise, trained labour and capital equipment. Unlike large multi-divisional firms, small firms often lack the scale and resources to conduct research, development, design and training in-house. As a result they are unable to reap the internal economies that large firms enjoy. Instead, (small and medium enterprises) SMEs are forced to use the market. Cooperation within networks offers SMEs the possibility to reap collective external economies and enables them to compete on equal terms with larger firms. (Blandy 2002, p. 64)

Also, while secondary research clearly indicates the need for metrification of units of analyses to ease policymakers' jobs, the debate on what spatial level best fits knowledge transfer for innovation agendas remains unresolved. There are early pointers in favour of regional and international spatial levels of analyses over national, but as such this remains a key future research issue. In this regard, Maggioni (2004, p. 1) indicates that

> in the meantime the current world-wide globalisation process, together with continental processes of economic integration, has gradually but crucially shifted the focus far from the national level toward the two extremes (the regions and the world) and the development and diffusions of high technologies (such as the ICTs) have highlighted the role of innovative industrial cluster as engine of local and national economic competitiveness and growth.

This chapter recognizes that there are several studies currently being conducted globally on regional, national, international clusters and knowledge transference within and among these with a view to promoting innovation through identification and harnessing of specific competitive advantages. Additionally, in light of key literature expositions and reviews conducted by this chapter, I attempt to put together a glossary of factors for consideration as a future research agenda, as well as knowledge management and innovation-promoting cluster mechanisms for review by policymakers. These are as follows:

1. Place the promotion of innovation as a key priority for the policy agenda of regional, national and international industry cluster governing bodies.
2. Develop an innovation culture within clusters, particularly less economically favoured clusters.
3. Increase the number of innovation projects in enterprises, particularly SMEs, in such industry clusters.
4. Promote public–private and interfirm cooperation and social–technological networks that facilitate the flow of knowledge needed for innovation in such industry clusters.
5. Increase the amount and, more importantly, the quality of public spending on innovation projects, e.g. structural funds assistance in particular, and thus promote a more efficient use of scarce public and private resources for the promotion of innovation.
6. Because of the nature of the knowledge economy, policymakers will have to expediently make available tangible and intangible economic support to relevant clusters given the impact of the digitization of Internet-based marketing and distribution systems; the windows of opportunity are short and fleeting.
7. Policymakers must support, if necessary, incubator models to kickstart innovation processes in clusters; specifically, this may involve sustaining activities and extending resources that encourage the import and

seeding of expertise in the not so economically advantaged and tacit-knowledge-stripped clusters.

8. Policymakers should also capitalize and promote diversity in the innovation process in knowledge-intensive industries to help create new genres and products in clusters.
9. Also, policymakers need to support activities that look at promoting cluster-relevant products, markets, brand equity and global awareness through brand names of production locations, among other measures.
10. Increase the roles of trade and industry associations in developing a sense of mutually beneficial goals and sharing of resources or projects for increased competitive advantage within and between clusters.

Each of these factors is cluster-specific and needs evaluation before, during and after implementation of supportive economic policy by relevant bodies.

References

Acs, Z.J. (ed). 2000. *Regional Innovation, Knowledge and Global Change*. London/New York: Printer.

Albino, V., N. Carbonar and G. Schiuma. 2000. 'Knowledge in inter-firm relationships in an industrial district'. *Industry and Higher Education* December:404–12.

Audretsch, D. and M.P. Feldman. 2003. 'Knowledge spillovers and the geography of innovation'. in *Handbook of Urban and Regional Economics*, vol. 4, edited by J.V. Henderson and J. Thisse. Amsterdam: North-Holland.

Bell, M. and M. Albu. 1999. 'Knowledge systems and technological dynamism in industrial clusters in developing countries'. *World Development* **27**:1715–34.

Bergman, E., E. Feser and S. Sweeny. 1996. *Targeting North Carolina Manufacturing: Understanding the State's Economy through Industrial Cluster Analysis*. Chapel Hill, NC: UNC Institute for Economic Development.

Blandy, R. 2002. *South Australian Business Vision 2010, Industry Clusters Program: A Review*. Adelaide, SA: Centre for Applied Economics, University of South Australia.

Boschma, R.A., J.G. Lambooy and V. Schutjens. 2002. 'Embeddedness and innovation'. Pp. 19–35 in *Embedded Enterprise and Social Capital: International Perspectives*, edited by M. Taylor and S. Leonard. Aldershot: Ashgate.

Braczyk, H.-J., P. Cooke and M. Heidenreich (eds). 1998. *Regional Innovation Systems*. London: UCL Press.

Breschi, S. and F. Lissoni. 2001. 'Localised knowledge spillovers versus innovative milieux: Knowledge "tacitness" reconsidered'. *Papers in Regional Science* **80**:255–73.

Byrant, K. and A. Wells (eds). 1998. *A New Economic Paradigm? Innovation-Based Evolutionary Systems: Discussions of Science and Innovation 4*. Canberra, ACT: Department of Industry, Science and Resources.

Camagni, R. (ed.). 1991. *Innovation Networks: Spatial Perspectives*. London and New York: Belhaven Press.

Carlsson, B. and R. Stankiewicz. 1991. 'On the nature, function and composition of technological systems'. *Journal of Evolutionary Economics* **1**:93–118.

Cecil, B.P. and M.B. Green. 2000. 'In the flagships' wake: Relations, motivations and observations of strategic alliance activity among IT sector flagship firms and their partners'. Pp. 165–88 in *Industrial Networks and Proximity*, edited by M.B. Green and R.B. McNaughton. Aldershot, UK: Ashgate.

Cowan, R. and D. Foray. 1997. 'The economics of codification and the diffusion of knowledge'. *Industrial and Corporate Change* **6**:595–622.

Dahl, M.S. 2001. 'Geographic clustering and the innovative activities of firms: Patenting in

Danish firms and regions'. Chapter presented at the Third Congress on Proximity, 'New Growth and Territories'. University of Paris South and Institut National de la Recherche Agronomique, Paris, 13–14 December.

Freeman, C. 1991. 'Networks of innovators: A synchapter of research issues'. *Research Policy* **20**:499–514.

Garlick, S. 1996. 'The incongruity of place and institution in spatial economic development: Some early thoughts'. Paper to the Regional Science Association of Australia and New Zealand Annual Conference. Australian National University, Canberra, 23–25 September.

Giuliani, E. 2003. 'Beyond localisation: The role of knowledge communities in wine clusters'. Chapter Presented at the Regional Studies Association Conference. Pisa, April.

Håkanson, L. 2003. 'Epistemic communities and cluster dynamics: On the role of knowledge in industrial districts'. Chapter presented at the Druid Summer Conference 2003 On Creating, Sharing and Transferring Knowledge: The Role of Geography, Institutions and Organizations: Copenhagen, 12–14 June.

Henton, D. and K. Walesh. 1998. *Linking the New Economy to the Livable Community*. San Francisco, CA: James Irvine Foundation.

Jacobs, J. 1969. *The Economy of Cities*. New York: Random House.

Leadbeater, Charles. 1999. *Living on Thin Air: The New Economy*. London: Penguin.

Lundvall, B.A. 1988. 'Interactive innovation as an interactive process: From user–producer interaction to the national system of innovation'. Pp. 349–69 in *Technical Change and Economic Theory*, edited by G. Dosi, C. Freeman, R. Nelson, G. Silverberg and L. Soete. London: Pinter.

Maggioni, M.A. 2004. 'High-tech firms' location and the development of innovative industrial clusters: A survey of the literature'. *Economia Politica*, 21(1): 127–66.

Martin, R. and P. Sunley. 2001. 'Deconstructing clusters: Chaotic concept or policy panacea?' Chapter presented at the Regional Studies Association Conference on Regionalising the Knowledge Economy. London, 21 November.

Meyer-Stamer, J. 2002. 'Clustering and the creation of an innovation-orientated environment for industrial competitiveness: Beware of overly optimistic expectations'. Revised version of paper prepared for International High-level Seminar on Technological Innovation, sponsored by the Ministry of Science and the Technology of China and United Nations University. Beijing, 5–7 September 2000.

Mulgan, G. 1997. *Connexity: How to Live in a Connected World*. London: Chatto & Windus.

Nelson, R.R. (ed). 1993. *National Innovation Systems: A Comparative Analysis*. Oxford: Oxford University Press.

Porter, M. 1998. 'Clusters and the new economics of competition'. *Harvard Business Review* **76**:77–90.

Uzzi, B. 1997. 'Social structure and competition in interfirm networks: The paradox of embeddedness'. *Administrative Science Quarterly* **42**:35–67.

11   Intellectual property rights in the knowledge economy
Peter Drahos

1. Introduction

In any economist's account of what makes a successful economy the institution of private property is never too far away and usually central. Douglass North, in answering his question 'why aren't all the countries in the world rich?' (1974, p. 15), concludes that countries create well-defined property rights that stimulate individuals into productive activity by raising the level of private return to meet the social return. Theories of economic development that advance an institutional explanation of development include widely distributed and enforceable property rights as a key feature of institutions that promote development (Acemoglu 2003).

Does the general case that can be made out for the economic benefits of private property apply to intellectual property rights (IPRs)? This is not an easy question to answer. Economic theory suggests that a society that had no intellectual property protection at all would almost certainly not be allocating resources to invention and creation at an optimal level (Landes and Posner 2003). But equally a society that went to extremes of protection would almost certainly incur costs that exceeded the benefits. Figure 11.1 captures the idea that one can have too much intellectual property protection.

In short, there is no easy jump from the general economic theory of property rights to IPRs. IPRs, like general property, give their holders a bundle of rights, most importantly the rights of exclusion, transfer and licensing. Like general property rights they facilitate bargaining and investment activity. But there are also important differences between IPRs and other types of property, differences that flow from the fact that the object of IPRs protection is, at base, information of one kind or another. An important characteristic of information for economic purposes is that it exhibits non-rivalry in consumption. The rules of arithmetic, for instance, can be used and reused endlessly. The act of using them does not prevent their further use in the way that the act of an eating an apple prevents the further use of that apple. The costs of excluding people from the use of information can be high, especially if potential copiers have technologies at their disposal that keep the cost of copying low. For example, the costs of excluding people from the use of the rules of arithmetic would be

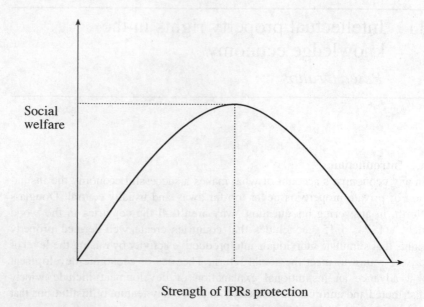

Figure 11.1   Benefits and strengths of IPRs protection

very high in economic terms and in terms of basic human freedoms. These public-good characteristics of information (a pure public good is said to be non-rivalrous and non-excludable) form the starting point of a complex economics of information and intellectual property rights.

Intellectual property rights have a fundamental and catalysing role in a knowledge economy. The technical and detailed nature of these rights has tended to mask this role, but it is clearly there. So, for example, patent rules determine when generic companies can enter a market in relation to a patented drug and under what conditions. This in turn determines what kind of industry structure will evolve in a given country and how competitive it will be. The rules of copyright affect the size of the public domain and therefore how much material creators have to pay for. In a knowledge economy it is the rules of intellectual property that determine who has access to informational resources, the terms and duration of that access and the price to be paid for the use of those resources. Intellectual property affects what kind of business models entrepreneurs can develop to compete with existing models (for example, Napster was at base an alternative business model).

The remainder of this chapter is organized as follows. Section 2 identifies the different kinds of IPRs and illustrates how IPRs have proliferated at national and international levels. Section 3 discusses IPRs from the perspective of the firm that is bound up in the process of innovation. Section 4 focuses on the danger that IPRs trigger high levels of rent-seeking behaviour.[1] Section 5 pursues the theme of rent-seeking in the context of the connection between trade and IPRs. Section 6 concludes.

2. Types of IPRs

IPRs can be divided into statutory and non-statutory systems of protection (Ricketson 1984, p. 4). The oldest forms of statutory IP are patents, copyright, trade marks and design protection. Patent statutes date back to the fifteenth century and copyright statutes to the eighteenth century. Newer forms of statutory protection that were developed in the second half of the twentieth century are plant breeder's rights and protection for the circuit layout for integrated circuits. Non-statutory systems of IPRs include protection for trade secrets and the protection of commercial reputation that attaches to signs/marks of various kinds. Within some jurisdictions such as the US, the courts have recognized a right of publicity. Roughly, this is the right of a person to protect his commercially valuable persona.

Each of these statutory systems consists of a complex body of rules that over time have been interpreted and developed by the courts. Essentially they all follow the same basic format. The relevant statute specifies criteria of eligibility for protection, a set of exclusive rights that attach to the protected subject-matter, rules on duration of protection, infringement of rights, exceptions to infringement and rules that relate to the licensing of the exclusive rights. The size and complexity of these statutory systems can in practical terms make life difficult for many classes of users of information. Librarians, for example, often find it very hard to find out the copyright status of an individual literary work and small to medium enterprises do not find the patent system especially user-friendly.

States continue to develop special kinds of IPRs. The European Community in 1996 passed a directive on the legal protection of databases and has continued to advocate a treaty on this subject-matter. The European Community has also been the greatest advocate of another kind of special IPR protection known as geographical indications. This form of protection has medieval origins and essentially allows producers within a geographical location exclusive rights over the use of the geographical name (for example, Bordeaux and Champagne) (van Caenegem 2003). While the expansion of intellectual property has been driven by developed economies, more recently developing countries have begun to push for intellectual property standards of interest to them. In particular, some developing states have gone down the path of protecting the traditional knowledge of their indigenous peoples (for example, Peru passed in 2002 a Regime for the Protection of the Collective Knowledge of Indigenous Peoples related to Biological Resources).

The one outstanding feature of IPRs has been their relentless expansion, especially in the second half of the twentieth century. Old forms of protection such as patent law and copyright have expanded their scope of protection to accommodate new types of subject-matter, such as business methods in the case of the former and computer software in the case of the latter. New types of protection have come along and at the international level there has been a steady growth in the number of international treaties. In the nineteenth century two important multilateral agreements on intellectual property were negotiated by some states: the Berne Convention for the Protection of Literary and Artistic Works (1886) and the Paris Convention for the Protection of Industrial Property (1883). Today the World Intellectual Property Organization administers some 23 treaties on intellectual property. There are hundreds of agreements at the bilateral and regional levels that contain chapters on intellectual property. Most importantly, all the members of the World Trade Organization (WTO) (currently 148) have to comply with the standards of protection that are set down in the Agreement on the Trade-Related Aspects of Intellectual Property Rights (TRIPS).

We can see that IPRs have become a pervasive feature of modern economies. Accompanying this global spread of IPRs' standards has been a vast growth in bureaucracies that administer IPRs. Patents, trade marks and designs are registration systems and therefore require a bureaucracy that examines applications for the rights, decides on eligibility and maintains a register of the rights. Patent Offices are not trivial operations. The United States Patent and Trademark Office has a staff of some 6500, the Japanese Patent Office some 2500 and the European Patent Office approximately 5000.[2] The costs of creating IPRs do not end with administration. Property rights that cannot be enforced are worth little. Enforcement requires the participation of civil courts and specialist tribunals. Increasingly criminal law enforcement agencies have begun to play a much greater role in enforcement as states have moved down the path of criminalizing infringement of IPRs.

3. Firms, innovation and IPRs

Justifications for IPRs can be divided into economic and moral kinds. Moral justifications tend to draw on a long tradition of moral theorizing about private property. The moral argument that can probably be said to have the greatest influence is the argument that there is a rights-based connection between a person's labour and the result of that labour (Drahos 1996, ch. 3). Even today this argument has enormous rhetorical force despite the fact that many objects of IPRs are the products of complex collective forms of origination and production. Any given piece of software or biotechnology has, for example, many 'authorial' inputs. Working out where one person's contributions and therefore rights begin and end is difficult. This moral argument would justify an ownership distribution of IPRs that was much more dispersed and collective in nature than the more concentrated distribution of ownership that currently prevails in many markets.

Economic justifications for IPRs begin from an *ex ante* perspective. That is, they ask under what conditions an economic agent would be willing to bear the risk of future losses when investing in the production of information. Economic agents are assumed to be rational profit-maximizers. An agent will only bear the R&D costs necessary for product innovation if it can 'lock up' the R&D information that leads to the innovative product. If it cannot lock up the information, competitors move in, acquire that information at zero cost and produce the innovative product at a price below that at which the first agent did so (primarily because the competitors save on the R&D cost). In a market without protection for R&D information it is rational for agents to free-ride on the R&D efforts of others, but not rational for them to undertake their own R&D. Society suffers overall because not enough resources are being allocated to invention. This has long-run implications for economic growth.

IPRs, on the face of it, provide a solution to this problem. Economic agents are given monopoly rights over the R&D information embodied in the new product. However, the strength of that monopoly is limited in various ways (for example, by limiting the right to a fixed number of years), so that others will eventually be able to compete in the making of the same product (assuming the market is still there). IPRs also have features that allow potential competitors to access the information while it is the subject of the exclusive right. The patent system, for example, releases the R&D information into the public domain in the form of patent specifications during the period of the monopoly so that others can make use of the information to produce non-infringing products. In this way the patent system is said to encourage the availability of useful information at zero cost, while at the same time helping to encourage the production of new information.

From a societal perspective IPRs are in essence a form of regulatory contract in which society agrees to give investors in innovation a set of temporary exclusive rights in exchange for acts of investment. If there is a demand for the relevant innovation and no real substitute for it, consumers will face prices well above marginal cost. The gain to consumers is access to innovation that would not have occurred in the absence of IPRs. Through IPRs a society restricts the operation of competitive markets and therefore allocative efficiency in order to achieve more dynamic efficiency. How great a restriction to impose and what the returns in terms of dynamic efficiency are likely to be are not easy to calculate. In truth, it is something of a gamble.

IPRs are, as many people have pointed out, an imperfect solution to the problem of ensuring that a society devotes sufficient resources to the creation or discovery of information. No legal system can ensure that information is completely appropriable (Arrow 1962, p. 615). There are enormous difficulties in defining the boundaries of information. Its boundaries are inherently fuzzy. For example, it is axiomatic in copyright law that copyright protects expression but not ideas. In cases of non-literal infringement this distinction turns out to be very difficult to draw. If I rewrite Peter Benchley's novel *Jaws* using a crocodile instead of a shark, have I infringed Benchley's copyright? Many corporations have turned to technological 'locks' as part of an appropriation strategy (for example, the use of encryption devices on CDs and DVDs and the use of genetic technologies to produce sterile plants).

There are many different kinds of markets and sub-markets in information where innovation occurs, and not all of them depend on strong IPRs. So, for example, there would be no gain in extending intellectual property protection to chess moves because chess moves are a by-product of an activity undertaken for reasons having nothing to do with intellectual property (the analysis, however, is different for markets in books about chess moves) (Frank 1996). Some markets can develop in the absence of IPRs. The market in computer software innovation was flourishing well before the use of copyright and then patents to protect software (Drahos and Braithwaite 2002, p. 170). The free software movement is an example of how a market in high technology can develop in the absence of IPRs. It is also possible that IPRs may actually inhibit innovative activity. If, for example, there are many separate owners of IPRs that relate to a particular piece of technology, a company may find that the cost of obtaining the licences is too great. Known as the theory of the anticommons, the effect of many IPRs may be that a resource remains underexploited (Heller 1998). There is a case for robust IPRs protection in some markets. The pharmaceutical market is usually cited as an example. But even here there is a range of complex questions about how strong IPRs should be. How long should the patent term be? Should patentees be given the right to patent processes and pharmaceutical compounds or just processes? What should be the rights of generic manufacturers in terms of accessing the patent in order to begin the process of manufacturing as the patent nears expiry? There are debates on all of these questions (Correa 2001).

We can conclude this section by noting that, as the scholarship on the nature of innovation has grown, more and more scepticism has been expressed about the need for strong IPRs in that process (Macdonald 2002; Mandeville 1998). Processual accounts of innovation start with Arrow's conclusion that innovation is 'about the production of information' (Mandeville 1996, p. 38). If innovation is about information rather than products, how is such information generated? The conventional view assumes single actors in antagonistic competition with each other. Real-life processes involve much more. No one firm can meet all its information needs through internal resources alone. Mechanisms develop to encourage the flow of information among them. Examples of such mechanisms are personal communication networks, open publication, collaboration between technology-supplying firms and, even more broadly, social institutions of knowledge such as the public domain and the university. These mechanisms exist because individuals can see the benefits in keeping them. Cooperation among individuals is just as important to the innovation process as competition. These kinds of mechanisms do not require IPRs and in fact their operation may be inhibited by them.

Many highly innovative industries are crucially dependent on flows of uncodified or tacit information.[3] (A recipe is an example of codified knowledge. Much of what an experienced cook knows is uncodified and may even be uncodifiable, existing as a good instinct.) Less innovative industries are characterized by a greater presence of codified information. Importantly, uncodified technological information requires resources to imitate. It follows that uncodified information enjoys a certain level of 'natural protection' (Mandeville 1996, p. 93). Codified information is much more vulnerable to free-riding problems. The patent system has a role to play in helping to facilitate the exchange of codified information, but essentially it performs no useful function in the case of those innovative processes that are largely dependent upon networks of economic agents participating in flows of uncodified information. Patent specifications rarely disclose what is really needed to make an invention work. Strengthening the patent system may have a negative effect on innovation, for stronger patent rights may disrupt the fragile networks of communication upon which innovation is dependent. More generally, strong IPRs may disrupt the exchange norms of the creative commons upon which much innovation depends.

4. IPRs and the problem of rent-seeking

One of the problems raised by IPRs that has perhaps not received as much attention as it deserves is the problem of rent-seeking, or what we might call unproductive property rights. Property rights are generally thought to be the best form of incentive for raising the rate of private return on activities that have a social return. But it does not follow from this that the presence of property rights always signals the presence of productive activity. Property rights can sometimes cause social losses.

There are strong incentives for individuals to seek unproductive property rights, especially if the property right in question confers a monopoly of some kind. For example, copyright owners in the USA during the 1990s successfully lobbied for a 20-year extension of the copyright term for subsisting copyrights.[4] The effect of the extension was to continue the copyright protection of lucrative works such as Fitzgerald's *The Great Gatsby*, Gershwin's *Rhapsody in Blue* and films such as *Gone with the Wind* and *Casablanca*. An *amici* brief filed by the Association of American Publishers and other copyright owners pointed out that an annual nationwide licence for a Gershwin song earns around the US$250 000 mark.[5] The gain of the 20-year extension to the owners of Gershwin songs is, therefore, considerable. From the point of view of efficiency it is hard to justify. The extension of the copyright term could only have an incentive effect on future works, not on works that were already in existence. These works had already been socially purchased, as it were, by the copyright term that existed before the extension. Extending the copyright term inflicts allocative efficiency losses with no compensating incentive effects. The allocative losses are likely to be high because many of these works were about to enter the public domain in the USA, meaning that the cost of continued monopoly pricing has to be worked out in present values rather than discounted future values. There are also dynamic efficiency losses. When a copyright work enters the public domain other creators no longer have to face the transaction costs of locating copyright owners or having to pay for the use of the work. They are free to adapt and innovate with those works. Famous copyright works that enter the public domain are, in effect, cultural standards for which there is high demand both by creators wishing to adapt them for their own projects and by consumers who wish to see the final product. The effect of extending the copyright term for works, especially those in the category of cultural standards, is to restrict the supply of cultural invention compared to the supply had the works not been the subject of copyright protection. A good example of the kind of dynamic efficiency gains that occur when a famous work enters the public domain is H.G. Wells's *The Time Machine*. It entered the public domain in the USA in 1951 and aside from being continuously in print has been the subject of five sequels, five films, two musicals, a ballet, video games and comic books.[6] In Europe, where the novel has yet to enter the public domain, the creators of all these follow-on works would have had to have obtained licensing permission.

The problem of unproductive property rights is not confined to copyright. Patent owners with lucrative patents and a shortage of new products in the pipeline have a strong incentive to invest in finding ways to extend their patent rights.[7] Often incumbents in industry face lower costs and greater benefits by investing in the extension of their existing property rights or the creation of new ones (for example database protection by publishers) rather than investing in innovation where they face higher costs and uncertain gains.

5.   Trade and IPRs – global rent-seeking?

Just as the attributes of information mean that information does not fit neatly into classical economic theory, so IPRs do not fit neatly into classical trade theory. IPRs are complex systems of rules that may in certain cases confer on their holders enormous economic power. For example, patents may in certain cases allow the patent owner the sole right to import goods into a market, meaning that the patent owner can price discriminate between markets (Heath 1997). The monopoly nature of IPRs, including their potential to affect the free movement of goods, sits at odds with the economic case for allowing the free movement of goods across borders.

One might then ask how it is that an agreement like TRIPS made it into the WTO. TRIPS sets minimum standards in patents, copyright, trade marks, geographical indications, industrial designs and layout designs of integrated circuits. TRIPS effectively globalizes the set of intellectual property principles it contains, because most states of the world are members of the WTO. Every member, for example, has to have a copyright law that protects computer programs as a literary work as well as a patent law that does not exclude micro-organisms and microbiological processes from patentability. The standards in TRIPS will profoundly affect the ownership of the twenty-first century's two great bodies of technology – digital technology and biotechnology.

The puzzle deepens when it is realized that in immediate trade terms the globalization of intellectual property really only benefited the USA and to a lesser extent the European Community (Maskus 2000).[8] Economic theory suggests that there will be a conflict of interests between countries that are net exporters of IPRs and those that are net importers (Subramanian 1991). The net importers will either have no interest in recognizing IPRs or will only recognize them in ways that discriminate in favour of domestic rights holders. Perhaps the only case where it might be rational for a net importer to recognize foreign IPRs is where by doing so the net importer triggers innovative activity in a foreign market that is important to the importer and would otherwise not have taken place. This presupposes that consumers in the importing country can pay. This is one reason why this approach was not used by developing countries in the context of pharmaceutical markets and patents.

At the time of the TRIPS negotiations the USA and the European Community had between them the world's dominant software, pharmaceutical, chemical and entertainment industries, as well as the world's most important trade marks. The rest of the developed countries and all developing countries were in the position of being importers with nothing really to gain by agreeing to terms of trade for intellectual property that would offer so much protection to the comparative advantage the USA and European Community enjoyed in intellectual-property-related goods. An Australian study of copyright royalty flows during the 1990s showed that Australia paid out to overseas copyright owners around $1.2 billion more than it received

(Office of Regulation Review 1995, p. 39). Another Australian study showed that the cost to Australia of the TRIPS provision which extended the patent term of 20 years to patents *already in existence* could be as high as $3.8 billion (Gruen et al. 1996). In Australia, as is the case in all small to medium-sized developed-country economies and developing-country economies, the vast bulk of patents is in foreign ownership.

The explanation for TRIPS lies in the global corporate interest group politics that increasingly permeates sectors of the global economy. Mancur Olson's (1965) analysis of the logic of collective action forms a useful starting point in developing the explanation. Concentrated interests are more likely to organize to gain a legislative outcome than diffuse interests because concentrated interests face lower costs of organization and greater individual gains. Diffuse interests face the reverse problem. The demand of concentrated interest groups for legislation will be affected by the relevant electoral structure. If money is important to re-election, the demands of those concentrated interests making generous donations to election campaigns are likely to be met. This logic explains why, for example, logging or mining interests can trump the preferences of citizens for higher levels of environmental public goods.

A body of scholarship has shown that TRIPS was the product of organized and coordinated activities of key international business players in the 1980s (Drahos and Braithwaite 2002; Matthews 2002; Ryan 1998; Sell 2003). In the early 1980s the CEOs of Pfizer, IBM and DuPont, sitting on the President's Advisory Committee on Trade Negotiations, began a campaign that led to the formation of a lobbying organization (the Intellectual Property Committee) and the enrolment of European business in an international business coalition that ultimately persuaded the US government and the European Community to make an international agreement on intellectual property their top priority. By contrast, the users and consumers of intellectual property rights, which represented a broad and diffuse constituency, were not organizationally represented at these negotiations.

The effects of TRIPS are likely to be debated for a long time. How productive the IPRs that it globalizes will be for developing countries' economies time will tell. There is every possibility, however, that TRIPS is a spectacular example of rent-seeking on a global scale.

6. Conclusion

The conventional *a priori* economic argument for IPRs looks plausible enough. Individual economic agents need incentives, and the exclusivity of property rights is a powerful incentive. Even on this argument, however, one can have too much intellectual property protection. At some point the costs outweigh the benefits. As the scholarship surrounding IPRs has grown, the problems of IPRs have become clearer and clearer. Markets in information do not always fail and in fact may thrive in absence of IPRs. Strong IPRs do not always promote innovation and in fact may interfere in the process for innovation. The economic case for strong IPRs depends on one's economic context. There seems to be no strong case for globalizing one set of IPRs standards. The setting of new IPRs carries with it the risk that it will deliver rents rather than stimulate socially productive investment. The challenge, for those who want a flourishing knowledge economy, is to minimize this risk. Most probably the answer lies in thinking about the form that democracy must take in the knowledge economy.

The current problem that faces emerging knowledge economies is that their law-making processes have been heavily influenced by owners of intellectual property. As a result the rights of ownership have strengthened. Many civil society groups have formed to oppose developments such as the patenting of genes, seeds and software and the extension of copyright into the digital environment, but they have had comparatively little success in strengthening rights of access to intellectual property. The explanation for this has everything to do with the way that multinationals with large intellectual property holdings have penetrated the corridors of legislatures, set up think tanks to influence public policy and financed re-election campaigns. The influence of big business over the setting of laws and standards is hardly a new phenomenon. But it is a potentially greater problem in a knowledge economy because the rules that are made under the auspices of organizations such as the WTO now have a genuinely global reach. There are no easy answers to this problem, but clearly if the knowledge economies of the future are not to be choked by intellectual property regimes and a lawyer-led approach to innovation, ways will have to be found to involve communities of users of intellectual property in the rule-making processes. Among other things, governments will have to open up to user representatives the membership of the thousands of technical committees and advisory bodies that steer the development of intellectual property policy. By encouraging and deepening the participation of user groups in the policy process governments at least create the opportunity for more bargaining to take place over the definition and scope of intellectual property rights. Democratic bargaining is the key to socially productive intellectual property rights.

Notes

1. 'Rent' refers to a 'payment that is not needed to elicit productive labour or the productive services of some other input'. See Baumol et al. (1991), p. 274.
2. This information was taken from the Trilateral Statistical Report 2001. The report can be accessed from the website of the US Patent and Trademark Office, the Japanese Patent Office or the European Patent Office.
3. For a classic discussion of the economic importance of tacit knowledge see Nelson and Winter (1982).

4. Copyright Term Extension Act of 1998.
5. See Brief of *Amici Curiae* Association of American Publishers et al. in support of Respondent, No. 01-618, in the Supreme Court of the United States, *Eldred* v. *Ashcroft*, 29, fn. 85.
6. See Brief of Intellectual Property Law Professors as *Amici Curiae* Supporting Petitioners, No. 01-618, in the Supreme Court of the United States, *Eldred* v. *Ashcroft*, 2
7. For a discussion of this in the context of pharmaceutical markets see Federal Trade Commission (2002).
8. See *Global Economic Prospects and the Developing Countries*, Washington, DC: World Bank, 2002, p. 133.

References

Acemoglu, Daron. 2003. 'Root causes: A historical approach to assessing the role of institutions in economic development'. *Finance and Development* June:27–30.
Arrow, K.J. 1962. 'Economic welfare and the allocation of resources for invention'. Pp. 609–25 in *The Rate and Direction of Inventive Activity*, edited by National Bureau of Economic Research. Princeton, NJ: Princeton University Press.
Baumol, W.J., S. Blackman and E. Wolff. 1991. *Productivity and American Leadership*. Cambridge, MA: MIT Press.
Correa, Carlos M. 2001. 'Public health and patent legislation in developing countries'. *Tulane Journal of Technology and Intellectual Property* 3:1–53.
Drahos, Peter. 1996. *A Philosophy of Intellectual Property*. Aldershot, UK: Dartmouth.
Drahos, Peter and John Braithwaite. 2002. *Information Feudalism: Who Owns the Knowledge Economy?* London: Earthscan.
Federal Trade Commission. 2002. 'Generic drug entry prior to patent expiration'. http://www.ftc.gov/os/2002/07/genericdrugstudy.pdf.
Frank, Björn. 1996. 'On an art without copyright'. *Kyklos* 49:3–15.
Gruen, Nicholas, Ian Bruce and Gerard Prior. 1996. *Extending Patent Life: Is it in Australia's Economic Interests?* Belconnen, ACT: Industry Commission, Commonwealth of Australia.
Heath, Christopher. 1997. 'Parallel imports and international trade'. *International Review of Industrial Property and Copyright Law* 5:623–32.
Heller, M. 1998. 'The tragedy of the anticommons: Property in the transition from Marx to markets'. *Harvard Law Review* 111:621–88.
Landes, William, M. and Richard A. Posner. 2003. *The Economic Structure of Intellectual Property Law*. Cambridge, MA: Belknap Press of Harvard University Press.
Macdonald, Stuart. 2002. 'Exploring the hidden costs of patents'. Pp. 13–39 in *Global Intellectual Property Rights: Knowledge, Access and Development*, edited by P. Drahos and R. Mayne. Basingstoke, UK and New York: Palgrave Macmillan.
Mandeville, Thomas. 1996. *Understanding Novelty: Information, Technological Change, and the Patent System*. Norwood, NJ: Ablex Publishing.
Mandeville, Thomas. 1998. 'An information economics perspective on innovation'. *International Journal of Social Economics* 25:357–64.
Maskus, Keith, E. 2000. 'Intellectual property rights and economic development'. *Case Western Reserve Journal of International Law* 32:471–506.
Matthews, Duncan. 2002. *Globalising Intellectual Property Rights: The TRIPs Agreement*. London and New York: Routledge.
Nelson, Richard R. and Sidney Winter. 1982. *An Evolutionary Theory of Economic Change*. Cambridge, MA: Harvard University Press.
North, Douglass C. 1974. *Growth & Welfare in the American Past*. Englewood Cliffs, NJ: Prentice Hall.
Office of Regulation Review. 1995. *An Economic Analysis of Copyright Reform*. Australia: Commonwealth of Australia.
Olson, Mancur. 1965. *The Logic of Collective Action*. Cambridge, MA: Harvard University Press.
Ricketson, Staniforth. 1984. *The Law of Intellectual Property*. Sydney: Law Book Company.

Ryan, Michael. 1998. *Knowledge Diplomacy: Global Competition and the Politics of Intellectual Property*. Washington, DC: Brookings Institution Press.

Sell, Susan K. 2003. *Private Power, Public Law: The Globalization of Intellectual Property Rights*. New York: Cambridge University Press.

Subramanian, Arvind. 1991. 'The international economics of intellectual property right protection: A welfare-theoretic trade policy analysis'. *World Development* **19**:945–56.

van Caenegem, William. 2003. 'Registered geographical indications: Between intellectual property and rural policy – Part II'. *Journal of World Intellectual Property* **6**:861–74.

PART III

IMPLEMENTATION

12   Information sharing

Donald M. Lamberton

Information sharing can be viewed as a practical matter at various levels: between people in their workplace or community, among managers, between firms or government departments or, in these times of somewhat fractured globalization, between nations. It is often tainted by collusion and constrained in a variety of ways, for example by costs, the desire to achieve or to retain competitive advantage, and not least by the different information using capabilities of donor and donee. The element in this complex process most often neglected which proves to be the crucial barrier is the different mindsets of the parties involved.[1] Because mindsets also characterize the relevant intellectual disciplines involved, for example economics, management studies and decision theory, this chapter is cast in terms of those disciplinary approaches and their literatures

Early recognition of the information revolution (see, e.g., Lamberton 1974; Machlup 1962), with its questioning about what kind of society it would shape, gave way to a heavy emphasis on ICT (information and communication technology), which only now seems to be challenged as the concept of the *social* is being re-examined (see, e.g., International Center for Advanced Studies). At the World Summit of the Information Society, the Secretary-General of the International Telecommunication Union said: 'Telephones will not feed the poor, and computers will not replace textbooks. But information and communication technologies can be used effectively *as part of the toolbox* for addressing global problems.' The UN Secretary-General noted that 'building the inclusive information society ... will require a multi-stakeholder approach' (United Nations and International Telecommunications Union 2003–5, italics added; see also Curtis 2004 for some probing of the rethinking and realignments taking place on the world stage). Although the heady rhetoric of the last decade or more has given way to this muted claim, such a multi-stakeholder approach raises major issues about information sharing and takes us back to earlier debates about information as a public good[2] and universal service in, for example telecommunications. Other developments, such as the continued growth and extension of intellectual property rights, cut across these paths, even as the data mountain grows and becomes more unequally distributed around the world (*The Economist Technology Quarterly* 2003). Nevertheless, there is widespread belief that information sharing is beneficial because it fosters collaboration, enables coordination, enhances capabilities and facilitates growth.

Information as oil

Some writers saw information as simply a lubricant. An early precursor of the information society with its primary and secondary information sectors (Crump 1934) explored the borderland between economics and business practice. Along with production, distribution and consumption, lubrication was seen as an essential stage of economic activity. This stage included all those not involved in extractive, productive or distributive work. 'Their function was to go around with the oil can, and to maintain the commercial machine in smooth operation . . . [e.g.] money, banking and finance . . . collection and publication of information . . . advertising experts . . . the journalist . . . the writer and author . . . [those] maintaining law and order and the government of the state' (Crump 1934, pp. 8–9).

We have left far behind the old notion of the business firm (or an administrative organization) being a *given* unit of coordinating capability but we are only now trying to cope with information as a structured quantity. This is necessary once we recognize that information is capital and that the structure of capital dictates many complementarities, sequences and lags. Add a time dimension and we are moving towards a historical, evolutionary process (Schumpeter 1953, pp. 631–2). Learning and unlearning are necessary; knowledge, that is, 'information of indefinite tenure' (Machlup and Mansfield 1983, p. 10), has to be managed and the task becomes even more intricate than is the case with physical resources. All this is done in a climate of uncertainty. The dominant decision theories have built upon ideas of probability, and empiricism has been directed to evaluating those probabilities.

Mindsets

This approach has been challenged. G.L.S. Shackle endeavoured to substitute a concept of possibility for probability (Shackle 1961). Instead of making sweeping assumptions about the decision-maker's information and optimizing capabilities, Shackle addressed the questions: can a person take all possible outcomes into account? Do people take them into account? A reviewer of Shackle's book wrote:

> After the initial shock to established conventions has been partly overcome, the suspicion begins to dawn that Professor Shackle's theory describes what *in fact* people do when they make a decision. Perhaps it is Professor Shackle who is the empiricist, and the frequency-theorists who are the metaphysical thinkers. (Dickinson 1963, p. 725)

Why is this important? The main reasons are that, first, it undermines the notion that people are insatiable information processors, ready and waiting to seize upon all the information to which they are granted access; and, second, it paves the way for us to consider mindsets, which are a major but sadly neglected barrier to information sharing. As an outgrowth of their experience as managers, consumers, researchers and politicians, and including their social relationships, people, individually or in groups, can become committed to mindsets that prove to be barriers to information sharing. At a high level of abstraction this has been recognized in several concepts:

- organizational obsolescence;
- lock-in;
- cognitive dissonance; and
- prejudices of education.

Arrow has argued that

> the combination of uncertainty, indivisibility, and capital intensity associated with information channels and their use imply (a) that the actual structure and behaviour of an organization may depend heavily on random events, in other words on history, and (b), the very pursuit of efficiency may lead to rigidity and unresponsiveness to further change. (Arrow 1974, p. 49)

Related reasoning has created concepts of lock-in and cognitive dissonance (see Akerlof 1984; Arthur 1989). Adam Smith appreciated the stultifying effects of the 'prejudices of education' (see Wightman and Bryce 1982, p. 21). And this wisdom was expressed by American comedian Will Rogers, who remarked that 'the trouble isn't what people don't know; it's what they do know that isn't so' (quoted by Boulding 1971, p. 21). These mindsets override tidy optimization calculations in a world where uncertainty waxes and wanes. This is not simply a restatement of bounded rationality – a point to be considered later in this chapter.

While we must emphasize that mindsets are only one barrier to effective information sharing, they are a major one and their neglect justifies further discussion and exploration. What are some of the other barriers? All information is costly: to create, assemble, transmit, receive, understand, use and store. These costs are not identified in most accounting practice, even by those who are willing to put values on intangible assets. Elaborate systems of intellectual property exist and are being extended in scope day by day. Information markets are inherently imperfect and suppression of information is likely an attractive competitive strategy – and one furthered through the structural characteristics of information.

Economists take time into account in some analyses but for the most part they take refuge in simplistic generalization, for example the distinction between the short run, where little or nothing can change, and the long run, where everything has changed. Actual learning and decision-making take place in clock time, where matching of capabilities and information in order to perceive and pursue opportunities may not be feasible, and in any case may not seem to be to the advantage of those making the decisions. These are not difficulties to be overcome through reliance on ICT. As Oettinger reminds us:

> Creative processing of substance to turn raw data into useful knowledge remains a monopoly of our flesh and blood minds . . . When it comes to thinking, IT still can't hack it. And . . . when it comes to thinking and acting collectively, we don't shine so brightly either. (Oettinger 2001, p. 12)

But before illustrating these Will Rogers-style mindsets, it might help if we look briefly at the long-term dynamics of economic growth and technological change. The neoclassical viewpoint makes the market central and the division of labour a consequence of exchange (Bortis 2001, p. 258; Smith 1976 (1776)). The standard reasoning is that the institutional structure, including Crump's lubrication, provides the framework for market activities. However, some parts of that structure are just as much actors on the economic stage as the buyers and sellers in markets. In particular, they can be the source and the upholders of major mindsets – and, of course, they can be major actors in market transactions. The mindsets can therefore be encumbered with vested interests and cultural trappings.

The information/knowledge economy, with its sprawling growth of information industries, is bringing a greater division of labour. In this process, the division of labour in information gathering 'is perhaps the most fundamental' (Arrow 1979, p. 310) because it underpins all other efficiency gains from specialization. Because of the limitations of markets in information, the organizations created to coordinate activities become larger, more complex and more costly. As a consequence of these changes, the problems of matching information flows with information use and hence the potential impacts of mindsets are magnified. It is here that one senses the hopes for the potential of a new breed of slave, the computer expert, who will be able to effect the matching that the new divisions of labour necessitate (see, e.g., Watts et al. 2002 on the searchability of social networks). Those entertaining such hopes should ponder carefully Oettinger's caution.

High hopes of many rest on machine capabilities. These dreams can be traced back to the development of so-called information theory that was developed for communications engineering.[3] The problem is that both size of organization and machine dependence may work with the characteristics of information to foster what Arrow called organizational obsolescence. One might well wonder whether the information revolution, with its over-emphasis on ICT, has managed to preserve a key role for that scarcest resource of all: curiosity (see Davies 1971). Neither successive waves of management fads nor the policy initiatives of governments in respect of education and innovation seem to have found the right balance. Specifically, more research on R&D collaboration is needed. While there are contrasting views on the way spillovers work and the extent to which they are socially advantageous (see Sena 2004), such research has to explore the very problems of mindsets discussed in this chapter.

Curiosity is the most valuable resource and must not be stifled by conformity. This is not palatable to those controlling decision processes, neither to managers nor politicians. Some recent developments are adding new pressures. The creation of the Department of Homeland Security in the USA made the DHS one of the major funding sources of R&D. This was achieved initially through transfers of existing programmes from Departments of Agriculture, Defense, Energy and Transportation. Bioterrorism R&D was scheduled to stay in the National Institutes of Health but with DHS having a priority-setting role (see Koizumi et al. 2003).

To illustrate the pervasiveness and importance of these entrenched ideas, some illustrations from major areas are provided, that is, science, economics, management and policy.

Robert Wright subjected three modern scientists to close scrutiny: Ed Fredkin (physicist/computer scientist), E.O. Wilson (biologist) and Kenneth Boulding (economist) (Wright 1988). While each was concerned in a fundamental way with information, Wright emphasized the mixture of inquiry and faith and 'the hazy line where scientific hypothesis passes over into fervent conviction'. Ann Moyal (2001) provides a fascinating account of the growth of Western knowledge of the platypus and the challenge the strange Australian creature was to the ideas of the scientific establishment in Europe – a mammal and at the same time laying eggs! As Macdonald explains:

> the platypus is the tool with which [Moyal] explores the rivalry and jealousy of scientific men, the can opener used to reveal the scientific worms. Names were to be made by more and more detailed classification of the denizens of the animal and plant kingdoms. The platypus defied classification and thus cast doubt on existing classification, and more fundamentally, on existing classification systems. Reputations were at stake, to be tested as much in philosophical and theological dispute as in scientific. (Macdonald 2003, p. 266)

Another revealing science story with rigidities and guessing games is that of the development of influenza vaccines, stimulated by the 1918–19 epidemic which killed more people than the guns and bayonets of World War I (Barry 2003).

Turning to economics, there is the role of the central analytical device, equilibrium, which reflects the wishes and efforts of those who saw themselves following in the physical scientist's footsteps. There is a joke around (see, e.g., Page 2003). Gather together 100 intelligent people and show them graphs of what has been going on: unemployment, interest rates, share prices, crime, election results, church attendance, TV viewing, rainfall and so on. Then ask them which of two words best describes the events portrayed: complex or equilibrium? Typically, 93 will pick complex. The other seven are economists.

Lighthearted as this may seem, it reflects deeply entrenched, centuries-old ideas about the economy and the way it functions. More specific illustrations can be offered. There are old-established notions of free trade and comparative advantage. Heavy emphasis was placed on natural resources and location and it has proved difficult to abandon these mindsets. Comparative advantage is still meaningful but it is to be found in new skills, new technology, quicker response times, and above all in changed education systems.

Subtle differences can prove to be very important. Carabelli and De Vecchi point to an underlying difference between Keynes and Hayek that has had profound influence on the broad mindsets shaping modern economic analysis and policy approaches (2001, p. 239). On their reading, for Keynes the cognitive horizon of the public sector is less limited than that of individuals or organizations. In contrast, Hayek's belief in spontaneous order led him to restrict public action 'to acts having particular, foreseeable or visible short-term effects'.

Changes in mindsets do not necessarily transmit between societies. In recent times, information economics developments have attracted attention worldwide but not so much so, for example, in Australia. A citation search of *The Economic Record*, the leading Australian economics journal, covering the decade leading up to the Nobel award to Joseph Stiglitz for his major contributions to information economics, revealed little interest. The search focused on the 111 sole-authored Stiglitz papers listed in his Nobel Lecture as given at Columbia University. Only five of those papers had been mentioned, each only once. One citation was by an American author; another was only listed in references but not mentioned in the text; and the other three were quite perfunctory mentions. Nowhere was there a hint that something big was stirring in the economics world.

Analysis and policy thinking are merged together by those contemplating longer-term trends. One of the most challenging statements comes from historian Carlo Cippolla in his introduction to *The Economic Decline of Empires*:

> While an empire is flourishing, its members show a strong inclination to delude themselves about its life-expectancy. History offers no examples of indestructible empires, yet most people are convinced that what happens to previous empires

cannot happen to their own. In so doing they just show a lack of imagination, a naïve incapacity to imagine new situations for which their tastes, inclinations and institutions will grow progressively inadequate. Once the decline starts, there are still optimistic people who stubbornly deny reality, but the number of those who realize what is happening is bound to enlarge progressively. Some then try to rationalize the events and to build theories around them. (1970, p. 15)

Why information systems fail

What bearing does all this have on management issues and their analysis? Information systems have many elements: environment, structure, history, cognitive abilities, politics and power, and technical processes. Some of the primary elements can be the interdependence amongst organizers, systems and stakeholders, and the tensions and trade-offs between the management of innovation and the management of support (see Sauer 1993). Sauer, *Why Information Systems Fail*, is an exception in the literature in that he is much concerned with process. As a reviewer of his book reasoned, 'The issue of how to incorporate uncertainty and chaos into our models is perhaps the most important current agenda items for sciences and humanities' (Dervin 1994, p. 270). It is a contention of this chapter that studying process and taking account of what is excluded by the mindsets is a step forward in what is a very big task.

Bounded rationality

Is this mindset approach just another name for bounded rationality? The answer is 'no'. Bounded rationality puts heavy emphasis on simple rules for search, stopping and decision. It allows for cultural systems of belief and claims to be inherently interdisciplinary:

The common denominator is that decisions need to be made with limited time, knowledge, and other resources, and in a world that is uncertain and changing. Thus, the framework of bounded rationality – the building blocks of heuristics; the notion of ecological rationality; the cultural acceleration of learning by social norms and imitation – may help to integrate fields that, so far, have been dissociated and did not access relevant knowledge outside their disciplines. (Gigerenzer and Selten 2001, p. 10)

As tends to happen, there is too little flow of thinking between the bounded rationality school and new work in information economics. The big issue is what happens when different views of the state of the world are used and viewing takes place from the vantage points of different mindsets in an evolutionary context where the path chosen determines the future events.

This is an old issue. Engels said he and Marx had grappled with 'all the interactions, the innumerable intersecting forces giving rise to the "historical event" '. He explained:

Marx and I are ourselves partly to blame for the fact that younger writers lay more stress on the economic side than is due to it. We had to emphasize this main principle in opposition to our adversaries, who denied it, and we had not always the time, the place or the opportunity to allow the other elements involved in the interaction to come into their rights. (Engels, quoted by Venable 1945, p. 31)

Where might this lead those who seek greater understanding of the role of information in society and, in particular, in knowledge management? Tucked away at the very end of John Laurent's *Evolutionary Economics and Human Nature*, there is a challenging essay by Jason Potts, who distinguishes two approaches to evolutionary economics (Potts 2003, p. 214). The first is that part of the current economics enterprise that 'deals with technological and institutional change, industrial dynamics and the statistical side of economic dynamics'. The second view is concerned with 'analysis of the growth-of-knowledge process'. In that mindsets have a central role in that process, they belong in this second mode of thought and are to be viewed as variously building blocks, direction signs, filters, and even as obstacles.

A thoroughgoing management analysis clearly has to rectify this omission by treating the organization and its processes. There would seem to be enough common ground for management studies/science to collaborate with new economics initiatives – specifically a merging of information economics and evolutionary economics. The focus needs to be on the individual agent, the organization and their histories, with first priority given to how information is used rather than who has access to what information.

Notes
1. Mindset: 'a habitual or characteristic mental attitude that determines how you will interpret and respond to situations'.
2. A public good is characterized by non-rivalrous consumption (the marginal costs of providing it to an additional person are zero) and non-excludability (the costs of excluding an individual from consumption are prohibitively high).
3. See Machlup and Mansfield (1983), p. 56, where this extension to human communication was described as 'a methodological disaster'. See also Mirowski (2002) reviewed by Mongiovi (2004).

References
Akerlof, G.A. 1984. *An Economic Theorist's Book of Tales*. Cambridge: Cambridge University Press.
Arrow, K.J. 1974. *The Limits of Organization*. New York: Norton.
Arrow, K.J. 1979. 'The economics of information', in *The Computer Age: A Twenty-Year View*, edited by M. L. Dertouzos and J. Moses. Cambridge, MA: MIT Press.
Arthur, W.B. 1989. 'Competing technologies, increasing returns, and lock-in by historical events'. *Economic Journal* **99**:116–31.
Barry, J.M. 2003. *The Great Influenza: The Epic Story of the Deadliest Plague in History*. New York: Viking.
Bortis, H. 2001. 'Notes on institutions, political economy and economics'. Pp. 249–64 in *Knowledge, Social Institutions and the Division of Labour*, edited by P.L. Porta, R. Scazzieri and A. Skinner. Cheltenham, UK and Northampton, MA, USA: Edward Elgar.

Boulding, K.E. 1971. 'The economics of knowledge and the knowledge of economics'. Pp. 21–36 in *Economics of Information and Knowledge*, edited by D.M. Lamberton. Harmondsworth, UK: Penguin Books. First published 1966 in *American Economic Review*, **56**:1–13.

Carabelli, A. and N. De Vecchi. 2001. 'Individuals, public institutions and knowledge: Hayek and Keynes'. Pp. 229–48 in *Knowledge, Social Institutions and the Division of Labour*, edited by P.L. Porta, R. Scazzieri and A. Skinner. Cheltenham, UK and Northampton, MA, USA: Edward Elgar.

Cippolla, C.M. (ed.). 1970. *The Economic Decline of Empires*. London: Methuen.

Crump, N. 1934. *A First Book of Economics*. London: Macmillan.

Curtis, T. 2004. 'Two views from the summit'. *Prometheus* **22**:259–65.

Davies, D. 1971. 'A scarce resource called curiosity'. Pp. 315–22 in *Economics of Information and Knowledge*, edited by D.M. Lamberton. Harmondsworth, UK: Penguin Books. First published 1967 in *The Listener*, 4 May:557–9.

Dervin, B. 1994. 'Review of Sauer, *Why Information Systems Fail*'. *Prometheus* **12**:268–70.

Dickinson, H.D. 1963. 'Review of Shackle, *Decision, Order and Time in Human Affairs*'. *Economic Journal* **292**:723–5.

Gigerenzer, G. and R. Selten (eds). 2001. *Bounded Rationality: The Adaptive Toolbox*. Cambridge, MA: MIT Press.

International Center for Advanced Studies. 'The authority of knowledge in a global age'. New York: New York University. http://www.nyu.edu/gsas/dept/icas/authority.htm.

Koizumi, K., J. Carney, D. Cooper and A. Teich. 2003. 'R&D in the United States Department of Homeland Security'. *Prometheus* **21**:347–53.

Lamberton, D.M. (ed.). 1974. 'The information revolution'. *The Annals of the American Academy of Political and Social Science* **412**:1–162.

Macdonald, S. 2003. 'Review of Moyal, *Platypus: The Extraordinary Story of How a Curious Creature Baffled the World*'. *Prometheus* **21**:265–6.

Machlup, F. 1962. *The Production and Distribution of Knowledge in the United States*. Princeton, NJ: Princeton University Press.

Machlup, F. and U. Mansfield (eds). 1983. *The Study of Information: Interdisciplinary Messages*. New York: John Wiley & Sons.

Mirowski, P. 2002. *Machine Dreams: Economics Becomes a Cyborg Science*. Cambridge: Cambridge University Press.

Mongiovi, G. 2004. 'Review of Mirowski, *Machine Dreams: Economics Becomes a Cyborg Science*'. *Economic Journal* **114**:347–50.

Moyal, A. 2001. *Platypus: The Extraordinary Story of How a Curious Creature Baffled the World*. Crows Nest, NSW: Allen & Unwin.

Oettinger, A.G. 2001. 'Knowledge innovations: The endless adventure'. *Bulletin of the American Society for Information Science and Technology* December/January:9–15.

Page, S.E. 2003. 'Review of David Colander, *The Complexity Vision and the Teaching of Economics*'. *Journal of Economic Behavior & Organization* **52**:601–3.

Potts, J. 2003. 'Towards an evolutionary theory of *Homo economicus*: The concept of universal nomadism'. Pp. 195–216 in *Evolutionary Economics and Human Nature*, edited by J. Laurent. Cheltenham, UK and Northampton, MA, USA: Edward Elgar.

Sauer, C. 1993. *Why Information Systems Fail: A Case Study Approach*. Henley-on-Thames, UK: Alfred Waller.

Schumpeter, J.A. 1953. *History of Economic Analysis*. New York: Oxford University Press.

Sena, V. 2004. 'The return of the Prince of Denmark: A survey on recent developments in the economics of innovation'. *Economic Journal* **114**:F312–F332.

Shackle, G.L.S. 1961. *Decision, Order and Time in Human Affairs*. London: Cambridge University Press.

Smith, A. 1976 (1776). *An Inquiry into the Nature and Causes of the Wealth of Nations*. Edited by R.H. Campbell and A.S. Skinner. Oxford: Clarendon Press.

The Economist Technology Quarterly. 2003. 'Measuring the data mountain.' *The Economist Technology Quarterly* December **6**:3.

United Nations and International Telecommunications Union. 2003–2005. *World Summit on the Information Society*: Available at http://www.itu.int/wsis/.

Venable, V. 1945. *Human Nature: The Marxian View*. New York: A.A. Knopf.
Watts, D.J., P.S. Dodds and M.E. Newman. 2002. 'Identity and search in social networks'. *Science* **296**:1302–5.
Wightman, W.P.D. and J.C. Bryce (eds). 1982. *Adam Smith Essays on Philosophical Subjects*: General Introduction. Indianapolis, IN: Liberty Classics.
Wright, R. 1988. *Three Scientists and Their Gods*. New York: Times Books.

13 Collaboration and the network form of organization in the new knowledge-based economy

Thomas Mandeville

The relatively recent quantum jump in the degree of cooperative activity between firms has been widely noted and commented upon in the economics and management literatures. Indeed, collaboration, the network form of organization, business alliances, industry–government collaboration, and inter-government cooperation have become commonplace in the knowledge-based economy (KBE). This chapter addresses a basic question of what is driving this phenomenon – why has this burst of collaborative activity and associated network of organizational forms in business and elsewhere become, as we shall see shortly, a defining feature of the new KBE era? Part of the answer, as will be shown, lies with widespread use of the Internet.

Our frameworks for analysis of networks and collaboration, namely the economics of information and evolutionary complexity theory, the latter including the concept of self-organization, differ considerably from most earlier work. Previously, Williamson's (1981) transactions-cost-based analysis of choices between markets and hierarchies has provided a basic framework for analysis of the economics of collaboration (Earl 2002). Here we also draw on that framework in places, but not greatly. In essence this chapter extends the transactions-cost-based analysis of collaboration by utilizing these two additional frameworks.

What's new about the new economy?

A working definition of the new economy, for our purposes here, is: a communications revolution based mainly on business use of the Internet. By about the early 1990s, business and private individuals across the OECD started to adopt the Internet as a commercial and recreational medium; thus this time frame represents an approximate starting point for the new economy era. Below we examine some of the central features of the new KBE in order to illustrate aspects of its fundamental and revolutionary change in the nature of business and economic activity.

Knowledge intensive

US Federal Reserve Chairman Alan Greenspan has called the new economy the 'weightless economy'. This reflects the growing importance of intangible knowledge activities and assets in the new KBE. Knowledge, which includes intangible assets such as intellectual property, human and social capital, technology (defined as knowledge applied to doing things in information economics), brand names, customer databases, core competencies and business relationships, is becoming the key resource in the new economy, just as land, buildings and physical capital were the key resources in the old economy. As Rooney et al. (2003) have put it, a KBE is an economy in which knowledge is the most important productive factor. Of course, knowledge does not render physical assets redundant; instead it builds on them.

Thus the KBE idea is part of the story of what is really new about the new economy. More precisely, though, the new economy is best considered a new evolutionary phase of the knowledge economy that information sector research (e.g. OECD 1981) showed was already beginning to emerge in advanced economies by the 1950s. The catalyst for this new phase was the widespread business and community take-up of the Internet, beginning in the 1990s (Hearn et al. 1998).

In any complex system, the level of complexity increases as knowledge (novelty) increases and the connectivity between system components (agents) increases. Thus further defining features of the new KBE are increased complexity (Hearn et al. 1998) and associated turbulence (Hearn et al. 2003). As complexity increases, so does uncertainty. This factor may also underpin organizational change in the new economy. According to Kranton and Minehart (2000), firms integrate when there is low uncertainty, but disintegrate to form networks when uncertaintly increases. If this is so, then inter-organizational networks should be the dominant organizational form in the highly complex, turbulent and uncertain new economy. We'll return to this point as this chapter unfolds.

Convergence

The new economy, or the new digital era, as Hearn et al. (1998) have termed it, emerged in part from the convergence of computers and telecommunications. Business IT usage shifted from the disconnectedness or stand-alone functions of the earlier era to the connectedness of networked personal computers linked to the Internet. Pervasive connectedness is: changing how companies deal with suppliers, customers and rival firms; changing how consumers buy things; revolutionizing firms' management and organizational structure; creating a whole set of new or transformed firms, as well as collaborative alliances between firms to capture Internet-based gains in efficiency and to create new Internet-based products and services. For example, convergence has enabled new opportunities for the e-delivery of services such as: e-commerce generally, e-banking and share trading in the finance sector, e-shopping in the retail sector, telemedicine and e-health in the health sector, flexible delivery in the education sector, and the e-provision of government services.

Clearly the Internet revolution would seem to rank alongside major events in economic history like the Industrial Revolution as a major transformer of economic and social life. Today, the Internet has become the workhorse of the modern economy (Barabasi 2002).

Convergence, or the breaking down of boundaries between formerly separate activities, is also occurring more generally, such as between industries, between work and leisure with 24/7 schedules, between industry and government, and between business and the community. For organizations and business, stakeholders that were once distinct now overlap, such as the roles of shareholders and employees (Hearn et al. 2003). As Potts (2001) explains, the boundaries between knowledge domains do not last long.

Services sector innovation based on ICTs
A radical change in the KBE era has been the rise of service industries as the main source of innovation in the economy. This innovation is not directly based on R&D but on investments in, and adoption of, new information and communication technologies (ICT) platforms and adapting these to produce new products and services or improved business processes. Before the business adoption of the Internet, there was limited capacity for productivity improvements in the services sector because a service was consumed almost immediately after it was produced. But the Internet has revolutionized the services sector and enabled it to become the major source of innovation in the economy by creating a space/time gap between the production and consumption of services (Freeman and Soete 1997). Previously services had tended to be consumed at the same time and in the same place as they were produced. This provides an opportunity to innovate as well as more readily enabling trade in services via the e-delivery of services on domestic and international markets. Much services sector innovation also involves collaboration between firms.

Rise of organizational networks and collaboration
This key feature of the new KBE is the main topic of this chapter. It could be hypothesized that a new form of capitalism, alliance capitalism, is emerging (Dunning 1995). Business collaboration and networking have become a key segment of corporate strategy. Indeed, the KBE is evolving into a networked economy (Kirman 1997) and networked society (Castells 1996) consisting of numerous ties and interdependences between people, organizations and

nations. In one view of the economy as a complex network, the nodes are companies, and the links are the various economic and financial ties connecting them (Barabasi 2002). These developments also have implications for the nature of the economic agent itself (Rohen 2003). The classical, conventional concept of the lone, self-interested economic actor with perfect information making rational decisions to maximize benefit for itself may have passed its use-by date. Increasingly, economic actors or agents are networks and alliances of firms collaborating to be more efficient, to innovate, or to access wider markets.

Networks may be defined as simply a linkage of points or nodes such that movement may occur from any point to any other point: networks as nodes connected by links (Barabasi 2002). This definition covers both pyhsical networks, such as the railway system, road network, or telecommunications networks, and organizational and social networks. In this chapter we are not so directly interested in physical networks or even in network typology – the description of possible communication within a network. Instead we are interested in explaining the increasing prevalence of the network form of industrial organization. These can be interorganizational networks, an organization adopting a network structure, or loose coalitions of individuals.

The network form of organization may be contrasted to hierarchies. Most organizations, be they firms, government agencies, unions, churches or universities, are still primarily hierarchical, with the traditional command-and-control, pyramid or triangular structure. But network organizational forms are not hierarchies. Instead, in a definition adapted from Dorothy Leonard-Barton and Everett Rogers (1981), with some sprinklings of Ken-ichi Imai (Kaneko and Imai 1987), we like to think of networks as: unstructured organizations comprising clusters of communicating agents sharing common interests, values or goals. Whereas hierarchies tend to work by coercion, networks primarily work by cohesion; hence the importance of shared values, goals, visions and trust in networks. Networks are more flexible than hierarchies, mainly for informational reasons, and thus may be more suited to the turbulent KBE.

Organizational networks may also be contrasted to other forms of resource allocation such as markets and hierarchies (firms) by drawing on the transactions cost framework. Richardson (1972) has made the triple distinction between firms, cooperation and market modes of resource coordination. Contrasting features of these three modes of organization – hierarchies, networks and markets – have been summarized by Kaneko and Imai (1987). They hypothesize that, on a continuum, networks fall somewhere between markets and hierarchies. Thus in terms of degree of flexibility, markets are high, hierarchies are low, and networks are medium. In terms of formal connections among participants, markets have none, hierarchies have strong connections, while networks have weak formal connections between members. In terms of communication media, markets rely on price signals, hierarchies have an implicit code system, while networks rely on context. For conflict resolution, markets rely on price mediation, hierarchies rely on authority or coercion, while networks utilize context or cohesion.

Organizational networks have become pervasive in the new KBE in at least five distinct areas, four of which explicitly involve business.

1. Interorganizational networks in business/collaboration between firms Examples include strategic alliances, geographic clusters of firms, joint ventures and industry associations. These arrangements can also include inter-locking directorships, partial shareholdings, and the process of trust building via regular trading relationships (Richardson 1972). Detailed studies by scholars such as Eric von Hippel (1982), Stuart Macdonald (1986), Everett Rogers (1982) and others have long been pointing out that various interorganizational network-like relationships between firms in highly innovative industries have been evolving since the 1960s. These include informal personal networks, supplier–user relations, user–user relations and supplier–supplier relations.

In the new economy the services sector, especially innovative services based on ICT platforms, has become a key source of innovation. Since the beginning of the 1990s, announcements of various strategic alliances or joint ventures in rapidly growing knowledge industries have become commonplace. A good example are the business-to-business e-commerce procurement alliances, some of which are mega-ventures including the world's biggest retailers, car manufacturers, miners, and food and drink groups. Thus novel collaborative business practices, previously only found in places like Silicon Valley, have become widespread in this KBE era. In the new, network economy, business collaboration is becoming necessary for competitiveness in most industries.

Kay (1997) points to a distinction between individual and multiple relationships between firms, the latter including strategic alliances and other network-like relationships involving multiple firms in multiple relationships. While there has been considerable interest in the economics literature in terms of modelling individual business level cooperative behaviour, such as between two firms, multiple relationships have been neglected. Kay notes that the latter is not something that the neoclassical perspective is well disposed to recognize, let alone analyse. Hence the need for new economic perspectives in the new economy, such as those utilized here.

2. The firm as a network Kaneko and Imai (1987) were among the first observers to point out that the modern business organization is becoming a combination of the interpenetration of the pure network form of organization with hierarchical elements. In other words, rather than a pure hierarchy or network, the firm is evolving into a hybrid, blending traditional hierarchical practices with network forms. Examples of the latter include quality circles; multiskilled work teams; virtual teams; intrapreneurship; the growing importance of shared visions, values and corporate culture; the rise of stakeholder capitalism and the triple bottom line. More fundamentally, perhaps, is the relatively recent emergence of flatter, lattice-like, web-like, or matrix-like forms of horizontally connected organizational structure, with lots of cross-links between the nodes, gradually replacing the triangle-shaped, vertically integrated, hierarchical chain of command. Overall, in terms of its internal organizational structure, the twenty-first-century firm is tending to look more like a network than a traditional hierarchy, but is still a hybrid, blending the two organizational forms.

3. *Citizen movements* Before the new KBE, clubs and societies were among the main social network forms of organization. However, these community forms of networks have also become more pervasive in the new economy. Citizen movements, such as Greenpeace, Amnesty International and the recent anti-globalization movement, are network-like organizations facilitated by the Internet that now wield enormous power and influence in advanced countries.

Terrorist organizations adopting the network form of loosely linked cells have become a major global force in the twenty-first century. One military response has been to adopt asymmetric warfare approaches utilizing network-like units within the military. In this sense, even the military, the ultimate hierarchy, is beginning to look less hierarchical in the new KBE.

4. *Goals and visions for nations, regions, industries and organizations*
Japanese futurist Yonegi Masuda (1980) hypothesized that, in the knowledge economy, society relies less on the invisible hand, or price system, to allocate resources, and more on vision/goal-setting firms and governments. Ambitious visions or goals can work via a process of self-organization to create networks for their fulfilment (Hearn et al. 1998). We'll return to this point later in the chapter.

5. *Converging collaborations* Breaking down of boundaries between formerly separate activities is a pervasive form of new economy convergence. This is reflected in growing numbers of collaborative arrangements across formerly separate segments of society or between formerly separate sovereign governments. Examples include business collaborations involving participants from different industries, collaborative arrangements between business and government such as public–private partnerships (PPPs), community–business partnerships, and the various forms of intergovernmental cooperation.

Informational considerations

Informational considerations are hypothesized here as a basic force driving the trend towards network organizational structures and collaborative arrangements in the KBE. Let's begin with some general observations on how information, and its growing pervasiveness in the economy, may be driving business towards the network form of organization. Such informational considerations may underlie this sea-change in the nature of business organization.

An information economics perspective on innovation (Mandeville 1998) suggests that as well as being a process of knowledge creation, innovation also involves the flow of technological information between participants during that creation process. With innovation, particularly in the services sector, becoming relatively more important in the new KBE, the growing importance of networks in organizational structure can be partly attributed to cost savings and competitive advantages gained from better information flows within and between firms.

Compared to hierarchies, networks are much more effective informational resource allocation mechanisms. Structurally, networks facilitate rapid information transfer by providing horizontal links cutting through former institutional and organizational boundaries to put people in direct contact with one another. Networks also help create new information as well as transmit it. New information often emerges spontaneously through interaction of network members. Also, as each person in a network receives information, it is synthesized and new ideas may spring forth. Networks thus share new ideas and help create them, and are therefore an ideal form of learning organization for acquiring timely, relevant, effective knowledge.

As already observed, the increasing complexity and turbulence of the new economy has also brought increased business uncertaintly. This uncertainty itself may in turn help explain the rise of the network form of organization in business, according to Kranton and Minehart (2000). From another perspective, as Arrow (1974) points out, information is the negative of uncertainty. Thus, as uncertainty increases, an organizational form that facilitates the creation and flow of information might be expected to flourish.

Finally, in terms of networks versus hierarchies, given that information is very different from ordinary goods, the organizational form most conducive to goods production – hierarchies – may not be as appropriate for information production. As the economy becomes more information-intensive, new organizational forms for business seem to be required.

The unique features of information, including its economic characteristics, illustrate the ways in which information and knowledge differ from ordinary goods and services. As the economy and society become more information-intensive, this factor alone will influence all activity. In order to aid in the understanding of some basic rationales for the recent upsurge in collaboration, some of the features of information originally indicated by Arrow (Arrow

1974, 1979), Lamberton (1986), Mandeville (1996), and others will be spelled out below. We will focus on those features with direct implications for networking and collaboration, and briefly indicate these aspects.

1. Information is accumulative

Information is expandable: it can grow and evolve. Information grows with use and enhances its social value through dissemination. The value of information can be amplified indefinitely and synergistically by the addition of new information to existing information. The source of synergy may be explained by Masuda's (1980) process of interactive joint production and shared utilization of information to produce a cumulative effect. Interfirm collaboration can extend the benefit of this process beyond the confines of the single firm. Thus a technology gradually evolves via the collective social action of many firms. Some of this collective social action involves explicit collaboration; some does not. An example of this process is the evolution of personal computers (Jackson et al. 2002). Such innovations rarely emerge full blown from a self-contained, single firm.

2. Information endowments among agents are asymmetrical

Information asymmetries are an important economic reality. In a market context one of the agents to a contract usually has a deeper knowledge than the other. For example, in a technology licensing agreement, sellers have more knowledge about the technology than buyers. Differences in information endowments can relate to possession of information, access to information and capacity to use information. Networks help ease these asymmetries for network members.

3. Acquiring information, or learning, takes time

There is a limit to the rate at which decision-makers can absorb information. This is partly due to inbuilt psychological characteristics, but it is also affected by barriers and efficiencies in the way organizations are structured. Networks appear to be more effective learning organizations than hierarchies.

4. Public-good aspects of information

Fundamentally, information has many of the features of a public good. That is, information, along with other public goods such as street lighting, roads, bridges, police and fire protection, national defence and environmental quality, exhibits features of non-exclusivity, non-rivalry in consumption and indivisibility. With regard to public-good resource allocation issues for information, Lamberton et al. (1982) declared that the limitations on information as a commodity dictate resort to organization as an alternative to markets. The KBE has extended this to the network form of organization.

5. *The cost of producing information is independent of the scale on which it is used*

The formula for a new pharmaceutical product has a given cost though it may be used by one person or a billion persons. A new way of putting more transistors into an integrated circuit may potentially be used by one semiconductor firm or by most semiconductor firms. Implications of this economic feature of information include advantages in sharing, that is, distributing information as widely as possible. This suggests advantages to organizations that cooperate to share information. Increasing returns to the use of information suggest competitive advantages to large organizations or collaborative groups, and provide strong incentives for, and considerable mutual advantage from, the joint sharing of information.

Overall it can be seen that information-based goods and services have fundamentally different characteristics in comparison with ordinary goods and services. A key implication, already mentioned, is that different forms of organizational structure, such as the network forms, may be more suited to dealing with these new commodities.

Finally, tacit knowledge and its growing importance in the innovative process should also encourage networking. In essence firms need easy access to other firms' tacit knowledge in order to successfully innovate, especially in relation to opportunities emerging from convergence.

ICTs, networking and collaboration

In the KBE, ICTs are encouraging the rise of network-like organizational forms and collaboration in business in a number of ways. The Internet is making it easier for firms to form relationships with suppliers, customers and rival firms locally, nationally or globally. With just-in-time technology and other factors, supply chain management and logistics developments are creating chains of business relationships spanning producers through transport and processing to retail distribution.

Castells (1996) suggests that the importance of the Internet is its creation of the technological basis for the organizational form of this new era – the network. While networks have long been important in the informal social context, in the more formal contexts of production and power, they were previously surpassed by the efficiency of centralized hierarchies in business and government. But the Internet has shifted the ground and brought about an organizational sea-change by creating a platform for sharing information that allows flexible networks to coordinate their activities around shared goals. As already observed, this phenomenon was partly foreshadowed many years ago by Masuda (1980), who pointed out that in the information society goals replace the market as the central coordinating mechanism in society.

Converging IT, telecommunications and media technologies are also bringing about industry convergence, that is, the bringing together of formerly separate industries. This, in turn, is leading to increased collaboration, as well as merger and acquisition (M&A) activities, between firms in these formerly separate industries to take advantage of the new opportunities. Firms require access to each other's technology, customer bases and capabilities.

Another important way in which ICTs are encouraging and facilitating the network form of organization is through their effects on transactions costs. The stand-alone IT of the 1960–80 period helped firms reduce their internal coordination costs, and thus favoured the firm over the market as a mechanism for resource allocation. However, from the 1990s, when business computers became connected to the Internet, ICTs have also been helping to reduce market transactions costs. One result has been increased outsourcing of activities once performed in house by large firms. Large firms are also becoming more 'virtual', itself an organizational form more closely resembling a network.

An interesting hypothesis that can be suggested here is that the network form of organization may be capturing both the efficiencies of reduced internal costs of coordination that IT has traditionally bestowed on organizations, plus reduced transactions costs that have come with the Internet. Organizational networks may thus enjoy some fundamental economic efficiency advantages over both hierarchical firms and markets, thereby transcending them both. If so, the Internet has provided the connective technological platform that has paved the way for the rise of the network form of business organization.

Self-organization can help shed light on the upsurge of collaboration in the new KBE. Self-organization is a process of spontaneous communication between parts of a system, bringing it to new patterns of coordination and concerted common behaviour. It creates new relationships among existing parts of the system to bring about a new pattern of organization. In business, this means the spontaneous formation of interest groups and coalitions around specific issues, communication about these issues, and collaboration and the formation of consensus and commitment to a response to these issues (Hearn et al. 1998). Thus self-organization itself is a form of collaboration involving the formation of network-like organizational structures between agents. So if the preconditions for self-organization improve, for example by the vastly improved communication linkages between economic agents that the Internet inexpensively brings, then, *ceteris paribus*, we should expect to see an upswing in this type of collaboration in the economy.

Management implications

The KBE and the concomitant pervasive emergence of network organizational forms such as business collaborative arrangements and the hybrid network–hierarchical structure for the firm itself, brings far-reaching implications for management. In essence the key questions become: how do you manage a network, and when is it essential to collaborate? Insights from evolutionary complexity theory suggest two respective principles.

1. Facilitate self-organization

Organizational networks are best understood as complex systems and, as such, are largely outside the direct control of economic agents, including managers (Hearn et al. 2003). In addition, knowledge is socially constructed (Rooney et al. 2003). It is about ideas and meanings that have evolved through social interaction and communication. These very acts are outside the control paradigm and, in addition, new knowledge, particularly in the form of innovations, introduces additional uncertainty and complexity. It follows that order cannot be imposed on a system.

So what should managers do? Basically the approach should be process-oriented focusing on system design (Byrant and Wells 1998). This includes recognizing that self-organization is a vital process of complex systems. Thus the appropriate role for managers is to help shape and create contexts in which appropriate forms of self-organization can occur so that desirable patterns can emerge. These contexts can be both within the firm and/or include other firms. Managers help shape the parameters that define the appropriate context, while allowing the details to unfold. This includes active involvement in the processes of setting visions or goals that are achieved by self-organizing processes. It also includes ensuring smooth and effective linkages between agents in the network. Encouraging or facilitating improved ICT infrastructure is an obvious step here. Less obvious is the necessity to encourage the development of appropriate soft infrastructure to enable the leveraging of benefits from the improved hardware. Trust, a form of social capital (Putnam 1993), is a key lubricant of networks. Collaborative arrangements need time to build trust.

2. Innovation, collaboration and M&A

Competitive pressures, both to innovate and to be able to respond to the demands of a constantly changing marketplace, imply that firms need to gain access to the complementary capabilities of other firms. Today's new product and service innovations are typically an amalgamation of several distinct and complex technical capabilities drawn from multiple industries. Thus it is not surprising that firms collaborate, especially in the early phases of the innovation cycle and that 40 per cent of breakthrough technologies are now developed by alliances (Duysters 1996). Given the critical importance of person-to-person transfer of tacit knowledge, collaborative networks help facilitate the knowledge creation process.

The strategic options for access to the complementary capabilities of other firms include arm's-length transactions in markets, collaborations or M&A. High transactions costs tend to preclude the transfer of tacit knowledge via the market mechanism (Mandeville 1996). The evolutionary complexity perspective sheds some light on the collaborative versus M&A options in the context of potential innovative capabilities and performance. This perspective emphasizes the new – new products, ideas, or firms that arise endogenously and then exert adaptive effects on other elements of the system. For complex systems this transformative innovation (Hearn et al. 1998) occurs best when the system has an abundance of microdiversity and variety. M&A reduces variety and thus may lead to a less competitive outcome than the collaborative option. Also the M&A option adds to the inertia of the firm while the turbulent environment of the new KBE demands flexibility.

References

Arrow, Kenneth. 1974. *The Limits of Organisation*. New York: Norton.
Arrow, Kenneth. 1979. 'The economics of information'. Pp. 306–17 in *The Computer Age: A Twenty Year View*, edited by M.L. Dertouzos and J. Moses. Cambridge, MA: MIT Press.
Barabasi, Albert-Laszlo. 2002. *Linked: The New Science of Networks*. Cambridge, MA: Perseus.
Byrant, K. and A. Wells (eds). 1998. *A New Economic Paradigm? Innovation-Based Evolutionary Systems: Discussions of Science and Innovation 4*. Canberra, ACT: Department of Industry, Science and Resources.
Castells, Manuel. 1996. *The Rise of Network Society*. Malden, MA: Blackwell.
Dunning, John H. 1995. 'Reappraising the eclectic paradigm in an age of alliance capitalism'. *Journal of International Business Studies* **29**:45–66.
Duysters, Geert. 1996. *The Dynamics of Technical Innovation: The Evolution and Development of Information Technology*. Cheltenham, UK and Brookfield, VT, USA: Edward Elgar.
Earl, Peter. 2002. *Information, Opportunism and Economic Coordination*. Cheltenham, UK and Northampton, MA, USA: Edward Elgar.
Freeman, Chris and Luc Soete. 1997. *The Economics of Industrial Innovation*. London: Pinter.
Hearn, Greg, Tom Mandeville and David Anthony. 1998. *The Communication Superhighway: Social and Economic Change in the Digital Age*. St Leonards: Allen and Unwin.
Hearn, Greg, David Rooney and Tom Mandeville. 2003. 'Phenomenological turbulence and innovation in knowledge systems'. *Prometheus* **21**:221–45.
Jackson, Mark, Tom Mandeville and Jason Potts. 2002. 'The evolution of the digital computation industry'. *Prometheus* **20**:323–36.
Kaneko, Ikuyo and Ken-ichi Imai. 1987. 'A network view of the firm'. *1st Hitotsubashi–Stanford Conference, Tokyo, March 29–April 1*.
Kay, Neil. 1997. *Pattern in Corporate Evolution*. Oxford: Oxford University Press.
Kirman, Alan. 1997. 'The economy as an evolving network'. *Journal of Evolutionary Economics* **7**:339–53.
Kranton, R.E. and D.F. Minehart. 2000. 'Networks versus vertical integration'. *Rand Journal of Economics* **31**:570–601.
Lamberton, Donald M. 1986. 'Information, economic analysis and public policy'. *Prometheus* **4**:174–86.
Lamberton, Donald M., Stuart Macdonald and Tom Mandeville. 1982. 'Productivity and technological change'. *Canberra Bulletin of Public Administration* **9**:23–30.
Leonard-Barton, Dorothy and Everett M. Rogers. 1981. *Horizontal Diffusion of Innovations: An Alternative Paradigm to the Classical Diffusion Model (Working Paper No. 1214)*. Cambridge, MA: Amherst: Sloan School of Management, MIT.
Macdonald, Stuart. 1986. 'Headhunting in high technology'. *Technovation* **4**:233–45.

Mandeville, Tom. 1996. *Understanding Novelty: Information, Technological Change, and the Patent System.* Norwood, NJ: Ablex.

Mandeville, Tom. 1998. 'An information economics perspective on innovation'. *International Journal of Social Economics* **24**:357–64.

Masuda, Yonegi. 1980. *The Information Society as Post-Industrial Society.* Tokyo: Institute for the Information Society.

Organisation for Economic Co-operation and Development (OECD). 1981. *Information Activities, Electronic and Telecommunications.* Paris: Organisation for Economic Co-operation and Development.

Potts, Jason. 2001. 'Knowledge and markets'. *Journal of Evolutionary Economics* **11**:413–31.

Putnam, Robert. 1993. *Making Democracy Work: Civic Traditions in Modern Italy.* Princeton, NJ: Princeton University Press.

Richardson, G.B. 1972. 'The organisation of industry'. *Economic Journal* **82**:883–96.

Rogers, Everett M. 1982. 'Information exchange and technological innovation'. Pp. 105–23 in *The Transfer and Utilisation of Technological Knowledge,* edited by D. Sahel. Lexington, MD: Lexington Books.

Rohen, Ella. 2003. *Identity, System Boundaries and Economic Agency.* Brisbane, QLD: School of Economics, The University of Queensland.

Rooney, David, Greg Hearn, Tom Mandeville and Richard Joseph. 2003. *Public Policy in Knowledge-Based Economies: Foundations and Frameworks.* Cheltenham, UK and Northampton, MA, USA: Edward Elgar.

von Hippel, Eric. 1982. 'Appropriability of innovation benefit as a predictor of a source of innovation'. *Research Policy* **11**:95–115.

Williamson, Oliver. 1981. 'The modern corporation: Origins, evolution, attributes'. *Journal of Economic Literature* **14**:1537–68.

14 Exploring the information space: a strategic perspective on information systems[1]

Max Boisot

1. Introduction

We can think about information systems (IS) in two ways. First, we can think of them normatively, that is, as organizational supports. They then tend to be defined in terms of organizational tasks and draw on a functionalist perspective characteristic of the engineer. This perspective, focused on technology, the computer, and well-defined input/output relationships, systems, customers, users and so on, has been the traditional one. It is the practitioner perspective. A second, alternative approach is to take an information system as a description of the way that information flows in and around different types of system. In this second approach the body has an information system – hormonal and/or nervous – and so does a city or an economic organization (Checkland and Howell 1998). This second perspective on information systems often operates at a higher level of abstraction than the first (Clarke 2001). Here, we adopt features of the second perspective to modify certain features of the first. We look at how the information flows in and around systems affect the nature of the information processing tasks that make up the IS function within organizations and the kinds of knowledge that can be generated from these.

Whether they are viewed normatively or descriptively, as has been the case with many other information-related intellectual disciplines, thinking on information systems has tended to conflate data, information and knowledge (Boisot and Canals 2004; McRae 1971). Strictly speaking, the raw material of any information system is data, that is, discernible differences between physical states of the world that get registered as such for some agent or agency. Data are always borne on some physical substrate, whether it be stone, paper, or pure electromagnetic waves. The challenge then becomes to extract information – recurrent regularities that can give rise to expectations – from the data through some definable operation. A computer program, for example, is typically designed to do just that and, if it is successful, the program's output data will then be more information-rich than its input data. But information has to be converted into knowledge if it is to have any effect at all. Like the pragmatists and the evolutionary epistemologists, we are inclined to associate knowledge more with a disposition to action than with the disinterested pursuit of truth; that is, we are more aligned with Pierce, James and Campbell than with Plato (Campbell 1974; James 2000; Pierce 1868). Although these two views of knowledge are not actually incompatible (Boisot and MacMillan 2004), the focus here is thus on the value of knowledge to an action system such as a living organism rather than on abstract truth conditions that need to be met in order to achieve a given level of certainty.

Intelligent agents convert data into information and thence into knowledge through a two-step filtering process that is guided by the possession of prior knowledge. In the first step, noise is filtered out from incoming signals by the agent's sensory apparatus and the latter gets registered as data by different senses. In the second, non-information-bearing data gets filtered out by the agent's conceptual apparatus, so that only information-bearing data are left to impact their action system and thus get metabolized into knowledge. Figure 14.1 is an adaptation of Newell, Shaw and Simon's model of information processing that illustrates the process (McRae 1971). As indicated in the figure, the perceptual and conceptual filters are activated by the agent's prior knowledge and experience.

Agents have finite brains and intelligence. They often encounter more data and information than they can process or store. How do they deal with the resulting overload without blowing a fuse? They have recourse to external processing and storage devices – that is, artefacts of various kinds – to overcome the problem. Stewart and Cohen call this use of external props extelligence, Gregory calls it 'potential intelligence', and Andy Clark calls it

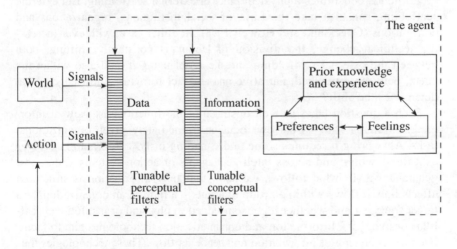

Figure 14.1   The agent and the world

'external scaffolding' (Clark 1997; Gregory 1981; Stewart and Cohen 1997). Networks of such artefacts, in effect, make up embryonic information systems that have the agent at their centre. Take, for example, a kitchen. The layout of a kitchen articulates a kind of 'script' with much information embedded in the physical form of the kitchen layout, in the equipment, and in the utensils to be found there (Schank and Abelson 1997). A well-designed kitchen communicates relevant information to its user and minimizes his or her search time: cutlery is likely to be found in drawers; pots and pans in the deeper cupboards; the hot water tap above the kitchen sink, and so on. There is one code for dealing with cookers, another one for dealing with refrigerators and a third for dishwashing machines. These codes are often set out in the manufacturers' instruction booklet. Note, however, that such information only registers with someone having prior familiarity with kitchens and thus having some knowledge of the design codes that are being used.

In sum, a kitchen can be considered an information system whose major components are embedded and distributed in artefacts. It was not explicitly designed as an information system, however, so that here we are using the term descriptively rather than normatively. The path-dependent design conventions that shaped the evolution of the kitchen as an information system incrementally 'decided' what information to embed in the external scaffolding – that is, the kitchen and equipment design – and what prior knowledge to require of the kitchen user. A process of natural selection operating on numberless small design decisions established the best division of labour between the different elements of the information system – those that are external and those that are internal to the user.

A kitchen constitutes a physical piece of external scaffolding. But external scaffolding can also take the form of social institutions, organizations and conventions (Checkland and Howell 1998). In either case, with ever-increasing technical change, the division of labour is constantly shifting, both between the external scaffolding and the agent using it, and also within the agent, between embodied, narrative and abstract forms of knowledge. What determines the shift?

Such a question takes us well upstream of the functionalist view of information systems with its narrow focus on immediately given organizational tasks. Answering it requires some understanding of how information evolves as it flows within and across intelligent agents or action systems at the most general level. In what follows we show that how information is structured affects how it flows within a group of agents – a family, an organization, or a larger society – and whether it gets embedded in physical or institutional scaffolds or in agents. Information and communication technologies aim to facilitate the structuring of information and hence its flow. These technologies thus materially modify the information environment within which an agent, or a group of agents, acts and interacts. We shall argue that the agenda for the future development of information systems needs to broaden out to encompass a wider conception of its mission, one that relates an agent's, or a group of agents' learning needs to the nature of the information environment that respectively confront them. In the next section, Section 2, we present a conceptual framework, the information space or 'I-Space', which will help us address the issue. We then apply the framework to the question in Section 3 and offer a brief conclusion in Section 4.

2. The I-Space

The I-Space builds on the proposition that the structuring of data facilitates its diffusion (Boisot 1995, 1998). The structuring of data, the process through which information is extracted from data, is achieved through acts of codification and abstraction.

Codification draws distinctions and articulates boundaries between states or around objects. Codification is a precondition for the creation of objects and categories. It will be harder to codify fuzzy boundaries or objects than those that are well formed; the amount of data processing required to do so will be greater.

Abstraction treats things that are different as if they were the same (Dretske 1981). It either associates or – if they are recurrent – correlates the objects or categories discerned or created by codification and allows one object or category to stand in for another, thus reducing the number of these needed for navigating in particular situations. As with codification, the amount of data processing required to perform an abstraction will be greater when objects or categories are only weakly correlated with each other than when they are strongly so.

Codification and abstraction are matters of degree. We can represent them as the two dimensions of an epistemological space, or 'E-Space', as indicated in Figure 14.2 (Boisot 1995). The vertical axis measures the ease with which the data of experience can be codified. At the top of the scale little data processing will be required to distinguish between objects and categories, whereas at the bottom of the scale a large amount – and possibly an infinite amount – of data processing will be required. We can apply the same data processing measures to the act of abstracting. Towards the left of the abstraction scale, we encounter the world of concrete experience, one in which a large number of potential categories present themselves. Here a large amount of data processing – and, again, possibly an infinite amount – will be required to establish a correlation between categories. Towards the right, we are dealing with relatively few categories so that less data processing will be called for.[2]

The E-Space of Figure 14.2 allows us to identify three types of knowledge

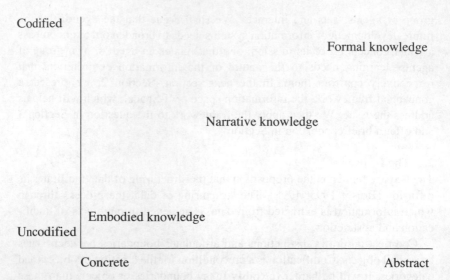

Figure 14.2   The E-Space

as a function of their degree of codification and abstraction: embodied knowledge, narrative knowledge and formal knowledge. Embodied knowledge is rooted in behaviours and experiences that are largely tacit in nature (Polanyi 1958) – playing tennis, riding a bicycle and so on. Although this kind of knowledge can be referred to, most of it cannot be articulated or placed into categories. Narrative knowledge can be thought of as an emanation of embodied knowledge. It covers those aspects of experience and behaviour that can be articulated into identifiable – though not always distinct – categories and hence, to some extent, shared with others. Whether because of a lack of coherence or a lack of recurrence, however, narrative knowledge is typically not systematic enough to allow for its formalization. Formal knowledge, in turn, arises out of narrative knowledge and is the product of either logical or recurrent associations that have been both established between categories and stabilized enough for correlations to emerge. These facilitate abstraction.

Intelligent agents with finite capacities will be concerned to economize on their scarce data processing resources (Deacon 1997). Moves towards greater codification and abstraction help them to achieve data processing economies. Codification and abstraction work in tandem and, over time, selectively shift limited quantities of embodied knowledge into a narrative mode. They subsequently allow a subset of such narrative to get formalized and thereby to acquire an abstract representation. The moves towards ever-higher levels of codification and abstraction can also be made to work in reverse. Abstract representations – universals, and so on – find their way back into narrative

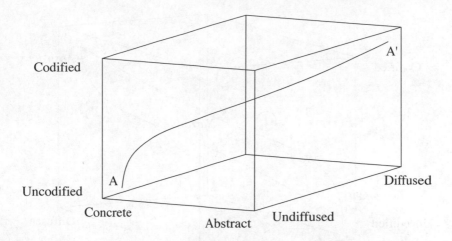

Figure 14.3   The I-Space

discourse and help to shape it. Narratives leavened by abstractions in turn give coherence and meaning to tacit experiences that would otherwise remain uninterpreted and perhaps even undetected. This process has been well described by Deacon in his book *The Symbolic Species* (Deacon 1997).

Note that abstract representations will travel further and faster within a population than 'situated' narratives whose particular meanings are anchored to time and place. They can only do so, however, by sacrificing the richness and nuance of context. Note also, by contrast, that embodied knowledge hardly travels at all, for the most part being confined to the context in which it arises. Thus whereas embodied and narrative knowledge gives rise to highly personalized and rich interactions between agents that relate to each other primarily face to face, abstract knowledge gives rise to an impersonal order in which interacting agents may never actually meet.

We illustrate the relationship between codification, abstraction and diffusion by means of a curve as indicated in Figure 14.3. The figure – labelled an information space or 'I-Space' – is just an E-Space augmented by a diffusion dimension that allows us to locate a given population of intelligent agents along a scale. Towards the origin only a small percentage of agents have access to a given item of information or knowledge. At the end of the scale, close to 100 per cent of the agent population will have access to a given item of information. What the curve tells us is that more agents can be reached in a given time period by codified and abstract knowledge than by uncodified and concrete knowledge. The diffusion curve constitutes half of a *social learning cycle* or *SLC* in which abstract representations are first extracted from narrative and embodied forms of knowledge and then work their way back into new

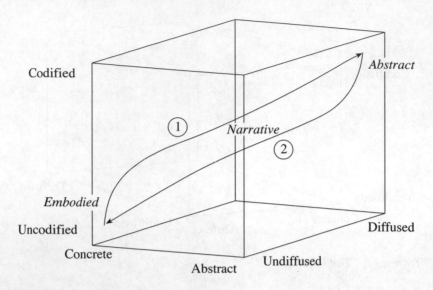

Figure 14.4   The social learning cycle

narratives which, in turn, help to shape tacit and embodied forms of knowledge that remains situated and undiffused. An SLC thus generates and subsequently integrates embodied, narrative and abstract forms of knowledge as

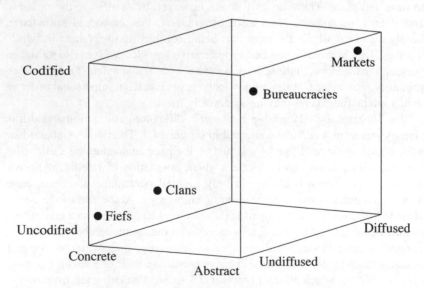

Figure 14.5   Institutional structures in the I-Space

Table 14.1   Characteristics of institutional structures

Bureaucracies	Markets
• Information diffusion limited and under central control	• Information widely diffused, no control
• Relationships impersonal and hierarchical	• Relationships impersonal and competitive
• Submission to superordinate goals	• No superordinate goals – each one for himself
• Hierarchical coordination	• Horizontal coordination through self-regulation
• No necessity to share values and beliefs	• No necessity to share values and beliefs

Fiefs	Clans
• Information diffusion limited by lack of codification to face-to-face relationship	• Information diffused but still limited by lack of codification to face-to-face relationships
• Relationships personal and hierarchical (feudal/charismatic)	• Relationships personal but non-hierarchical
• Submission to superordinate goals	• Goals are shared through a process of negotiation
• Hierarchical coordination	• Horizontal coordination through negotiation
• Necessity to share values and beliefs	• Necessity to share values and beliefs

indicated in Figure 14.4. Many different shapes of SLC are possible within an I-Space, signalling either the presence of blockages or catalysts to the flow of knowledge.

What might these blockages or catalysts look like? Information and knowledge move through the space either through the cognitive efforts of individual agents or through a process of social exchange or transactions between agents. Both activities are either facilitated or hindered by the presence of institutional structures designed to lower data processing and transmission costs in a given region of the information environment captured by the I-Space. We identify four of these – markets, bureaucracies, clans and fiefs – in Figure 14.5 and briefly summarize some of the information and cultural characteristics of these transactional structures in Table 14.1.

How might the emergence of new information and communication technologies (ICTs) affect the flows of information and knowledge in the I-Space?

Could they affect the evolution of institutional structures? The new ICTs increase data processing and data transmission capacity of agents located along the diffusion dimension. At whatever level of codification or abstraction an agent operates, he or she can reach more agents with more data in a given time period than hitherto. We can think of this as a shift to the right of the diffusion curve of Figure 14.3 in the I-Space. Whether these data are information-bearing, whether they then get internalized by receiving agents and then converted into knowledge is another matter, one that concerns the behaviour of agents with respect to the SLC as a whole.

Figure 14.6 identifies two quite different effects of a rightward shift in the diffusion curve. The first is indicated by the arrow labelled A, that is parallel to the diffusion axis; it is the one that we can intuitively grasp since all it is telling us is that for a given level of codification and abstraction, a larger population can be reached with the new ICTs than with the old ones. The second effect, indicated by the downward-pointing arrow, B, is less intuitively obvious. Arrow B tells us that for whatever size of population one is trying to reach with a message, this can now be done at a lower level of codification and abstraction than hitherto.

The explanation of this second effect is that messages have a much wider bandwidth available for their transmission than hitherto so that much of the

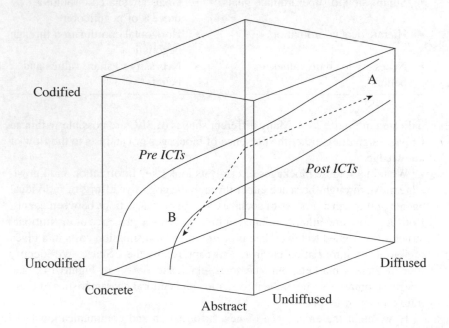

Figure 14.6   The impact of ICTs in the I-Space

richness and context of face-to-face communication might now be restored between parties even if these are transacting at some distance from each other. Pictures, videoconferencing and Internet telephony will, by degrees, either replace or complement written text and numbers. In this way, the new ICTs will infuse a degree of personalization to distant communications[3] by restoring to these the embodied and narrative components that were lost in the move towards greater codification and abstraction.

3. The I-Space applied to IS

We are now in a position to address the question that we posed at the end of Section 1, namely, what is an appropriate division of labour between information systems that are internal to agents and those that are external to them? The question builds on a more basic one: what is an appropriate division of labour between embodied, narrative and abstract forms of knowledge given the shape and flow dynamics of a given SLC and the constraints imposed by a given configuration of institutional structures in the I-Space? How might such a division of labour evolve over time and what should be IS's contribution to that evolution?

IS has its origins in the disciplines of accounting, management science and decision sciences (Anthony 1964; Galbraith 1973; Scott Morton 1991), all disciplines that exhibit a strong bias in favour of codification and abstraction. The bias was to confine many practitioners' conception of the IS mission to a very specific region of the I-Space, one that favoured an impersonal abstract order as well as technological solutions to the problem of generating and regulating information flows. Practitioners of the new discipline of knowledge management today inherit this bias – and find themselves limited by it.[4] Other disciplines – ergonomics, human–computer interaction and so on – focus on the region of the I-Space which gives rise to the kind of embodied knowledge that makes for good kitchen design. The intermediate region, the one inhabited by narrative knowledge, has also been attracting attention of late.[5]

No one discipline covers the SLC as a whole and none of the ones just cited talk much to each other. The result is a lack of integration across the different stages of the SLC. One discipline that is well placed to address the challenge of integration turns out to be IS, but to do so effectively, IS would have to come to terms with and manage *the whole* of the information environment as defined by the I-Space and not just the limited region it currently occupies. There is thus no need to choose between a technological and a humanist view of IS, as has been suggested by certain authors such as Clarke (2001), with each view located in a different region of the I-Space. The need is to recognize which view is appropriate to what circumstances and then to reconcile them. Such a contingency approach to IS would entail shifting the emphasis from an almost exclusive concern with static efficiency – a traditional focus of the discipline as it came to be constituted – to accommodate more dynamic issues of effectiveness and of learning. The new ICTs are now making this increasingly possible.

An effective IS system would aim to develop an integrated approach to managing the metamorphosis of data from embodied to narrative forms and thence to abstract forms of representation – and back again. In other words, it would take the management and development of an organization's or a community's learning processes – that is, its SLCs – as its prime mission. Such an approach would require the answers to three questions:

- What kind of knowledge are we dealing with and where is it located in the I-Space? How does it blend embodied, narrative and abstract forms of representation? These questions could be answered by mapping an organization's or a community's critical knowledge assets in the I-Space (Boisot 1998).
- What phase of the learning cycle are we dealing with? The question could be answered by mapping an organization's or a community's critical SLCs in the I-Space.
- What institutional and cultural processes are acting to support or impede their operation? The question could be answered by mapping an organization's or a community's institutional and cultural structures in the I-Space.

IS's core competence would then consist of integrating and then interpreting in a cost-effective way the maps so created. If successful, the exercise would result in the adaptation of ICTs to an organization's or a community's learning processes instead of having things the other way round as so often happens today.

4.   Conclusion

In this chapter, we have presented a conceptual model, the I-Space, that would help us to study information and knowledge flows as well as the different information environments that such flows give rise to. Our analysis turns out to constitute something of a challenge to the IS community.

By asking questions that typically lie upstream of conventional IS concerns, this chapter has argued for a significant broadening of the IS agenda to incorporate forms of knowledge – embodied, narrative – that it has hitherto tended to underplay or ignore, and to pay more attention to how, with learning, one form of knowledge evolves into the other. The proposed approach does not invalidate the discipline's current practices; nor does it render its current skills base obsolete. But by going beyond what might today be covered by the term 'information system', it suggests a rethink of the IS mission.

The argument in favour of a rethink is becoming compelling. With the development of ambient computing, for example – the distribution of computational capacity to everyday artefacts – ICTs are bursting their banks, spilling out of the boxes to which they have hitherto been confined by computing preconceptions, and spreading out to occupy every nook and cranny of our environment. As a result, much embodied and narrative knowledge is now slowly becoming 'computable'. If IS remains locked in its computing era paradigms, then it will miss the opportunities that are currently opening up all around it to redefine itself.

Notes

1. The author wishes to thank Agusti Canals and Ramon O'Callaghan for their useful comments and suggestions on earlier drafts of this chapter.
2. We are here applying Chaitin's concept of algorithmic information complexity (AIC) to the measurement of both codification and abstraction (Chaitin 1974).
3. Note that in contrast to Evans and Wurster, we do not argue that the trade-off between 'richness' and 'reach' has been abolished; it has merely been attenuated (Evans and Wurster 2000).
4. The emphasis here is on practitioners, most of whom come out of the IT stable. Academics in knowledge management such as Nonaka and Takeuchi have a more balanced view of knowledge managment (Nonaka and Takeuchi 1995).
5. The newly created Cynefin Centre for the Study of Organizational Complexity, for example, takes a focus on narrative knowledge as its point of departure.

References

Anthony, R. 1964. *Management Accounting: Text and Cases*. Homewood, IL: Richard D. Irwin Inc.

Boisot, M. 1995. *Information Space: A Framework for Learning in Organizations, Institutions and Cultures*. London: Routledge.

Boisot, M. 1998. *Knowledge Assets: Securing Competitive Advantage in the Information Economy*. Oxford: Oxford University Press.

Boisot, M. and A. Canals. 2004. 'Data, information, and knowledge: Have we got it right?' *Journal of Evolutionary Economics* 14:1–25.

Boisot, M. and I. MacMillan. 2004. 'Crossing epistemological boundaries: Managerial and entrepreneurial approaches to knowledge'. *Long Range Planning* 37: 505–24.

Campbell, D. 1974. 'Evolutionary epistemology', in *The Philosophy of Karl Popper*, edited by P.A. Schlipp. La Salle, IL: Open Court.

Chaitin, G.J. 1974. 'Information-theoretic computational complexity'. *IEEE Transactions on Information Theory* 20:10–15.

Checkland, P. and S. Howell. 1998. *Information, Systems, and Information Sytems*. Chichester, UK: John Wiley & Sons.

Clark, A. 1997. *Being There: Putting Brain, Body, and World Together Again*. Cambridge, MA: MIT Press.

Clarke, S. 2001. *Information Systems Strategic Management: An Integrated Approach*. London: Routledge.

Deacon, T.W. 1997. *The Symbolic Species*. New York: Norton and Co.

Dretske, F. 1981. *Knowledge and the Flow of Information*. Cambridge, MA: MIT Press.

Evans, P. and T. Wurster. 2000. *Blown to Bits*. Boston, MA: Harvard Business School Press.

Galbraith, J. 1973. *Designing Complex Organizations*. Reading, MA: Addison-Wesley.

Gregory, R.L. 1981. *Mind in Science: A History of Explanations in Psychology and Physics*. Harmondsworth, UK: Penguin Books.

James, W. 2000. *Pragmatism (1907)*. New York: Penguin Books.

McRae, T.W. 1971. *Management Information Systems*. Harmondsworth, UK: Penguin Books.
Nonaka, Ikujiro and Hirotake Takeuchi. 1995. *The Knowledge Creating Company: How Japanese Companies Create the Dynamics of Innovation*. New York: Oxford University Press.
Pierce, C.S. 1868. 'Questions concerning certain faculties claimed for man'. *Journal of Speculative Philosophy* **2**:103–14.
Polanyi, M. 1958. *Personal Knowledge: Towards a Post-Critical Philosophy*. London: Routledge and Kegan Paul.
Schank, R. and R. Abelson. 1997. 'Scripts, plans and knowledge', in *Thinking: Readings in Cognitive Science*, edited by P. Johnson-Laird and P. Wason. Cambridge: Cambridge University Press.
Scott Morton, M. 1991. *The Corporation of the 1990s: Information Technology and Organizational Transformation*. New York: Oxford University Press.
Stewart, I. and J. Cohen. 1997. *Figments of Reality: The Evolution of the Curious Mind*. Cambridge: Cambridge University Press.

15 'Tacit knowledge' versus 'explicit knowledge' approaches to knowledge management practice

Ron Sanchez

Introduction

Managers concerned with implementing knowledge management in their organizations today face a number of challenges in developing sound methods for this still emerging area of management practice (Sanchez 2001). Both the growing literature on knowledge management and the advice offered by various knowledge management consultants, however, seem to advocate forms of knowledge management practice that often appear incomplete, inconsistent and even contradictory. This chapter suggests that the current lack of coherence in the diverse recommendations for knowledge management practice results from the fact that the development of both theory and practice in this emerging field is being driven by two fundamentally different approaches to identifying and managing knowledge in organizations. These two approaches are characterized here as the 'tacit knowledge' approach and the 'explicit knowledge' approach.

This chapter first clarifies how these two fundamental approaches differ in both their philosophical premises and derived recommendations for practice, and it summarizes the main strengths and weaknesses of each of the two approaches in practice. We then suggest that sound knowledge management practice requires a creative synthesis of the two approaches that enables the strengths of one approach to offset the inherent limitations of the other approach, and vice versa.

Tacit knowledge versus explicit knowledge approaches

Even a casual review of the many articles and consulting recommendations on knowledge management practice today soon reveals a plethora of recommended processes and techniques. Unfortunately – especially for the many managers looking to researchers and consultants for insights to guide development of sound knowledge management practices – many of these recommendations seem unconnected to each other, and in the worst cases many seem to be quite at odds with each other. Close analysis of these recommendations, however, usually reveals that the many ideas for practice being advanced today can be grouped into one of two fundamentally different views of knowledge itself and of the resulting possibilities for managing knowledge in organizations. These two views are characterized here as the 'tacit knowledge' approach and the 'explicit knowledge' approach. Let us consider the basic premises and the possibilities for knowledge management practice implied by each of these two views (see Table 15.1 for a summary of the differences in the two approaches).

The tacit knowledge approach
The salient characteristic of the tacit knowledge approach is the basic belief that knowledge is essentially personal in nature and is therefore difficult to extract from the heads of individuals. In effect, this approach to knowledge management assumes, often implicitly, that the knowledge in and available to an organization will largely consist of tacit knowledge that remains in the heads of individuals in the organization.[1]

Working from the premise that knowledge is inherently personal and will largely remain tacit, the tacit knowledge approach typically holds that the dissemination of knowledge in an organization can best be accomplished by the transfer of people as 'knowledge carriers' from one part of an organization to another. Further, this view holds that learning in an organization occurs when individuals come together under circumstances that encourage them to share their ideas and (it is hoped) to develop new insights together that will lead to the creation of new knowledge.

Table 15.1   Basic beliefs in tacit versus explicit knowledge management approaches

Tacit knowledge approach	Explicit knowledge approach
Knowledge is personal in nature and very difficult to extract from people.	Knowledge can be articulated and codified to create explicit knowledge assets.
Knowledge must be transferred by moving people within or between organizations.	Knowledge can be disseminated (using information technologies) in the form of documents, drawings, best practices, etc.
Learning must be encouraged by bringing the right people together under the right circumstances.	Learning can be designed to remedy knowledge deficiencies through structured, managed, scientific processes.

Recommendations for knowledge management practice proffered by researchers and consultants working within the tacit knowledge approach naturally tend to focus on managing people as individual carriers of knowledge. To make wider use of the tacit knowledge of individuals, managers are urged to identify the knowledge possessed by various individuals in an organization and then to arrange the kinds of interactions between knowledgeable individuals that will help the organization perform its current tasks, transfer knowledge from one part of the organization to another, and/or create new knowledge that may be useful to the organization. Let us consider some examples of current practice in each of these activities that are typical of the tacit knowledge approach.

Most managers of organizations today do not know what specific kinds of knowledge the individuals in their organization know. This common state of affairs is reflected in the lament usually attributed to executives of Hewlett-Packard in the 1980s: 'If we only knew what we know, we could conquer the world.' As firms become larger, more knowledge-intensive, and more globally dispersed, the need for their managers to 'know what we know' is becoming acute. Thus a common initiative within the tacit knowledge approach is usually some effort to improve understanding of who knows about what in an organization – an effort that is sometimes described as an effort to create 'know-who' forms of knowledge.[2] An example of such an effort is the creation within Philips, the global electronics company, of a 'yellow pages' listing experts with different kinds of knowledge within Philips' many business units. Today on the Philips intranet one can type in the key words for a specific knowledge domain – say, for example, knowledge about the design of optical pickup units for CD/DVD players and recorders – and the yellow pages will retrieve a listing of the people within Philips worldwide who have stated that they have such knowledge. Contact information is also provided for each person listed, so that anyone in Philips who wants to know more about that kind of knowledge can get in touch with listed individuals.

An example of the tacit knowledge approach to transferring knowledge within a global organization is provided by Toyota. When Toyota wants to transfer knowledge of its production system to new employees in a new assembly factory, such as the factory recently opened in Valenciennes, France, it typically selects a core group of two to three hundred new employees and sends them for several months' training and work on the assembly line in one of Toyota's existing factories. After several months of studying the production system and working alongside experienced Toyota assembly-line workers, the new workers are sent back to the new factory site. These repatriated workers are accompanied by one or two hundred long-term, highly experienced Toyota workers, who will then work alongside all the new employees in the new factory to assure that knowledge of Toyota's finely tuned production process is fully implanted in the new factory.

Toyota's use of Quality Circles also provides an example of the tacit knowledge approach to creating new knowledge. At the end of each work week, groups of Toyota production workers spend one to two hours analysing the performance of their part of the production system to identify actual or potential problems in quality or productivity. Each group proposes 'counter-measures' to correct identified problems, and discusses the results of counter-measures taken during the week to address problems identified the week before. Through personal interactions in such Quality Circle group settings, Toyota employees share their ideas for improvement, devise steps to test new ideas for improvement, and assess the results of their tests.

This knowledge management practice, which is repeated weekly as an integral part of the Toyota production system, progressively identifies, eliminates and even prevents errors. As improvements developed by Quality Circles are accumulated over many years, Toyota's production system has become one of the highest-quality production processes in the world (Spear and Bowen 1999).

The explicit knowledge approach
In contrast to the views held by the tacit knowledge approach, the explicit knowledge approach holds that knowledge is something that can be explained by individuals – even though some effort and even some forms of assistance may sometimes be required to help individuals articulate what they know. As a result, the explicit knowledge approach assumes that the useful knowledge of individuals in an organization can be articulated and made explicit.

Working from this premise, the explicit knowledge approach also believes that formal organizational processes can be used to help individuals articulate the knowledge they have to create knowledge assets. This approach also holds that explicit knowledge assets can then be disseminated within an organization through documents, drawings, standard operating procedures, manuals of best practice, and the like. Information systems are usually seen as playing a central role in facilitating the dissemination of explicit knowledge assets over company intranets or between organizations via the Internet.

Usually accompanying the views that knowledge can be made explicit and managed explicitly is the belief that new knowledge can be created through a structured, managed, scientific learning process. Experiments and other forms of structured learning processes can be designed to remedy important knowledge deficiencies, or market transactions or strategic partnering may be used to obtain specific forms of needed knowledge or to improve an organization's existing knowledge assets.

The recommendations for knowledge management practice usually proposed by researchers and consultants working within the explicit knowledge approach focus on initiating and sustaining organizational processes for generating, articulating, categorizing and systematically leveraging explicit knowledge assets. Some examples of knowledge management practice in this mode help to illustrate this approach.

In the 1990s, Motorola was the global leader in the market for pagers. To maintain this leadership position, Motorola introduced new generations of pager designs every 12–15 months. Each new pager generation was designed to offer more advanced features and options for customization than the preceding generation.[3] In addition, a new factory with higher-speed, more flexible assembly lines was designed and built to produce each new generation of pager. To sustain this high rate of product and process development, Motorola formed teams of product and factory designers to design each new generation of pager and factory. At the beginning of their project, each new team of designers received a manual of design methods and techniques from the team that had developed the previous generation of pager and factory. The new team would then have three deliverables at the end of their project: (1) an improved and more configurable next-generation pager design, (2) the design of a more efficient and flexible assembly line for the factory that would produce the new pager, and (3) an improved design manual that incorporated the design knowledge provided to the team in the manual it received – plus the new and improved design methods that the team had developed to meet the product and production goals for its project. This manual would then be passed on to the next design team given the task of developing the next generation of pager and its factory. In this way, Motorola sought to make explicit and capture the knowledge developed by its engineers during each project and to systematically leverage that knowledge in launching the work of the next project team.

In addition to its tacit knowledge management practice of moving new employees around to transfer knowledge of its production system, Toyota also follows a highly disciplined explicit knowledge management practice of documenting the tasks that each team of workers and each individual worker is asked to perform on its assembly lines. These documents provide a detailed description of how each task is to be performed, how long each task should take, the sequence of steps to be followed in performing each task, and the steps to be taken by each worker in checking his or her own work (Spear and Bowen 1999). When improvements are suggested by solving problems on the assembly line as they occur or in the weekly Quality Circle meetings of Toyota's teams of assembly-line workers, those suggestions are evaluated by Toyota's production engineers and then formally incorporated in revised task description documents.

In addition to developing well-defined and documented process descriptions for routine, repetitive production tasks, some organizations have also created explicit knowledge management approaches to support more creative tasks such as developing new products. In the Chrysler unit of DaimlerChrysler Corporation, for example, several 'platform teams' of 300–600 development engineers have responsibility for creating the next-generation platforms[4] on which Chrysler's future automobiles will be based. Each platform team is free to actively explore and evaluate alternative design solutions for the many different technical aspects of their vehicle platform. However, each platform team is also required to place the design solution it has selected for each aspect of their vehicle platform in a 'Book of Knowledge' on Chrysler's intranet. This catalogue of developed design solutions is then made available to all platform teams to consult in their development processes, so that good design solutions developed by one platform team can also be located and used by other platform teams.

Other firms have taken this explicit knowledge management approach to managing knowledge in product development processes even further. For example, GE Fanuc Automation, one of the world's leading industrial automation firms, develops design methodologies that are applied in the design of new kinds of components for their factory automation systems. In effect, instead of leaving it up to each engineer in the firm to devise a design solution for each new component needed, GE Fanuc's engineers work together to create detailed design methodologies for each type of component the firm uses. These design methodologies are then encoded in software and computerized so that the design of new component variations can be automated. Desired performance parameters for each new component variation are entered into the automated design program, and GE Fanuc's computer system automatically generates a design solution for the component. In this way, GE Fanuc tries to make explicit and capture the design knowledge of its engineers and then to systematically re-use that knowledge by automating most new component design tasks.

Advantages and disadvantages of tacit versus explicit knowledge approaches

Like most alternative approaches to managing, each of the two knowledge management approaches we have discussed has advantages and disadvantages, briefly summarized below, and in Table 15.2.

Advantages and disadvantages of the tacit knowledge approach
One of the main advantages of the tacit knowledge approach is that it is a relatively easy and inexpensive way to begin managing knowledge. The essential first step is relatively simple – identify what each individual in the organization believes is the specific kind of knowledge he or she possesses. Managers

Table 15.2   Advantages and disadvantages of tacit versus explicit knowledge management approach

Tacit knowledge approach	Explicit knowledge approach
Advantages:	**Advantages:**
Relatively easy and inexpensive to begin.	Articulated knowledge (explicit knowledge assets) may be moved instantaneously anytime anywhere by information technologies.
Employees may respond well to recognition of the (claimed) knowledge.	
	Codified knowledge may be pro-actively disseminated to people who can use specific forms of knowledge.
Likely to create interest in further knowledge management processes.	
Important knowledge kept in tacit form may be less likely to 'leak' to competitors.	Knowledge that has been made explicit can be discussed, debated and improved.
	Making knowledge explicit makes it possible to discover knowledge deficiencies in the organization.
Disadvantages:	**Disadvantages:**
Individuals may not have the knowledge they claim to have.	Considerable time and effort may be required to help people articulate their knowledge.
Knowledge profiles of individuals need frequent updating.	
	Employment relationship with key knowledge workers may have to be redefined to motivate knowledge articulation.
Ability to transfer knowledge constrained to moving people, which is costly and limits the reach and speed of knowledge dissemination within the organization.	
	Expert committees must be formed to evaluate explicit knowledge assets.
An organization may lose key knowledge if key people leave.	Application of explicit knowledge throughout an organization must be assured by adoption of best practices.

can then use this knowledge to assign individuals to key tasks or to compose teams with appropriate sets of knowledge to carry out a project, to improve performance in current processes, or to try to create new knowledge in the organization. As Philips did with its intranet-based 'yellow pages,' managers may also elect to create an open database listing the knowledge claimed by individuals in the organization to facilitate knowledge sharing between individuals.

A tacit knowledge approach may also lead to improvements in employee satisfaction and motivation when an organization 'officially' recognizes and makes visible in the organization the kinds of knowledge that individual workers claim to have. In addition, the tacit knowledge approach is likely to avoid some of the practical and motivational difficulties that may be encountered in trying to secure the cooperation of individuals in making their knowledge explicit (discussed below).

A further advantage often claimed for tacit knowledge management approaches derives from the view that making knowledge explicit increases the risk that knowledge will be 'leaked' from an organization, so that leaving knowledge in tacit form also helps to protect a firm's proprietary knowledge from diffusing to competing organizations. (The potential disadvantages of leaving knowledge in tacit form are summarized below.)

Although relatively easy to begin, the tacit knowledge approach also has some important long-term limitations and disadvantages. One is that individuals in an organization may claim to have knowledge that they do not actually have or may claim to be more knowledgeable than they really are (Stein and Ridderstråle 2001). The knowledge that various individuals have is likely to evolve over time and may require frequent updating to correctly communicate the type of knowledge each individual in the organization claims to have now. In addition, if knowledge only remains tacit in the heads of individuals in an organization, then the only way to move knowledge within the organization is to move people. Moving people is often costly and time-consuming and may be resisted by individuals who fear disruptions to their careers or family life. Even when knowledgeable individuals are willing to be moved, an individual can only be in one place at a time and can only work so many hours per day and days per week, thereby limiting the reach and the speed of the organization in transferring an individual's knowledge. Moreover, sometimes transferred individuals may not be accepted by other groups in the organization or may otherwise fail to establish good rapport with other individuals, and the desired knowledge transfer may not take place or may occur only partially.

Most seriously, leaving knowledge tacit in the heads of key individuals creates a risk that the organization may lose that knowledge if any of those individuals becomes incapacitated, leaves the organization, or – in the worst case – is recruited by competitors.[5]

Advantages and disadvantages of the explicit knowledge approach

In general, the advantages and disadvantages of the explicit knowledge approach constitute a 'mirror image' of the advantages and disadvantages of the tacit knowledge approach. Whereas the tacit knowledge approach is relatively easy to start and use, but has important limitations in the benefits it can bring, the explicit knowledge approach is much more challenging to start, but offers greater potential benefits in the long term. Let us first consider the long-term advantages of the explicit knowledge management approach, and then the challenges that have to be overcome to start and sustain this approach in an organization.

Perhaps the main advantage of the explicit knowledge approach is that once an individual articulates his or her knowledge in a document, drawing, process description, or other form of explicit knowledge asset, it should be possible through use of information systems to quickly disseminate that knowledge throughout an organization or indeed anywhere in the world. In effect, converting tacit knowledge into explicit knowledge creates an asset that is available 24/7 and is free from the limitations of time and space that constrain the dissemination of tacit knowledge by moving individuals.

Moreover, knowledge that has been made explicit within an organization can often be more carefully codified and more effectively leveraged than tacit knowledge assets. To codify some forms of knowledge is to categorize and order the knowledge so that important interrelationships between different kinds of knowledge within the firm can be identified. For example, forms of knowledge that are related by sharing a similar theoretical or practical knowledge base can be identified, as can forms of (complementary) knowledge that are interrelated by being used together in an organization's processes. Once the various forms of explicit knowledge in an organization are codified in this way, knowledge created in one part of an organization can be proactively leveraged through information systems to people and groups elsewhere in the organization that can benefit from having that knowledge.

Moreover, by disseminating some instance of explicit knowledge to other individuals who have expertise in that knowledge domain, the explicit knowledge can be discussed, debated, tested further and improved, thereby stimulating important 'incremental' forms of organizational learning processes. Such processes also help to identify which individuals in the organization are capable of making significant contributions to the organization's knowledge base, and which are not.

An important further advantage of systematically articulating and codifying an organization's knowledge is that this process makes an organization's current knowledge base more visible and analysable, and this helps an organization to discover deficiencies in its knowledge assets. In effect, by making an organization's current knowledge base more visible, so that the organization can begin to see more clearly what knowledge it does have, it should be possible for that organization to begin to see more clearly what knowledge it does not have. Focused, structured, managed learning processes to remedy important knowledge deficiencies can then be launched and may lead to more 'radical' forms of organizational learning.

Once an organization establishes processes for articulating, codifying and leveraging explicit knowledge assets, the systematic dissemination of explicit knowledge within the organization should minimize the risk that it will lose vital knowledge if key individuals become unavailable or leave the organization.

To obtain the potentially significant benefits of an explicit knowledge management approach, however, a number of organizational challenges must be overcome. These challenges arise primarily in assuring adequate articulation, evaluation, application and protection of knowledge assets.

Individuals may not have sufficient skill or motivation to articulate their useful knowledge. Individuals vary greatly in the precision with which they can state their ideas, and some individuals – perhaps many – may need organizational support to adequately articulate their knowledge into useful knowledge assets.[6] Providing organizational support to individuals to articulate their knowledge may have a significant financial cost and inevitably takes time.

An even more fundamental challenge arises when an individual is capable of articulating his or her knowledge, but resists requests by the organization to do so. At the heart of such resistance is usually a belief that an individual's job security or position of influence in an organization depends on the tacit knowledge that he or she has and that the organization needs. Such beliefs result in fear that full revelation of an individual's important knowledge will be followed by dismissal or loss of influence in an organization, because – presumably – the individual will no longer be as necessary or important to the organization. Overcoming such fears is likely to require a profound rethinking of the employment relationship in many organizations, especially with regard to key knowledge workers. New employment norms may have to be defined and institutionalized that both seek and reward ongoing learning by individuals and their continuing contributions of explicit knowledge to the organization.[7]

Organizations must also meet the challenge of adequately evaluating knowledge that has been made explicit by individuals. Individuals with different backgrounds, education and organizational roles may have varying sets of knowledge, with resulting differences in their deeply held ideas about the most effective way to get something done. Such differences will be revealed in the process of making their ideas and knowledge explicit, and managers implementing explicit knowledge approaches must establish a process for evaluating the individual knowledge that has been made explicit and for resolving conflicting knowledge beliefs of individuals. Organizations with experience in managing this process have found that the people involved in such evaluation processes must be respected within the organization for their expertise, objectivity and impartiality. In most organizations, the time of such people is usually both very valuable and in short supply, and involving such people in evaluating explicit knowledge in many forms may impose a significant cost on the organization (although the resulting benefits may far outweigh the costs).

Since knowledge is useful to an organization only when it is applied, a further challenge in implementing explicit knowledge management approaches is assuring that knowledge articulated in one part of the organization is not rejected or ignored by other parts of the organization simply because they prefer to stay close to their own familiar knowledge base – that is, because of an intra-organizational 'not invented here' syndrome. One approach to managing this concern is the implementation of organizational 'best knowledge' and 'best practice' practices.

In this practice, the committee of experts responsible for a knowledge evaluation process (discussed above) examines both the theoretical knowledge and practical applications of knowledge articulated within the organization, and defines the 'best knowledge' and 'best practice' in applying that knowledge currently available within the organization. The various groups within the organization to whom this knowledge or practice applies are then required either to adopt and use the currently defined 'best knowledge' and 'best practice', or to demonstrate convincingly to the committee of experts that they have developed better knowledge or better practice in applying knowledge. If a group persuades the expert committee that their knowledge or practice is better than the currently defined 'best knowledge' or 'best practice' in the organization, the expert committee then modifies the current 'best knowledge' or 'best practice' for the organization in light of the new knowledge they have received from the group. Implementing such a process for assuring that an organization's best knowledge and practice are actually used requires a high degree of organizational discipline in adhering to the organization's current best knowledge and best practice, and such discipline will normally require building a high degree of organizational trust that the process of the expert committee for deciding best knowledge and best practice is objective, impartial and transparent.

Finally, an organization that creates explicit knowledge assets must take care that those assets remain within the boundaries of the organization and do not 'leak' to other organizations, especially competitors. Security measures of the type most organizations now routinely use to protect their databases must be extended to provide security for the organization's explicit knowledge base.

Conclusions

As described above, the tacit and explicit knowledge management approaches involve quite different emphases and practices, and one might naturally be led to ask 'Which approach is right?' As with most alternative approaches to management issues, however, the answer is 'Both are right – but in the right combination.' As the discussion in this chapter has suggested, there are important advantages to be obtained through both the tacit and explicit knowledge management approaches, and in many respects, the advantages of each approach can be used to help offset the disadvantages of the other. In any organization, therefore, the goal is to create a hybrid design for its knowledge management practice that synthesizes the 'right' combination and balance of the tacit and explicit knowledge management approaches.

What the 'right' combination and balance may consist of will vary with a number of factors – the technology the organization uses or could use, the market conditions it faces, the 'knowledge intensity' of its strategies and operations, the current attitudes of its key knowledge workers toward the organization, the degree of geographical dispersion of its knowledge workers, the resources available to the organization to invest in developing infrastructure and processes for its knowledge management practice, and so on. However, some basic guidelines may be suggested.

Organizations that have not implemented systematic knowledge management approaches should in most cases begin with tacit knowledge management practices of the type discussed in this chapter. Such practices are relatively inexpensive, fast to implement, and less challenging organizationally than full-blown explicit knowledge management practices, and they often create surprising organizational interest in and energy for developing more extensive knowledge management practices. In any event, implementation of tacit knowledge management practices should be seen and communicated within the organization as only the first step in an evolving management process that will eventually include more formal and systematic explicit knowledge management practices. Achieving some initial organizational successes through use of tacit knowledge practices also helps to build confidence that the much greater organizational demands involved in implementing explicit knowledge management practices will be worth the effort.

We have discussed here a number of reasons why in the long run organizations that manage to implement effective explicit knowledge approaches will not only be more effective at leveraging their knowledge, but will also become better learning organizations. When the respective advantages of tacit and explicit knowledge management practices can be combined, an organization should be able to develop and apply new knowledge faster and more extensively than organizations that do not try to manage knowledge or that use only tacit or only explicit knowledge management practices. Thus the eventual goal for most organizations will be to devise and implement hybrid knowledge management practices in which explicit knowledge management practices complement and significantly extend their initial tacit knowledge practices.

Notes

1. Some writers and consultants have even gone so far as to argue that *all* knowledge is tacit in nature. The irony in trying to communicate to others the 'knowledge' that all knowledge is tacit, however, should be obvious.
2. *Know-how, know-why* and *know-what* forms of knowledge can also be described (see Sanchez 1997).
3. Using modular product architectures to create increasingly configurable product designs, Motorola was able to increase the number of customizable product variations it could offer from a few thousand variations in the late 1980s to more than 120 million variations by the late 1990s.
4. A platform includes a system of standard component types and standardized interfaces between component types that enable 'plugging and playing' different component variations in the platform design to configure different product variations (see Sanchez 2004).
5. Of course, under patent, copyright or trade secrecy laws, an organization may have intellectual property rights in the tacit knowledge developed by individuals in the organization, and these rights may discourage – though not entirely prevent – individuals from sharing such knowledge with other organizations.
6. Of course, the more knowledge-intensive an organization's work is, and the more an organization is populated by 'knowledge workers' with advanced education and training in formally communicating their ideas, the less difficult the articulation of explicit knowledge within the organization should be.
7. Further, not all knowledge of individuals will necessarily be worth more to the organization than it may cost the organization to help or to reward individuals who try to articulate their knowledge. Essentially, managers must try to understand when the marginal cost of articulating knowledge is becoming greater than the marginal benefit of extracting the next bit of knowledge from an individual. Since no one currently knows exactly how to make such a cost–benefit analysis at the margin, as a practical matter organizations that implement the explicit knowledge approach do not strictly try to optimize this process and tend to prefer to 'err' on the side of articulating more – rather than less – knowledge.

References

Sanchez, Ron. 1997. 'Managing articulated knowledge in competence-based competition'. Pp. 163–87 in *Strategic Learning and Knowledge Management*, edited by R. Sanchez and A. Heene. Chichester, UK: John Wiley & Sons.

Sanchez, Ron. 2001. 'Managing knowledge into competence: The five learning cycles of the competent organization'. Pp. 3–37 in *Knowledge Mangement and Organizational Competence*, edited by R. Sanchez. Oxford: Oxford University Press.

Sanchez, Ron. 2004. 'Creating modular platforms for strategic flexibility'. *Design Management Review* Winter:58–67.

Spear, Steven and H. Kent Bowen. 1999. 'Decoding the DNA of the Toyota production system'. *Harvard Business Review* September–October:97–106.

Stein, Johan and Jonas Ridderstråle. 2001. 'Managing the dissemination of competences'. Pp. 63–76 in *Knowledge Management and Organizational Competence*, edited by R. Sanchez. Oxford: Oxford University Press.

16 Knowledge and social identity
Thomas Keenan

Introduction

If we accept that post-industrial economics is knowledge-based and that effective knowledge management is a necessary (though not sufficient) condition for the survival of modern organizations, then it is essential that we have as complete an understanding as possible of the nature of knowledge creation and diffusion in organizations. To do this, we must have a sophisticated and well-considered sense of what knowledge is and how it comes to be. This is not necessarily an easy task; in fact, the nature of knowledge has been the subject of considerable debate for millennia (Welbourne 2001). What is emerging in modern research about the nature of knowledge is an appreciation of its relational aspects. Individuals do not create knowledge in isolation. Rather, knowledge emerges out of the complex webs of relationships that individuals form throughout their lifetimes, including relationships with other individuals, with animate and inanimate objects, and with ideas themselves (Rooney et al. 2003; Stacey 2001).

The growing interest in the relational nature of knowledge is opening up new avenues for knowledge research. For organizational researchers, the relational conceptualization of knowledge suggests that there are issues in terms of sociology, social psychology and organizational behaviour that must be considered if the way in which knowledge is created and diffused effectively is to be understood fully. In this chapter I focus on social identity (i.e. that part of our self-concept that is derived from the social groups to which we perceive we belong (Vaughan and Hogg 2002)) and the role that it plays in the creation and diffusion of knowledge. I use data gathered from a not-for-profit, community-based creative organization to illustrate the effects that the social identity variables of identity salience, status and belonging have on knowledge processes in knowledge-intensive organizations.

The nature of knowledge

The traditional epistemological definition of knowledge is 'justified true belief' (Nonaka et al. 2000; Steup 1996). However, in applied terms, this definition is insufficient because it fails to address even the most fundamental cognitive, social and cultural issues of what knowledge is and how it comes to be (Nonaka et al. 2000). I have adopted the definition of knowledge offered by

Rooney et al. (2003, p. 16), who, reflecting the influence of Whitehead (1978) and Vygotsky (1986), suggest that knowledge is the result of the process of knowing, which is an 'evolving and variable constellation of the conceptual, intellectual, cognitive, intuitive, emotional, spiritual, axiological and motor bases to achievement that is an emergent property of relations, and that is regarded as a reliable basis for action'. The definition proposed by Rooney et al. (2003) suggests that knowledge does not have an independent existence outside the processes of knowing, and that the unit of analysis should there-fore be the (living) process (Whitehead 1978).

The acceptance of the concept of knowledge as the result of a process rather than an objective 'thing' has implications for the way in which we might go about 'managing' knowledge. In addition to relying on the traditional knowl-edge management assumption that knowledge can be 'owned, measured and controlled' (Stacey 2001, p. 3), knowledge management efforts should consider ways in which processes of knowing can be facilitated effectively in organizations.

The relational conceptualization of knowledge suggests that an important source of knowledge creation and diffusion is the relationships individuals form with each other (Berger and Luckmann 1966; Morton 1997; Nonaka et al. 2000). Importantly, what we come to know is often a product of what we are told in our interactions with others (Welbourne 2001). Without this testi-monial knowledge we run the risk of continually having to 'reinvent the wheel' (Shapin 1994). Furthermore, it would seem reasonable to assume that some of the relationships we form are more effective knowledge-creating and -diffusing relationships than others.

Research reported in the social capital literature (see e.g. Cohen and Prusak 2001; Lesser 2000; Nahapiet and Ghoshal 1998; Yli-Renko et al. 2001) suggests that effective relationships for creating and diffusing knowledge are characterized by mutual trust, understanding, feelings of reciprocity, compat-ibility of values and a willingness to communicate openly. These types of rela-tionships are important as they facilitate the effective and efficient exchange of information in social networks within and across organizational boundaries, an important precursor to knowledge creation and diffusion (Adler and Kwon 2000; Anand et al. 2002; Bouty 2000; Gant et al. 2002; Lesser 2000; Nahapiet and Ghoshal 1998; Yli-Renko et al. 2001). Consequently, if we wish to manage knowledge effectively in organizations, we need to understand the factors that affect the formation of effective knowledge-creating and -diffus-ing relationships. I argue that one such factor is the social identity of each participant in the relationship. In order to substantiate this claim, it is impor-tant to examine the essential tenets of social identity theory (SIT) (Hogg and Abrams 1988; Tajfel and Turner 1979).

Social identity theory

SIT is a theory aimed at explaining the nature of group membership and inter-group relations. It is based primarily on four assumptions: (1) interpersonal and group behaviour are not synonymous; (2) cognition is about 'simplifying processes of the social world in socially adaptive and meaningful ways' (Vaughan and Hogg 2002, p. 14); (3) society is divided into categories that have perceived differences in terms of power and status; and (4) people generally have a need for self-esteem (Hogg and Abrams 1999; van Dick 2001; Vaughan and Hogg 2002). The proponents of SIT argue that it is the relationship between perceived social groups that defines the behaviour of people within groups, and, consequently, people behave differently in groups from the way they behave as individuals (Vaughan and Hogg 2002). Further, inter-group comparison allows people to gain individual self-esteem while at the same time defining their social identity (i.e. the part of the self-concept based on the groups to which they belong). The need for both positive self-esteem and a positive self-concept motivates people to view their 'ingroups' more favourably than their 'outgroups' (Deschamps and Devo 1998; Operario and Fiske 1999; Sherman et al. 1999; van Dick 2001; Vaughan and Hogg 2002).

Because we belong to various social groups (e.g. work, religious, recreational and family groups) we have a number of different social identities (Ashforth and Mael 1989; Hogg 1996). Which group we identify with at a particular time depends on which is most salient in the context in which we find ourselves. The need for a positive self-concept and positive self-esteem prompts people to seek membership of perceived high-status groups, and (or) to protect and enhance the status of groups to which they already belong (Vaughan and Hogg 2002). This behaviour results from group comparison and occurs because the status of the group to which people belong or aspire to belong to reflects their self-concept (Ashforth and Mael 1989; Drigotas et al. 1998; van Knippenberg and van Schie 2000). Membership of groups is defined by adherence to group norms (i.e. the attitudes, values and behaviours of the group members). These group norms govern individual behaviour if a person identifies with the group (van Knippenberg 2000; van Knippenberg and van Schie 2000; Vaughan and Hogg 2002). Therefore, the behaviour of individuals is socially influenced (van Knippenberg 2000; van Knippenberg and van Schie 2000; Vaughan and Hogg 2002).

SIT offers some important insights for knowledge management. Ashforth and Mael (1989) argue that one of the consequences of SIT in an organizational context is that people choose to engage in activities, or exhibit specific behaviours or sets of behaviours, that match the salient parts of their social identity. It would seem reasonable to extend this concept to knowledge-creating and -diffusing activities, such as forming effective relationships and cooperating for learning.

According to SIT, if people identify with a particular group, they are more likely to engage in behaviour that protects and enhances both the status of that group and their own sense of identification with that group. This protection and enhancement behaviour has important implications for knowledge creation and diffusion. This sort of behaviour is likely to result in the formation of positive interpersonal relationships with ingroup members. If we identify with a group, and people accept us as group members, then we generally have some form of active connection to people within that group and a mutual understanding of and commitment to the norms and the shared values of that group (Hornsey and Hogg 2002). Identification with a group stimulates people in the group to increase their mutual understandings and shared values, promoting trust between group members. A corollary of this membership and identification is the fulfilment of the need for positive self-esteem and self-concept. In terms of knowledge, the strong ties that result from this group identification facilitate the effective and efficient creation and diffusion of knowledge within the ingroup.

The desire for group identification may also have negative consequences for knowledge creation and diffusion. It would seem that the social identity of people may determine with whom they form relationships, as people may only expend energy to form potential knowledge-creating and -diffusing relationships if they perceive that by doing so they will protect and enhance the status of the groups to which they belong, thereby enhancing their own esteem and self-concept; or that doing so will enable them to join a higher-status group (Ashforth and Mael 1989; Vaughan and Hogg 2002). Therefore, unless people in an organizational context perceive social identity benefits for themselves in terms of their own power, status or prestige, they may withdraw from engaging in knowledge-creating and -diffusing relationships, thus limiting the potential for knowledge creation and diffusion. Also, this desire for group identification may inhibit the forming of 'weak ties' with people who are not group members. Weak ties play an important role in knowledge processes because 'those to whom we are weakly tied are more likely to move in circles different from our own and will thus have access to information different from that which we [normally] receive' (Granovetter 1973. p. 1373). The ability to access these weak ties reduces the amount of redundant information that exists within a social network and enables access to a broader and deeper knowledge base, thus increasing the chances that new knowledge will be created or diffused (Burt 1997; Eastis 1998; Granovetter 1973; Putnam 2000).

The relationship between knowledge and social identity – some empirical evidence
My ethnographic study of knowledge processes in a not-for-profit, community-based choral group (Keenan 2002) provides evidence of the effect that the

social identities of members of an organization can have on the creation and diffusion of knowledge. Effective knowledge creation and diffusion is essential for the successful functioning of a performance-oriented creative organization such as this one. The analysis of data collected for this study demonstrates that although knowledge is created and diffused in this organization, as evidenced by its ability to produce its creative 'products' (i.e. concerts, musical productions, recordings, etc.), the effectiveness of knowledge processes is impeded by a number of factors. In particular, social-identity-related factors result in recurrent acts of incivility, which not only affect the ability of members to form and sustain effective knowledge-creating and -diffusing relationships, but also the quality of their lived experiences within the organization.

Identity salience is one issue that emerged as a potential impediment to effective knowledge processes in this organization. For some members, the choir is their primary social outlet, and as such, forms an important part of their social identity. These people tend to be those who are heavily involved in the management of the organization. They are often older members, who have retired from work and have adult children who have moved out of the family home. These members tend to be uncivil to those who fail to display as much commitment to the organization as they do, while members who do have commitments away from the choir can be uncivil to others because they feel that the more 'committed' members of the choir fail to appreciate the fact that they have other pressures in their lives apart from the choir. Extracts from the interview transcripts acknowledge these salience conflicts:

> The powers that be have to realise that a lot of us . . . have got very stressful jobs, extremely stressful jobs, everyone wants you to work one and a half or two people instead of just one, that's just how jobs are. So when you go to choir you don't want to go to be like a sergeant major in a concentration camp. You want to go and work, do your thing, have that bit of fun, work hard, but have a bit of fun, so you get home and say that was a great night, we got a lot done, we had a lot of fun, but you're not going home feeling like that anymore, it's just hard work. The recreational fun side, I think we've all got to remember that the choir, we are a community choir, we are not being paid to do this. We go because we love going. We don't want to be paid either, but it's not our job. It's there for our recreation, to do a good job, but to enjoy ourselves as a group. Somehow I think we've got to find a way to put that back in but I don't know how to do that.

> . . . but you've got to make a line, a distinction in that way, that people don't recognise sometimes and you often hear it said that 'there's more to life than choir'. They've got to work, they've got families, other things that the choir as an organisation has got to realise. Choir's not it. For some people it is, that's their life apart from maybe their husband or wife, perhaps they're divorced or whatever, perhaps retired, this is their outlet and they don't understand that people have different ways of thinking about things.

The interviewees are suggesting that the 'powers that be' in the organization fail to recognize that members of the organization, like all people, have multiple social identities, apart from their identity as a member of the choir. SIT suggests that the social identity that is most salient to a person will depend on the context in which they find themselves. Therefore a choir member's social identity as a member of the organization will not always be the only salient part of their social identity, and this has implications for how they behave. The transcript evidence suggests that for some choir members other social identities, such as work identity and family identity, are often more salient than their choir-related identity, but for others their choir-related social identity is predominant. In this context, this salience conflict hampers the ability of members to form the types of positive relationships that are essential for the effective creation and diffusion of the performative and aesthetic knowledge that is required for the choir to function at its peak. It is not unreasonable to assume that similar conflicts may arise in any organization where members have differing levels of social identity salience related to their membership of that organization. Consequently, problems associated with social identity salience differences is an issue that should be considered by knowledge managers.

Status seeking and maintenance behaviour was another social-identity-related issue that affected the ability of the members of the choir to form effective knowledge-creating and -diffusing relationships. As suggested by SIT, members of formal groups in the choir engage in group status protection and enhancement behaviour (including uncivil behaviour) as a means of maintaining their own positive self-concept and self-esteem. The choir is formally divided into soprano, alto, tenor and bass sections, with the soprano and bass sections further divided into first and second parts. This division is based on vocal range and is necessary for the choral arrangements the choir performs. Interview respondents were asked whether there were identifiable subgroups in the organization, and whether or not they identified with these subgroups. All respondents were able to identify the various groups and subgroups within the organization. As anticipated, given the amount of time they spend interacting with members of their formal organizational group, members tend to identify with their particular vocal line

> I think you do a little bit. I think you do, yes, because when you go and sit there you're a tenor or a bass. I think you do identify yourself in that way.

> The group I sit with in the altos . . . To be honest, I should probably be singing in the second sopranos rather than the alto section but that's another thing.

> Formally, I do certainly identify as a bass. I think most basses do to avoid being labelled with the tenors, which is not necessarily a good thing, but I think that's how it is. And there are people who could be singing second tenor or who are singing

first bass just to avoid being labelled as a tenor, which seems to be a derogatory term in the organisation I think.

The last two extracts are important in terms of social identity because they represent examples of group status issues. In this organization, the tenors and the second sopranos are lower-status groups. The low status of these sections in the choir is related to their smaller numbers, their lack of recognized soloists, and their under-representation at a management level. The senior people in the organization are altos or basses. SIT suggests that people would avoid being labelled with these low-status sections if at all possible as a means of self-concept and self-esteem protection. This is indeed the case. For example, as one respondent noted,

> let's face it, the tenors are the weaker section, it doesn't matter where you go the tenors are the weaker section because the people who could possibly be the second tenors are the baritones anyway [i.e. the first bass line].

This lower status is particularly evident for the tenor line. For example, during one rehearsal, it was noted that

> the tenors were having problems with their notes. As usual, this was accompanied by sarcastic comments from the bass line and general noises of disapproval. At one stage, the deputy pianist pointed out to the tenors that there was a rest in the music that they were not observing. One bass quipped (with regards to the 'rest') 'Which doesn't mean that you go to sleep'.

As is evidenced in this field note extract, the tenors are really the 'whipping boys' for the rest of the sections, especially the bass line. The bass line actively reinforces the low-status position of the tenor line through its negative treatment of the tenors at practically every rehearsal. In this organization, this status maintenance behaviour limits the possibility of the development of positive relationships between the groups, which in turn affects their ability to engage in effective knowledge creation and diffusion.

Informal or social group identification also affects knowledge processes in the choir. In the choir, social groups form either through extended contact with others at choir (and consequently, they are usually based around vocal lines or family groups – who have been in the organization for many years), or as a result of non-choir-related activities (e.g. there is a strong sense of professional identification among the music teachers in the choir; also, some members currently work together or have done so in the past). Interview respondents often identified the existence of these groups before they were asked whether or not they felt there were identifiable subgroups within the organization. The term 'clique' was often used to describe the nature of the social groups within the choir.

Cliquey. There seems to be a big, like a clique.

With every organization you always get cliques, you always get people who become friendly and if one of the people in the particular group becomes defensive, people are looking for slights or somebody doing something . . .

It's a close knit group and that most probably can be a negative as well because if a new person was coming into the choir I'm sure they would find it hard to get into a particular group and start to mingle because I know for a fact that we all have our cliquey little groups and it would be extremely hard.

This strong identification among members of social groups within the organization results in people behaving in an uncivil manner to people who are not seen as 'one of us'. This hampers knowledge diffusion and creation in this organization as it inhibits the ability of people to form network ties with others, and increases the chance of redundant information exchange among group members. The uncivil treatment of outgroup members is particularly evident among members of the so-called 'elite' or ' "A" List' group within the organization. This social subgroup contains a number of the leading soloists, several of the senior management personnel and family groups who have been in the organization for a considerable length of time, in some cases since the founding of the organization. One interviewee suggested, in reference to this group, that

> there's a clique in the choir that's not terribly accepting. I didn't find it with me and I think it may have been, and this is confidential, but I think it may have been because I was brought in by one of the elite, one of the older members. I was approached to come in, I didn't voluntarily join, it wasn't a let's go out and get her kind of thing, but there is a certain clique in the choir that does make the decision on whether to accept or not to accept others . . . I find it rather regrettable, but it's there . . . I think it does have an impact in the communication, I think it has a detrimental effect.

This quote clearly establishes that social group identification has an effect on the manner in which people interact in this organization. The interviewee highlights that members of a group behave in a manner that identifies them as group members and protects and enhances the status of the group. Another interviewee, a member of the 'elite' group, expanded on this point, stating that

> there are different groups within the organization and some people you don't like and some people you don't share a common history or heritage with, so it's often difficult to communicate when you have a lack of commonality, but some people you just don't like. To a certain extent that gets reinforced in the group in that there are people 'we' don't like, and sometimes I try to avoid that. Sometimes, I don't do it very well and I think it's a laziness thing more than anything else. It becomes too difficult to manage your relationships with the people you do need to interact with more frequently if you're seen to be sleeping with the enemy . . . A reasonably fine

example is someone who's got a role in the particular production we're doing and some of the people in my group don't like that person because they got a role over one of the group members. I find the person who got the role quite pleasant to deal with personally and I don't have a problem with her whatsoever, so I treat her that way, despite the pressure to be rude to her because 'we' don't like her.

This quote clearly shows that the individual behaviour of this group member is often determined by group norms. What is interesting in terms of knowledge is that a norm of this group appears to be 'we do not like people who have offended other group members, and we treat them accordingly'. Therefore, uncivil interpersonal interaction is actually a group norm. As a result, it may be difficult for members of this group to engage in effective knowledge-creating and -sharing relationships with people outside the group who have offended another group member, even though the group member has not had any personal negative experiences with the person in question. This is obviously a problem in terms of the effective management of knowledge in the choir if the group that essentially 'controls' the organization both formally and informally has uncivil behaviour as one of its group norms.

The relationship between knowledge and power is clearly raised by SIT because it foregrounds issues to do with elites, status, control and punishment. Power can manifest itself most damagingly in the unreflexivity of the elite. There is a perception that members of the elite group in this organization are allowed to behave in an uncivil manner without sanction. For example, one interviewee noted that as a member of this particular social group

You get a lot of leeway, like if you play up or you're naughty, for want of a better word, at rehearsals you're not penalised or punished in this group as much as other people might be.

The respondent is suggesting that uncivil behaviour (i.e. 'playing up' or being 'naughty' at rehearsals) is tolerated if you are a member of the elite group. Although this issue is related to the social identity notion of ingroups and outgroups, it is also a power-related issue, given the status of the people who are members of this group. Rooney et al. (2003) argue that issues of power have largely been ignored in the literature on knowledge management and the knowledge economy. SIT provides an avenue for introducing power concepts into this literature, as it suggests that one of the primary motives for engaging in any activity (including knowledge creation and diffusion) in an organizational context is the desire to build, maintain or protect power, status and esteem through favourable intergroup comparisons.

Finally, an understanding of what it means to 'belong' in, or to be 'identified' as a member of the choir also affects the ability of people to engage in effective knowledge-creating and -diffusing relationships. To be perceived as a 'true' or 'good' member of the choir, you need to have joined in a particular manner (e.g. by being introduced by someone who is already a member and not through general, publicly announced membership drives), you must display a high degree of loyalty and commitment to the group, and you must attempt to integrate into the culture of the choir (rather than attempt to change it). This conceptualization of an 'ideal' member type can be understood in terms of SIT. The discussion of SIT has so far been limited to subgroups within the organization. The ideal member type is related to the social identity of the choir as a whole. People are expected to behave in a particular way if they want to be perceived as a choir member, and it is perceived that behaviour such as loyalty and commitment enhance and protect the power and status of the choir compared to its outgroups. In this study, high levels of intolerance of non-ideal members was a source of conflict and missed opportunities. For example, as one interviewee said, '[t]here seems to be a feeling that you have to be here for a while before you can voice your opinions'.

People who act in a way that contravenes this generalized notion of belongingness, whether deliberately or through ignorance, are perceived to be acting uncivilly. If these people act in this unsanctioned manner, then other members treat them uncivilly. This is a problem in terms of knowledge processes, not only because of the general detrimental effect incivility has on the formation and maintenance of effective knowledge relationships, but also because people who are not 'ideal' members are often disregarded even when they possess information that might be useful for the creation and diffusion of beneficial knowledge, the equivalent of the 'not-invented-here' syndrome. The conceptualization of an 'ideal' member type is further linked to SIT in that it reflects the perception of how members should behave if they want to be perceived as part of the group. Members who do not match this conceptualization are treated in an uncivil fashion because they are perceived to be failing to act in a manner that enhances or protects the status of the group.

Implications and conclusion

The importance of effective knowledge management is increasingly recognized by both management researchers and practitioners. One issue that requires further consideration by both groups is the relational nature of knowledge. If we are going to manage knowledge effectively in organizational contexts, we must accept that one of the most important ways that knowledge is created and diffused is through interpersonal and intergroup relationships. One of the prime goals of knowledge management should therefore be to facilitate the formation and maintenance of effective knowledge-creating and -diffusing relationships. To do this, managers must understand, first, what constitutes these types of relationships, and second, that there are numerous factors that affect their formation and maintenance. I have argued that one such factor is the social identity of people who are the parties to these relationships. Through my examination of data collected in a knowledge-intensive creative organization, I have endeavoured to demonstrate how the social identity variables of salience, status and belonging influence the manner in which people interact in this organization and, consequently, the effect that this has on their ability to engage in effective knowledge-creating and -diffusing relationships.

It is also interesting that the organization at the centre of this study is quite literally a performance-based one. There is an imperative for this organization to produce highly competent public performances on specific occasions (e.g. concerts). This creates an imperative that demands that the group focus on specific goals and tasks. Received wisdom suggests that such pressure should act to 'concentrate the (organizational and individual) mind' in the pursuit of these goals. Importantly, this study demonstrates that the reality of creative knowledge work – at least in this organization – is rather more messy and distracted than many assume it to be, and does not come without considerable 'tensions' (Gulbrandsen 2004). In this case, it is important to note that despite the incivility and distraction, public performances continued successfully. While it is safe to assume that no organization will ever be without messy social-identity-driven impediments to the perfection of performance, there is very little we can say about these tensions in the absence of more research except to point out that while some tensions may be good, too many are likely to be unhelpful (Gulbrandsen 2004). In the interim, knowledge managers should be alert to the social messiness and tension in knowledge work and the fact that social identity is a key factor in creating that messiness and tension.

SIT suggests that if knowledge managers want knowledge to be created and diffused effectively in their organizations, they should examine ways of ensuring that social identity benefits accrue to those members of the organization who engage in activities that result in the effective creation and diffusion of knowledge. This has implications for knowledge management practice. Managers need to assess which social groups are salient for organizational members, and which groups within the organization have a perceived high status. In terms of knowledge processes, identity salience and group status are not only potential issues in relation to intergroup conflict within an organization (which, owing to its effect on civil relations between organizational members, is detrimental to effective knowledge creation and diffusion); they also determine the values and attitudes that guide individuals' behaviour. For this reason, it would seem particularly important for effective knowledge management to ensure that salient and/or high-status groups within the organization maintain the creation and diffusion of knowledge within and between social groups as a key group value. If, after the assessment of the salience and status of social groups within the organization, managers find that salient or perceived high-status groups do not hold effective knowledge creation and diffusion as a core value, then action will need to be taken to rectify this situation. In this instance, effective leadership would be required to either change the salience or perceived status of groups within the organization to ensure that groups who hold knowledge creation and diffusion as a core value become more salient or higher-status groups, or alter the values of the existing salient or high-status groups to incorporate knowledge creation and diffusion as a key group value. SIT offers a number of potential strategies to achieve these aims (see e.g. Hornsey and Hogg 2002).

SIT also suggests that it is important for knowledge managers to understand how notions of belonging are conceptualized within the organization. The data gathered from the choir suggest that the conceptualization of what it is to truly be a member of the group affects group members' interactions, in that those who are not perceived as being 'ideal' type members are treated in an uncivil manner, thus limiting the possibility of both the formation of effective knowledge-creating and -diffusing relationships and the chance to access new and potentially beneficial sources of information. Again, it would seem important for knowledge managers to attempt to ensure that part of what it means to belong to the organization as a whole, or to salient or high-status groups within the organization, is a desire to create and diffuse knowledge in a manner that is beneficial for the success of the organization.

SIT foregrounds power as a key dynamic in knowledge work. In this study it is evident that social dynamics can close an organization to new knowledge and make relationships less functional. Protecting status and prestige can manifest itself in the form of narrow-mindedness, intolerance, conceit and so on, preventing intellectual growth even if it does not entirely stifle performance. Organizational politics is therefore relevant to knowledge management. These politics are not easy, though. We cannot eliminate politics and power from organizations, only use them better. Importantly, identity-based status is not all bad in knowledge management. For example, organizations in some sectors of the creative industries are likely to be well rewarded for according high status to the pursuit and application of aesthetic knowledge. SIT therefore suggests that managers need to develop quite sophisticated attitudes to the role of power in knowledge work.

The social identity of organizational members is only one of many factors that need to be considered if knowledge is to be managed effectively in organizations. However, owing to its potential importance in determining whether or not organization members engage in effective knowledge-creating and -diffusing relationships, it is a significant issue that knowledge managers and knowledge researchers must examine seriously. The analysis presented here highlights the relationship between knowledge and social identity. However, examining the effects that the relationship between knowledge and other types of identity (e.g. place identity) have on effective knowledge creation and diffusion; the effect that social identity has on processes related to knowledge, such as creativity; and the role of other factors such as power play in knowledge processes are also important to knowledge management and research.

References

Adler, Paul S. and Seok-Woo Kwon. 2000. 'Social capital: The good, the bad and the ugly'. Pp. 89–115 in *Knowledge and Social Capital: Foundations and Applications*, edited by E.L. Lesser. Boston, MA: Butterworth-Heinemann.

Anand, Vikas, William H. Glick and Charles G. Manz. 2002. 'Thriving on the knowledge of outsiders: Tapping organizational social capital'. *The Academy of Management Executive* **16**:87–101.

Ashforth, Blake E. and Fred Mael. 1989. 'Social identity theory and the organization'. *The Academy of Management Review* **14**:20–39.

Berger, Peter L. and Thomas Luckmann. 1966. *The Social Construction of Reality*. Harmondsworth, UK: Penguin.

Bouty, Isabelle. 2000. 'Interpersonal interaction influences on informal resource exchanges between R&D researchers across organizational boundaries'. *The Academy of Management Journal* **43**:50–65.

Burt, Ronald S. 1997. 'The contingent value of social capital'. *Administrative Science Quarterly* **42**:339–65.

Cohen, Don and Laurence Prusak. 2001. *In Good Company: How Social Capital Makes Organizations Work*. Boston, MA: Harvard Business School Press.

Deschamps, Jean-Claude and Thierry Devo. 1998. 'Regarding the relationship between social identity and personal identity'. Pp. 1–12 in *Social Identity: International Perspectives*, edited by S. Worchel, J.F. Morales, D. Paez and J.-C. Deschamps. London: Sage.

Drigotas, Stephen M., Chester Insko and John Scholper. 1998. 'Mere categorization and competition: A closer look at social identity theory and the discontinuity effect'. Pp. 180–98 in *Social Identity: International Perspectives*, edited by S. Worchel, J.F. Morales, D. Paez and J.-C. Deschamps. London: Sage.

Eastis, Carla M. 1998. 'Organizational diversity and the production of social capital'. *The American Behavioral Scientist* **42**:66–77.

Gant, Jon, Casey Ichniowski and Kathryn Shaw. 2002. 'Social capital and organizational change in high-involvement and traditional work organizations'. *Journal of Economics and Management Strategy* **11**:289–328.

Granovetter, Mark. 1973. 'The strength of weak ties'. *American Journal of Sociology* **78**:1360–80.

Gulbrandsen, Magnus. 2004. 'Accord or discord? Tensions and creativity in research', in *Creative Knowledge Environments: The Influences on Creativity in Research and Innovation.*, edited by S. Hemlin, M.C. Allwood and B.R. Martin. Cheltenham, UK and Northampton, MA, USA: Edward Elgar.

Hogg, Michael A. 1996. 'Intergroup processes, group structure and social identity'. Pp. 66–93 in *Social Groups and Identities: Developing the Legacy of Henri Tajfel*, edited by W.P. Robinson. Oxford: Butterworth-Heinemann.

Hogg, Michael A. and Dominic Abrams. 1988. *Social Identifications: A Social Psychology of Intergroup Relations and Processes*. London: Routledge.

Hogg, Michael A. and Dominic Abrams. 1999. 'Social identity and social cognition: Historical backgrounds and current trends'. Pp. 1–25 in *Social Identity and Social Cognition*, edited by D. Abrams and M.A. Hogg. Oxford: Blackwell.

Hornsey, Matthew J. and Michael A. Hogg. 2002. 'The effects of status on subgroup relations'. *The British Journal of Social Psychology* **41**:203–18.

Keenan, Thomas M. 2002. 'Discord: Incivility and knowledge processes in a community choir', Honours Thesis, UQ Business School. St Lucia: University of Queensland.

Lesser, Eric L. 2000. 'Leveraging social capital in organizations'. Pp. 3–16 in *Knowledge and*

Social Capital: Foundations and Applications, edited by E.L. Lesser. Boston, MA: Butterworth-Heinemann.

Morton, Adam. 1997. *A Guide Through the Theory of Knowledge*. Malden, MA: Blackwell.

Nahapiet, Janine and Sumantra Ghoshal. 1998. 'Social capital, intellectual capital and the organizational advantage'. *The Academy of Management Review* 23:242–64.

Nonaka, Ikujiro, Ryoko Toyama and Noboru Konno. 2000. 'Seci, *ba* and leadership: A unified model of dynamic leadership'. *Long Range Planning* 33:5–34.

Operario, Don and Susan T. Fiske. 1999. 'Integrating social identity and social cognition: A framework for bridging diverse perspectives'. Pp. 26–54 in *Social Identity and Social Cognition*, edited by D. Abrams and M.A. Hogg. Oxford: Blackwell.

Putnam, Robert D. 2000. *Bowling Alone: The Collapse and Revival of American Community*. New York: Simon and Schuster.

Rooney, David, Greg Hearn, Tom Mandeville and Richard Joseph. 2003. *Public Policy in Knowledge-Based Economies: Foundations and Frameworks*. Cheltenham, UK and Northampton, MA, USA: Edward Elgar.

Shapin, Steven. 1994. *A Social History of Truth: Civility and Science in Seventeenth-Century England*. Chicago, IL: University of Chicago Press.

Sherman, Steven J., David L. Hamilton and Amy C. Lewis. 1999. 'Perceived entitativity and the social identity value of group memberships'. Pp. 80–110 in *Social Identity and Social Cognition*, edited by D. Abrams and M.A. Hogg. Oxford: Blackwell.

Stacey, Ralph D. 2001. *Complex Responsive Systems in Organizations: Learning and Knowledge Creation*. London: Routledge.

Steup, Matthias. 1996. *An Introduction to Contemporary Epistemology*. Upper Saddle River, NJ: Prentice Hall.

Tajfel, Henri and John C. Turner. 1979. 'An integrative theory of intergroup conflict'. Pp. 33–47 in *The Social Psychology of Intergroup Relations*, edited by S. Worchel and W.G. Austin. Monterey, CA: Brooks/Cole.

van Dick, Rolf. 2001. 'Identification in organizational contexts: Linking theory and research from social and organizational psychology'. *International Journal of Management Review* 3:265–83.

van Knippenberg, Daan. 2000. 'Work motivation and performance: A social identity perspective'. *Applied Psychology: An International Review* 49:357–71.

van Knippenberg, Daan and Els C.M. van Schie. 2000. 'Foci and correlates of organizational identification'. *Journal of Occupational and Organizational Psychology* 73:137–47.

Vaughan, Graham M. and Michael A. Hogg. 2002. *Introduction to Social Psychology*. Sydney, NSW: Prentice-Hall.

Vygotsky, Lev S. 1986. *Thought and Language*. Translated by T.A. Kouzulin. Cambridge, MA: MIT Press.

Welbourne, Michael. 2001. *Knowledge*. Chesham, UK: Acumen.

Whitehead, Alfred North. 1978. *Process and Reality*. Translated by D.R. Griffin and D.W.E. Sherburne. New York: The Free Press.

Yli-Renko, Helena, Erkko Autio and Harry J. Papienza. 2001. 'Social capital, knowledge acquisition and knowledge exploitation in young technology-based firms'. *Strategic Management Journal* 22:587–613.

17 Managing creativity in the knowledge economy

Mark Banks

Introduction

In the knowledge economy creativity is widely promoted as a key resource for securing competitive advantage, yet precisely how firms define and manage this elusive attribute continues to attract diverse opinions (Amabile 1996; Davis and Scase 2000; Florida 2002). This chapter first accounts for the emergence of creativity as a desirable corporate asset before examining varied workplace definitions of creativity and strategies for creative management. Since it is often argued that, in the 'new' economy, 'knowledge is in the networks' (Cooke 2002, p. 2), priority is given to the social and interactive – rather than the individualistic – nature of the creative process. It is argued that the popular idealization of the individual creative, as the impulsive harbinger of new ideas, is, for the most part, a partial and reductive one. This is because it disclaims the organizational and institutional forms of interaction that are necessary for the effective mobilization of creativity (Amabile 1996), as well as ignoring the ways in which creativity is contested, disciplined and, indeed, often negated, in the contemporary firm (Nixon 2003; Prichard 2002). In drawing upon empirical research undertaken with managers working in 'new media' SMEs from the north-west of England (Banks et al. 2002), the chapter contends that creativity is a contested *social* process – and in doing so emphasizes both the local and specific character of creativity discourses and the centrality of power relations in defining and managing creativity.

Creativity, production and consumption

Arguably, the creative impulse has been stimulated by the mooted transition to an informational mode of production (Castells 1996), whereby competitiveness is increasingly seen to be determined by the ability to tap into new knowledge, ideas and innovations. Here, cutting-edge ideas are not only crucial to the production of new material commodities, but also to the generation of a burgeoning range of non-material goods, that is, those primarily valued as cultural signs and symbols, or as providers of knowledge and information (Scott 2000). This mode of production not only relies on the increased 'flexible specialization' (Piore and Sabel 1984) of the firm, but is further made possible through global networks and infrastructures that enable the effective flow of people, information, commodities, finance and services across real and abstract space. In this emergent knowledge economy, creativity is seen as a potential source of competitive advantage rather than, as in the 'old' (Fordist) economy, an unaffordable luxury or additional cost (Jeffcut and Pratt 2002).

Additionally, shifts in the nature of consumption are central to an understanding of the emergence of the creativity issue. If Fordist mass production was characterized by product standardization and the fulfilment of basic consumer 'needs', then post-Fordism is concerned with the flexible disorganization of capitalism in order to fulfil increasingly differentiated and individualistic wants and desires (Amin 1994; Lash and Urry 1994). In contrast to the 'mass consumer' of the past, the contemporary consumer enjoys a 'lifestyle' that is particularistic and privatized, and is now more concerned with consuming images and signs as well as increasingly differentiated ranges of material goods (Featherstone 1991). In markets where consumer demands are difficult to define and categorize, and behaviour often impossible to predict, firms and entrepreneurs must themselves become more open-minded, self-reflexive and open to radical change (Lash and Urry 1994) – hence the need to instil a creative dynamic at the core of corporate enterprise.

Within the knowledge economy, it is argued that firms are compelled to develop a creative, innovative capacity that can generate new ideas, solutions and products (Florida 2002). Increasingly, keeping ahead of one's competitors is seen as a problem to be solved by 'unlocking' creative potential or mobilizing 'knowledge assets', as much as one necessitating application of more traditional measures such as cutting costs (Davis and Scase 2000; Jeffcut and Pratt 2002). To oversee a 'learning', 'knowledge-rich' or 'creative' firm is not only seen as a widespread managerial aspiration, but is increasingly judged a necessity for creating a competitive firm (Florida 2002).

Creativity at work
Creativity is often idealized as individual capriciousness (Rickards 1999), the product of some innate disposition that eludes the 'non'-creative (McFadzean 1998; Tan 1998), or simply a fundamental part of being human (Russell and Evans 1992). A widespread, common sense conviction is that creativity is essentially an individualistic enterprise, rooted in psychological aspects of behaviour, articulated at crucial moments of inspiration (Boden 1990).

Yet, in the workplaces of the knowledge economy, the genesis of creativity increasingly takes place within the context of collective interaction and communicative exchange – the project group or team meeting, the 'away-day', the networking event or in the informal networks and social spaces outside of the workplace environment (Davis and Scase 2000; Granovetter 1973). What is more, the content of creativity – that initial seed of an idea, plan or process

– is only judged to *be* creative within the context of existing and established procedures and protocols that are socially produced, maintained and mediated. Put simply, it can be argued that what counts as creativity is determined by managerial priorities and goals and what we might call the 'workplace culture' – as much as through the force of creative personality or any innate qualities contained within an idea itself.

Jeffcut and Pratt (2002) refer to the need to develop analyses that move beyond the 'atomistic assumptions' inherent in much creativity research, recognizing that firms and organizations are actively implicated in the social construction of creativity in particular settings and contexts. This is not to say, as they are quick to point out, that creativity is *all* context, but rather to recognize that the creativity problematic tends to be configured in dynamic organizational contexts, where multiple stakeholders are seeking to secure strategic advantages, and where normalizing and disciplining discourses around creativity will tend to produce 'devices that identify, classify and regulate' creativity and its outcomes (Prichard 2002, p. 266). Idealizing the creative as the 'individual subversive' or the 'lone voice at the margins' is not necessarily helpful with regard to understanding the interplay of actors and the organizational conditions under which creativity is constrained or permitted to flourish.

Creativity, communities and clusters
There are a number of options open to a firm or organization that wishes to become more creative. While this usually involves the importing of formal training or specific techniques of creative thinking (see McFadzean 1998), what we address here is how embedded and routinized social and organizational structures can act as incubators or generators of creativity, ones that have no explicit connection to managing 'behaviour' as such, but are more concerned with enhancing communication and providing opportunities for interaction among diverse sets of actors involved in the production process.

To this end, it can be argued that firms are, to a greater or lesser extent, implicated in what various commentators have labelled 'communities of practice' (Amin 2000; Brown and Duguid 1991; Wenger 1998). This term describes the range of formal and informal, social and organizational collectives that make up the workings of an organization. Such communities, as Amin (2000) notes, are seen as vital mechanisms for enabling both routine and strategic learning through processes of social interaction, as well as providing the conditions for the development of both tacit and formal organizational knowledge. Brown and Duguid (1991, p. 76) claim that 'it is from the site of such interactions that new insights can be coproduced' – suggesting that communities of practice may have a key role to play in organizational creativity and innovation.

In its ideal state, a community of practice works as a group of people informally bound together, sharing knowledge in order to pursue a goal or to solve problems in an organization. Yet, while these communities might ideally be informal and resistant to overt supervision, they cannot exist without management support and structure (Wenger 1998; Wenger and Snyder 2000). To that end we can argue that organizational creativity is a latent potential, the realization of which is determined partly by the range and efficacy of the 'communities of practice' in which a firm engages, and partly by the effectiveness of strategies employed by managers to facilitate this engagement. Thus creativity may be effectively realized through a range of strategies, the most obvious of which are team-working, collective learning and development exercises, 'free' time for 'blue skies' thinking, rotating or switching of roles and responsibilities, and research and development initiatives. Ensuring that workers are provided with opportunities to explore and articulate new ideas and solutions, and to develop personal and collective knowledge is increasingly seen as crucial in constructing a creative, learning organization and an effective community of practice (Amin 2000).

While developing an internal creative capacity is crucial, as these arrangements are often bounded, to varying degrees, within the bureaucratic organization of the firm, it is often found that the limits to the creative capacity may be quickly reached. In this scenario, developing 'external' communities of practice may be a solution to problems of creative underperformance.

The shift towards the employment of external experts – contractors, freelancers and consultants – has been one of the characteristics of the knowledge economy, where jobs and projects often require a range of knowledge inputs not necessarily housed within the confines of the firm itself. The role of external artists, designers, advertisers and marketers has grown in recent years, first as a result of a general expansion in 'creative industries', but also as a wider range of 'traditional' manufacturing firms look to factor the 'creative' dimension into products and the production process. These external experts may be members of close-knit and informal networks, often (though not necessarily) geographically 'clustered' around the firm, but usually linked by a history of collaboration, shared experience and industry knowledge. Managing and facilitating the effective integration of external experts into the organizational creative process is now seen as a crucial skill (Russell et al. 2003).

While 'communities of practice' may offer one solution to the problem of exploiting social creativity, another is to enhance the development of less structured, more informal social networks. Here, 'network' describes the web of traded and untraded relations and associations between individuals and firms, maintained through the production and exchange of goods, knowledge and information. Networking allows both the dissemination of relevant information and the generation of new contexts through which creativity and production can ferment. Effective networks allow firms to combine 'local' knowledge and tap into more distant 'global' resources on order to aid production processes (Castells 1996). In this respect, an important emergence has been the creative 'cluster' (Porter 1990), defined as an agglomeration of geographically proximate and interconnected firms, institutions and ancillary services working within a distinct field of production. The literature on clusters is extensive, though much of it points to the importance of co-location and shared sense of place as crucial in the construction of knowledge-rich sectors and the necessity of interfirm collaboration for the effective, collective accumulation of wealth (Cooke 2002; Porter 1990; Scott 2000; Sennett 2001). Local social relations, developed over time, help underwrite new productive coalitions, and geographical proximity provides a compelling basis for maintaining networking and collaborative activities. This can lead to the development of a 'Marshallian' local industrial complex of close personal relationships and productive relations of trust (Amin and Thrift 1992; Banks et al. 2000; Cooke 2002; Maskell et al. 1998) that provides the necessary 'atmosphere' for further creative ideas and knowledge transfer. Examples include the leading production complexes of Hollywood, Silicon Valley and Boston USA, Cambridge UK, Lombardy and Emilia-Romagna in Italy. These are places where sectors such as ICT, hi-tech manufacturing or cultural production have blossomed, underwritten by myriad social networks where intense knowledge exchange, 'weak ties' (Granovetter 1973) and webs of association (Scott 2000) take precedence over more traditional, Fordist firm cultures and practices.

We have suggested that in the knowledge economy creativity may be located within discrete patterns of social relations which we have idealized as 'communities of practice' – structures that are contained by the firm but also externally located in formal collaborations and informal networks of cooperation, dialogue and exchange. But even if firms can identify the potential sources of creativity, be it in the creative individual, or (as we have suggested here) in the matrix of social and organizational interactions and structures, precisely how to mobilize and manage creativity remains a key issue. It is to this problem we now turn.

How managers define and locate creativity

The way in which creativity is defined and managed varies considerably across industrial sectors. More surprising, it also varies markedly within sectors; indeed, there may be disagreement at the level of the individual firm as to what constitutes creativity and who possesses it. To illustrate this I draw briefly on our own research on managers of small and medium enterprises (SMEs) working in the 'creative industries' sector in the north-west of England (see Banks et al. 2002). As a sector that has a strong and self-

conscious perception of being 'creative' and 'cutting edge', one would anticipate that organizational debate around the creativity issue would be somewhat
more developed than in 'non'-creative sectors. Yet even in a sector where
creativity is argued to be central to securing competitive advantage, definitions
of creativity were often vague, partial and contested.

We interviewed a range of managers working in what are broadly referred
to as 'new media' SMEs – firms involved in the production of Internet-based
designs, services and applications (see Pratt 2000; Preston and Kerr 2001 for
comparative work). Managers (variably) defined creativity as a loose combination of individual skills, personality attributes and organizational capacity.
Few managers differentiated between the concepts of creativity, innovation
and problem-solving; indeed they were seen as interchangeable and closely
linked. When asked to suggest who possessed creativity, or where creativity
was located in the context of the firm, managers' responses fell broadly into
three categories. First, we found what we call 'managerial creativity', where
managers tended to emphasize their own creative qualities in areas of client
management and corporate marketing, and downplay the role of creativity at
other stages of the production process – an assumption contested by other
employees. Creativity was defined as the individual ability to negotiate the
deal, manage the client and deliver the 'whole package' – rather than a quality inherent in the team-based design or planning of the product itself. Second,
we identified 'content creativity' in firms working in areas such as e-learning,
training or human resource management, where creativity was defined in relation to the development of products that contained useful 'learning content' or
provided efficacious mechanisms for promoting new knowledge and understanding. Creativity here was team-based and dialogic, conceived as the
outcome of a series of intellectual challenges to the product – from tutors,
designers, programmers and clients. A third definition of creativity offered by
managers within more digital-art-based activities, or those managing small
graphic design firms, we labelled 'aesthetic creativity'. Here, a more traditional notion of 'pure' creativity where the individual freedom and autonomy
to pursue creative designs was prioritized and made distinctive from more
mundane or functional elements of the business.

This variability has important implications for those wishing to promote
and enhance creativity through strategic sector or firm-based interventions – a
one-size-fits-all approach will have limited purchase, for any intervention
must recognize the varied and contested nature of creativity. As well as
contrasting definition, within our small cluster of firms we found considerable
variation in suggestions as to how creativity could be managed.

How managers manage creativity
As Jeffcut and Pratt (2002) note, we should avoid stereotyping management

roles in organizations: the dichotomy of the 'rational bureaucrat' at the helm of the monolithic corporation against the free-wheeling creative anarchist facilitating the 'no-collar' workplace (Ross 2003) is not a true representation of the range of management practices embedded within either 'old' or 'new' economy firms. Despite claims that the creative company is one where traditional management protocols have been largely superseded by new forms of flexible (dis)organization (Davis and Scase 2000; Florida 2002), there is considerable variation in the ways in which creativity is managed. We would argue that such claims underestimate, for example, the role of workplace conflict in creative organizations and the ways in which traditional hierarchical structures remain prominent even in so-called creative, 'network' organizations; the end of formal hierarchy and top–down management is still some way off (Moule 1998). Our research revealed approaches to the management of creativity that varied between facilitative and enabling, formal and traditional, and completely 'hands-off' – depending on who the 'creatives' were deemed to be and how important creativity was perceived to be relative to other inputs.

In our study virtually all managers insisted that creativity required direct management (Banks et al. 2002). However, within this broad consensus approaches to management did vary – again three broad 'types' or styles were identified. One group exhibited an 'open' democratic style, whereby managers were concerned with developing and managing opportunities for creative exchanges and interactions among staff, in effect creating 'communities of practice' for creativity. This was often underpinned by informal codes of toleration, mutual respect and deliberative negotiations rather than formal control. In contrast, a significant number of managers relied on what might be dubbed the 'traditional' approach, where 'creative' staff were subjected to close monitoring and discipline, and found their work under constant scrutiny to ensure conformity to managerial priorities and provision of customer satisfaction. Experimentation and autonomy for the 'creatives' had to be curtailed as designers were often judged to be 'designing for themselves' and not for the client. Creatives were identified as more 'problematic' than non-creative staff and, while certain forms of personal expression and autonomy were tolerated, as one manager put it, errant creatives ran the risk of being identified as the 'bad apple'. We described a third type as a 'formal rejection' of any managerial obligation for managing creativity. Here creatives had the 'choice' of either fulfilling managerially prescribed targets or losing their job – there was no room for experimentation, discussion and debate within these firms. While creativity was recognized, it was not seen as a crucial input in securing competitive advantage. At the extreme end of this perspective some firms even rejected the idea that they were in fact 'creative' or worked in the 'creative sector' – creativity played no part in the discourse or practice of the firm.

Creativity, therefore, is a key asset in the knowledge economy, but as our findings suggest, even in 'creative industry' firms there may be little consensus on what creativity is, who possesses it, where it is applied and how best to manage it. Some would even deny it has value, or even exists in the context of what is widely regarded elsewhere as creative or knowledge work. Any attempts to stimulate creativity in firms must be mindful of the divergent and context-specific uses and understandings of the term.

Yet, despite this apparent diversity, there appears to be a set of common understandings that underpin managerial approaches to creativity and the management of 'creatives', assumptions that perhaps bring into question the ability of firms to mobilize and manage creativity in an effective – and indeed equitable and egalitarian – manner.

Barriers to change
Notwithstanding opportunities offered by the development of creative and interactive communities of practice, perhaps the most significant barrier to the development of a creative knowledge economy remains the reluctance of firms and managers to disengage from traditional, formal, organizational and managerial structures. Even when firms do espouse the 'no-collar' principles of the 'new' economy (Florida 2002), it is often the case that the discourse of creative freedom may only serve to mask managers' strategies of oppression – the 'freedom' to create offered by firms may be illusory in so far as it forces employees to work long and unsocial hours, accept 'flexible' contracts and embody a lifestyle that may be alien to their experience or culture (McRobbie 2002; Richards and Milestone 2000; Moule 1998; Sennett 1998). It is widely acknowledged that working conditions are often oppressive (McRobbie 2002) and much work in the creative sector remains casual, unstable, informal and underpaid. Further, as Nixon (2003) confirms in his study of advertising practitioners, because there is a tendency for managers' definitions and understandings of creativity to remain shackled by stereotypical understandings of who creatives are (usually young men), how they should look and behave (wild, eccentrically) and how they should be treated (over-indulged and/or over-disciplined), this often influences managerial strategies and techniques for team-building among 'creatives' in the firm. As our research confirmed, the internal culture of creative project teams, competing to win briefs or design contracts, is often masculinist in orientation, based on a heightened sense of conflict, competitiveness and 'edge'. Further, as others have noted, many external team-building initiatives tend to be male-centred in terms of being based around evening socializing/networking, sports-based 'away-days' or, in extreme cases, 'bonding' sessions involving crude and obvious appeals to mores of hegemonic masculinity (see Nixon 2003; Richards and Milestone 2000). Adkins (1999) argues that the mooted shift towards a new,

'de-traditionalized', knowledge-based economy may in fact be activating a process of *re*-traditionalization in terms of gender roles, whereby women who are often less able to 'fit in' and adequately embody the model of the new all-flexible, all-networking creative worker may find themselves displaced into more traditional work and domestic roles away from the heat of 'reflexive, knowledge intensive occupations' (1999, p. 126). Indeed, the consequences for those who generally fail to live up to the creative ideal may be stigmatization, marginalization (Prichard 2002), or, ultimately, the loss of their job. Avoiding such retrogressive practices clearly involves tackling some of the fundamental assumptions embedded in the culture of creative industry management.

Key questions for creativity
Given the poor state of knowledge about creativity in the workplace, managers are often unprepared to deal with it. In fact, they may not even know where to begin to approach managing creativity or what questions to ask about it. It would seem that the best place for managers and firms wishing to stimulate creative thinking to begin is with these broad questions:

- How is creativity defined in the context of the firm?
- Who possesses it and in what form is it expressed?
- What value is placed on creativity as an internal resource?
- How do intrinsic and extrinsic organizational structures enhance or undermine creativity?

By considering these questions, managers and firms might begin to develop a more reflexive, inventive approach to the management of creativity – one that may lead to new forms of project and team organization, human resource management, and a workplace culture that can empower rather than oppress or inhibit creative impulses. As Davis and Scase (2000) note, in the contemporary economic climate, management processes and the design of organizations have had to adapt to accommodate the needs of the growing number of creative, knowledge-based employees – managing creativity has become a necessity rather than a choice. The benefits of becoming more reflexive, innovative and creative have been widely reported – and many problem-solving techniques and creativity 'gurus' can now be called upon (McFadzean 1998, 2000). Yet, while specific tools and techniques may well make individual organizations more creative, the volatility of the market suggests that the real problem may lie in the ongoing tendency for managers and firms to view creativity solely as a calculable and manageable aspect of psychological behaviour, amenable to a quick fix. Such an assumption not only tends to negate the possibility of more pluralistic and reflexive analyses of creativity at the level of practice and within the wider workplace culture, but also wholly disclaims the socially constructed and mediated character of creativity.

Evaluation of industry and workplace context, structures of social and interpersonal interaction and managerial and organizational understandings of 'creativity' should be seen as vital components of any academic or corporate attempts to understand or stimulate creativity in contemporary organizations. The idea that 'creative activity in the economy is the next stage in the long-term development of our society' (Kelly 2004, p. 22) is a pervasive one, and so securing more detailed understandings of the general and firm-specific negotiations involved in the contested politics of creativity is a clear priority.

References

Adkins, L. 1999. 'Community and economy. A retraditionalization of gender?' *Theory, Culture and Society* **16**:119–39.

Amabile, T.M. 1996. *Creativity in Context*. Boulder, CO: Westview Press.

Amin, A. 1994. *Post-Fordism: A Reader*. Oxford: Blackwell.

Amin, A. 2000. 'Organisational learning through communities of practice', in *Millennium Schumpeter Conference*. University of Manchester.

Amin, A. and N. Thrift. 1992. 'Neo-Marshallian nodes in global networks'. *International Journal of Urban and Regional Research* **16**:571–87.

Banks, M., D. Calvey, J. Owen and D. Russell. 2002. 'Where the art is: Defining and managing creativity in new media SMEs'. *Creativity and Innovation Management* **11**:255–64.

Banks, M., A. Lovatt, J. O'Connor and C. Raffo. 2000. 'Risk and trust in the cultural industries'. *Geoforum* **31**:453–64.

Boden, M.A. 1990. *The Creative Mind: Myths and Mechanisms*. London: Weidenfeld and Nicolson.

Brown, J.S. and P. Duguid. 1991. 'Organizational knowledge and communities of practice'. *Organization Science* **2**:40–57.

Castells, M. 1996. *The Rise of the Network Society*. Oxford: Blackwell.

Cooke, P. 2002. *Knowledge Economies: Clusters, Learning and Cooperative Advantage*. London: Routledge.

Davis, H. and R. Scase. 2000. *Managing Creativity: The Dynamics of Work and Organisation*. Buckingham, UK: Open University Press.

Featherstone, M. 1991. *Consumer Culture and Postmodernism*. London: Sage.

Florida, R. 2002. *The Rise of the Creative Class*. New York: Basic Books.

Granovetter, M. 1973. 'The strength of weak ties'. *American Journal of Sociology* **78**:1360–80.

Jeffcut, P. and A. Pratt. 2002. 'Managing creativity in the cultural industries'. *Creativity and Innovation Management* **11**:225–33.

Kelly, J. 2004. 'Time to take a risk'. *The Independent* 4 March.

Lash, S. and J. Urry. 1994. *Economies of Signs and Space*. London: Sage.

Maskell, P., H. Eskelinen, I. Hannibalsen, A. Malmberg and E. Vatne. 1998. *Competitiveness, Localised Learning and Regional Development: Specialisation and Prosperity in Small Open Economies*. London: Routledge.

McFadzean, E. 1998. 'The creativity continuum: Towards a classification of problem solving techniques'. *Creativity and Innovation Management* **7**:131–9.

McFadzean, E. 2000. 'What can we learn from creative people? The story of Brian Eno'. *Management Decision* **38**:51–6.

McRobbie, A. 2002. 'Clubs to companies: Notes on the decline of political culture in speeded up creative worlds'. *Cultural Studies* **16**:516–31.

Moule, C. 1998. 'Regulation of work in small firms: A view from inside'. *Work, Employment and Society* **12**:635–53.

Nixon, S. 2003. *Advertising Cultures*. London: Sage.

Piore, M. and C. Sabel. 1984. *The Second Industrial Divide: Possibilities for Prosperity.* New York: Basic Books.

Porter, M.E. 1990. *The Competitive Advantage of Nations.* Basingstoke, UK: Macmillan.

Pratt, A. 2000. 'New media, the new economy and new spaces'. *Geoforum* 31:425–36.

Preston, P. and A. Kerr. 2001. 'Digital media, nation states and local cultures: The case of new media content production'. *Media, Culture and Society* 23:109–31.

Prichard, C. 2002. 'Creative selves? Critically reading creativity in management discourse'. *Creativity and Innovation Management* 11:265–76.

Rickards, T. 1999. *Creativity and the Management of Change.* Oxford: Blackwell.

Richards, N. and K. Milestone. 2000. 'What difference does it make? Women's pop cultural production and consumption in Manchester'. *Sociological Research Online* 5. http://www.socresonline.org.uk/5/1/richards.html.Russell, D., D. Calvey and M. Banks. 2003. 'Creating new learning communities: Towards effective e-learning production'. *Journal of Workplace Learning* 15:34–44.

Ross, A. 2003. *No Collar: The Humane Workplace and its Hidden Costs.* New York: Basic Books.

Russell, D., D. Calvey and M. Banks. 2003. 'Creating new learning communities: Towards effective e-learning production'. *Journal of Workplace Learning* 15:34–44

Russell, P. and R. Evans. 1992. *The Creative Manager.* San Francisco, CA: Jossey-Bass.

Scott, A.J. 2000. *The Cultural Economy of Cities.* London: Sage.

Sennett, J. 2001. 'Clusters, co-location and external sources of knowledge: The case of small instrumentation and control firms in the London region'. *Planning Practice and Research* 16:21–37.

Sennett, R. 1998. *The Corrosion of Character: The Personal Consequences of Work in the New Capitalism.* New York: W.W. Norton.

Tan, G. 1998. 'Managing creativity in organizations: A total systems approach'. *Creativity and Innovation Management* 7:23–31.

Wenger, E. 1998. *Communities of Practice: Learning, Meaning and Identity.* Cambridge: Cambridge University Press.

Wenger, E.C. and W.M. Snyder. 2000. 'Communities of practice: The organisational frontier'. *Harvard Business Review* January:139–45.

18 Inexperience and inefficiency in information transactions: making the most of management consultants

Stuart Macdonald

Experience with management consultants

There can be few organizations of any size, in any sector of a developed economy, that have not at some time hired management consultants. The management consultant is a creature of the knowledge-based economy. On the face of it, the function the consultant performs in this economy is simple and self-evident: the consultant sells the client the information required to manage the organization. But information transactions are seldom simple and this one is no exception. In this chapter, an information perspective, rather than the conventional management perspective, is applied to explore just what is going on.

While there is much the organization can gain from management consultants, there are also problems inherent in hiring them, often deep-rooted and seldom acknowledged. Management consultants can easily become addictive, each successive consultancy increasingly likely to lead to another. Management consultancy can as easily become incestuous, consultants being hired because other managers hire them. And management consultants can encourage dependency, managers desperate to meet the expectations made of them hiring consultants and finding that this only increases the expectations. Together, these ingredients make a powerful cocktail, and yet its effects are not often appreciated. The explanation would seem to be that management consultants are now so pervasive that it is hard to remember ever being without them. To be sure, there is dissatisfaction with the performance of management consultants (e.g. Dwyer 1993), and consequently prescriptive tips galore on how to get more from your management consultant. Generally, the assumption seems to be that those who have most experience of management consultants are best placed to proffer advice. But if hiring management consultants has indeed become compulsive, even compulsory, this may not be so.

Not all the considerable growth of the management consultancy industry in the 1990s is explained by regular clients hiring more management consultants (Clark 1995). There was also much new business, and some of it from organizations that might be considered unlikely customers for consultants. This chapter looks at three such cases. First it investigates the use of management consultants in the former Soviet bloc, specifically Poland. The rise of capitalism following the fall of communism was to be facilitated by despatching management consultants from the West, an uncompromising introduction to the realities of Western business. The chapter then turns to a trade union, examining the use of management consultants by the Communication Workers' Union in the UK. Lastly, the chapter considers the use of management consultants in the Church of England, not exactly their customary terrain. Are these new clients innocents cast to the wolves, or do they somehow manage to survive, and even profit from, their experience with the management consultant?

This chapter is based on research that hypothesized that the information transaction between consultant and client cannot be effected by the market because of the nature of information. The relationship between consultant and client can help compensate for this market failure (Macdonald and Simpson 2001). Basically, it was argued, if an information transaction is to occur, the management consultant and the hiring manager have to collude. The closer their relationship, the easier and more likely such collusion. But the collusion that facilitates an information transaction also allows benefits to be bestowed on consultant and client rather than on the organization that pays them both. Here there was no established relationship between management consultant and client, and no expectation on the part of the client that a relationship was of any importance. Thus, there was little opportunity for collusion. Some forty interviews were conducted, mostly in Poland, where managers from several organizations participated in the study. Ten management consultants were also interviewed because they had experience of dealing with novice clients, though not necessarily these clients. The chapter is laden with quotations from these interviews, offered to illustrate, rather than prove, theory. The conclusions are necessarily no more than thoughts, though interesting thoughts, and perhaps even significant.

Theory

The management consultant earns his living – and some make a very good living – by advising managers how to manage. The rationale is that the external consultant's advice is different from, but complementary to, information already available inside the organization. The consultant, it is argued, can look at the organization from a new perspective, one directed by experience in comparable organizations, and informed by the latest management methods. When clients re-hire the same consultants – and they often do – they would seem to be eroding the impartiality, and hence much of the value, of the information they might receive (Robinson 1982). The explanation may be that such value was always more likely to be realized in theory than in practice and that managers hiring consultants are generally seeking other benefits altogether, benefits that the usual consultant, the regular man, the one already 'up to speed', understands he is expected to provide (Huczynski 1993).

On the face of it, the client simply has a need and the consultant the means of satisfying the resultant demand. But buying and selling information is rarely simple, as this volume makes clear. The problems reflect the peculiar characteristics of information as an economic good, and particularly the difficulty of expressing demand for information in ignorance (Clark 1993). After all, the putative client cannot know what he does not know, nor can he be allowed to know what the management consultant does know. If the consultant reveals what he knows before he is hired, then there is no need to hire him to acquire his knowledge. So, clients are in no position to express demand, and management consultants find difficulty displaying supply. This fundamental problem of matching supply to demand tends to be overlooked by those who study the activities of management consultants. Many take a prescriptive approach to the subject, proffering advice either on how to be a management consultant, or on how to use one (e.g. Corcoran and McLean 1998; Covin and Fisher 1991; Frankenhuis 1977; Litwin et al. 1996; Mitchell 1994; Nelson and Economy 1997; Schlegelmilch et al. 1992; Shapiro et al. 1993; Washburn 1989). While such advice may be wise and welcome – and is infinitely more entertaining than a mechanistic approach to the topic (e.g. Kolb and Frohman 1970) – it does tend to disregard the difficulties inherent in the information transaction between management consultant and client. More particularly, it neglects the exploitation of this relationship that is required to overcome these difficulties, · and the consequences of this exploitation.

A small subset of the literature on management consultancy is more reflective (see, e.g., Clark and Fincham 2002). For example, some challenging work explores the link between management consultancy and management method. While the 'churn' of fads is clearly in the consultant's interest, it would seem that the client has even more incentive to welcome the latest management fashion with open arms (Abrahamson 1996; Collins 2000; Fincham 1995; Gill and Whittle 1992; Huczynski 1993, 1996). Much is expected of managers these days, and the manager who does not embrace change as demonstrably as other managers is showing little regard for his career (Clark and Salaman 1998a). This trickle of querying literature looks at the provenance of management consultancy in the huge auditing firms of the USA, with their diversification into the provision of advice, first on IT and then on strategy (Kipping 1996; McKenna 1995) and relates this development to the domination of the world's management thinking by the American school of management (Furusten 1995; Watson 1994). It also reflects on the issue of particular concern in this chapter – the relationship between the management consultant and the manager who hires the consultant.

Given the pressure on the manager to be seen to perform, not hiring a consultant may be an unrealistic option (Ginsberg and Abrahamson 1991). The explanation runs much deeper than managers seeking extra authority for their decisions, or somewhere to pass the buck if things go wrong. It lies in the spiral of expectation and dependency established by the hiring of management consultants, especially expensive ones. The manager can easily find himself trapped, the confidence to manage insidiously but surely dissipating (Sturdy 1997).

> Dependency is increased by using consultants. You can get hooked on consultants. You can become consultant-happy.
>
> Management consultant

> I would not have wanted to rely on my own judgement.
>
> Experienced client

Key to understanding the workings of management consultancy is not just that the relationship with clients is important, but also that it is information that is being bought and sold (Gummesson 1978). Inevitably, this entails difficulties, and where there are difficulties there are also opportunities. It is because market signals are so faint and distorted in the sale of the consultant's information that the relationship is allowed to compensate for, and guide, the transaction (Clark and Salaman 1998b). So, a tacit understanding develops, neither party wishing to examine the failure of the market and the consequent reliance on the relationship between consultant and client to compensate (Easley and Harding 1999). While such understandings have a major part to play in organizational life, and are explored in the theory of the convention (Orléan 1994; Salais et al. 1998), the theory has yet to be applied to the study of management consultancy. This chapter retreats from such a monumental task. Instead, it explores but one nook of the situation: what happens when management consultants meet managers who do not appreciate the convention, who may not even realize that there is one. The following studies suggest very strongly that, in the absence of the relationship, and the understanding that goes with it, management consultant and client struggle to effect an information transaction. This struggle may be inefficient, but it may be necessary if the hiring organization, rather than the hiring manager and the hireling, is to reap benefits from the transaction.

The Poles

With the collapse of communist governments in Eastern Europe, the enterprises of the former Soviet bloc were suddenly exposed to capitalism incarnate – the management consultant. Western governments argued that the conversion of Eastern enterprises to Western capitalism would be most thoroughly and speedily accomplished by sending in Western management consultants, and various programmes – most prominently the Phare Programme of the European Commission – were concocted to do just this (Jack 1991). Of the 2 billion euros spent by Phare to the end of 1994, between 30 per cent and 40 per cent went on consultants (Marsh 1995). These seem to have been less successful than the programmes promised, but then the transition to a very different sort of economic and social system has been much more difficult than Western enthusiasm allowed (Hopsicke 1999).

> I met Western management consultants. They try to help. They came here with a feeling of mission and vision. I met these people with full respect for their knowledge. They were always surprised that we could manage. They started from the point that only we know, we will save you.
>
> Polish client

It is hard to find Polish managers uncritical of Western management consultants working in Eastern Europe. Much of this criticism focuses on the disregard for cultural differences displayed both by Western management consultants working in the East, and by the government programmes that sent them there (see, e.g., Fisher 1991). Among the cultural obstacles facing consultants in Poland was the notion, no longer common in the West, that bringing in management consultants suggested that an organization was in trouble, much like sending in the bailiffs. Similarly, hiring consultants was taken to be a sign of inadequate management.

> [Managers] buy consultants because they are not competent. If they were competent, they would not. It's as simple as that. Or if they are competent, they have not yet proven themselves. If some manager comes to me with a problem, it signals he has reached his competence level.
>
> Polish management consultant

Equally quaint is the notion prevalent in Poland that management consultants are hired simply for the advice they give and for no other reason. In the West, management consultants are hired for a plethora of reasons; to obtain advice is but one, and probably not even a very important one (Clark and Salaman 1996; Huczynski 1993). But in Poland, what the consultant will do for the organization is all that matters. In Polish organizations, an expectation prevails that would seem strange in the West and that astonished the first Western consultants to work in the country. It is that management consultants should know something about their client's industry, and that they should have practical experience rather than just a mastery of theory.

> I would rather hire a 40 or 50 year-old with business experience than someone young and dynamic.
>
> Polish client

> I am watching carefully how they [McKinsey] recruit people in Poland. Usually they are just-graduated students. I don't trust 24 year-old consultants who tell me how badly I am managing the company.
>
> Polish client

In the West, organizations hire the big consultancies at least partly for the credibility the reputation of these firms lends their advice; their very presence can lend credibility. Although foreign investors in Poland and foreign managers there may welcome the involvement of a name they recognize, the name has no great value among Polish managers. This reality may not yet have dawned on some Western consultancies, even those with Polish staff (see Merwin 1987).

> There is general suspicion against consultants, especially foreign consultants. It is felt that all this money is going to people who do nothing. No one would praise me for hiring Coopers and Lybrand as such.
>
> Polish client

It can be argued that the squads of management consultants that arrived in Eastern Europe have actually delayed its transition to capitalism. Because their advice was culturally inappropriate, its implementation met with little success among clients and discouraged other enterprises from taking similar courses. In Poland, managers are unanimously scathing about the 'Marriott Brigade', the term adopted for Western consultants rarely seen outside Warsaw's best hotel, and the condescension of at least some Western consultants seems thoroughly deserving of their scorn.

> Foreign consultants came here not because someone identified a need, but because foreign schemes had money to spare. This helped create the Marriott Brigade.
>
> Polish client

Not only did Western management consultants give consulting a bad name among their potential clients; they also undercut prices in the local market – a fee reversal made possible by the subsidies of Western governments (Saunderson-Meyer 1992). In consequence, growth of the local industry remained stunted until Western consultancies turned to hiring local staff and working with Polish consultancies.

The Polish experience is instructive. It allows an examination of management consultancy stripped of many of the new clothes it wears in the West. Without the support of reputation, the working methods of management consultants attract a level of suspicion and criticism not common in the West.

> I was told you have to be very careful [with management consultants]. They send you names of senior people then, when the contact is signed, you never see these people.
>
> Polish client

Their job is to find problems so even if the one you think you have isn't, they will find one.

Polish client

But most impressive in the Polish experience is the simple insistence of Polish clients that the management consultant should do precisely what the management consultant promises to do, so that the organization really will benefit from the consultant's efforts. Polish managers expect to work their consultants hard.

I pay for a consultant and get this feeling I can demand that they do the job. I can't demand this of my own staff.

Polish client

The trade union

The period in the UK when the trade unions were said to be holding the country to ransom is well within living memory. The threat was in some part responsible for the rise of Thatcherism in the 1980s, a right-wing reaction that was replicated in many other countries and that was accompanied by a philosophy that easily accommodated the management consultant. The new, privatized, market-led economy elevated the manager to heroic status as leader, visionary and entrepreneur, and where the manager went, the consultant was sure to follow. It is little wonder that the vast increase in the use of management consultants coincided with their political acceptability.

A return to left-wing government during the 1990s in Britain and elsewhere might have been expected to bode ill for management consultants. Not so. The 'Third Way' is somewhat removed from red-blooded socialism and the UK government has long encouraged the private sector's use of consultants (Segal Quince Wicksteed 1989), especially in SMEs, and has become a heavy user itself. Perhaps more surprising still is that even the trade unions are now employing management consultants. These consultants advise not just on the customary concerns of unions, but also on corporate strategy, the traditional preserve of senior management. Trade unions hire management consultants so that they may – as their consultants might put it – operate on a level playing field, as well briefed and informed as management itself. Equally surprising is the skill with which the inexperienced trade union seems to use its consultants.

Consider the example of the Communications Workers' Union (CWU), anxious to protect its members not simply against the machinations of management, but also against the government's plans for the Post Office. The Post Office suffered a decline in business throughout the 1990s. Senior managers and government responded by closing many of the Crown post offices – post offices in public ownership – to reduce costs and to make the whole organization more attractive for privatization. The pay and working conditions of union members – indeed, their very jobs – were threatened and the CWU called in consultants.

The Communication Workers' Union is the product of the amalgam of the Union of Communication Workers and the National Communications Union in 1995. The privatization issue arose just after the 1992 election. In response, the Union of Communication Workers had seen fit to approach a political lobbyist, an expensive exercise but entirely successful. In those days, only a slim majority remained to the Conservative government, and many Conservative MPs were concerned about their prospects of being returned to Parliament at the next election. Those from rural constituencies were reminded by the lobbyist just how unpopular closing hundreds of country post offices would be and the privatization issue was dropped. When it reared its head again, the Labour Party was in power with a huge majority and unlikely to be swayed by political lobbyists arguing the case of voters in the shires. A new strategy was required, one that needed resources beyond those of the Communication Workers' Union. Through John Kay at London Business School, the CWU approached London Economics to undertake the task.

> I knew they were credible. In no way was he fishing for business. Kay was also a friend of a friend. I just sort of talked my way round my network of mates. I may have started out with an idea. John Kay clinched it.
>
> Trade union client

> We have a reasonable size research department here and could have done the work, but we needed the credibility of London Economics.
>
> Trade union client

Credibility seems to have been the quality most valued by the trade union client, but within this was included influence with those that mattered, in this case the government rather than management.

> London Economics [1998] produced a superb document which cost us a great deal of money. In terms of credibility in the highest echelons of government, it was invaluable to us. It is no exaggeration to say that the London Economics report was a crucial part of the argument we used to keep the Post Office in the public sector.
>
> Trade union client

To reinforce this credibility, the CWU co-sponsored a report from the Institute of Public Policy Research on the public corporation model (Robinson and Rubin 1999). This contributed to the model's legitimacy and acceptability, but the consultant's report had established the principle. The fundamental problems of the Post Office remain in that its strategic options are constrained by limitations on its borrowing as long as it remains in the public sector, but efforts are now being made to find innovative solutions to these problems. In that brute privatization no longer appears to be an option, the union and its use of consultants have been outstandingly successful.

Just why should a trade union have proved so proficient in its use of management consultants? Could it be that while client managers in other organizations are at least in part concerned about what the management consultant can do for them as individuals, trade unionists who hire management consultants cannot have quite the same interest? They are responsible, either directly or indirectly, to a membership unlikely to be impressed by management consultants *per se*, and perhaps with an instinctive distaste for them (see Labour Research Department 1988; Transport and General Workers' Union 1983). Moreover, unions are fundamentally democratic organizations whose members must be persuaded. Management consultants are accustomed to catering for the needs of senior managers, for clients who exert control over their employees. When management consultants work for trade unions, their whole rhetoric and value system are redundant; they have to prove their worth by the advice they give. It may also be that the deep suspicion unionists can feel for management consultants spurs them on – much like clients in Poland – to ride the consultants hard, extracting every ounce of benefit they can. To be sure, management consultants who have worked for trade unions do not regard them as a soft touch.

The Church
The Church of England also employs management consultants and also makes effective use of them. One use is advising on the training requirements of vicars. The modern Church of England considers itself to be as much in need of management, and consequently all the trappings of management (of which management consultants are but one), as any other global organization. And the Church is also a decidedly political organism. It would be quite impossible for any external consultant to proffer any sort of advice anywhere in such an organization without threatening the prevailing balance of power.

> We have just conducted a telephone survey of rural deans . . . Rural deans are now much more into management. . . . Some of the magnet is contact with bishops, which everybody wants.
>
> Church client

If ever there were an organization whose managers might be forgiven their anxiety to hire the usual consultants, it must be the Church of England. It would be difficult to imagine a more Byzantine organization, one in which subtleties of precedence and position have greater influence over performance, in which behaviour is as much determined by conditioning and culture as by code. One would have expected a fundamental requirement of management consultants working for the Church to be that they are thoroughly inured in its ways. Instead, the Church's consultants are not even expected to be Christians; such a requirement is seen as irrelevant, even a disadvantage.

> There are a lot of Christian consultants whom I would not hire.
>
> Church client

> The team wanted someone who was not in the Church to provide a different perspective.
>
> Church client

A large part of the explanation seems to lie in the unwillingness and perhaps sheer inability of the Church of England to pass itself off as an organization just like any other. It may need management, and therefore management consultants, like other organizations, but the Church of England can hardly pretend to be a learning organization getting itself close to its global customers with a just-in-time, total quality product. If such notions make little sense in other organizations, they make none at all in the Church. The problem for management consultants who might work for the Church – a problem they encounter when working for trade unions – is that these notions are often inherent in the way they think, how they work, and what they advise (Kolb and Frohman 1970, p. 52; Werr et al. 1997). Many management consultants are unable to work on any other basis, in any other currency. Such consultants find they cannot treat the Church like other organizations without seeming slightly silly.

> Questions 4 and 5 – on spirituality – need to be up front.
>
> Management consultant

In the light of the strong intellectual tradition of the Church and its limited familiarity with management methods, many management consultants run the risk of actually being told they are silly. Consider the hard-nosed approach to volunteers as sources of external advice for the Church.

> The problem with using volunteers as consultants is that you can't bollock them; they just walk away.
>
> Church client

The consultant's reluctance to explore the hostile terrain offered by the Church of England is conventionally and conveniently explained in terms of money: the Church is unable to afford the high consultancy fees of the commercial consultant, and the commercial consultant is unwilling to accept lower fees. But the disjunction is really much more fundamental. Most management consultants would be, at the very least, disturbed by the apparent chaos they would encounter in the Church of England. They would certainly be frustrated in their attempts to make its systems and structure more conventional. For example, while Church expenditure is necessarily a formal commitment, much Church income is alarmingly informal and uncommitted. And while much of the Church workforce might be committed, it too is informal; parishioners cannot be forced to work longer or harder, or even to retain their membership of the organization. Such workers might well take exception to performance indicators or measures of efficiency. What measures should be used to determine, say, whether a funeral is conducted efficiently? What indicators disclose level of performance in coping with bereavement? The very order and efficiency that is central to so much consultancy advice sits awkwardly with an ecclesiastical tradition that values diverse opinion and encourages criticism of the sort that would lead to instant dismissal in other organizations (see Baritz 1987; Oliver 1998).

There is absolutely no point, then, in the Church of England administrators hiring bright young MBAs from the large consultancies, or even hiring more experienced consultants from smaller firms (Coghlan 1987). There is little tolerance in the Church of peddlers of fads and fashions (Abrahamson 1996; Armstrong 1994). A rather special person is always required, and such consultants are found through personal recommendations and individual networks, much as the trade unions find consultants. A person is sought who can supplement the Church's own resources with a very specific skill, rather than provide a complete package of assistance (Cummings et al. 1990). Above all, someone whom people in the Church will respect and whose skills they will value is essential. The sort of management consultant most valued in most other large organizations does not satisfy these requirements at all.

Bringing in people in serious professions helps people in the Church to listen.
Church client

Thoughts
One would expect new clients of management consultants to be ineffective users of their services, less able than experienced clients to make the most of what management consultants have to offer. Those who hold management consultants in particularly low esteem might even expect consultants to take advantage of these novices. And yet the examples offered here suggest that such clients are perfectly able to look after themselves and to make good use of consultants. Indeed, they would seem to be much more capable than many experienced clients of extracting value from management consultants. Why might this be?

It is always possible that novice clients strike a sympathetic chord in consultants, inspiring them to work especially hard on their behalf, almost out of charity. This is possible, but not probable. It is only slightly more likely that consultants work hard to attract repeat business by impressing new and uncommitted clients. But by far the most probable explanation is that the very innocence of these new clients means that they strike a deal with management consultants very different from that struck by more practised clients. The latter, it would seem, are primarily concerned with what the management consultant will do for them as individuals (Sturdy 1997). The organization facilitates this transaction and might well benefit eventually, at least indirectly, but the primary beneficiary is the hiring manager acting in collusion with a consultant well aware of this tacit arrangement. Novice clients are ignorant of this understanding, this convention; they actually believe that management consultants are hired for the direct benefit of the organization, and they do their utmost to ensure that the consultants they hire provide this benefit.

If this hypothesis is correct, one cannot help but speculate on how long it will be before these innocents become sufficiently practised to achieve the same relationship with management consultants as experienced clients (Edvardsson 1990). The transition may not be a simple function of time, but may also depend upon the acceptance of management method, of management itself, in areas and activities in which these would not previously have been considered appropriate. In other words, the intervention of the management consultant in all things may be contingent on the acceptance of all things being manageable and the subsequent argument that methods are essential to management (see Pascale 1990). From this position, it is but a small step to the management consultant, and but short hops from the first consultancy to the second, and the third, and the fourth.

This is not an inevitable progression, of course. It is quite possible that taking on management consultants will always be exceptional in some organizations and that there will always be novice clients. The problem with such a scenario is that it would probably require the determined intervention of management, especially senior management, to restrict or prohibit the use of consultants. It is hard to imagine such intervention being effective without the use of management consultants. Put bluntly, a strategy not to use management consultants would be unlikely to prevail unless it were devised, justified and implemented by management consultants (see Ginsberg 1986). Profligate use of management consultants in the British Broadcasting Corporation was stemmed only by management consultants advising against the use of management consultants (*The Economist* 1997).

It seems that those organizations that make much use of management consultants may have lessons to learn from those that make much less use, that there is something like an inverse learning curve. All these novice clients were able to take advantage of their inexperience to gain benefits from their consultants that might have eluded experienced clients. They saw the function of the consultant and their relationship with the consultant as disarmingly obvious. It followed from this – especially in Poland – that the consultant could not do the job properly unless he knew something of the client's business, or – as in the other cases – made the client's business central to the advice offered. In most cases, the consultant's value to the client lay in his ability to complement organizational knowledge with his own experience and expertise, and to work with this combination in the outside world. There was no interest whatsoever in any of the management methods with which management consultants belabour their more experienced clients. These novice clients were already suspicious of management consultants in general and would not have been impressed by the latest in management fashion. It would take a brave and foolish management consultant to offer the Church of England a mission statement, or to tout empowerment to a trade union. These clients were similarly unimpressed by the reputations of management consultants, an attitude which made apparent how very little else some consultancies have to offer. Each of these clients sought a custom product from the consultant, not a pre-packaged one and certainly not one that had already been used elsewhere. It is striking how different this is from the requirements of many practised clients. This is the demand that has fuelled the vast growth of the management consultancy industry. A possible consequence may be that those organizations long accustomed to using consultants have become increasingly consultant-friendly, as attuned to the requirements of the consultant as to those of the market. In this happy world, supply of consultancy services creates its own demand for yet more consultancy services.

These examples of individuals who are not steeped in the ways of management consultants reveal something of the essence of consultancy. Its weaknesses become evident, but so too do its strengths. In each of these cases, the consultant was skilful and flexible enough to play an essentially political role, and with great success (see Gattiker and Larwood 1985). Each was expected to devise solutions that were intellectually robust and that would withstand vigorous criticism. And each was expected to devise these solutions for an environment that – like most organizations in practice – was in a state of working disarray. It may be that experienced clients are not making the most of their consultants when they allow them to shape the organization to suit the consultant's methods, when they are timorously respectful of the consultant's credentials (Poulfelt and Payne 1994). Demanding what is fashionable circumvents some of the problems inherent in effecting the information transaction between consultant and client; the relationship between the two avoids most of the others. Where there is no relationship, client and consultant struggle to match information demand to information supply, but with real benefit for the hiring organization. There are surely lessons here for all organizations that hire management consultants.

Acknowledgements

This research was financially supported by the Economic and Social Research Council in the UK (grant number H52427500297). The author is extremely grateful to the very many managers and management consultants kind enough to provide information for the study. Neither they nor the organizations to which they belong are responsible for the arguments and opinions presented here. These, and whatever errors the chapter contains, are the responsibility of the author alone.

References

Abrahamson, E. 1996. 'Management fashion'. *Academy of Management Review* 21:254–85.
Armstrong, J. 1994. *Why Management Fads Persist: On Experience Curves: The BCG Matrix, Escalation Bias, and Such.* Philadelphia, PA: University of Pennsylvania.
Baritz, L. 1987. *The Servants of Power. A History of the Use of Social Science in American Industry.* New York: John Wiley & Sons.
Clark, T. 1993. 'The market provision of management services, information asymmetries and service quality – some market solutions: An empirical example'. *British Journal of Management* 4:235–51.
Clark, T. 1995. *Managing Consultants: Consultancy as the Management of Impressions.* Birmingham, UK: Open University Press.
Clark, T. and R. Fincham. 2002. *Critical Consulting: New Perspectives on the Management Advice Industry.* Oxford: Blackwell.
Clark, T. and G. Salaman. 1996. 'The management guru as organizational witchdoctor'. *Organization* 3:85–107.
Clark, T. and G. Salaman. 1998a. 'Telling tales: Management gurus' narratives and the construction of managerial identity'. *Journal of Management Studies* 35:137–61.
Clark, T. and G. Salaman. 1998b. 'Creating the "right" impression: Towards a dramaturgy of management consulting'. *Services Industries Journal* 18:18–38.
Coghlan, D. 1987. 'Corporate strategy in Catholic religious orders'. *Long Range Planning* 20:44–51.
Collins, D. 2000. *Management Fads and Buzzwords: Critical–Practical Perspectives.* London: Routledge.
Corcoran, J. and F. McLean. 1998. 'The selection of management consultants: How are governments dealing with this difficult decision? An exploratory study'. *International Journal of Public Sector Management* 11:37–54.
Covin, T. and T. Fisher. 1991. 'Consultant and client must work together'. *Journal of Management Consulting* 6:11–19.
Cummings, P., D. White and S. Wisniowski. 1990. 'Strategic simplicity'. *McKinsey Quarterly* 3:80–90.
Dwyer, J. 1993. 'Who gains but the gurus from the business bull market?' *Works Management* January:12–15.
Easley, C. and C. Harding. 1999. 'Client vs. consultant: Fishbowl or foxhole?' *Journal of Management Consulting* 10:3–8.
Edvardsson, E. 1990. 'Management consulting: Towards a successful relationship'. *International Journal of Service Industry Management* 1:4–19.
Fincham, R. 1995. 'Business process reengineering and the commodification of managerial knowledge'. *Journal of Marketing Management* 11:107–19.
Fisher, A. 1991. 'Chipping away at mountainous problems in the East: Germany'. *Financial Times* 15 May:vii.
Frankenhuis, J. 1977. 'How to get a good consultant'. *Harvard Business Review* December:133–9.
Furusten, S. 1995. *The Managerial Discourse: A Study of the Creation and Diffusion of Popular Management Knowledge.* Uppsala, Sweden: Department of Business Studies, Uppsala University.

Gattiker, U. and L. Larwood. 1985. 'Why do clients employ management consultants?' *Consultation* **4**:119–29.

Gill, J. and S. Whittle. 1992. 'Management by panacea: Accounting for transience'. *Journal of Management Studies* **30**:281–95.

Ginsberg, A. 1986. 'Do external consultants influence strategic adaptation? An empirical investigation'. *Consultation* **5**:93–102.

Ginsberg, A. and E. Abrahamson. 1991. 'Champions of change and strategic shifts: The role of internal and external change advocates'. *Journal of Management Studies* **28**:173–90.

Gummesson, E. 1978. 'The marketing of professional services: An organisational dilemma'. *European Journal of Marketing* **13**:308–18.

Hopsicke, D. 1999. 'Masters of the universe'. Broadcast 5 September in the UK on Channel 4.

Huczynski, A. 1993. 'Explaining the succession of management fads'. *International Journal of Human Resource Management* **4**:443–63.

Huczynski, A. 1996. *Management Gurus*. London: Routledge.

Jack, A. 1991. 'New realism sets in: Eastern Europe'. *Financial Times* 15 May:vi.

Kipping, M. 1996. 'The US influence on the evolution of management consultancies in Britain, France, and Germany since 1945'. *Business and Economic History* **25**:112–23.

Kolb, A. and A. Frohman. 1970. 'An organization development approach to management consulting'. *Sloan Management Review* Fall:51–65.

Labour Research Department. 1988. *Management Consultants: Who They Are and How to Deal with Them*. London: LRD Publications.

Litwin, G., J. Bray and K. Lusk Brooke. 1996. *Mobilizing the Organization: Bringing Strategy to Life*. London: Prentice-Hall.

Macdonald, S. and M. Simpson. 2001. 'Learning from management consultants: The lesson for management researchers'. *Prometheus* **19**:117–33.

Marsh, V. 1995. 'The unique tasks of transition: Eastern Europe'. *Financial Times* 12 September.

McKenna, C. 1995. 'The origins of modern management consulting'. *Business and Economic History* **24**:51–8.

Merwin, J. 1987. ' "We don't learn from our clients, we learn from each other" '. *Forbes* 19 October:122–8.

Mitchell, V.W. 1994. 'Problems and risks in the purchasing of consultancy services'. *Service Industries Journal* **14**:315–39.

Nelson, B. and P. Economy. 1997. *Consulting for Dummies*. Foster City, CA: IDG Books.

Oliver, N. 1998. 'Rational choice or leap of faith? The creation and defence of a management orthodoxy'. *Iconoclastic Papers* **1**.

Orléan, A. 1994. *Analyse Economique des Conventions*. Paris: Presses Universitaires de France.

Pascale, R. 1990. *Managing on the Edge*. New York: Simon and Schuster.

Poulfelt, F. and A. Payne. 1994. 'Management consultants: Client and consultant perspectives'. *Scandinavian Journal of Management* **10**:421–36.

Robinson, P. and M. Rubin. 1999. *The Future of the Post Office*. London: Institute of Public Policy Research.

Robinson, R. 1982. 'The importance of "outsiders" in small firm strategic planning'. *Academy of Management Journal* **25**:80–93.

Salais, R., E. Chatel and D. Rivaud-Danset. 1998. *Institutions et Conventions*. Paris: Ecole des Hautes Etudes en Sciences Sociales.

Saunderson-Meyer, W. 1992. 'Under pressure: The strategy boutiques'. *Financial Times* 21 October.

Schlegelmilch, B., A. Diamantopoulos and S. Moore. 1992. 'The market for management consulting in Britain'. *Management Decision* **30**:44–54.

Segal Quince Wicksteed. 1989. *Evaluation of the Consultancy Initiatives*. London: HMSO.

Shapiro, E., R. Eccles and T. Soske. 1993. 'Consulting: Has the solution become part of the problem?' *Sloan Management Review* Summer:89–95.

Sturdy, A. 1997. 'The consultancy process: An insecure business?' *Journal of Management Studies* **34**:389–413.

The Economist. 1997. 'A very British coup'. *The Economist* 30 August.

Transport and General Workers' Union. 1983. *Management Consultants: Friends or Enemies?* London: TGWU Research Bulletin 1.

Washburn, S. 1989. 'The many ways to hire prospective clients'. *Journal of Management Consulting* **5**:34–40.

Watson, T. 1994. 'Management "flavours of the month": Their role in managers' lives'. *International Journal of Human Resource Management* **5**:893–909.

Werr, A., T. Stjernberg and P. Docherty. 1997. 'The functions of methods of change in management consultancy'. *Journal of Organizational Change Management* **10**:288–307.

19 The knowledge worker: a metaphor in search of a meaning?
Richard Joseph

Introduction

The concept of the knowledge worker has now been around for over 40 years. Given the importance of the knowledge economy in present policy discussions, one could be excused for thinking that the knowledge worker, as an academic topic, would have been well and truly settled and now a feature of management practice. However, ironically, this would seem not to be the case. Of three major international handbooks published late in 2003, *The Blackwell Handbook of Organizational Learning and Knowledge Management* (Easterby-Smith and Lyles 2003), *The International Handbook on Innovation* (Shavinina 2003) and *New Economy Handbook* (Jones 2003), only one makes reference to knowledge workers and knowledge work in its index. If anything, the knowledge worker appears to be subsumed within more generally accepted terms such as organizational learning, the learning organization, organizational knowledge and knowledge management. What might this be indicative of? This chapter explores the concept of knowledge worker as a metaphor and asks if the meanings commonly associated with it may need revitalization. Weick (2003, p. xviii) has remarked that

> The concepts of learning that we now work with may seem more complex than their predecessors because we have made more refined differentiations of what we inherited. But it is also true that what we have inherited are simplified solutions to what originally were much more complex problems. The solutions have been simplified as they go from investigator to investigator and become farther removed from their origins. To go back to earlier work, to devolve from what we understand now, is not just an exercise in nostalgia that revisits earlier simplicities. Going back is also a chance to see in more detail a complex basic issue, a crucial turning point, a choice that turned out to result in the simplifications we now work with.

In order to explore the knowledge worker metaphor, I intend to follow two streams of argument. First I will draw on the work of Jacques (2000) and discuss what it means to talk about knowledge worker as a metaphor. Essentially, metaphors are linguistic or symbolic devices for interpreting complex phenomena in terms of something that may be familiar to us. Metaphors can play a significant role in political language (Edelman 1977).

Second, I will follow Weick's advice on the benefits of 'going back' and revisit two seminal thinkers, Machlup, the economist and Drucker, the management expert. Both of these well-known scholars are attributed with making a major contribution to the genesis of the knowledge worker concept over 40 years ago (Cortada 1998).[1] From the vantage point of the past, it is hoped that a 'choice point', in other words a turning point, can be identified and hence a way of rethinking the path already taken. The argument put forward in this chapter is that, for whatever reason, we have inherited an interpretation of the knowledge worker substantially influenced by Drucker. The future research agenda seems more promising, however, if we are willing to accept a greater intellectual debt to Machlup.

The knowledge worker as a metaphor
In this section I wish to acknowledge the work of Jacques (2000), who urges us to return to two fundamental questions, 'What creates value?' and 'Who has a right to it?' These two questions owe much to Karl Marx, but as Jacques argues, they have been substantially ignored in much recent management writing, which has promoted a Taylorist line of thought that 'the interests of employers are presumed congruent with the interest of all' (2000, p. 200). Jacques (ibid., p. 204) notes, 'to date, academic writing about knowledge work has predominantly treated knowledge work, the knowledge worker, the knowledge organisation and the knowledge economy (the "knowledge ___ terms") as new categories to understand within the existing interpretive frameworks of organisation studies. This project is probably futile.'

Jacques (ibid., p. 203) expands on what he calls the 'knowledge ___ terms':

- *'The knowledge worker*: Individuals who presumably differ in their relationship to employing organizations from the traditional characteristics of management inquiry: the generic employee and the manager.
- *Knowledge work*: as an intersubjective phenomenon this is not simply the work that knowledge workers do. Knowledge work may be an element of work done by those not defined as knowledge workers and vice versa.
- *The knowledge organisation*: Organisations whose competitive advantage is lodged more critically in forms of knowledge than in forms of capital and labour.
- *The knowledge econom(y/ies)*: Sociopolitical entities whose most critical economic factor is related to knowledge rather than to land, labour or (working) capital.'

These four terms are referred to by Jacques as objects of investigation that have led management writers away from questions of value and its ownership. Rather, these terms have created 'a dialogue about knowledge that has been largely presumed. Rather than creating a dialogue about the meaning of knowledge in organisations, this literature has – predictably – skimmed over substantive issues, going immediately to prescriptive tomes on building a "knowledge organisation" '. To the four objects of investigation above, Jacques (ibid.) argues that we need to add a fifth:

- '*Knowledge as a "root metaphor" for understanding work*: This has been less discussed in the literature. Understanding of emergent phenomenon in post-industrial systems of production requires that we treat knowledge as a metaphor for understanding work, rather than as a mere element of the work relationship.'

In sum, Jacques provides us with a valuable perspective for interpreting the knowledge worker and knowledge work. By sidestepping the value questions, the 'knowledge ____ terms' do not threaten the management *status quo*. They also prevent us from really appreciating knowledge and its meaning in organizations. If we can accept Jacques's line of thinking, then why has so much management thinking avoided these key questions? In the next section I will review briefly the work of two seminal thinkers, Drucker and Machlup, and identify the 'choice point' that has contributed to where much management writing on the matter has gravitated. I will not attempt to analyse why this is the case, save the more obvious point that certain ideas favouring existing powerful interests have a greater likelihood of surviving. Recent work by Scarbrough and Swan (2003) points to ways in which such self-reflexive questions might be answered. However, for the purposes of the discussion here, it may have been that the difficulty of articulating 'knowledge' into management practice was (and still is) rather problematic. Nevertheless, the upshot, as we shall see below, is that Drucker's Taylorist influence seems to have won out over Machlup's concern for the economics of knowledge. This has had some limiting consequences.

Drucker and Machlup: orginators of the knowledge worker concept [2]

Drucker
Peter Drucker has held a pre-eminent position in the field of organizational studies over a long period. His work has been described as 'a thoughtful, insightful focus on the nature of corporations, their behavior, and the workforce that breathes life into them' (Guy and Hitchcock 2000). Within this context, the idea of knowledge work and the knowledge worker has been an enduring theme. Drucker (1994) himself claims that the term knowledge

worker was unknown until he coined it in his 1959 book *The Landmarks of Tomorrow* (Drucker 1959). Drucker's writings on the knowledge worker cover many dimensions but in the short discussion which follows, I wish to emphasize one aspect that gives it a distinguishing feature: Drucker's concern with 'increased productivity through the application of science in management and the need for rationality and purpose in the workplace' (Guy and Hitchcock 2000).

Drucker's work echoes a strong post-industrial society feel as he sees the emerging knowledge society heralding the rise of a new class of workers – the knowledge workers. This new middle class of workers would have different goals and outlook compared with the old blue-collar industrial workers. The centrality of economic power around knowledge meant that organizations had to change to meet these new demands. Drucker had great faith in the work of Frederick Taylor on scientific management, and he saw this applying to knowledge work:

> The principles and concepts which automation applies to mechanical production-work had earlier been developed for non-mechanical work in the business enterprise. They are fast becoming the rule for the work of all those who are not 'workers' in the traditional usage of the word, but who work productively as technicians, professionals and managers. (Drucker 1959, pp. 50–51)

Even in his 1959 book, Drucker was struggling with issues that would be a recurring theme for his later work on the knowledge worker. First, Drucker saw existing personnel management theories as being inadequate for managing knowledge workers (Drucker 1959, p. 93). Second, teamwork would replace workers acting as individuals in a knowledge society and it was a major challenge to organizations to manage the integration of professionals and managers in the one organization (ibid., pp. 46 and 51). Finally, work done with the hands was becoming increasingly unproductive: 'Productive work, in today's society and economy, is work that applies vision, knowledge and concepts – work that is based on the mind rather than the hand' (ibid., p. 91).

Drucker's work therefore gives the organization a central place in understanding the knowledge worker. He is much less concerned with knowledge *per se* and more with how it can be managed productively. The following three quotes from a more recent article by Drucker highlight this emphasis:

> knowledge workers work in teams, and if knowledge workers are not employees, they must at least be affiliated with an organization.

> Only the organization can provide the basic continuity that knowledge workers need in order to be effective. Only the organization can concert the specialized knowledge of the knowledge worker into performance.

In the knowledge society it is not the individual who performs. The individual is a cost center rather than a performance center. It is the organization that performs. (1994)

In short, Drucker's interpretation seems to give weight to the observations of Jacques noted above. The emphasis is on Taylorist logic rather than a specific search for how knowledge creates value. Indeed, knowledge is not treated explicitly and it is the organization that is in control. Knowledge workers do not have a real definition if they are not associated with an organization.

Machlup

Machlup's (1962) *The Production and Distribution of Knowledge in the United States* is primarily concerned with the economic contribution of knowledge in the USA as measured through the system of national accounting used in that country. Machlup does not specifically use the term knowledge worker but alludes to this when he explores the tensions between knowledge industries and occupational structure. Some of these tensions are discussed below, keeping in mind that his immediate focus was national account statistics.

Unlike Drucker, Machlup does not conceptualize the problem of knowledge and work simply in terms of a special class of worker.

In other words, speaking of labor input alone, should an 'occupation' approach be used, or an 'industry' ('product') approach . . . If the phrase 'knowledge industry' were to be given an unambiguous meaning, would it be a collection of industries producing knowledge or rather a collection of occupations producing knowledge in whatever industries they are employed? (Machlup 1962, p. 45)

Thus Machlup's view, with hindsight, appeals to a way of interpreting knowledge and work rather than a special element of work.

A second problem that Machlup addressed is whether knowledge is a production, investment or cost item. How one sees knowledge will have an impact on its economic significance. Machlup identified knowledge production with communication – 'all the procedures by which one mind can affect another' (1962, p. 30). Machlup is averse to making a distinction between workers based on whether the work is intellectual work as opposed to physical work. For him, 'what counts is not the knowledge *required* for a particular activity but only whether or not this activity consists largely in *communicating* knowledge' (ibid., p. 326, original emphasis). So, for example, not all medical practitioners (e.g. dentists and surgeons) qualify as knowledge producers in Machlup's view. A dentist primarily manipulates teeth and there is very little 'information and advice' in this activity. Machlup's view is at odds with Drucker, who takes the more stylized view that knowledge work is with the head rather than the hand.

Third, another problem Machlup identified is the extent to which we can see knowledge production as being undertaken by different occupations. The management occupation cannot ever be entirely the preserve of a management consulting industry since 'decision-making is one activity which the firm must perform internally, or it stops being a firm' (Machlup 1962, p. 46). This too puts Machlup at odds with Drucker in that it undermines the notion of a single category called knowledge worker.

Finally, the management of knowledge (a topic of considerable interest today) was not a central theme in the 1962 book. As mentioned above, Machlup was primarily concerned with statistical aspects and did not have a goal-oriented approach of harnessing knowledge for productive output, although he certainly saw this aspect of knowledge production to be significant. I suspect Machlup's reticence on this theme reflects the fact that he saw knowledge in a greater totality than purely as an investment item. This totality and the difficulty of 'fitting' knowledge to organizational objectives obviously made Machlup cautious of simple management solutions (Machlup 1962, p. 6).

Discussion

The argument thus far has suggested that there are considerable differences between Drucker and Machlup. Machlup's analysis of knowledge and work is much more open to its applicability as a 'root metaphor' for understanding work. Despite this, it would seem that Drucker's work has influenced many 'prescriptive tomes on building a "knowledge organisation" ' (Jacques 2000, p. 202). Examples include Awad and Ghaziri (2004, p. 414), who place emphasis on knowledge workers 'leveraging products and services' and Becerra-Fernandez et al. (2004), who take a very technical approach to the issue. While it is evident that the knowledge worker is an emerging concept, the traditional metaphors of the 'knowledge ___ terms' would not appear to have served us well in answering the questions of how knowledge creates value and who owns it.

Towards an agenda for the future

Having established, I hope, that the metaphor of the knowledge worker may have held some promise years ago, the 'choice point' is worth reflecting on. It is my contention here that Drucker prefers a static conceptualization of the knowledge worker whereas Machlup alludes to a dynamic one. Drucker appeals to managerial hierarchy whereas Machlup sees a less hierarchical process of how knowledge is communicated as important. It is this difference that I see as the 'choice point' and one that is most significant. If one can accept this view, the observation by Jacques (2000, p. 208) is most appropriate:

Today, the importance of learning may indicate a comparable watershed. Unlike knowledge, which is not easily capitalized, learning is the property of the worker or the workgroup, until it is applied. Once applied, it becomes knowledge and can be capitalized, but if every situation is unique, it is learning and not the knowledge that is the primary source of value. As the shelf life of an item of knowledge approaches zero, knowledge ceases to be power; the ability to change knowledge – to learn – becomes the source of power.

In sum, the knowledge worker concept, at least in terms of how it is often portrayed in the literature, has been rather reticent on matters of power and control. It has achieved this largely through a debt to Drucker, who, either intentionally or not, avoided addressing the question of what was the primary source of value. Machlup, on the other hand, is more open to knowledge as part of a learning process, and this in turn directly challenges the organization's locus of control (Macdonald 1995). Jacques (2000, p. 214) notes that 'We cannot, in other words, add knowledge to our understanding of work. We must learn to understand work as a form of "doing knowledge". To this, we must return to the question long-buried in management discourse: "What adds value?" And "Who has a right to it?" .' Having retraced our steps some 40 years, what might be some reasonable suggestions for the future?

If a revitalized metaphor for the knowledge worker can be accepted, then, following the line of Jacques above, identifying a knowledge theory of value seems particularly productive. As Jacques (2000, p. 209) puts it:

> Organisations perform complex tasks. Within organisations people with differing interests and perspectives must collectively determine *what* tasks to perform and *how* to perform them effectively. They must then *distribute* the value produced among those involved in the production'. (Original emphasis)

The 'what and how' of the knowledge worker presents us with some interesting challenges: it opens up the possibility of questioning existing patterns of control in organizations; it suggests the need for a more detailed understanding of the epistemological links between knowing and doing; and it also suggests the need to be self-reflexive about why this discourse has come about.

First, with respect to existing patterns and assumptions about control in organizations, if we no longer see knowledge workers as an elite group and compliant to the wishes of management control, then knowledge management of the future may need to accept a degree of management without or at least with only limited control (Macdonald 1995). Asking what and how opens up the issue of what knowledge workers actually do, as opposed to sidestepping this point, as Drucker would lead us to do. Many years ago Machlup identified different types of communicators, or knowledge producers: 'the transporter;

the transformer; the processor; the interpreter; the analyzer; and the original creator' (Machlup 1962, pp. 32–3). Likewise, Wilensky (1967, pp. 8–40) identified 'contacts men', 'facts and figures men', slogans and preconceptions as important elements of intelligence in organizations. Evidently, these are themes that have been identified in the past that seem worth pursuing despite the fact that this knowledge-based way of categorizing workers is not prominent in organizational studies.

Second, the link between knowing what to do and how to do it is a difficult issue. In recent years much discussion has revolved around tacit and codified knowledge (Tsoukas 2003). This association of knowing what to do and how to do it reflects different sorts of knowledge, for example, knowledge at the level of the individual; knowledge associated with teamwork; and knowledge that is shared (Farr et al. 2003). However, it extends beyond this into management itself. If knowledge workers are not an elite and distinct category of employee, then all workers to some extent are involved in knowledge as work. From the point of view of the innovation process, this may open up the process to be more dynamic and influenced by different levels in the organization, from the shop floor to senior management (Macdonald 1997). This perspective, in practice, allows us to subject management to a knowledge-type of analysis as well, effectively blending management knowledge together in a seamless fashion with the knowledge worker that managers are supposed to manage. This demands an epistemological approach that theoretically links personal and organizational knowledge as well as know-what and know-how (Brown and Duguid 2003; Cook and Brown 2003). The knowledge worker now not only exhibits different ways of communicating but also different ways of knowing in an organizational context. This, in turn, potentially enhances our understanding of the manager as a knowledge worker (Introna 1997).

Third, the above analysis also suggests that there is value in reflecting on what choices led us to thinking about knowledge workers in the way we do today and what might need to be done to change this. This is the self-reflexive stance of management studies and one worth exploring (Prichard 2000; Scarbrough and Swan 2003). As a consequence, by being self-reflexive, management academics may see why the historical side of the knowledge worker seems to have been neglected in recent years (Cortada 1998). Indeed, this would be a useful way of analysing not so much knowledge workers but knowledge as work (Jacques 2000; Thomas 1999).[3]

Conclusion

While the knowledge worker concept has been around for over 40 years, there is a pressing need to reflect critically on it. Interpreting the knowledge worker as a metaphor is a useful way of getting a better picture of its historical significance. It is a highly value-laden term that needs revitalization. If anything, the knowledge worker needs to be made more relevant to a knowledge economy. I have suggested some areas for future research that may be useful. The process may need to start with management academics reflecting on their own knowledge work. What this means is a greater awareness of academic knowledge as being not exogenous to society, but shaped by the political, economic and social forces giving rise to it.

Notes
1. Ironically, though, a literature review by Easterby-Smith and Lyles (2003) identifying 'watersheds' in academic research dealing with organizational learning and knowledge management makes no reference to the work of either Machlup or Drucker.
2. This section dealing with Drucker and Machlup is a paraphrase of a similar section from Joseph (2004).
3. I am indebted to Don Lamberton, who has made this point in conversation and referred me to Thomas (1999).

References
Awad, Elias M. and Hassan M. Ghaziri. 2004. *Knowledge Management*. Upper Saddle River, NJ: Pearson.

Becerra-Fernandez, Irma, Avelino Gonzalez and Rajiv Sabherwal. 2004. *Knowledge Management: Challenges, Solutions and Technologies*. Upper Saddle River, NJ: Pearson.

Brown, John Seely and Paul Duguid. 2003. 'Organizing knowledge'. Pp. 19–40 in *Managing Knowledge: An Essential Reader*, edited by S. Little, P. Quintas and T. Ray. London: Sage.

Cook, S.D.N. and John Seely Brown. 2003. 'Bridging epistemologies: The generative dance between organizational knowledge and organizational knowing'. Pp. 68–101 in *Managing Knowledge: An Essential Reader*, edited by S. Little, P. Quintas and T. Ray. London: Sage.

Cortada, James W. 1998. 'Where did knowledge workers come from?' Pp. 3–21 in *Rise of the Knowledge Worker*, edited by J. W. Cortada. Boston, MA: Butterworth-Heinemann.

Drucker, Peter F. 1959. *The Landmarks of Tomorrow*. London: Heinemann.

Drucker, Peter F. 1994. 'The age of social transformation'. *The Atlantic Monthly* 174:53–80.

Easterby-Smith, Mark and Marjorie A. Lyles. 2003. *The Blackwell Handbook of Organizational Learning and Knowledge Management*. Oxford: Blackwell.

Edelman, Murray. 1977. *Political Language: Words that Succeed and Policies that Fail*. New York: Academic Press.

Farr, James L., Hock-Peng Sin and Paul E. Telsuk. 2003. 'Knowledge management processes and work group innovation'. Pp. 574–86 in *The International Handbook of Innovation*, edited by L.V. Shavinina. Amsterdam: Elsevier Science.

Guy, Mary E. and Janice R. Hitchcock. 2000. 'If apples were oranges: The public/nonprofit/business nexus in Peter Drucker's work'. *Journal of Management History* 6:30.

Introna, Lucas D. 1997. *Management, Information and Power*. London: Macmillan.

Jacques, Roy. 2000. 'Theorising knowledge as work: The need for a "knowledge theory of value" '. Pp. 199–215 in *Managing Knowledge: Critical Investigations of Work and Learning*, edited by C. Prichard, R. Hull, M. Chumer and H. Willmott. New York: St Martin's Press.

Jones, Derek C. 2003. *New Economy Handbook*. Amsterdam: Elsevier.

Joseph, Richard. 2004. 'The knowledge worker: Getting the organizational and informational balance right: A review'. *Innovation: Management, Policy and Practice* 6:85–97.

Macdonald, Stuart. 1995. 'Learning to change: An information perspective on learning in the organization'. *Organization Science* 6:557–68.

Macdonald, Stuart. 1997. *Information for Innovation*. Cambridge, UK: Cambridge University Press.

Machlup, Fritz. 1962. *The Production and Distribution of Knowledge in the United States*. Princeton, NJ: Princeton University Press.

Prichard, Craig. 2000. 'Know, learn and share! The knowledge phenomena and the construction of a consumptive-communicative body'. Pp. 176–98 in *Managing Knowledge: Critical Investigations of Work and Learning*, edited by C. Prichard, R. Hull, M. Chumer and H. Willmott. New York: St Martin's Press.

Scarbrough, Harry and Jacky Swan. 2003. 'Discourses of knowledge management and the learning organization: Their production and consumption'. Pp. 495–512 in *The Blackwell Handbook of Organizational Learning and Knowledge Management*, edited by M. Easterby-Smith and M.A. Lyles. Oxford: Blackwell.

Shavinina, Larisa V. 2003. *The International Handbook on Innovation*. Amsterdam: Elsevier Science.

Thomas, Keith. 1999. *The Oxford Book of Work*. Oxford: Oxford University Press.

Tsoukas, Haridimos. 2003. 'Do we really understand tacit knowledge?' Pp. 410–27 in *The Blackwell Handbook of Organizational Learning and Knowledge Management*, edited by M. Easterby-Smith and M.A. Lyles. Oxford: Blackwell.

Weick, Karl E. 2003. 'Foreword'. Pp. xvii–xx in *The Blackwell Handbook of Organizational Learning and Knowledge Management*, edited by M. Easterby-Smith and M.A. Lyles. Oxford: Blackwell.

Wilensky, Harold L. 1967. *Organizational Intelligence: Knowledge and Policy in Government and Industry*. New York and London: Basic Books.

20 How to be productive in the knowledge economy: the case of ICTs

Greg Hearn and Thomas Mandeville

The knowledge economy has a number of defining features (Rooney et al. 2003), namely:

1. it is characterized by progressive waves of innovation;
2. products and services have pronounced externalities; and
3. production involves compound multidisciplinary knowledge regimes.

Productivity in the knowledge economy is therefore affected by these factors as much as by traditional issues of cost minimization and control of resources. For example, Arthur (1996) has argued that knowledge industries often have dynamics that approximate natural monopolies. For a start they tend to have high research and/or development costs but relatively low variable costs. Their products are often 'heavy' in knowledge but 'light' in material; hence they enjoy extraordinary profit margins per unit cost. In addition they often exhibit network externalities. This means that the advantages of using a particular product accrue not solely from the characteristics of the product but from the fact that other agents are also using that product (Leff 1996).

The significantly different dynamics which operate within sectors dealing with intangible knowledge products and services highlight the need for a different approach to thinking about productivity for strategic managers, policy-makers and those interested in industry development in these sectors. Information and communication technologies (ICTs) illustrate these dynamics clearly and therefore are an important exemplar of general issues in knowledge productivity. In this chapter, we will examine productivity issues in the deployment of ICTs and then develop a general model of the management of different knowledge regimes in the productive process. From this model, principles for the strategic management of productivity in knowledge sectors are offered.

The wave of innovation in information and communication technologies is affecting all sectors (Engelbrecht 1997; Mulgan 1991). This digital wave is changing the way all sectors operate by reshaping transaction costs, changing access to consumers and other stakeholders, making existing procedures smarter and creating totally new processes and products. This is as true in those sectors based on engineering and technology as it is in the services, entertainment and cultural sectors. As a result there is a good deal of 'boosterism' in discussions about ICTs and productivity and a common argument is that ICTs are important enabling technologies that generate productivity gains across sectors.

However, there has been an ongoing debate over several decades concerning the so-called productivity paradox of new information technologies (e.g., *The Economist* 1999), and recent literature (Baily 2004; McKinsey Global Institute 2003) suggests that the simple equation of ICTs = productivity gains is wrong. It is clear, for example, that productivity levels across the service sector did not vary much throughout the 1970s and 1980s whilst heavy investment in information technology was ongoing (Makridakis 1998). Castells argues (1996a, 1996b) that in general, across the developed nations, productivity from 1973 to 1993 stagnated compared to the pre-ICT era of 1950–73. There is some evidence also that the widespread diffusion of ICTs has coincided with a significant reversal of long-term trends in productivity gains (Preissel 1997; Soete 1981).

Since the mid-1990s these trends appear to be reversed. Some growth in productivity at the national level, directly attributable to information technologies, may be occurring because of the growth of IT as a sector in its own right rather than its deployment in other existing sectors (Gordon 2000; *The Economist* 1999). A number of empirical studies have argued that clear productivity advances across sectors from the mid-1990s can be attributed to ICTs (Gretton et al. 2003; Oliner and Sichel 2000; Parnham 2003). Even these findings are debatable, however, because they are based on correlational measurement which really cannot sort out whether the growth in productivity is caused by deployment of ICTs or whether deployment of ICTs is caused by growth in productivity (Baily 2004).

The difficulty with the productivity paradox debate is that it is often fought on the basis of aggregated statistics which do not reveal the logic of how productivity gains may be occurring, rather than on the basis of case studies which do suggest possible mechanisms. When we shift focus and interrogate specific cases, the logic of productivity and ICTs is revealed and it is clear that there is significant variation in mechanisms of how ICTs might yield productivity gains. Consider a trivial case. Will purchasing a new computer and updated version of *Word* enhance the productivity of a small business, for example? Or consider a more complex example. Most e-commerce developments have primarily been about new logistics for existing products rather than new products and services. The spectacular activity in e-commerce has most often been about competing for dominance in existing consumer markets (for example, amazon.com) by using technology for logistical and marketing advantage. This has generated productivity for the IT sector more than for the retailers themselves. Business-to-business e-commerce does not create new domestic consumer markets but rather sees the substitution of new procedures and, therefore, firms in the logistics of production and distribution (Lucking-Reily and Spulber 2001). Therefore, ICTs have probably not been responsible for the productivity gains in retailing (Foster et al. 2002).

So we suggest examining firm-level strategies. As a consequence, a degree of insight into the productivity paradox of ICTs can be gleaned and principles for understanding productivity and knowledge can be deduced. We propose that ICTs could in principle enhance the productivity of enterprises in five main ways. They can:

1. reduce the transaction costs of the enterprise;
2. expand and enhance the relationship of the enterprise to its stakeholders;
3. 'informate' the processes of the enterprise making them 'smarter' and thus more robust, accurate or attractive to clients;
4. stimulate completely new products or services for the enterprise; and
5. enhance the reputation of the enterprise as progressive (regardless of the results of 1 to 4).

However, we also propose that it is equally true that ICTs can produce the opposite effect for each of these functions. That is, they can:

1. increase the transaction costs of the enterprise;
2. negatively affect the relationship of the enterprise to its stakeholders;
3. make the processes of the enterprise needlessly complex, in effect 'dumber', and, therefore, less robust and attractive;
4. eliminate existing products or services for the enterprise; and
5. damage the reputation of the enterprise as technocratic (regardless of the results of 1 to 4).

This is the core of the productivity paradox and we will illustrate it by examining each of these productivity functions in turn. In this examination, when using terms such as 'ICTs improve', we are not implying a form of technological determinism in which the technology itself brings about the consequence. Rather, we are using shorthand to describe the frequently observed consequences of the deployment of ICTs in various ways. Indeed, as we will shortly argue, a more sophisticated frame of reference – one that does not only privilege technological knowledge – is needed to manage ICTs toward productivity.

Transaction costs
Every enterprise incurs transaction costs in the execution of its core activities.

A component of these transaction costs is informational in nature. For example, the exchange of material goods requires logistical information and the delivery of health services requires patient information. ICTs may improve the handling of information by, for example, eliminating logistical steps in the supply chain, reducing multiple handling of information, making information easier to find, or speeding up the transfer of information. These improvements may also involve the elimination of labour and thus the associated costs. Prime examples of this reduction in transaction costs can be found in the banking sector and transport logistics. Baily (2004) suggests that this is the mechanism which large retailers (e.g., Wal-Mart and Costco) have used successfully.

Alternatively, ICTs may increase transaction costs by adding additional steps in the production process, through increases in the level of technology and/or staff needed to process logistical information. ICTs may also increase the amount of information that has to be collected. A key factor in this derives from the externalities of ICTs we have already referred to. The need for an informational connection to others, or to conform to the standards of an industry, are drivers of increased information collection and transmission (ICTs may also, of course, result in increasing the amount of needless information collection and collation. This will be dealt with later as an example of unnecessary complexity). Examples of this occur throughout the services sector, conferring advantage on larger firms which can 'afford to play'. In general medical practice, the introduction of ICTs is a significant cost which often necessitates the amalgamation of practices. For example, in Australia, the Department of Health and Ageing established a GP Links program from March 1999 to September 2000, to assist in the amalgamation of general practices in Australia. The program was to aid those practices that could not maintain appropriate levels of efficiency and patient services. A significant hidden transaction cost of establishing an information platform is the human resource cost, that is, the cost of building capacity to exploit the technology via training, recruitment or, in some cases, simple increases in the number of staff required to run more complex systems.

Relationship to stakeholders

All enterprises must communicate with a range of stakeholders. Two significant groups are customers and staff. ICTs can enhance and expand communication with these two stakeholder groups. For example, new markets to customers can be opened. Also, the quality of communication with staff can be improved through, for example, the transparency of processes and feedback of timeliness and accuracy. Put in a nutshell, time and space dis-substantiation enables the services of the enterprise to be available in more places more often. Successful examples here include amazon.com and the University of Phoenix, and e-bay.

Alternatively, ICTs can negatively affect the relationship of the enterprise to its stakeholders. Competitors can enter the enterprise's territory, for example. ICTs can also divert resources away from other more effective communication channels. A prime example here from regional Australia is the failure of banks to understand attachment of their customer base to real rather than virtual branches.

Informating or complexifying

Informating can be defined as the addition of information to a product or service that improves it in significant ways. Basic 'industrial age' products have been made smarter. For example, agriculture was once a matter of 'growing stuff'. Now plant growth is controlled by ICT-directed nourishment systems. Plant readiness is a function of information about markets and so on. Similarly, pizza delivery competitiveness is a function of information capability as well as product quality and innovation. Informating also occurs in less direct ways, for example, via market research. Informating adds cost to products but also potentially improves the viability of the product by making it more robust, attractive or timely. Speciality retailers such as J. Crew use IT in sophisticated ways to track customer tastes and match inventory on a store-by-store basis (Baily 2004).

Alternatively, information intensity can add significant costs to an enterprise without improving quality. Transaction costs in modern organizations are significantly increased by information collection and analysis in the name of quality assurance, improved decision-making, or simply the fact that ICTs make information collection possible. The cheapness of information storage means that organizations err on the side of collection rather than sorting, adding to the information complexity of the organization and to the bureaucratizing of processes in some cases. In addition, the complex layer of information can sometimes distance individual decision-makers from intuitive or more natural information (for example, in military accidents involving 'friendly fire'). The costs in this info-glut scenario are sometimes long-term and difficult to assess. Long-run productivity stagnation in the service sector, despite large investments in ICTs, may in part be explained by such phenomena. ICTs get in the way of service quality in some sectors where the human element is still as crucial. Education is one sector where the evidence suggests that the need for expert personal interaction cannot be completely replaced by ICTs.

New products and services

ICTs have engendered completely new products and services in the form of digital content and applications. Moreover, optimizing opportunities depends on understanding how all sectors affect each other because:

- the demand for broadband content will not just be from the IT sector nor from the technical sectors. Rather, because service delivery will in part move on-line, the consumption of services in general will also underpin demand for broadband content and applications;[1]
- ICTs will provide enabling technology and distribution for all sectors; and
- entertainment and culture will shape the form and scale of consumption of services in all sectors, through communication, marketing and advertizing functions in particular.[2]

The computer gaming industry is growing at 5 per cent per annum and now outgrosses movies (Global Information 2003). Other software products have been developed and deployed in many consumer domains. More generally, content for broadband ICT applications is an important new player in the ICT productivity equation. Content applications have spawned new industries, let alone new companies.

Alternatively, ICTs have eliminated some product classes and companies altogether. For example, online share trading has changed the way brokers operate and resulted in the demise of a number of notable companies (e.g., Charles Schwab). Film-making and graphic design have been completely transformed, with older analogue components being replaced by digital versions and by completely different processes in some cases.

Enterprise reputation
Finally, the deployment of ICTs may at times be more to do with their symbolic value rather than their informational capacities. In effect, the ICT platform, particularly through web interfaces, is an important indicator of a progressive and effective corporation. But more than this, ICTs carry with them connotations of power and supremacy. As with previous surges in technological development, Hand and Sandywell (2002, p. 198) note how the relatively recent advent of ICTs has elevated them to 'central agents of history'. While Hand and Sandywell present such claims as clearly contestable, they do nevertheless identify that ICTs and 'digitized knowledge' are 'synonymous with power'. So aside from claims from corporations and organizations about ICTs and improved productivity, access and client service, ICTs also represent opportunities to demonstrate organizations being part of the era of 'e-topia'.

While the use of technology as a rhetorical strategy for an enterprise/organization may carry affirming attitudes towards it, it can also carry a 'cold' inhuman subtext. A prime example here is automatic voice response systems and the promotion by many institutions to steer clients towards virtual service options, rather than face-to-face service. Call centres (controversially labelled the 'new sweatshops' by Fernie and Metcalf 1998) with high ICT demands on staff performance are another case in point, as they have sometimes left a legacy of damaged client relations and poor corporate health outcomes for staff, in spite of increased processing efficiencies (Bain and Taylor 2000; Kinnie et al. 2000). Even such efficiencies are open to uncertainty, and damage to reputation is a possibility, as was the case with Centrelink and the Child Support Agency in Australia. Both federal agencies introduced a heavy reliance on call centre culture and investment in related IT in the early 2000s, resulting in decreases in corporate health and adverse publicity about client outcomes (Community and Public Sector Union (CPSU) 2003; LaborNET 2002; *Sydney Morning Herald* 2004).

When each of the factors that could enhance productivity is examined carefully it becomes clear that ICTs in and of themselves are no guarantee of a more productive enterprise. What is needed is a clearer understanding of what factors affect the path that the deployment of ICTs will take. Moreover, it may be that seeking to maximize one of the productivity functions described above will have negative effects on others. That is, the functions are mutually interactive. In addition, we will suggest that productive deployment of ICTs requires synchronization of compound knowledge regimes. We approach this by building a heuristic model of the productive deployment of ICTs. In this model we suggest that organizational learning is missing in many essential prescriptions of ICT deployment in conjunction with investment in human *and* cultural capital. We illustrate the model under three productivity-related scenarios, namely: disaster, downsize and innovation.

The disaster scenario
The starting-point here is the recognition that through what is called the 'Xerox effect', ICTs may erode overall informational efficiency (Lamberton et al. 1982). Organizations adopt new ICTs to perform specific tasks. However, the enormous capacity potential inherent in these technologies enables them to perform a number of other tasks. The more tasks that the technology performs, the more strain is placed on the existing structure of the organization, and the greater is the necessity for the organization to adjust and adapt – otherwise information will be produced indiscriminately and will be used inefficiently (Baily 2004). Changes in organizational structures to use newly available information may be difficult and expensive (Arrow 1974). However, if the organization fails to adapt the efficiency with which it handles all its information, it may be impeded, with consequent reduction in productivity. While the productivity of a specific task may increase, overall organizational productivity may decline (Baily 2004).

One can envisage a vicious circle in organizations attempting to cope with a flood of internally generated information by hiring more knowledge workers, accountants, forecasters, analysts, programmers, consultants, researchers, administrators and coordinators – who in turn generate more information and demand more support from IT. Normally the market mechanism would weed out organizations bogged down in self-generated work, unless the cause of the work is a prerequisite for remaining in the market and competitors are experiencing similar novel difficulties.

Our heuristic model in Figure 20.1 illustrates the Xerox effect hypothesis of the productivity paradox. Imagine during time (T), an organization has an established technical infrastructure. In this case its capital and technical labour costs stay constant. Also the knowledge required to efficiently and effectively run the organization has stabilized, as has productivity. At the end of time (T) management decides to invest in new technical infrastructure. ICT investments are often lumpy/discontinuous – thus the capital curve jumps significantly in Figure 20.1. As the firm enters period $T + 1$, labour costs rise (or at least they don't decrease) and productivity falls, as discussed above. At the same time, and this is a new explicit element to the Xerox effect hypothesis, the knowledge utilization curve will decrease in period $T + 1$. This is due to the decline in the knowledge for running the technical infrastructure effectively. Recent evidence suggests that it takes at least two years for organizations to learn how to use new ICTs effectively (Baily 2004; Gordon 2000; Mandeville and Rooney 1996). In addition, changes in operating systems often create internal chaos. Much of the knowledge potential in the organization is directed towards managing this turbulence. Also, bounded rationality – the limitations of people's memory for new operating procedures in this instance – contributes to the drop in knowledge.

Of course the issue here is basically a learning problem – organizations need time to learn to use their new ICTs effectively. This process involves

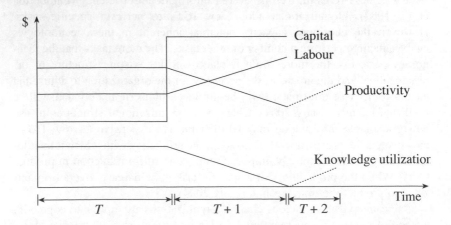

Figure 20.1   The disaster scenario

both unlearning old habits as well as learning new ways (Rooney et al. 2003). Normally at time $T + 2$, one would expect the knowledge and productivity curve to rise and labour costs to level out (see dotted lines in Figure 20.1). However, rapid technological change in ICTs and associated competitive pressures to upgrade (more lumpy investments in ICTs) forces the firm back to the earlier position at the end of time period T. Thus we have a possible explanation for how enormous investments in ICTs have been accompanied by a slowdown in productivity growth for long periods.

Downsizing scenario
Both manufacturing and financial services experienced considerable employment contraction from 1989–90 until about 1993, as ICT-led downsizing initiatives took hold. Subsequently the downsizing fashion began to fall out of favour as firms become less than enamoured with outcomes (e.g., see Abernathy 1997; Gollan 1997). Our model can also shed some light here. At $T + 1$ (Figure 20.2) productivity does rise, but simply because labour costs have fallen with deliberate downsizing. However, as labour departs, knowledge falls may be even greater than in Figure 20.1 (see also Baily 2004). Eventually, at $T + 2$, productivity falls, for similar reasons as in Figure 20.1.

Innovation scenario
Finally, the model in Figure 20.3 also depicts the dynamics of productivity growth when it does occur (for example, see Baily 2004; *Financial Review* 1997; Parnham 2003; Ryan 1997a, 1997b).

Over time, more organizations adapt and learn to use ICTs better (Tylecote 1995). This involves continuous investment in knowledge/training/ organizational restructuring/soft infrastructure, along with the occasional traditional lumpy investments in hardware. Another way of referring to this effect is the impact of investment in intangible capital on productivity (as in,

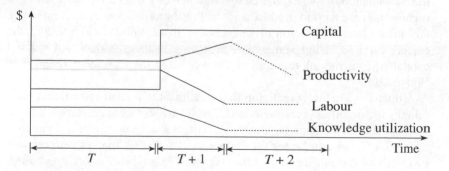

Figure 20.2   The downsizing scenario

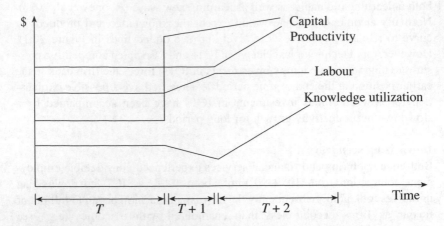

Figure 20.3   The innovation scenario

e.g., Baily 2004; Brynjolfsson 2003; Gordon 2000). The argument is essentially that it takes time and human resources to learn how to apply technologies effectively. These stocks of knowledge constitute intangible capital (Baily 2004).

In addition, the innovation required potentially includes the development of new products or services, or new modes of delivery. Indeed, a key factor emerging from recent productivity studies is the importance of competitive pressure to innovate (Baily 2004). This also necessitates strong market reconnaissance as well as positioning and promotional strategies. Rarely is technology alone a sufficient driver of innovation. Rather, successful commercialization of innovation comes via a combination of new technology plus service market opportunity plus cultural packaging (branding). Moreover, it is the combination of these three factors – all deriving from different knowledge regimes that are hard to produce and can thus become a source of competitive advantage. In an innovation-driven scenario, in all periods in Figure 20.3, the capital curve is rising somewhat, as it now includes human and cultural capital investments more explicitly, compared to the traditional situation in Figure 20.1.

Industry is gradually realizing that investment in human and cultural capital is as important as investment in ICT hardware. For example, recent US and German studies are showing a strong link between the degree of a company's investment in its employees on the one hand and stock market performance, productivity and profits on the other (Gollan 1997). These factors suggest that once a lumpy investment is made in ICTs at the end of time T, the adjustment period $T + 1$ is a good deal shorter than has traditionally been the case. Thus over time the economy experiences rising productivity associated with investments in ICTs – in principle, it moves out of the productivity paradox era.

Conclusions

The ICT sector is of central importance in knowledge economies and illustrates many of the principles of productivity growth and decline. The idea that ICTs drive productivity through cost cutting – of transactions and people – is deeply ingrained in the management psyche. And of course this is indeed one mechanism at play. However we have illustrated here that productivity dynamics in the knowledge economies are much more complicated. Not only have we shown that the evidence for a strong and straightforward relationship between investment in ICTs and productivity does not exist, but we have also shown why this may be the case. Productivity increases may be derived from increased efficiencies or from innovations in product service or their cultural package. The challenge in delivering sustained productivity growth is to be able to combine the different knowledge regimes that are necessarily involved in innovation in knowledge economies.

Notes

1. See Cunningham (2002a, 2002b) and Howkins (2001).
2. See Florida (2002).

References

Abernathy, M. 1997. 'Downsizing leaves many companies down and out'. *Financial Review* 4 July: 61.

Arrow, K. 1974. *The Limits of Organization*. New York: W.W. Norton.

Arthur, W.B. 1996. 'Increasing returns and the new world of business'. *Harvard Business Review* 74:100–109.

Baily, M. 2004. 'Recent productivity growth: The role of information technology and other innovations'. Pp. 35–42 in *FRBSF Economic Review 2004*. San Francisco, CA: Research Dept, Federal Reserve Bank of San Francisco.

Bain, P. and P. Taylor. 2000. 'Entrapped by the "electronic panopticon"?: Worker resistance in the call centre'. *New Technology, Work and Employment* 15:2–28.

Brynjolfsson, E. 2003. 'The IT productivity gap'. *Optimize* July. http://ebusiness.mit.edu/erik/Optimize/pr_roi.html.

Castells, M. 1996a. 'Megacities and the end of urban civilisation'. *New Perspectives Quarterly* 13:12–15.

Castells, M. 1996b. *The Rise of the Network Society*. Cambridge, MA: Blackwell.

Community and Public Sector Union (CPSU). 2003. 'CSA: Comcare Serves Improvement Notice in CSA'. http://www.cpsu.org.au/news/1057799950_23059.html.

Cunningham, S. 2002a. 'Culture, services, knowledge or is content king, or are we just drama queens?'. *Communications Research Forum* 2–3 October.

Cunningham, S. 2002b. 'From cultural to creative industries: Theory, industry, and policy implications'. *Media Information Australia Incorporating Culture & Policy* 102:54–65.

Engelbrecht, H.J. 1997. 'The international economy: Knowledge flows and information activities'. Pp. 19–42 in *The New Research Frontiers of Communication Policy*, edited by D. Lamberton. Amsterdam: Elsevier.

Fernie, S. and D. Metcalf. 1998. *(Not) Hanging on the Telephone: Payments Systems in the New Sweatshops*. London: Centre for Economic Performance, London School of Economics.

Financial Review. 1997. 'Paradox of productivity'. Editorial, 18 September:20.

Florida, R. 2002. *The Rise of the Creative Class.* New York: Basic Books.

Foster, L., J. Haltiwanger and C.J. Krizan. 2002. 'The link between aggregate and micro productivity growth: Evidence from retail trade'. *NBER Working Paper No. W9120* http://papers.ssrn.com/sol3/papers.cfm?abstract_id=325946.

Global Information. 2003. 'Game industry dynamics, data, figures & forecasts'. http://www.the-infoshop.com/press/fi14850_en.shtml.

Gollan, P. 1997. 'Training and the bottom line'. *Financial Review* 14 July:16.

Gordon, R.J. 2000. 'Does the "new economy" measure up to the great inventions of the past?'. *Journal of Economic Perspectives* **14**:49–74.

Gretton, P., J. Galia and D. Parnham. 2003. 'The effects of ICTs and complementary innovations in Australian productivity growth'. Canberra, ACT: Productivity Commission, Australian Government.

Hand, M. and B. Sandywell. 2002. 'E-topia as cosmopolis or citadel: On the de-democratizing logics of the Internet, or, toward a critique of the new technological fetishism'. *Theory, Culture and Society* **19**:197–225.

Howkins, J. 2001. *The Creative Economy: How People Make Money from Ideas.* London: Allen Lane.

Kinnie, N., S. Hutchinson and J. Purcell. 2000. 'Fun and surveillance: The paradox of high commitment management in call centres'. *International Journal of Human Resource Management* **11**:967–85.

LaborNET. 2002. 'CUBA crisis hits child support'. *LaborNET* http://www.labor.net.au/news/1860.html.

Lamberton, D., S. MacDonald and T. Mandeville. 1982. 'Productivity and technological change: Towards an alternative to the Myers hypothesis'. *Canberra Bulletin of Public Administration* **9**:23–30.

Leff, N. 1996. 'Externalities, information costs, and social benefit–cost analysis for economic development: An example from telecommunications'. Pp. 500–21 in *The Economics of Communication and Information*, edited by D. Lamberton. Cheltenham, UK and Brookfield, VT, USA: Edward Elgar.

Lucking-Reily, D. and D.F. Spulber. 2001. 'Business-to-business electronic commerce'. *Journal of Economic Perspectives* **15**:55–68.

Makridakis, S. 1998. 'The forthcoming information revolution: Its impacts on society and firms'. *Futures* **27**:799–822.

Mandeville, T. and D. Rooney. 1996. *The Business Use of E-mail: Organisation and Workpractice Impact: Research Report No. 4.* Brisbane, QLD: The Communication Centre, Queensland University of Technology.

McKinsey Global Institute. 2003. 'Perspective: Improving European competitiveness'. McKinsey Global Institute.

Mulgan, G.J. 1991. *Communication and Control: Networks and the New Economies of Communication.* New York: Guilford Press.

Oliner, S. and D. Sichel. 2000. 'The resurgence of growth in the late 1990s: Is information technology the story?', in *Finance and Economics Discussion Series.* http://www.federalreserve.gov/pubs/feds/2000/.

Parnham, D. 2003. 'Australia's productivity surge and its determinants'. Revised draft of a paper presented to the 13th Annual East Asian Seminar on Economics, Melbourne, 20–22 June 2002.

Preissel, B. 1997. 'Information technology: A critical perspective on its economic effects'. *Prometheus* **15**:2–26.

Rooney, D., G. Hearn, T. Mandeville and R. Joseph. 2003. *Public Policy in Knowledge-Based Economies: Foundations and Frameworks.* Cheltenham, UK and Northampton, MA, USA: Edward Elgar.

Ryan, C. 1997a. 'Low inflation pumps up US economists'. *Financial Review* 14 July:10.

Ryan, C. 1997b. 'Living to the new paradigm'. *Financial Review* 5 September:32.

Soete, L. 1981. 'Technological change, international competition and employment', in *Papers Presented for the Joint Conference on Technological Industrial Policy in China and Europe.* Lund, Sweden: Research Policy Institute.

Sydney Morning Herald. 2004. 'Centrelink's "one million errors"'. *Sydney Morning Herald* 14 February.

The Economist. 1999. 'The new economy: Work in progress'. *The Economist* 24 July:19–22.

Tylecote, A. 1995. 'Technological and economic long waves and their implications for employment'. *New Technology, Work and Employment* **10**:3–18.

21 Digital rights management (DRM): managing digital rights for open access[1]
Brian Fitzgerald and Jason Reid

Introduction

As Mandeville and Drahos point in this volume, information is a non-rivalrous good. Think of the often quoted statement by Thomas Jefferson to the effect that 'as he who lights his taper at mine, receives light without darkening me' (Jefferson 1813/1854, pp. 180–81). He goes on to say 'that if nature has made any one thing less susceptible than all others of exclusive property, it is the action of the thinking power called an idea . . .' (ibid.; see generally Lessig 1999).

As a result of the non-rivalrous nature of information, the law plays a role in commodifying and packaging information in the marketplace through intellectual property law, which is discussed in detail by Drahos in this volume (Fitzgerald 2001b). A concise and recent international restatement of the scope of intellectual property law is found in the Agreement on Trade-Related Aspects of Intellectual Property Rights (TRIPS), which is an annex to the World Trade Organization Agreement of 1994. It explains that the key intellectual property regimes cover: copyright, trademarks, geographical indicators, industrial designs, patents, layout designs of integrated circuits and the protection of undisclosed information. In some countries consumer protection, competition/antitrust and/or unjust enrichment laws may also act to reinforce rights in information along with *sui generis* database laws in the European Union.

Technological and contractually created information rights

However, more and more it is technology that is being used as means of regulating our behaviour in relation to informational products. Stanford University law professor Lawrence Lessig, in his seminal book *Code and Other Laws of Cyberspace* (1999), highlights how the digital environment is not a given but rather a construction of code writers. The 'nature' we inhabit in the digital world is that constructed through technology and technologists. In Lessig's theory there are four modalities of regulation: customary norms, the market, law and architecture. If I want to stop someone speeding I can employ the four modalities of regulation by encouraging a customary norm that speeding is bad through means such as advertising; raise the price of petrol (market); enact a law to say speeding is an offence; and build a restraining architecture such as a mechanical limit in the car or speed bumps. It is as simple as speed bumps. Lessig explains that just as architecture in real space can constrain our action, architecture in the digital world (code) can regulate what we do.

Therefore, instead of relying solely on law (e.g. copyright law) to protect my IP (e.g. software) I should consider what technological mechanisms are available to regulate access and use of my informational product. The big players have already begun this process and we will hear more and more about the role encryption will serve in the distribution of digital entertainment informational products. And while many advocate that technological restraints need to be principled and give balanced access to the public – in the way copyright legislation does – the legislatures have enacted laws, such as the Digital Millennium Copyright Act of 1998 ('DMCA') in the USA and the Copyright Amendment (Digital Agenda) Act 2000 (Cth) in Australia, which serve to buttress technological constraints by making it a crime to deal in or provide devices that circumvent technological protection measures. These types of laws combined with code will make technological protection measures popular in the new environment.

For example, some new software products contain technological or coded restraints that make it very difficult to copy and load the software on to a second machine. This technological constraint is designed to enforce copyright in the software. Likewise, Digital Versatile Discs (DVDs) are distributed with anti-copying CSS encryption, which will only allow them to be accessed through an authorized player. There is significant fear that these types of coded restraints could become a law unto themselves and slant protection too far in favour of the property holder.

Along with technology or code we have also seen the increasing importance of contract to the digital environment. A contract is an agreement between two or more parties that allows for a privately ordered legal foundation. Contract can be used to construct rights in information or to further structure or leverage existing rights. In Australia, the Copyright Law Review Committee has recently questioned the power of contract to oust or override public domain freedoms embodied in the Copyright Act (Copyright Law Review Committee 2002). Contract along with code is crucial to understanding the control of information in the digital environment (Fitzgerald 2001a).

Managing rights for open and closed distribution
Rights in relation to information might be used to restrict access to that information or to further open access to that information. The classic model in which the owner of intellectual property seeks maximum economic reward will entail the management and control of owners' rights in such a way as to limit access to those users willing to pay the licence fee or price. In contrast,

an open source or information commons approach might seek to manage and control owners' rights in such a way as to open up and guarantee further access.

The powerful insight that Richard Stallman and his associates at the Free Software Foundation discovered was that if you want to structure open access to knowledge you must leverage off or use as a platform your intellectual property rights. Stallman's genius was in understanding and implementing the ethic that if you want to create a community of information or creative commons you need to be able to control the way the information is used once it leaves your hands. The regulation of this downstream activity was achieved by claiming an intellectual property right (copyright in the software code) at the source and then structuring its downstream usage through a licence (GNU GPL). This was not a simple 'giving away' of information but rather a strategic mechanism for ensuring the information stayed 'free' (as in 'free speech', not price).

In the classic free software scenario embodied in the GNU General Public License (GPL) software source code is distributed in a manner that is open and free, allowing software developers (usually many hundreds, known broadly as the 'hacker community') further down the line to modify and improve upon the initial software product. The initial distributor of the code controls its presentation and further dissemination through copyright and contract law (contractual software licence). As a consequence the down-the-line developer and modifier is required to make source code of any derivative work that they distribute available for all to see. In this process copyright law is used to create a 'copyleft' effect as opposed to a 'copyright' effect by mandating that code should be open and free for all to use in innovation and development of software. By way of contrast, in a proprietary or closed distribution model source code is not released and can only be ascertained through decompilation or reverse engineering (see generally Fitzgerald and Bassett 2001).

The free and open source model for software development is now being expanded into the area of digital content. The context for this is the under-utilization of significant amounts of digital content and the 'cut-and-paste negotiability' of digital networked environments. Through concepts such as 'digital repositories or conservancies' like Australian Creative Resources Online (ACRO; see http://www.uq.edu.au/acro/) or merely distributed networks of information open content licensing projects such as the Creative Commons will allow people to access digital commons content for the purpose of reutilization and further innovation with a minimum of legal knowledge and transactional and physical effort. Taking digital content from the commons, as under the free and open source model, may carry obligations such as attributing the author of the digital content or sharing any derivative product back to the commons. In this Creative Commons model owners of intellectual property rights manage and control their rights at the source to structure open access downstream.

As Lessig pointed out, the power of technology or code to act as a mode of behavioural regulation is often underestimated (1999). Managing digital rights for open access may not only require the use of IPRs such as copyright to structure the digital commons but may also require technologies that can facilitate and augment such open access. It has already been suggested that projects such as Creative Commons may need to be augmented by technological measures that further its goals. This is the issue we need to examine further in redefining DRM to include managing digital rights for open access.

The role of technology in implementing open IPR management

What contribution can technology make to open IPR initiatives such as the Creative Commons project?[2] Technological approaches such as encryption and watermarking are more commonly associated with the enforcement of IPRs to maximize financial gain through restrictions on dissemination and use (see for example Stefik 1997). The context of their application is typically as a 'weapon' to combat the piracy of digital content. Comparatively little consideration has been given to the application of technological mechanisms to support open IPR regimes where the primary goal is to encourage the dissemination of intellectual property.

Open IPR regimes achieve their goals by conditionally reserving a carefully selected subset of IP rights. In the example of the GNU GPL licence, the right to make and distribute derivative works (adaptations that build on the original source code) is conditionally given on the proviso that the derivative work, upon distribution, will also be made available under the same terms. In this fashion, the GNU GPL encourages and perpetuates open distribution and contribution to a 'commons' by structuring downstream use.

Using watermarking to communicate licence terms

Arguably, the most important requirement for an effective open IPR regime is effective communication of the fact that a subset of IP rights has been reserved. Potential users of the IP need to be reliably notified of the licence conditions that govern its use. A common and simple approach to rights communication, particularly for digital sound and image content, is to include the conditions or a reference to where they can be found in the header of the digital file.[3] However, there is a practical problem with this approach. The reference to the licence can be easily separated from the content, for example through changes in file format or digital to analogue conversion. This separation need not be intentional. Indeed, it is often an unintended result of the normal handling and usage of digital files. The communication of licence terms would be more reliable if the licence reference were encoded in the content data itself rather than in a tag or header field, where it can be easily lost. In this manner, the licence reference becomes an intrinsic part of the work. This type of data embedding is possible using the technique of public digital watermarking, which is described in more detail in a later section (for a more detailed treatment of watermaking, see, e.g., Cox et al. 2001).

Describing licence terms

Technology can also contribute to open IPR regimes by describing licence terms in a form that computers can read. Computer-readable licences have a number of benefits. They allow automated searching for content that has been made available under particular licence terms. For example, using a search engine, a user could specify search criteria to restrict matches to only those images that are available without licence fee for non-commercial use. IP rights description conventions that are computer-readable are commonly called rights expression languages (REL). Much research and development effort has focused on these. The goal is to create a language which has fine enough granularity to enable the expression of all types of rights, for use in both open and closed environments. The language needs to be simultaneously descriptive and flexible. The International Organization for Standardization has recently ratified a standard for a rights expression language that is based on XrML (Extensible Rights Markup Language)[4]. The Open Digital Rights Language (ODRL) is an open source language with no licensing requirements.

Enforcing licence terms with technological measures

In addition to communicating usage conditions, technological measures can also be used to enforce them. An example of enforcement of a usage restriction (from a restrictive DRM scheme) is not being able to listen to a song unless you have paid for a licence to do so. This can be achieved through technological measures such as encryption and access control implemented in a content player device. This type of active licence enforcement can have a number of undesirable consequences with regard to privacy and freedom of access that are arguably inconsistent with the ideology that underpins open schemes such as the Creative Commons. For instance, most active enforcement DRM schemes involve both user and creator identification and registration, and the ability to monitor individual accesses to creative works. As many commentators have noted, the consequent loss of anonymous access is a high price to pay for effective copyright enforcement (for a detailed discussion of the importance of anonymous modes of access see Cohen and Burk 2001; for a treatment of the privacy threatening aspects of active DRM systems see Garnett and Sander 2002). It can therefore be argued that the relevant usage restrictions from open schemes that might benefit from technological enforcement are quite different to those of closed schemes, particularly if the undesirable privacy-invasive side-effects of active copyright enforcement are to be avoided.

Open scheme usage restrictions tend to lend themselves to passive rather than active enforcement. This is largely due to the divergent view that each regime takes of the 'user' and the nature of 'use'. In closed schemes, the user is generally seen as a paying, passive consumer of pre-packaged creative works whereas open schemes envisage forms of use that may involve interaction, modification and adaptation, often without requiring payment. The typical closed scheme requirement of payment before access lends itself to a form of active technological enforcement that tightly restricts access to the underlying data – the raw digital representation of the work. The security of the active enforcement mechanism works by ensuring that these raw data are not directly available to the consumer, since such access would allow bypassing of the active protection. This is a key reason why active technological enforcement is less appropriate in open schemes. Open schemes embrace the possibility of creative forms of interaction, modification and adaptation of a work and this requires access to the raw data. This does not mean that technological protection has nothing to contribute to open schemes. It does mean, however, that applicable technological measures tend more toward a passive supporting role than an active 'gatekeeper' style of enforcement.

Consider the Creative Commons licence terms as an example. There are four key protocols or terms governing usage:

1. Attribution required: the IP is authorized for use as long as the originator/creator is acknowledged.
2. No commercial use: the IP is authorized for use as long as the use is not commercial.
3. Share alike: the IP is authorized for use in an adapted or derived form as long as the derived work is made available under the same terms as the original work.
4. No derivative uses: the IP is authorized for use as long as it is not changed or altered.

Creative Commons licences can include any single term or combination of the four terms (except 3 and 4, which are incompatible).

One of the more compelling applications of technological measures in support of open IPR scheme usage conditions relates to the attribution-required constraint. The originator's identity can be embedded in the work via a digital watermark. The digital work itself carries the identity of the creator, so the obligation to ensure attribution can be discharged automatically, where users of the work have access to watermark detection software. This would require the inclusion of detectors in media authoring, editing and presentation software. Here, technology contributes by passively conveying information in a reliable manner. It reduces the possibility that the attribution will be lost in some downstream use as the attribution is an intrinsic part of the digital work. In doing so, it facilitates compliance with the licence terms.

The reserved rights combination of attribution required and no derivative uses can be technologically assisted by a combination of two watermarks with different properties. The first implements the attribution-required stipulation via a robust, redundant mark that embeds a reference to the licence terms and the creator's identity. The second mark is fragile. A fragile watermark is one that is destroyed by modifications to the work. Any derivative use would result in removal of the second mark, signalling that the work has been changed, thereby contravening the licence terms.

Watermarking can also be used in a more traditional manner[5] to support compliance with the 'no-commercial-use' right. The identity of the licensor of the work and a reference to the licence itself can be embedded in the work using a robust watermark. When an unauthorized commercial use of the work is detected (e.g. the work is being offered for sale on the Internet), the watermark serves to assert ownership in support of a claim of licence infringement. A watermark technique known as fingerprinting can also be used to help enforce the no-commercial-use right. Fingerprinting embeds information that can be used to identify an individual licensee of a work. Hence each copy is individually personalized to its licensee. The knowledge that the work carries the licensee's identity acts to discourage infringing uses by the licensee. The requirement that each licensee of a work be identified presents a clear disadvantage for fingerprinting since it limits opportunities for anonymous access.

Robust watermarking
Watermarks used to support the attribution-required licence term should be robust to survive without compromising the fidelity of the work. Robustness describes the ability of the watermark to survive common media manipulation and signal processing operations. Increased robustness typically comes at the cost of reduced fidelity. This means that the more robust the watermark, the more likely that it will be perceptible, compromising the subjective experience of the work. Ideally a robust watermark should survive any transformation that does not significantly impair the perceptible quality of the content, including digital to analogue to digital conversion and data compression (e.g. jpeg or mp3 conversion). Robust watermarks are an active area of research where many challenges remain, with the result that 'robust' must be used in a relative, rather than absolute, sense. Their short history has been somewhat of an 'arms race', where schemes are proposed and subsequently shown to be vulnerable to attack. As we note in a later section, it is questionable whether

watermarks can ever be made sufficiently robust to withstand removal by a motivated and technically sophisticated attacker.

Increased robustness also reduces the watermark's data payload. Payload refers to the amount of data that the watermark can carry. Practical robustness constraints mean that it will generally be impractical to embed the licence terms themselves because of their size. Instead, a watermark can encode a (shorter) reference to where the creator's identity and licence terms can be accessed, for example via a URL (uniform resource locator – the globally unique address of a file or web page accessible on the Internet). Where robustness is not a requirement, greater payloads are possible.

Redundant watermarks to attribute derivative use

Where the no-derivative-use constraint is not invoked, the Creative Commons licence supports 'sampling', a common creative process in the audio and visual arts. Sampling involves using portions of another creator's work in a derivative work. This permission for derivative use is commonly given with an attribution-required constraint. Some authors encourage sampling of their work as a means of increasing personal exposure. Robust public watermarking can be used to redundantly embed attribution data that could survive the types of processing and manipulation that are common in sampling. Again, the primary goal is not active enforcement; rather, it is increased convenience. The derivative author is freed from the attribution responsibility as the sample retains the ability to identify itself through a robust public watermark.

Robustness of public watermarks

The use of watermarks to provide reliable access to rights information and creator identity implies that the watermark must be able to be detected by any interested party. Such a watermark is known as a public watermark. Robustness is a challenging property to guarantee in public watermarks. In many schemes, the ability to detect a watermark implies the ability to remove it. A number of researchers have questioned whether a public watermark can ever be made strongly robust (see, e.g., Hachez and Quisquater 2002), as the watermark detector must be made available to potential adversaries. An adversary who wishes to disable the watermark can make incremental changes to the work and test whether each manipulation has disabled the mark using the public watermark detector. Clearly, the watermark can be removed if enough of the bits in the underlying work are changed. The challenge for the watermark designer is to ensure that watermark removal necessarily results in a sufficiently serious degradation of the subjectively perceptible qualities of the work to the point where it is destroyed. Improving the robustness of watermarks is an active area of research where many serious challenges remain.

Where the watermark is being used in the more traditional active DRM usage restriction context (e.g. to restrict copying), it should be expected that adversaries will expend considerable effort in disabling a watermark, in order to bypass the active protection and therefore the need for payment for a licence. Arguably, usage of watermarking to communicate Creative Commons licence terms does not require the same degree of robustness as the incentives to remove the mark are less compelling. They must survive common signal processing techniques that derivative authors and users can be expected to apply in the course of normal handling of the work, but they need not be strong enough to resist a motivated, malicious adversary. This is because, unlike closed schemes, open schemes typically provide access to the raw data that represents the work so that the envisaged forms of interaction, modification and adaptation are possible. In this context, watermarking plays a passive, supporting role that makes it easier for the users of a work to comply with the licence terms.

Conclusion: contemplating the role of technology in managing digital rights for open access

The open source community is not generally well disposed to technological measures such as watermarking and encryption. This reaction is due in part to the fact that technological approaches have been championed by organizations seeking to commercially exploit copyright in a closed system of knowledge distribution. To help overcome such immediate reactions, this chapter has sought to highlight how technology might be used to promote the goals of open IP regimes and to stimulate debate on the issue.[6] Increasingly we will be forced to recognize that digital rights management (DRM) is both an open and closed story and that we need to better understand the power of code to underpin and implement open content models.

Notes

1. This research has been undertaken pursuant to a QUT Strategic Collaborative Grant designed to enhance cross-disciplinary research across the Faculties of Law, IT and Creative Industries. We owe thanks to: Professors Bill Caelli and Ed Dawson, Fred von Lohmann, Dr Lauren May, Susanna Leisten, Nic Suzor and Rachel Cobcroft for their feedback.
2. 'Creative Commons is devoted to expanding the range of creative work available for others to build upon and share.' See http://creativecommons.org/
3. For example, to reference the licence in MP3 files the Creative Commons recommends including the URL where the licence can be found in the ID3 copyright field. See http://creativecommons.org/technology/mp3
4. ISO/IEC 21000-5:20 adopts MPEG 21 Part Five.
5. This feature is already supported by some content-authoring tools, e.g. Adobe Photoshop.
6. As shown, watermarking techniques can be used to robustly bind licence conditions to a work, enhancing communication of licence terms. Attribution required and sampling with attribution are two examples where robust public watermarking potentially offers significant benefits in allowing the derivative author to comply with the licence terms more easily and reliably.

References

Cohen, J. and D. Burk. 2001. 'Fair use infrastructure for rights management systems'. *Harvard Journal of Law and Technology* **15**:42–83.

Copyright Law Review Committee. 2002. 'Copyright and contract'. http://www.clrc.gov.au.

Cox, I., J. Bloom and M. Miller. 2001. *Digital Watermarking: Principles & Practice*. San Francisco: Morgan Kaufmann Publishers.

Fitzgerald, A. and B. Fitzgerald. 2004. *Intellectual Property in Principle*. Sydney: LBC/Thomson.

Fitzgerald, B. 2001a. 'Digital property: The ultimate boundary?' *Roger Williams University Law Review* **7**:47–150.

Fitzgerald, B. 2001b. 'Intellectual capital and law in the digital environment'. *Southern Cross University Law Review* **5**:206–20.

Fitzgerald, B. and G. Bassett. 2001. 'Legal issues relating to free and open source software'. *Journal of Law and Information Science* **12**:59.

Garnett, N. and T. Sander. 2002. 'Fair use by design: What DRM can and cannot do and what it is or isn't doing today', in *12th Conference of Computers, Freedom and Privacy*, San Francisco, CA: ACM Press.

Hachez, G. and J.J. Quisquater. 2002. 'Which directions for asymmetric watermarking?', in *Invited talk at the XI European Signal Processing Conference (EUSIPCO 2002)*. Lausanne: EURASIP.

Jefferson, Thomas. 1813/1854. 'Letter from Thomas Jefferson to Isaac McPherson, 13 August 1813'. Pp. 180–81 in *VI Writings of Thomas Jefferson*, edited by H. Washington. Washington, DC: The Thomas Jefferson Memorial Association of the United States.

Lessig, L. 1999. *Code and Other Laws of Cyberspace*. New York: Basic Books.

Stefik, M. 1997. 'Shifting the possible: How trusted systems and digital property rights challenge us to rethink digital publishing'. *Berkeley Technology Law Journal* **12**:137.

Index

DATE DUE

FEB 2 8 2008			